STERLING
Test Prep

AP
European History

Complete
Content Review

2nd edition

www.Sterling-Prep.com

2   1

ISBN-13: 978-0-9977782-0-5

Sterling Test Prep products are available at special quantity discounts for sales, promotions, academic counseling offices and other educational purposes.

For more information contact our Sales Department at:

Sterling Test Prep
6 Liberty Square #11
Boston, MA 02109

info@sterling-prep.com

© 2018 Sterling Test Prep
Published by Sterling Test Prep

We want to hear from you

Your feedback is important to us because we strive to provide the highest quality prep materials. If you have any questions, comments or suggestions, email us, so we can incorporate your feedback into future editions.

Customer Satisfaction Guarantee

If you have any concerns about this book, including printing issues, contact us and we will resolve any issues to your satisfaction.

info@sterling-prep.com

Congratulations on choosing this book as part of your AP World History preparation!

Scoring well on AP exams is important for admission to college. To achieve a high score on AP European History exam, you need to develop historical thinking skills to properly analyze historical evidence and quickly respond to the exam's questions. You must learn to apply chronological reasoning, draw comparisons and contextualization and craft arguments from historical evidence.

This book provides a thorough and curriculum-oriented review of all periods and Key Concepts per the College Board's most recent AP European History course outline. The content is organized into four historical periods and is centered around all Key Concepts tested on the AP European History exam.

The information is presented in a clear and easy to understand style. You can focus on one historical period or one Key Concept at a time to fully comprehend and internalize important historical relationships.

This book can be used both as accompanying text during your AP course and as a review guide before the exam. By using it as your study tool you will develop the necessary skills and will be well prepared for the course and the exam.

The content is developed and edited by highly qualified history teachers, scholars and education specialists with an emphasis on the curriculum and skills outlined by the College Board for the AP European History course. It was examined for quality and consistency by our team of editors who are experts on teaching and preparing students for standardized tests.

We wish you great success in your future academic achievements and look forward to being an important part of your successful preparation for the AP European History!

Sterling Test Prep Team

180408gdx

Our Commitment to the Environment

Sterling Test Prep is committed to protecting our planet's resources by supporting environmental organizations with proven track records of conservation, environmental research and education and preservation of vital natural resources. A portion of our profits is donated to support these organizations so they can continue their important missions. These organizations include:

 For over 40 years, Ocean Conservancy has been advocating for a healthy ocean by supporting sustainable solutions based on science and cleanup efforts. Among many environmental achievements, Ocean Conservancy laid the groundwork for an international moratorium on commercial whaling, played an instrumental role in protecting fur seals from overhunting and banning the international trade of sea turtles. The organization created national marine sanctuaries and served as the lead non-governmental organization in the designation of 10 of the 13 marine sanctuaries.

 For 25 years, Rainforest Trust has been saving critical lands for conservation through land purchases and protected area designations. Rainforest Trust has played a central role in the creation of 73 new protected areas in 17 countries, including Falkland Islands, Costa Rica and Peru. Nearly 8 million acres have been saved thanks to Rainforest Trust's support of in-country partners across Latin America, with over 500,000 acres of critical lands purchased outright for reserves.

 Since 1980, Pacific Whale Foundation has been saving whales from extinction and protecting our oceans through science and advocacy. As an international organization, with ongoing research projects in Hawaii, Australia and Ecuador, PWF is an active participant in global efforts to address threats to whales and other marine life. A pioneer in non-invasive whale research, PWF was an early leader in educating the public, from a scientific perspective, about whales and the need for ocean conservation.

Thank you for choosing our products to achieve your educational goals.

With your purchase, you support environmental causes around the world.

Table of Contents

AP European History Exam

The AP European History Exam is 3 hours and 15 minutes long and includes both a multiple-choice/short-answer section (105 minutes) and a document-based/long-essay section (90 minutes). Each section is divided into two parts, as shown in the table below. Student performance metrics on these four parts are compiled and weighted to determine an overall AP Exam score.

Section	Question Type	Number of Questions	Timing	Percentage of Exam Score
I	Part A: Multiple-choice questions	55 questions	55 minutes	40%
	Part B: Short-answer questions	4 questions	50 minutes	20%
II	Part A: Document-based question	1 question	55 minutes	25%
	Part B: Long-essay question	1 question (chosen from a pair)	35 minutes	15%

The content of the new AP European History curriculum and exam is divided into four chronological periods. The table below shows the specific years included in each of the four periods and their approximate presence on the exam.

Period 1:   1405 – 1648

Period 2:   1648 – 1815

Period 3:   1815 – 1914

Period 4:   1914 – Present

Students write at least one essay—in either the document-based question or long essay—that examines long-term developments spanning historical time periods.

Assessment of Student's Learning on the Exam

The following are general parameters about the relationship between the components of the curriculum framework and the questions on the AP Exam. AP European History exam assesses:

- Students' competence of the thematic learning objectives.
- Students' capability using the historical thinking skills.
- Students' grasp of the four time periods of European history.

Multiple-Choice Questions

The multiple-choice section contains several sets of questions with 2-5 questions per set. These sets ask students to respond to stimulus materials (primary or secondary sources) including texts, images, charts, graphs, maps, etc. The stimulus material reflects the types of evidence that historians use in their research. The set of multiple-choice questions draws upon knowledge required by the curriculum framework, and each question addresses one of the learning objectives for the course. While a set may focus on one particular period of European history, the individual questions within that set may ask students to make connections to thematically linked developments in other periods.

Multiple-choice questions assess students' ability to evaluate the stimulus material *in tandem with* their knowledge of the historical issue at hand. The possible answers for a multiple-choice question reflect the level of detail present in the required historical developments found in the concept outline for the course. Events and topics contained in the illustrative example boxes of the curriculum framework do *not* appear in multiple-choice questions (unless accompanied by text that fully explains the topic to the student).

Short-Answer Questions

Short-answer questions directly address one or more of the thematic learning objectives for the course. At least two of the four questions have elements of internal choice, providing opportunities for students to demonstrate what they know best. All of the short-answer questions require students to use historical thinking skills to respond to a primary source, a historian's argument, non-textual sources such as data or maps, or general propositions about European history. Each question asks students to identify and analyze examples of historical evidence relevant to the source or question; these examples can be drawn from the concept outline or from other examples explored in depth during classroom instruction.

Document-Based Question

The document-based question measures students' ability to analyze and synthesize historical data and to assess verbal, quantitative, or visual materials as historical evidence. As with the long essay, responses to the document-based question are judged on students' ability to formulate a thesis and support it with relevant evidence. The documents included in the document-based question are not confined to a single format, vary in length, and illustrate interactions and complexities within the material.

Where suitable, the documents include charts, graphs, cartoons, pictures and written materials. In addition to calling upon a broad spectrum of historical skills, the diversity of materials allows students to assess the value of different sorts of documents. The document-based question typically requires students to relate the documents to a historical period or theme and, thus, to focus on major periods and issues. For this reason, outside knowledge beyond the specific focus of the question is important and must be incorporated into the student's essay to earn the highest scores.

Long Essay Question

To provide opportunities for students to demonstrate what they know best, they are given a choice between two comparable long essay options. The long essay questions measure the use of historical thinking skills to explain and analyze significant issues in European history as defined by the thematic learning objectives. Student essays must include the development of a thesis or argument supported by an analysis of specific, relevant historical evidence. Questions are limited to topics or examples specifically mentioned in the concept outline but are framed to allow student answers to include in-depth examples of large-scale phenomena, either drawn from the concept outline or from topics discussed in the classroom.

Tested Skills

There are nine historical thinking skills that students must demonstrate on the AP European History exam. They are grouped into four skill types as shown in the table below.

Skill Type	Historical Thinking Skill
Analyzing Historical Sources and Evidence	• Analyzing Evidence: Content and Sourcing • Interpretation
Making Historical Connections	• Comparison • Contextualization • Synthesis
Chronological Reasoning	• Causation • Patterns of Continuity and Change over Time • Periodization
Creating and Supporting a Historical Argument	• Argumentation

Skill Type: Analyzing Historical Sources and Evidence

Analyzing Evidence: Content and Sourcing – the ability to describe, select and evaluate relevant evidence about the past from diverse sources and draw conclusions about their relevance to different historical issues.

Proficient students are able to:

- explain the relevance of the author's point of view, purpose, audience, format or medium and/or historical context, as well as the interaction among these features, to demonstrate understanding of the significance of a primary source.

- evaluate the usefulness, reliability and/or limitations of a primary source in answering particular historical questions.

Interpretation – the ability to describe, analyze, evaluate and construct diverse interpretations of the past.

This skill asks students to both describe and evaluate varied historical interpretations while being aware of how particular circumstances and contexts in which individual historians work and write also shape their interpretation of past events. Historical interpretation requires analyzing evidence, reasoning, determining the context and evaluating points of view found in both primary and secondary sources. To help students create their own interpretation of European history, students should examine changing historical interpretations over time.

Proficient students are able to:

- analyze diverse historical interpretations.
- evaluate the effectiveness of a historian's argument by analyzing their argument and explaining how the argument has been supported through the analysis of relevant historical evidence.

Skill Type: Making Historical Connections

Comparison – the ability to describe, compare and evaluate multiple historical developments.

This skill asks students to compare related historical developments and processes in various chronological and geographical contexts within one society or between different societies. This skill also involves the ability to identify and compare multiple perspectives on a given historical experience.

Proficient students are able to:

- compare diverse perspective represented in primary and secondary sources in order to draw conclusions about one or more historical events.

- compare different historical individuals, events, developments and/or processes, analyzing both similarities and differences in order to draw historically valid conclusions.

Contextualization – the ability to connect historical events and processes to specific circumstances of time and place and to broader regional, national, or global processes.

The "context" for European history is Europe in general. The skill of contextualization therefore takes on different forms depending on the scope of time and geography. One of the central questions of European history is: How does the history of a particular group, region or era fit into the larger story of the development of Europe?

Proficient students are able to:

- situate historical events, developments or processes within the broader regional, national or global context in which they occurred in order to draw conclusions about their relative significance.

Synthesis – the ability to develop meaningful and persuasive new understandings of the past by applying all of the other historical thinking skills

This skill asks students to demonstrate an understanding of the past by making an argument that draws appropriately on ideas from different fields of inquiry or disciplines and creatively fuses evidence from different works.

Proficient students are able to:

- make connections between a given historical issue and related developments in a different historical context, geographical area, period or era, including the present.

- make connections between different course themes and/or approaches to history (political, economic, social, etc.) for a given historical issue

- use insights from a different discipline or field of inquiry (economics, politics, anthropology, etc.) to better understand a given historical issue.

Skill Type: Chronological Reasoning

Causation – the ability to identify, analyze and evaluate the relationships among multiple historical causes and effects, distinguishing between those that are long-term and proximate, and among coincidence, causation and correlation.

Proficient students are able to:

- explain long- and/or short-term causes and/or effects of a historical event, development or process.

- evaluate the relative significance of different causes and/or effects on historical events or processes, distinguishing between causation and correlation and showing an awareness of historical contingency.

Patterns of Continuity and Change over Time – the ability to recognize, analyze and evaluate the dynamics of historical continuity and change over periods of time.

Proficient students are able to:

- identify, analyze and evaluate historical patterns of continuity and change over time.

- connect patterns of continuity and change over time to larger historical processes or themes.

Periodization – the ability to describe, analyze, evaluate and construct models that historians use to organize history into discrete periods.

Students should be familiar with different ways that historians divide time into historical periods and identify turning points in the past. Students may develop this skill by examining and evaluating the model of periodization provided in this framework. Students may then compare this periodization against competing models, such as the one used in their textbook.

Proficient students are able to:

- explain ways that historical events and processes can be organized within blocks of time.

- evaluate whether a particular event or date could or could not be a turning point between different periods when considered in terms of particular evidence.

- analyze and evaluate competing models of periodization of European history.

Skill Type: Creating and Supporting a Historical Argument

Argumentation – the ability to define and frame a question about the past and to address that question through the construction of an argument.

Over the span of the course, students should move from describing to evaluating the conflicting historical evidence used in making plausible historical arguments. In European history, the skill of historical argumentation often operates in conjunction with other skills and with course themes that transcend several periods. A plausible and persuasive argument requires a clear, comprehensive and analytical thesis supported by relevant historical evidence—not simply evidence that supports a preferred or preconceived position. In addition, argumentation involves the capacity to describe, analyze and evaluate the arguments of others in light of available evidence.

Proficient students are able to:

- articulate a supported historic claim in a clear and effective thesis that evaluates multiple factors and acknowledges disparate, varied or contradictory evidence/perspectives.

- develop and use evidence to buttress an argument by conducting a close reading and analysis of relevant evidence, framing the argument through the use of a chosen historical thinking skill.

- adroitly link evidence to claims or theses by explaining the specific relevance they possess.

- cohesively relate varied historical evidence to acknowledge contradictions, corroborations and qualifications in argument development.

Period 1: c. 1450 to c. 1648

198 year difference

Major historical events of the period:

1400s: Gunpowder begins to be adapted into European armies

1440: The printing press is invented by Johannes Gutenberg

1478: The Spanish Inquisition begins

1488: Portuguese explorer Bartholomew Diaz reaches the Cape of Good Hope

1492: Christopher Columbus' journey to the New World

1494-1559: The (eight) Italian Wars begin, involving a rotating series of competing regional Italian states and their respective European allies (France, Spain, the Holy Roman Empire, England, the Ottoman Empire, Saxony and Brandenburg)

1497: Vasco da Gama leads expedition and successfully finds direct route to India

1517: The Protestant Reformation begins

1519: Religious Calvinism movement begins in Switzerland

1524-1525: The Peasant War in Germany

1545: The Catholic Counter-Reformation begins

1560s: Dutch revolt against Spanish rule begins

1562-1598: French Wars of Religion

1580: Portugal is annexed by Spain in the Iberian Union

c. 1580-1650: Peak period of witchcraft allegations

1588: England defeats the Spanish Armada invasion force

1572: St. Bartholomew's Day massacre in Paris

1600: The British East India Company is founded

c. 1600: The Baroque artistic period begins; The General Crisis begins

1602: The Dutch East India Company is founded

1606-1609: Zebrzydowski's Rebellion in the Poland-Lithuanian Commonwealth

1618-1648: Thirty Years' War between the Holy Roman Empire and its coalition of Spain, Hungary, Croatia, Denmark and the Polish-Lithuanian Commonwealth against German Protestant princes (Saxony, The Palatinate, Brandenburg-Prussia, Brunswick-Lüneburg) and their coalition of Sweden, France, the Dutch, England, Scotland, Transylvania, the Ottoman Empire and Russia

1640-1659: The Catalan Revolt in Spain

1642-1651: The English Civil War

Period 1: 1450-1648

> **Key Concept 1.1: The worldview of European intellectuals shifted from one based on ecclesiastical and classical authority to one based primarily on inquiry and observation of the natural world.**

Renaissance intellectuals and artists revived classical motifs in the fine arts and classical values in literature and education. Intellectuals—later called humanists—employed new methods of textual criticism based on a deep knowledge of Greek and Latin and revived classical ideas that made human beings the measure of all things. Artists formulated new styles based on ancient models. The humanists remained Christians while promoting ancient philosophical ideas that challenged traditional Christian views. Artists and architects such as Brunelleschi, Leonardo, Michelangelo and Raphael glorified human potential and the human form in the visual arts, basing their art on classical models while using new techniques of painting and drawing, such as geometric perspective. The invention of the printing press in the mid-15th century accelerated the development and dissemination of these new attitudes, most notably north of the Alps (the northern Renaissance).

During the 16th and 17th centuries, Europeans developed new approaches to and methods for looking at the natural world, in what historians have called the Scientific Revolution. Aristotle's classical cosmology and Ptolemy's astronomical system came under increasing scrutiny from natural philosophers (later called scientists) such as Copernicus, Galileo and Newton. The philosophers Francis Bacon and René Descartes articulated comprehensive theories of inductive and deductive reasoning to give the emerging scientific method a sound foundation.

Bacon urged the collection and analysis of data about the world and spurred the development of an international community of natural philosophers dedicated to the vast enterprise of what came to be called natural science. In medicine, the new approach to knowledge led physicians such as William Harvey to undertake observations that produced new explanations of anatomy and physiology and to challenge the traditional theory of health and disease (the four humors) espoused by Galen in the second century. The articulation of natural laws, often expressed mathematically, became the goal of science.

The unexpected encounter with the Western hemisphere at the end of the 15th century further undermined knowledge derived from classical and biblical authorities. The explorations produced new knowledge of geography and the world's people through direct observation, and this seemed to give credence to new approaches to knowledge more generally. Even as they developed inquiry-based epistemologies, Europeans also continued to use traditional explanations of the natural world based on witchcraft, magic, alchemy and astrology.

A revival of classical texts led to new methods of scholarship and new values in both society and religion.

Humanism was a belief system of the newly-created *bourgeoisie,* a social category mainly connected to the urban economy, which held the capital and much of the decision-making power in society. In the Middle Ages, they were inhabitants of cities, or *bourgs* (France); at the same time, humanism was a reaction against the social superiority of the feudal nobility and against medieval mysticism. The bourgeoisie, who at this time were found mostly in the Italian city-states, Flanders (present-day Belgium) and the German communal republics, were not content only to spread the privileges of medieval society to larger portions of the populace; rather, they sought to reorganize society according to a new set of values.

This process could not be fulfilled without the belief in a determined sense of life and in a hierarchy of values which were expressed in a new life style. A new ideal of culture was constructed, characterized by the glorification of earthly life, through the valorization of nature and of man and by studying classical Antiquity. Humanism was the expression of this ideal, which was radically opposed to medieval asceticism (i.e., strict self-discipline and avoidance of all forms of indulgence).

Marcus Tullius Cicero, Roman philosopher

Roman philosopher Marcus Tullius Cicero had used the term *humanitas* to imply "education." The admirers of classical Antiquity at the end of the 14th century were talking about *studia humanitatis,* by which they understood the Greek-Roman ideal of culture that had the virtue to make a better man. The term *humanista* first appeared in the Latin texts from the end of the 15th century and began to appear in Italian texts from 1530 onwards.

The word *humanism* (which dates from the 19th century) had two distinct meanings: first, the idea of an ideal education creating a perfect man and, second, the study of classical Antiquity, a period of notable accomplishments where contemporaries believed there had existed a superior idea of the human. As such, *humanitatis* competed with the belief that the human ideal was complete and, therefore,

Antiquity must be the only inspiration source for any system of rational education. Humanism and classicism are synonymous. In the second half of the 15th century, humanism gained the acceptance of the lay culture, which opposed the scholastic philosophy and mysticism of the Church.

Due to the rise in popularity of humanism (both critical and erudite) there was an increased interest in the culture, research methods, manuscripts and other works of Antiquity. This gave an impetus for cultural activity in all the domains: literature, philosophy, history, the natural sciences and art. The representatives of the humanist movement—restless researchers and collectors of manuscripts—distinguished themselves through their belief in the superiority of reason. The scholastic spirit, which was based on old dogmas, was replaced more and more with open dialogue, critical spirit and free thought.

Italian Renaissance humanists promoted a revival in classical literature and created new philological approaches to ancient texts. Some Renaissance humanists further the values of secularism and individualism.

Italian literature formed within the school of Provençal poetry. The troubadours, scattered by the crusade against the Albigensian, found refuge at Frederic II's court and, along with the autochthon poets, formed the first school of Italian poetry. At the end of the 13th century, a new school of poetry, *dolce stil novo*, appeared around the city-states of Bologna and Florence. As part of this school, Dante and Petrarch learned the art of spiritualizing love, to transform it in a subtle poetic theory and to search for inspiration not in foreign models, but in their own roots and souls.

Dante Alighieri, Italian poet

The founder of Italian poetry, Dante Alighieri (1265–1321), belonged to the medieval context of civilization, as judged by his religious enthusiasm and conception of the world. At the same time, he was a harbinger for the dawn of a new era. In his *Divine Comedy*, led by Virgil (who in the Medieval period was considered a prophet), Dante crosses the inferno—where the forever doomed expiate their sins—and climbs the purgatory mountain where, by painful purifications, the souls of the penitent can attain the state of innocence of the first men.

Dante revived the very sentiment of the ancient world. In the inferno vestibule, he placed the souls of the sages and heroes of Antiquity who, even though they had not sinned, could not be saved because they had not been christened. Moreover, Dante expressed a new sentiment of nature and a new conception of man; the hero of Antiquity thus became the model for the Renaissance ideal of manhood (*virtù*).

Just as Dante showed a great nostalgia for Antiquity, Petrarch (1304-1374) was a proponent for the intellectual atmosphere of ancient Rome. The Italians were direct descendants of the Romans and one of Petrarch's strongest desires was to revive the glory of ancient Rome. He wrote *Africa*, whose hero was Scipio the African, and *De Viris Illustribus*, which included twenty-four biographies of famous men, most of them Romans.

With a desire to retain the pure ideas of Antiquity, Petrarch based his expositions on classical documents that had been researched from a rational perspective. With his use of sources and rational thinking, Petrarch defined the critical spirit and set the base for humanist historiography. "*Ad fontes*!" became the humanists' mission statement and the fecund principle of philological critics. Due to Petrarch's influence, the study of Antiquity as the ideal of human culture became the fundamental element of education in the later period, not in contradiction to, but in harmony with, Christian doctrine. ✶

Lorenzo Valla (c. 1407–1457) was a representative of Renaissance thought and a true humanist. In his *De Elegantiis Latinae linguae*, he brought the study of Latin to a new level, and continued research of other classic authors. Valla's originality and knowledge of classical Latin enabled him to write an essay which proved, for the first time, that the historical document *Donatio Constantini*, which justified the papacy's rights to temporal rule, was a forgery; this provoked passionate debates in the religious and political circles of the time. The paper appeared in 1440 and was strongly rejected by the Church. Valla also compared the translation of the Bible made by St. Jerome with the Greek language version of the New Testament, laying the foundation for critical biblical scholarship and the attacking of Aristotelian thought from a linguistic perspective.

Marsilio Ficino (1433–1499) was a priest, doctor and musician, best known for his work as a translator of classic works of Antiquity. His patron, Cosimo de Medici, encouraged Ficino to study Greek and Latin. Among other things, Ficino provided the first Latin translations of Plato's works. He led the Florentine Platonic Academy, which had an enormous impact on European philosophy. Ficino was also a tutor for Cosimo de Medici's grandson, Lorenzo de Medici, and for Giovanni Pico della Mirandola (1463–1494).

Due to the influence of Ficino, Italian philosopher and humanist scholar Giovanni Pico della Mirandola embraced Plato's philosophy, in opposition to the Aristotelian tradition, and became one of the most active participants in debates that searched for unity between Platonic idealism and Christian spirituality. In 1486 Pico della Mirandola left for Rome and published 900 theses on various philosophical and theological themes, under the title *Conclusiones philosophicae, cabalisticae et theologicae*. Its introduction, *"Oratio de hominis dignitate,"* later became one of the most renowned texts of Italian humanism.

Marsilio Ficino, Italian humanist
8th

Pope Innocent VIII declared 13 of the 900 theses to be heretical. Although Pico della Mirandola tried to defend himself, he was condemned and forced to seek refuge in France. The Pope's emissaries found and arrested him but he was freed as a result of Lorenzo de Medici's intervention. Although he returned to Florence, he lived in ever-growing solitude, influenced by the sermons of Savonarola, who criticized the mores of the time, and envisioned the foundation of a fundamentalist ecclesiastical state.

Lorenzo de' Medici (Lorenzo the Magnificent),
ruler of the Florentine Republic 1469-1492

The humanist revival of Greek and Roman texts, spread by the printing press, challenged the institutional power of universities and the Roman Catholic Church and shifted the focus of education away from theology toward the study of the classical texts.

The new and enthusiastic group of advocates for classic Antiquity created an intellectual atmosphere that rejected medieval asceticism and scholars' reclusiveness. The identification of humanism with lay society and with the superior interests of the Florentine republic raised new ethical, philosophical and artistic issues, which were solved in accordance with lay society's interests.

The humanists gave public sermons, which previously had been the province of clerics or members of the clergy, actively defending the sovereign rights of individual human beings. References to the Romans' heroic deeds were no longer simply rhetorical themes, but examples meant to justify the measures of public salvation and to support the resistance against the powers which threatened the political independence and the civic rights of the Florentine republic. Civic humanism, which included the basic Renaissance principles, appeared in this context.

At critical political moments, the Florentine republic proclaimed the ideal of a free man and citizen, a notion prominent in the classics of Antiquity. The study of these works became, from then on, the foundation of the educational system. Classical studies and the humanist educational system threatened the institutional power of universities and the spirit of theological learning, so it was not long before they faced resistance from the clergy. Some of the greatest representatives of humanism, who founded their studies on classical texts and supported the new educational curricula, were Leonardo Bruni, Leon Battista Alberti and Niccolò Machiavelli.

Leonardo Bruni (1369–1444) was the most important representative of civic humanism and a model humanist historian. He was a true historian, consulting original sources, eliminating miracles and legends and seeking to establish the causal connection of events. He recognized the importance of general conditions in history and was wise enough to appreciate the active forces in history. Unlike the medieval chroniclers, who aggregated facts without any logical coherence, Bruni methodized information according to a rational plan.

Admiration for Greek and Roman political institutions supported a revival of civic humanist culture in the Italian city-states and produced secular models for individual and political behavior.

Along with a new conception of history, the Renaissance brought up new ideas about the nature of society and the art of governance. From his own observations and the study of the classics, Niccolò Machiavelli (1469–1527) built a system which reflected on the political experience and thinking of his time. The central issue, towards which all his ideas converged, was that the idea of a unified Italy was being subordinated to the centralized states. In *The Prince*, he demonstrated that only a unified and reorganized Italy could regain and maintain its independence.

Machiavelli described the portrait of an ideal prince who, first of all, had to be cunning and powerful. The prince had to master the art of war, to build a national army (rather than an army of mercenaries) and be motivated only by reason and the interests of the state. Justice, honor and morality were not to be regarded unless they were necessary and useful. Religion was nothing but another instrument of government. This total indifference to morality was named Machiavellianism, as if political amorality dated only from Machiavelli. He wrote a political treatise that exposed the political and religious hypocrisy and promoted the complete secularization of thought. He defined the very essence of humanism.

Niccolò Machiavelli, Italian Renaissance philosopher, writer and politician

Francesco Guicciardini (1484–1540) was the first Italian author to approach the subject of universal history. As the ambassador of the Florentine republic in Spain and governor of the papal state under Clement VII, Guicciardini was involved in all the great events of Italian history from the beginning of the 16th century until his death in 1540. *The History of Italy* is a memoir he wrote in order to justify his activity as the Pope's general lieutenant in the Cognac League War, which ended with the famous *sacco di Roma* of 1527. Unlike Machiavelli, Guicciardini considered only facts and created a general history of the struggle for supremacy over Italy. He understood the interdependence of the European states and he exposed the Italian events in international politics. It is no wonder he was dubbed "the father of modern historiography."

One important author who raised the issue of sovereign states was Jean Bodin (1530 – 1596), a French jurist, member of the Parliament from Paris and law professor at Toulouse. He is considered by Europeans to be the founder of political science because of his contributions to the development of the sovereign theory. Moreover, Jean Bodin discussed the problem of religious intolerance in the paper *Colloquium septaplomeres de rerum sublimum*.

Baldassare Castiglione (1478–1529) was an Italian diplomat, author and courtier who lived most of his life in Milan and Urbino. He was sent to Ludovico's court from Milan at the age of 18. He held several posts in the great courts of Italy and Spain and became a diplomat after an ankle injury prevented him from being a soldier. He spent over ten years at the court of Urbino, where he wrote *The Book of the Courtier*, which found immediate success. Published in Venice in 1528, the book became the vehicle through which the values of Italian humanism were spread throughout Europe, eventually having a large impact on the Renaissance.

The invention of printing promoted the dissemination of new ideas.

The popularization of intellectual activity was stimulated at the beginning of the 15th century with the invention of the printing press and the subsequent growth of the number of readers. The printing press allowed readers to discover critical texts directly instead of through adaptations. By multiplying them, it created new possibilities for mass education.

Due to the various vernacular languages of Europe, humanists used the more widely understood Latin language when spreading their ideas using the Gutenberg Press. Until the invention of the printing press, the manuscript was the only means of spreading the written word and was rare, often incomplete and expensive. The crucial step in the invention of the printing press was the new ability to acquire metal in sufficient quantities to make large machinery, which became a reality between 1440 and 1450.

A printing press was a device that applied pressure on an inked surface resting upon paper or cloth. Generally used for texts, the printing press is considered one of the most influential inventions of the millennium. The printing press was invented around 1440 by Johannes Gutenberg, in the Holy Roman Empire. A goldsmith by profession, Gutenberg created a hand mold, which was meant to create metal movable type. He adapted screw presses and other existing technologies to create a full printing system.

By the end of the century, the printing press had spread to more than two hundred cities throughout Europe. The use of the press led to the production of over twenty million volumes. In the 16th century, with printing activity flourishing, the number of copies produced increased to approximately 150–200 million. The activity of a printing press became synonymous with the enterprise of printing and lent its name to a new branch of media called "the press." In 1620, the English philosopher Francis Bacon asserted that the printing press was one of the three inventions that had changed the world.

The invention of the printing press in the 1450s aided in spreading the Renaissance beyond Italy and encouraged the growth of vernacular literature, which would eventually contribute to the development of the national cultures.

At the end of the 15th century, there were 73 printing presses in Italy, 51 in Germany and 39 in France. They stimulated the development of national languages, forcing editors to establish the orthography and grammar of each printed language and, by extension, each national culture. Johannes Gutenberg's work on the printing press began in approximately 1436 when he partnered with Andreas Dritzehn—a man who had previously trained in gem-cutting—and Andreas Heilmann, owner of a paper mill. However, it was not until a lawsuit against Gutenberg in 1439 that an official record of his work existed; witnesses' testimony discussed Gutenberg's types, an inventory of metals (including lead) he was using and his type molds.

Johannes Gutenberg,
Inventor of the printing press

As he had already worked as a professional goldsmith, Gutenberg was skilled at using the knowledge of metals he had learned as a craftsman. He created a durable type from an alloy of lead, tin and antimony, which was essential for producing high-quality printed books and proved to be much better suited for printing than other materials. To create these lead types, Gutenberg used an ingenious invention, a special matrix that enabled the precise molding of new type blocks from a uniform template. His type case is thought to have contained approximately 290 separate letter boxes, most of which were required for special characters, ligatures or punctuation marks.

Gutenberg was also responsible for the introduction of an oil-based ink which was more durable than the water-based inks previously used. He used both paper and a high-quality parchment as printing material. In some copies of the Gutenberg Bible, Gutenberg experimented with colored printing for a few of the page headings. A subsequent work, the Mainz Psalter of 1453 (which is presumed to have been designed by Gutenberg though published under the imprint of his successors), had elaborate red and blue printed initials.

The printing press was an important factor in the scientific revolution. It led to the establishment of a community of scientists who could easily disseminate their discoveries via widely read scholarly journals. Because of the printing press, authorship became more meaningful. Up to this point, the author of a given text was not widely known, since, for example, a handwritten copy of Aristotle made in Paris would not be exactly identical to one made in Bologna. In many cases, the names of authors of works produced prior to those printed on a press have been entirely lost.

The printing process ensured that information fell on the same pages in each copy, which is how page numbering, tables of contents and indices became common. The process of reading also changed, gradually transforming from a largely oral tradition that was done in groups, to a more solitary endeavor that one undertook in silence. The wider availability of printed material also led to a dramatic rise in the literacy rate among adults throughout Europe.

The printing press represented an essential and critical step towards the democratization of knowledge. Within fifty or sixty years of its invention, the entire classical canon had been reprinted and widely disseminated throughout Europe. Now that more people had access to knowledge both new and old, more people could discuss these works. Furthermore, now that book production was a more commercial enterprise, the first copyright laws were passed to protect what today is called intellectual property rights. On the other hand, the printing press was criticized for allowing the dissemination of information which may have been incorrect.

Due to this popularization of knowledge, Latin began to lose its prominence; works could be published in the local vernacular of the region in which the work was created and/or printed. The printed word also helped to unify and standardize the spelling and syntax of these vernaculars, in effect decreasing their variability. This rise in importance of national languages, as opposed to pan-European Latin, is cited as one of the causes of the rise of nationalism throughout Europe. *No more Latin produces individual nationalism*

Protestant reformers used the press to disseminate their ideas, which spurred religious reform and helped it to become widely established.

The printing press had an important role in the Protestant movement because of the intellectual climate it enabled, which contributed to the spread of the Bible and theological and humanist papers. It ensured wide access to the discoveries which shattered the official positions of the Church. Erasmus of Rotterdam retranslated the Bible into Latin after highlighting the faults of Jerome's 4th century translation of the Old Testament. Jerome's translation, which had errors, had been considered "official" edition and was the basis of some very important Catholic dogma. The printing press helped reformers to disseminate their ideas, allowing them to become more widely known throughout society.

During the Reformation, the spread of propaganda throughout Europe was aided by the printing press. In particular within Germany, it caused new ideas, thoughts and doctrines to be made available to the public in ways that had never been seen before the 16th century. By the time the Reformation unfolded in 1517, there were printing centers in over 200 major European cities. These centers became the main producers of Protestant Reformation documents and also, in some cases, anti-Reformation books put forth by Roman Catholics.

Erasmus of Rotterdam, Catholic theologian

There was a number of different methods of propaganda used during the Reformation, including pamphlets/leaflets, texts, letters and translations of the Bible/New Testament. Pamphlets or leaflets were among the most common forms of propaganda during the Reformation and were usually between eight and sixteen pages long. They were quite small and easy to conceal from authorities, thus making them very practical to reformers whose ideas were not accepted by the Roman Catholic authorities. Most of these pamphlets promoted Protestant ideas and—although not with the same effect—were also used by Roman Catholic propagandists.

Protestant and Roman Catholic propaganda during the Reformation attempted to sway the public into adopting new religious practices or continuing the established ones. Propagandists from both groups tried to publish documents about church doctrine, to either retain their believers or influence new believers. Occasionally, these printed texts also acted as manuals for lay people about the appropriate way to conduct themselves within church and society.

Protestant propaganda and church doctrine broke away from the traditional conventions of the Catholic Church. They called for a change in the way that the Church was run; insisting that the buying and selling of indulgences and religious positions be stopped, as well as putting an end to the corruption of the papacy. In addition to this, reformers questioned the authority of the Church and, in particular, the pope. Protestants believed that the main authority of their church should be the Gospel or Scripture, as understood through private interpretation and not from the dictates of the papacy.

Another dominant message that was found in Protestant propaganda was the idea that every person should be granted access to the Bible as a means to interpret it for themselves. This was the primary reason why Luther translated and published numerous copies of the New Testament during the Reformation years. Protestants questioned the belief that the pope had the sole authority to interpret Scripture. This can be seen in Luther's publication *To the Christian Nobility of the German Nation*, which criticized the Catholic belief that the pope was supreme and could interpret Scripture however he saw fit. To combat this, Luther put forth arguments from the Bible that indicated that everyone had the ability to interpret Scripture, not just the pope.

Reformation messages were very controversial and were frequently banned in a number of Catholic cities. Despite this attempt by the Catholic Church to contain and repress Protestant propaganda, Protestants found effective ways of disseminating their messages to believers. The use of pamphlets became the primary method of spreading Protestant ideas and doctrine; they took little time to produce and could be printed and sold quickly, making them more difficult for authorities to track. The sheer number of pamphlets produced during this time period indicates that during the Reformation Protestant works were available on a consistent basis and on a large scale, making controversial ideas accessible to the masses.

The visual arts incorporated the new ideas of the Renaissance and were used to promote personal, political and religious goals.

The new tendencies and ideas of the Renaissance were manifested with increased power and magnificence in the field of art. The history of civilization in this period remained an age of unequalled beauty. The contrast between the medieval world and the

Renaissance is all the more striking in the arts, which offered Europe a new vision of the world, a new conception of form and a new rapport between man and space. Starting in the 14th century, art began to be emancipated from the spiritual tutelage of the Church. Art became popular, even when it worked for the Church. Artists, like humanists, no longer approached the world in accordance with the idea of redemption, but instead as an activity field of assertion and joy for man. Art became more and more realistic. Although a lot of themes were still religious, they represented scenes from everyday life and political events.

In the Middle Ages, monks produced illuminated manuscripts. The change from this type of activity to the art of the Renaissance was a great step. From Giotto in the 13th century to Leonardo da Vinci and Raphael Sanzio at the beginning of the 16th century, this was the richest period in Italian art, when *chiaroscuro* techniques were used to create the illusion of three-dimensional space.

"Small Prison Scene" by Joseph Wright of Derby: example of chiaroscuro art

The artists from northern Europe were influenced by the Italian school. Among the most successful and famous were Hans Holbein the Younger from Germany, Jan van Eyck from Belgium and Pieter Bruegel the Elder from the Netherlands. In order to achieve depth and light, they used glazing techniques through the utilization of oils. In the 17th century, some of the great Dutch masters appeared such as Rembrandt, especially famous for his portraiture and Biblical scenes, and Vermeer, who specialized in interior scenes of Dutch life.

The Baroque period started after the Renaissance, lasting from the late 16th century to the end of the 17th century. One of the most famous artists was Caravaggio, who used tenebrism intensively. Peter Paul Rubens was a Flemish painter who studied in Italy, worked for local churches in Antwerp and also painted a series of paintings for Marie de' Medici. Annibale Carracci was influenced by the characteristics of the Sistine Chapel and created a type of illusionistic ceiling painting. Much of the development that happened in the Baroque period was because of the Protestant Reformation and the resulting Counter-Reformation. The most expressive characteristics of this art were dramatic lighting and overall visuals.

Princes and popes, concerned with enhancing their prestige, commissioned painting and architectural works based on classical styles and often employing the newly invented technique of geometric perspective.

Civil architecture also bloomed during this time, and wherever the laic element became powerful, like at the courts of princes and with the urban leaders, it transformed in order to satisfy the desire for elegance and comfort. The great nobles, tired of the morose severity of their military castles, now wanted houses which combined practical defense measures with the style, beauty and comfort of the age.

Michelangelo Buonarroti, Renaissance artist

Art excited the sacral and festive spaces of public monuments (churches, communal palaces) and entered the private realm as well. Its instructive and educative function was compounded by the esthetic one. At the same time, art gained prestige. Works of art became luxuries, which enhanced the social prestige of the acquirer. Many architects, painters and sculptors were known by their first names, such as is the case with Raphael, Michelangelo and Donatello. A new and original style was created—the Renaissance style—which combined elements of the admired architecture of Antiquity with the more recently fashionable romantic and gothic styles.

Since popes had relocated to Avignon or had been divided by the schism since 1309, Rome had remained architecturally underdeveloped, from both utilitarian and artistic perspectives. The patronage of the arts and architecture became a matter of papal policy—to increase the institution's prestige as a whole—and of certain popes' personal preferences. Leo X was well known for his patronage of Raphael, whose paintings played a large role in the renovation of the Vatican. Pope Sixtus IV initiated a major action to redesign and rebuild Rome, widening the streets and destroying the crumbling ruins, commissioning the Sistine Chapel and summoning many artists from other Italian city-states and giving them commissions. Pope Nicholas V founded the Vatican Library.

Popes and princes ordered works of art. Cities were embellished with various harmoniously proportioned constructions: palaces, villa, municipal buildings, libraries, squares. Religious constructions were represented by domes and funerary monuments. The architectural characteristic of the day was the cupola, a creation of the Florentine Filippo Brunelleschi who used it at the Dome of Florence, a monumental construction with enormous dimensions and synchronized proportions. The most important construction of the Renaissance was St. Peter's Cathedral in Rome, which was worked on by the prominent artists Donato Bramante and Michelangelo Buonarroti. Michelangelo (1475–1564) also created *David,* in which he represented the ideal of energy and manly beauty. In Rome, for Pope Julius II's tomb, he created *Moses* and *The Slaves,* in which he expressed human suffering and resistance in the face of death.

Julius II, pope from 1503–1513, commissioned a series of highly influential art and architectural projects in Rome. He ordered projects like the painting of the Sistine Chapel's ceiling, the reconstruction of St. Peter's Basilica and the frescoes of the Raphael Rooms' *Stanza della Segnatura* and *Stanza d'Eliodoro*, which included the painting *The School of Athens.* The painting on the ceiling of the Sistine Chapel by Michelangelo and Raphael's *Stanze* in the Vatican are considered among the masterworks of the High Renaissance in Rome.

Julius' decision to rebuild St. Peter's led to the construction of the massive basilica that can be seen at the Vatican to this day. His reasons for these projects were varied and they served political, spiritual and aesthetic purposes. During his papacy, the increasing influence of the Protestant Reformation produced ever-growing tension within Christianity, which caused the Catholic Church to lose influence and political power in Europe. Several of the previous popes had been poor, unjust and impious. Because of their behavior, the papal seat and the Vatican's monopoly on religion had been weakened. For these reasons, among others, Julius requested the magnificent and powerful images that are still so recognizable today.

Three of the most successful and revered artists of Renaissance Florence are Donatello, Michelangelo and Raphael. Donatello (1386 – 1466) was an early Renaissance sculptor from Florence. He contributed to the decoration of the Cathedral of Florence and created a huge statue of St. John the Evangelist, seated. He completed numerous other remarkable sculptures, including *Donatello's David* (not to be confused with Michelangelo's more famous *David*).

Michelangelo Simoni (1475 – 1564) was an artist and an engineer who lived in Florence during the Renaissance. He was a student and protégé of Leonardo DaVinci. His achievements are the highest of the period. They include the Genesis scenes on the ceiling of the Sistine Chapel and the famous statue of David. He was revered by his community because of his powerful talent, at a time when artists and artisans were considered the lowest level of society.

Ceiling of the Sistene Chapel in Rome

Raphael (Raffaello Urbino, 1483 – 1520) was an Italian Renaissance painter. He painted in many cities, including a large amount of time in Florence. He painted the "Raphael Rooms" in the Vatican Palace. He developed a much different style than Michelangelo, who is considered by many to be Raphael's rival.

A human-centered naturalism that considered individuals and everyday life appropriate objects of artistic representation was encouraged through the patronage of both princes and commercial elites.

Art became realist and naturalist, with representations of figures capturing the real-life model more and more faithfully. Artists were able to express their conceptions even though they were under the patronage of princes and commercial elites. The main innovation was the invention of a technique to the third dimension in art, which had initially been meant to express the volume of the human body and the perspective of the surrounding space. Leonardo da Vinci (1452–1519) was preoccupied with new solutions to the problem of perspective, light and composition.

In his paintings, *La Gioconda* (*Mona Lisa*) for example, he glorified feminine beauty, the nobility of the soul and maternity. *The Last Supper* (Milan), commissioned by Ludovico Sforza il Moro ("The Dark"), was a mural painting with a religious theme. In order to prevent the idealization of the characters in the painting, he created men whose faces reflected both their qualities and defects. He was a brilliant portraitist, illustrating with great talent the personage's character (Leon X, Julius II, etc.).

Other famous artists whose naturalism was centered on man and nature were: Jan van Eyck, Pieter Bruegel and Rembrandt. Jan van Eyck (1390–1441) was an early Dutch painter who worked in Bruges and was one of the most significant northern artists from the 15th century. He painted *Portrait of a Man in a Turban*. Pieter Bruegel the Elder (1525–1569), from Brabant, the Netherlands, was famous for his landscapes and peasant scenes, such as *The Harvesters* and *Netherlandish Proverbs*. Rembrandt (1606–1669) was the greatest painter in Dutch history. Among his works, with a wide thematic array, are *The Storm in the Sea of Galilee, A Polish Nobleman* and *The Abduction of Europe*.

Mannerist and Baroque artists employed distortion, drama and illusion in works commissioned by monarchies, city-states and the Church for public buildings to promote their stature and power.

The second part of Michelangelo's work did not belong to the Renaissance. The violence with which he treated the bodies, the seriousness which made it seem that joy was inaccessible to him and the contrast between the superhuman strength of some limbs and the inertia of others, made him the "founder of Baroque." Baroque was the artistic style of the Counter-Reformation. The Catholic reaction against Protestantism also manifested itself in the artistic field, by the tendency to resurrect medieval devoutness. In all of its art, the papacy tried to eliminate all the elements with pagan or heretical influence from the religious historiography. The clergy, and especially the Jesuits, sought to reinstate art in the service of the Church. Thus, they favored the representation of scenes of ecstasy and martyrdom which would arouse the imagination and religious ardor of the faithful.

Baroque art was characterized by the exaggeration of mass, light and movement. It was a process which made the passage from the purity of line to the exaggeration of mass, from severe lines to unrestrained picturesqueness of form, from symmetric and balanced forms to movement which violates lines. This movement started in Italy around 1530. It was the expression of the new conditions created by the loss of independence, economic decline and the Catholic Church's offensive against Protestantism.

Lorenzo Bernini, an Italian painter, sculptor and architect, embellished cities like Venice and Rome with architectural works and construction specific to the Baroque style. Examples of his work include the colonnades around the famous St. Peter's square in Vatican City, numerous constructions in Spanish squares, the *Triton Fountain* in Navona Square and the *Trevi Fountain*, which was modeled on Bernini's drawings. In this century, many statues were constructed of princes, cardinals and other prominent individuals; special attention was given to church altars. A wonderful altar built by Bernini, *St. Teresa's Ecstasy*, is remarkable because of the expression of beatitude of this famous abbess.

Trevi Fountain

El Greco (1548–1614), was born in Crete, studied in Venice and by 1577 was established in Toledo. From Greece, he brought a strong Byzantine influence which can be noticed in the prolonged and hieratic figures and in the two registers he painted, the earthly and the heavenly. He represented dramatic scenes, with contorted bodies and tormented faces, like *The Burial of the Count of Orgaz* in which, on Earth, a procession of the deceased's friends leads to a succession of portraits, while on the superior register, the soul of the dead count is received in paradise. The most important painter from Flanders was Peter Paul Rubens (1577–1640) who was responsible for over 2,000 paintings: scenes from reality, family scenes, self-portraits, children, scenes from everyday life, hunting images, wild animals, allegories and mythological and religious paintings. Rubens was Flemish and had his studio in Antwerp. He painted in the Baroque style, with dramatic movement and light in his scenes and is known for counter-Reformation subject matter.

New ideas in science based on observation, experimentation and mathematics challenged classical views of the cosmos, nature and the human body, although folk traditions of knowledge and the universe persisted.

Science was no longer the sum of knowledge transmitted, unvarying, from one generation to the next, but became information obtained from direct observation of nature and society, through research and reason. Against the absolute cult of authority, be it the Bible or classical Antiquity, the sovereignty of reason and experience was asserted. The concept of science itself changed. The shift, which determined the entire subsequent progress of science, was that experience came to replace authority. At the foundation of Renaissance science stood the idea of perfect correspondence between the human spirit and the material reality.

The pre-established harmony between nature and reason allowed for objective knowledge, which found its superior expression in mathematics, physics, anatomy and the application of new practical techniques. Leonardo da Vinci studied the properties of movement, equilibrium and falling objects. He formulated the idea of wave formation and propagation, and through his numerous studies established the basis of comparative anatomy. He believed in the sovereign value of science which allows man to discover the secrets of nature and put them in the service of mankind.

During the Renaissance period, great advances occurred in geography, astronomy, chemistry, physics, mathematics, manufacturing, anatomy and engineering. The rediscovery of ancient scientific texts was accelerated by the fall of Constantinople in 1453 and by the invention of the printing press, which encouraged learning and allowed a faster and wider propagation of new ideas. However, some historians see in the Renaissance a scientific backwardness, at least in its initial period. Humanists favored human-centered subjects like politics and history over the study of natural philosophy or applied mathematics. Others have focused on the positive influence of the Renaissance, pointing to outcomes like the rediscovery of lost and obscure texts and the increased emphasis on the study of language and the correct reading of texts.

New ideas and methods in astronomy led individuals such as Copernicus, Galileo and Newton to question the authority of the ancients and religion and to develop a heliocentric view of the cosmos.

In the late Middle Ages, astronomy was based on the geocentric model, which had been put forth by Claudius Ptolemy in Antiquity. It was likely that few practicing astronomers or astrologers actually read Ptolemy's *Almagest*, which had been translated into Latin by Gerard of Cremona in the 12th century. Instead of reading him directly, they based their beliefs on the Ptolemaic system described in papers like *De sphaera mundi* by Johannes de Sacrobosco, or *Theorica planetarum*. For the prediction of the planetary motions, they relied on the Alfonsine Tables, a set of astronomical tables based on the *Almagest* models, which also incorporated some later modifications. Contrary to popular belief, until Copernicus, astronomers of the Middle Ages and Renaissance did not resort to "epicycles on epicycles" in order to correct the original Ptolemaic models.

New experimental ideas also influenced astronomy. The efforts made in mathematics enhanced the work of Nicolaus Copernicus (1473–1543). Born in Thorn, Poland, Copernicus studied medicine and mathematics in Krakow and astronomy in Bologna. In Italy, he familiarized himself with the theories of Pythagoras, which led him to the discovery of the heliocentric system. He was among the first generation of astronomers to be trained with the *Theoricae novae* and the *Epitome*. Shortly before 1514, he began to explore the extraordinary new idea that the Earth revolved around the sun. He spent the rest of his life searching for the mathematical proof of heliocentricity.

In *De revolutionibus orbium coelestium* (*On the Revolutions of the Heavenly Spheres*), finished in 1507 and published in 1543, Copernicus proved the roundness of the earth, the rotation around its axis and the planets' revolutions around the Sun which forms the center of the universe. When the work was finally published in 1543, Copernicus was on his deathbed. A comparison of his work with the *Almagest* shows that Copernicus was in many ways a Renaissance scientist rather than a revolutionary, because he followed Ptolemy's methods and even his order of presentation.

Nicolaus Copernicus, Polish mathematician

Regarding astronomy, the science of the Renaissance ended with the serious works of Johannes Kepler (1571–1630) and Galileo Galilei (1564–1642). Galileo Galilei (1564–1642) proved Copernicus' theories and found evidence for the law of universal gravity by using the scientific method. However, it took time for the value of the experimental method to be recognized and the importance of Copernicus and Galilei's discoveries to be accepted beyond the narrow circle of the intellectual elite. In the middle of the 16th century, the papacy unleashed its offensive against the Reformation and against all of the ideas which threatened the dogmatic system and authority of the Church. The Jesuit order and the Inquisition reestablished the control of the Church over intellectuals. Galileo was twice questioned by the Inquisition for promoting Copernicus' ideas.

In 1616, the Catholic Church—which until then had tried to adapt its positions to the new knowledge, fearing that it might lose adepts—condemned all the writings that promulgated the notion of heliocentricity. Another decisive factor in the Catholic authorities' change of attitude was the severe theological implications of Copernican heliocentricity. According to heliocentrism, Earth was a simple planet among others. Yet a crisis was provoked by the theory of the infinite universe because of the hypothesis of the existence of several worlds and solar systems speculated about by Giordano Bruno. For the entire Catholic and Protestant religious hierarchy, even more important and threatening than the heliocentricity hypothesis proposed by Copernicus was his audacity in putting scientific or philosophic speculation above the teachings of the Bible.

Anatomical and medical discoveries by physicians, including William Harvey, presented the body as an integrated system, challenging the traditional humoral theory of the body and of disease espoused by Galen.

The experimental method also discredited scholastic authority (the belief that valid knowledge only comes from the ancient classical writings) in the field of natural sciences. Important progress was registered in medicine; the anatomy of the human body was discovered by dissection which, for a long period of time, had been strictly forbidden and severely punished by the Church. The development of modern neurology began in the 16th century with Vesalius, who described the anatomy of the brain and other organs. He had little knowledge of the brain's function, thinking that intellect resided mainly in the ventricles. Understanding of medical sciences and diagnoses improved, but with little direct benefit to health care. Beyond opium and quinine, few effective drugs existed. The most useful medical tomes at the time were *materiae medicae* and *pharmacopoeia*.

The Swiss Paracelsus (1493–1541) derived his fundamental therapeutic principle from the stimulation of "man's vital force." This method involved the physician intervening at the point at which a person's vital force was weakened. Paracelsus refuted formal scholastic knowledge, emphasizing the importance of the chemical and physical processes of live beings.

Emperor Charles V's physician, Andreas Vesalius (1514–1564), founded the study of modern human anatomy. Named professor of anatomy at the University of Padua, he suffered during the Inquisition because of his dissection of human corpses. His fundamental work, *De Humani Corporis Fabrica* (*On the Fabric of the Human Body*), introduced the system of macroscopic anatomy, which remains valuable to this day.

Vesalius, Belgian anatomist

William Harvey (1578–1657) was an English physician in the court of Kings James I and Charles I who became famous for elaborating on the theory of sanguine circulation. In 1628, he published the paper *De Motu Cordis*, which defended his theory of blood circulation in the human body. Harvey disproved Galen's theory about the role, origins and movement of blood which, for a long time, had been a dogma few had dared to question. Harvey's paper contained a description of the circulatory system, whose basic element was the heart. He also proved that the liver, which had the main role in Galen's theory, was not able to produce the high quantity of blood necessary for the entire organism. As the king's personal physician, and given his loyal Royalist opinions, Harvey suffered during the civil war when Cromwell's men demolished his house and burned most of his notes. Despite these difficulties, he continued his research.

Francis Bacon and René Descartes defined inductive and deductive reasoning and promoted experimentation and the use of mathematics, which would ultimately shape the scientific method.

Science was based on the idea of perfect correspondence between the human body and material reality, with objective knowledge finding its superior expression in mathematics and in shaping the scientific method. The English philosopher Francis Bacon (1561–1626) was the creator of empiricism and the first scientist to receive the title of "knight." Bacon asserted that the senses gave indubitable knowledge and that real knowledge could be obtained only by the methodical, rational processing of what was observed.

In his main paper, *Novum Organum*, Bacon introduced the inductive method, characterized by the use of analysis, observation and experimentation. In considering the world as material in nature, and movement as an inalienable characteristic of matter, Bacon recognized the existence of multiple forms of movement and of qualitative diversity in nature. Bacon outlined the role played by induction and analysis in knowledge, to the detriment of synthesis and deduction. This conception of a purely analytical experiment conferred on the Baconian method a non-dialectic character.

René Descartes, French philosopher and mathematician

The French philosopher and mathematician René Descartes lived from 1596 to 1650. (Cartesius was his Latin name, from which the term "Cartesian numbers" is derived.) He had a great influence on the study of western philosophy. He made great contributions to mathematics, by founding the Cartesian coordinate system and analytical geometry (a discipline which connects algebra and geometry). He also had a crucial role in the discovery of infinitesimal calculus. In philosophy, Descartes laid the basics of what is now called *rationalism*, in opposition to the empiricist school of thought represented by Bacon, Hobbes and Locke. He is best known for his philosophical statements, like *"Cogito ergo sum"*—"I think, therefore I am"—from his work *Discourse on Method* and for using the deductive method of knowing God.

Alchemy and astrology continued to appeal to elites and some natural philosophers, in part because they shared with new science the notion of a predictable and knowable universe. In the oral culture of peasants, a belief that the cosmos was governed by divine and demonic forces persisted.

At the beginning of the 16th century, the scientific disciplines were still hard to discern. Overlap existed between science and speculative thinking and between astrology and alchemy. Occult science first appeared in ancient Egypt and developed during the Medieval Ages. Medieval alchemy had such purposes as finding the elixir of life and the miraculous "philosopher's stone," which could allegedly transform all metals into gold.

Medicine, alchemy, natural sciences and astrology formed a kind of symbiosis. Among the first alchemists were Heinrich Cornelius Agrippa and Nicholas Flamel, who did not have a strong influence, but to whom all subsequent alchemists made reference.

The most important representative of alchemy was Paracelsus. He gave alchemy a new direction, freeing it from occultism and directing it towards experimentation and scientific observation, especially for the purpose of understanding the human body. He rejected the magical and gnostic traditions, adhering instead to hermetical, neoplatonic and Pythagorean philosophies.

According to his theory, the human body was a chemical system in which the basic elements sulfur, mercury and salt, played a fundamental role. He believed that illness was caused by a disequilibrium between these principal chemicals and not because of "humors," as Galen's adepts believed. His theory posited that remedies should be of a mineral nature, as opposed to organic. Organic chemistry later dealt a decisive blow to Paracelsus' theory and to the hope of finding the elixir of life by demonstrating the toxicity of the substances with which the alchemists were working.

Other alchemists and astrologists of the time included Johannes Kepler (1571-1630)—who demonstrated that the orbit of the celestial bodies is an ellipse and calculated the time for their revolutions—and Sir Isaac Newton (1643–1727), a famous English scientist, alchemist, mathematician and astronomer. He studied alchemical literature, hoping that he could clarify the structure of the micro-universe and find correlations with that of the cosmological system.

In 1687 he published *Philosophiae Naturalis Principia Mathematica*, in which he described the law of universal attraction and established the basis of classical mechanics, by studying the laws which governed the movement

Sir Isaac Newton, English scientist

of objects. Newton was the first to demonstrate that the laws of nature govern both the movements of the terrestrial globe and of other celestial objects, intuiting that their orbits might be not only elliptical, but also hyperbolical or parabolic. In modern times, alchemy has become more and more marginalized as science demands experimentation as the only way to verify the truth.

Period 1: 1450-1648

Key Concept 1.2: The struggles for sovereignty within and among states resulted in varying degrees of political centralization.

Three trends shaped early modern political development: (1) from decentralized power and authority toward centralization; (2) from a political elite consisting primarily of a hereditary landed nobility toward one open to men distinguished by their education, skills and wealth; and (3) from the prevailing religious norms toward secular norms of law and justice.

One innovation promoting state centralization and the transformation of the landed nobility was the new dominance of the firearms and artillery on the battlefield. The introduction of these new technologies, along with the changes in tactics and strategy, amounted to a military revolution that reduced the role of mounted knights and castles, raised the cost of maintaining military power beyond the means of individual lords and led to professionalization of the military on land and sea under the authority of the sovereign. This military revolution favored rulers who could command the resources required for building increasingly complex fortifications and fielding disciplined infantry and artillery units. Monarchs who could increase taxes and create bureaucracies to collect and spend them on their military outmaneuvered those who could not.

In general, monarchs gained power vis-à-vis the corporate groups and institutions that had thrived during the medieval period, notably the landed nobility and the clergy. Commercial and talented personas, acquired increasing power in the state—often in alliance with the monarchs—alongside or in place of these traditional corporate groups. New legal and political theories, embodied in the codification of the law, strengthened state institutions, which increasingly took control of the social and economic order from traditional religious and local bodies. However, these developments were not universal. In eastern and southern Europe, the traditional elites maintained their positions in many polities.

The centralization of power within polities took place within and facilitated a new diplomatic framework among sires. Ideals of a universal Christian empire declined along with the power and prestige of the Holy Roman Empire, which was unable to overcome the challenges of political localism and religious pluralism. By the end of the Thirty Years' War, a new state system had emerged based on sovereign nation-states and the balance of power.

The new concept of the sovereign state and secular systems of law played a central role in the creation of new political institutions.

"New monarchy" is the concept used to describe the type of government that appeared in the 16th century, which bridged medieval monarchy and the absolutist monarchy of the 17th century. The power of the monarch increased gradually while extending his domination of local institutions that represented law and justice in the Middle Ages. Following this development, the rights of cities were drastically restricted, as were those of landlords and quasi-independent regional assemblies. Ferdinand and Isabella of Spain, Henry VII of England and Gustav Vasa of Sweden were considered typical new monarchs. Still, the medieval institutions demonstrated a remarkable resilience; many of them survived to modernity.

Ferdinand and Isabella of Spain before Christopher Columbus

During the 16th century, there was an obvious tendency towards a stronger state. In Europe, the royal government extended beyond the limits it had had in the Middle Ages. The king's functionaries applied his rules with efficiency. Still, in most of the states this evolution encountered obstacles, especially from privileged groups that felt most threatened by the expansion of royal authority. The drive for a stronger state was based on the king's need to gather larger and larger amounts of money, especially for paying the armies of mercenaries. For the French monarchy of the Renaissance, there was a direct connection between this financial necessity and the creation of a more centralized and powerful government.

The royalty tried to maintain the idea that the monarchy had a consultative character. Royal laws and decrees were preceded by a declaration, in which it was indicated that the king had considered the opinions of the most important men in the state. The most frequently used instrument was the royal council, but this organization was too small and generally made up of the king's henchmen. So other organizations, such as parliaments and assemblies of notables, came to be consulted about important decisions.

In international relations and law, a sovereign state was defined as a nonphysical juridical entity that was represented by a centralized government, which had sovereignty over a geographic area. International law further defined the sovereign state as having a permanent population, a defined territory, one government and the capacity to enter into relations with other sovereign states. It was also normally understood that a state was neither dependent nor subject to any other power or state.

The appearance or disappearance of a state was a question of fact. According to the declarative theory of state recognition, a sovereign state could exist without being recognized by other sovereign states, but unrecognized states often found it difficult to negotiate with their counterparts if a question could be raised as to their legitimacy. The concept of Westphalian sovereignty was defining the nation-state based on territoriality and the absence of external actors inserting themselves into domestic matters. It was an international system of states, multinational corporations and organizations that was established during the Thirty Years' War and began with the Peace of Westphalia in 1648.

New Monarchies laid the foundation of the centralized modern state by establishing a monopoly on tax collection, military force and the dispensing of justice, and gaining the right to determine the religion of their subjects.

The new monarchy was a regime in which the power of the king was absolute and unquestioned. Its limits resulted only from his responsibility to God—the only source of monarchical authority. The Catholic Church and the Inquisition contributed to the consolidation of this type of authoritarian government. The monarch had the right to carry out justice and legislate as he pleased. French absolutism was characterized by the strengthening of the role of the state and by identifying the institution of the Crown with the state, through attempting to control all levels of social interaction, the conduct of commerce, the practice of religion and the development of intellectual life.

The control of subjects was a central issue. Moreover, the monarchy had a monopoly on tax collection. Some rulers reorganized the collection of demographic statistics in order to have better evidence of the number of subjects, to facilitate gathering taxes and to have a clear idea of their military potential. Monarchs also tried to control their peoples' beliefs, by Catholic religious leveling, as a method of attaining their political aims. In time, politics led to a succession of religious conflicts in all the European kingdoms.

Masimilian I, Roman emperor

Given the centralization process of the western European states and the privileges of the Church, the pope's interference in internal affairs was incompatible with the state. In England, the royalty embraced the Reformation, as it was interested in the secularization of the Church's property. In Germany, the princes feared the centralization attempts of Emperors Maximilian I and Charles Quint, so they embraced the ideas of the Reformation, which contributed to a strengthening of their authority at the expense of the Habsburgs. In the Religious Peace of Augsburg (1555), both Catholic and Lutheran confessions were declared to be equally legitimate.

The French kings acted as if their obligation to defend the Church conferred on them the right to act as they pleased in ecclesiastic affairs. In 1302, when Pope Boniface VIII reminded Philip IV of France that the pope had a superior authority over the Church, the king ordered him arrested. During the next 150 years, Philip's descendants profited from a long period of papal weakness and obtained from Rome the recognition of their vast powers in the Church. The Concordat of Bologna (1516) gave the king the right to name approximately one hundred bishops and archbishops and nearly five hundreds abbots. The king's enormous level of power and control, compared to the largely symbolic authority of the pope, transformed the hierarchy of the French Church into a docile instrument in the king's hands.

Religious wars dominated all of Europe during the 16th century and were mostly fought between Catholics and the Protestants. The most dramatic event was *The Night of Saint Bartholomew*, a massacre committed against the French Protestants (Huguenots), which was unleashed by the state on the night of August 23–24, 1572. The massacre lasted several days in Paris and later extended to twenty other towns and continued for weeks. Almost 30,000 Huguenots were killed. Some historians consider it the largest massacre of the century.

This tragic episode of the religious wars was the result of a series of political, religious and social factors. It was a consequence of the civil and military conflicts between the Catholic and Protestant French nobles. It had, as a result, a wild popular reaction that was ultra-Catholic and hostile to the king's reconciliation politics. Realizing the evil influence of the civil religious wars which plagued his kingdom, Henry IV tried to reconcile the two sides, as that was the only way to face powerful pressures from abroad.

The Edict of Nantes (13th April 1598) put a temporary end to these religious conflicts. Composed of four separate treaties, it granted the Huguenots complete freedom of conscience and to practice their religion in public, but with substantial restrictions. If the Edict of Nantes set France's religious affairs in order, it did so only because the king willed it. When Louis XIV no longer considered it appropriate to tolerate the Huguenots in 1685, severe persecution appeared again.

Religion was an issue in Spain, whose rulers, Ferdinand of Aragon and Isabella of Castile, were named "Reyes Católicos" by Pope Alexander VI. Along with Spain's territorial expansion, Ferdinand and Isabella desired a religious unification of their kingdom under Roman Catholicism. The Inquisition was institutionalized as a part of this process. Isabella's confessor, Cisneros, was named Archbishop of Toledo. He played an important role in the rehabilitation program of Spain's religious institutions, setting the base for the future Counter-Reformation.

The Peace of Westphalia (1648), which marked the effective end of the medieval ideal of universal Christendom, accelerated the decline of the Holy Roman Empire by granting princes, bishops and other local leaders control over religion.

The Thirty Years' War was the first conflict to take place in a pan-European context. It began as an internal conflict within the Holy Roman Empire, between the emperor and the Protestant princes. The emperor, supported by Catholic lords, Spain and the papacy, desired to consolidate his central power and install absolutism in Germany. For that purpose, he led a Catholicization campaign. The Protestant princes, supported by France, opposed those goals. The Thirty Years' War had four phases, Czech, Dane,

Swedish and French; following the victories of the French and the defeat of the Roman-German emperor, it ended in 1648 with the Peace of Westphalia.

Scene from the Thirty Years' War

The Peace of Westphalia was composed of a series of peace treaties signed between May and October 1648 in the cities of Osnabrück and Münster. These treaties ended the Thirty Years' War (1618–1648) within the Holy Roman Empire and the Eighty Years' War (1568–1648) between Spain and the Dutch Republic. Spain subsequently recognized the independence of the Dutch Republic.

The Peace Treaty of Westphalia was marked by two major events: the conclusion of the Peace Treaty of Münster between the Dutch Republic and the Kingdom of Spain on January 30, 1648, and the signing of two complementary treaties on October 24, 1648, namely The Treaty of Münster between the Holy Roman Emperor, France and their respective allies, and the Treaty of Osnabrück (*Instrumentum Pacis Osnabrugensis*), which involved the Holy Roman Empire, the Kingdom of France, Sweden and their respective allies.

The treaties did not restore peace throughout Europe, but they did create a basis for national self-determination. They were concluded after a large diplomatic congress, which initiated a new system of political order in central Europe, later called *Westphalian sovereignty*, which was based upon the concept of co-existing sovereign states. Inter-state aggression was to be held in check by a balance of power. A covenant was established against interference in another nation's domestic affairs. As European influence spread across the globe, these Westphalian principles, especially the concept of sovereign states, became central to international law and to the prevailing world order.

The stipulations of the Religious Peace of Augsburg (1555), by which the Catholic and Protestant (Lutheran) religions were considered equally entitled, were reasserted in the Peace of Westphalia. These stipulations were extended and the emperor had to admit the religious freedoms of the Protestant and Calvinist minority and the right of the two sects to have their place in the imperial Diet. This decision strengthened the independence of the Protestant princes, a fact that accentuated the empire's political disintegration.

Negotiating the Religious Peace of Augsburg

France obtained the episcopacies of Metz and Verdun and a part of Alsace. Spain had lost its supremacy on the European continent to France, but continued to hold a vast colonial empire. The independence of the United Provinces and of Switzerland were recognized. Sweden became a great European power and obtained control of the Baltic Sea, and the territories of Brandenburg and Saxony expanded, thus setting the base for the future Prussian state. The Peace of Westphalia marked the end of the ideal concept of "Christendom" and combined a series of dynastic, economic, political and religious interests, while applying the principle of European equilibrium. With small differences, the boundaries of the states remained unchanged until the French Revolution.

Across Europe, commercial and professional groups gained in power and played a greater role in political affairs.

Economic and technical progress, the increase of production and exchange, the intensification of monetary circulation and the disintegration of the classical medieval society led to the appearance of new market relations. This process was not consistent throughout Europe. It started in England, the Netherlands and France and later expanded to the rest of Europe. Capital represented an amount of money which, if invested, brought profit. The owners of capital were called investors. Immense sums of money were made from commerce, lending and (after the discovery of America) the exploitation of gold and silver mines and the population of the new territories.

The increase in manufacturing and the growing needs of the urban population resulted in the flourishing of commerce and the development of markets, trade and banking activity. It is possible that the special political structures of late Middle Ages Italy led to this rare cultural efflorescence. Italy did not exist as a political entity in the Early Modern period. Instead, it was divided into smaller city-states and territories, which often fought against one another: the Kingdom of Naples controlled the south, the Republic of Florence and the Papal States were in the center, the Milanese and the Genoese occupied the north and northwest, respectively, and the Venetians held the northeast. In the 15th century, Italy was one of the most urbanized areas in Europe. Since many of its cities stood among the ruins of ancient Roman buildings, it seems likely that the classical nature of the Renaissance owed much to its origin in the Roman Empire's heartland.

Historian and political philosopher Quentin Skinner underlined that Otto of Freising (c. 1114–1158), a German bishop who visited northern Italy in the 12th century, noticed a widespread new form of political and social organization. He noted that Italy seemed to have transcended feudalism so that its society was now based on merchants and commerce. Linked to this was anti-monarchical thinking. This was represented in the famous early Renaissance fresco cycle *Allegory of Good and Bad Government in Siena* by Ambrogio Lorenzetti (painted c. 1338–1340). The strong message in the work is its emphasis on the virtues of fairness, justice, republicanism and good administration. Holding both the Church and empire at bay, these city republics were devoted to notions of liberty.

Allegory of Good and Bad Government in Siena (detail) by Ambrogio Lorenzetti

City-states beyond central Italy were also notable for their merchant republics, especially the Republics of Florence and Venice. Although in practice they were oligarchical and bore little resemblance to a modern democracy, they did have democratic features and were responsive states, with forms of participation in governance and some belief in liberty. The relative political freedom they afforded encouraged and stimulated academic and artistic advancement. Likewise, because many Italian cities such as Venice were great trading centers, they served as intellectual crossroads. Merchants brought with them ideas from far corners of the globe, particularly the Levant. Venice was Europe's gateway to trade with the East and a producer of fine glass, while Florence was a capital of textiles. The wealth such businesses brought to Italy meant that large public and private artistic projects could be commissioned and individuals had more leisure time to devote to study.

The Italian (Frescobaldi, Strozzi) and German (Fugger, Wesler) financiers made so much profit and were so affluent that they became creditors of the European monarchs. The bourgeoisie was composed of wealthy citizens (owners of manufactures, merchants, loaners, craftsmen, even workers who became owners), new intellectuals (jurists, physicians and functionaries) and prosperous countrymen who had made their fortunes as farmers.

In England, along with the ancient nobility (who did not adapt to the changing economy), there appeared a new gentry interested in manufacturing and commerce, similar to the bourgeoisie found elsewhere in Europe. The two social classes became so rich and powerful that soon they did not feel the need for an absolutist regime's protection. In France, the great nobility became scarce—a consequence of the centralization of the state and of civil wars. Some of the nobility became nobles of the court. The most affluent were the Nobles of the Robe, who worked in administration, justice and the parliament. The nobility was not a closed social group, but an open elite, often accepting alliances with the bourgeoisie, which led to an increase of its economic power and political influence.

Under the Old Regime (*Ancien Regime*), the Nobles of the Robe or Nobles of the Gown (French: *Noblesse de robe*) were French aristocrats whose rank came from holding certain judicial or administrative posts. As a rule, these positions did not of themselves give the holder a title of nobility, such as baron, count or duke (although the holder might also have such a title), but were almost always attached to a specific function. The offices were often hereditary, and by 1789 most Nobles of the Robe had inherited their positions.

The most influential were the 1,100 members of the thirteen parliaments, or courts of appeal. They were distinct from the "Nobles of the Sword" (French: *Noblesse d'épée*)—whose nobility was based on their families' traditional function as the knightly class and whose titles were usually attached to a particular feudal fiefdom—a landed estate awarded in return for military service. Together with the older nobility, the Nobles of the Robe made up the Second Estate in pre-revolutionary France. Since these nobles, especially the judges, had often studied at a university, they were called Nobles of the Robe after the robes worn by scholars.

Originally given out as rewards for services to the king, the offices became venal, a commodity to be bought and sold (under certain conditions of aptitude). This practice became official with the edict of *la Paulette*, the Paulette being the tax paid by the holder to keep the office hereditary. As hereditary offices, they were often passed from father to son, creating a marked class consciousness. Nobles of the Robe were often considered by Nobles of the Sword to be of inferior rank because their status was not derived from military service and/or land ownership. The elite Nobles of the Robe, such as the members of parliament, fought to preserve their status alongside the Nobles of the Sword in pre-revolutionary society. Across Europe, the new social groups, gaining in wealth due to the profound transformations in the economy, became increasingly powerful and began to play an important role in political affairs.

Secular political theories, such as those espoused in Machiavelli's The Prince, provided a new concept of the state.

For six decades, Italy was not only the battlefield of international rivalries, but also the proving ground of European diplomacy. The pragmatic political combinations, the propaganda methods and the financial strategies that had been applied in Italy were transposed into European politics. The principle of equilibrium was adopted as a defense against the expansion of a power which threatened to break the rapport between the competing powers. It was first applied in order to weaken the opposition of the forces which clashed in the internal struggles of the Italian communal republics and principalities. The political context in which the Renaissance occurred led to the appearance of a new theory on the art of governance.

Cover of Machiavelli's
The Prince (1550 edition)

In *The Prince,* Niccolò Machiavelli (1469–1527) showed that in his essence man is artificial, greedy and frightened when in danger. These characteristics impel the prince not to consider what is good or bad for the individual when the interests of the state are at stake. Machiavelli argued that a prince's mission was only to maintain and save the state, which was the highest moral objective. There was nothing above the state, and the prince, who personifies the state, had to subordinate all his other preoccupations, even his personal morality, to this. Often he had to work against good faith, love, men and religion—the purpose justified the means. Later on, without renouncing the same general conception of politics, Machiavelli proposed that a republic was a more appropriate system of government than a monarchy to preserve the state, the functioning of which must be founded on the respect for law.

Jean Bodin (1530–1596) defined the concept of sovereignty before the appearance of constitutional law as a juridical science. Fearing tyranny and anarchy, Bodin promoted the king's absolute sovereignty and also respect for justice and tolerance, which he considered the two necessary conditions for internal peace. In his *Treaty on the Republic,* Bodin wrote that the preservation of kingdoms, empires and all peoples depended upon good princes and wise governors. He distinguished five manifestations of sovereignty: the power to legislate (which is the essence of the state); the right to declare war and negotiate peace; the right to name high magistrates; the recognition by the subjects of the sovereignty titular; and the right to absolve and give amnesty. Still, the sovereign's power had limits; it had to respect the divine and natural law and the country's justice, stability and traditions. For Bodin, the republic was just only if it ensured the happiness of its subjects.

Hugo Grotius (1583–1645) was one of the original theorists of public international law and natural rights, which he said had its origins in human nature, characterized by the instincts of sociability and reason. According to Grotius, "right" was based on four foundations: respecting what belongs to another; respecting agreements; reparation of damages inflicted on others; and equitable punishment of those who violated these principles. According to his theory of the natural right, Grotius analyzed the right of a society to punish those who did not respect its laws and who threatened its existence. This must not be arbitrary, like revenge, but it must be a manifestation of reason and exerted between the limits of justice and humanity. Thus, Grotius derived the principle of the liberty of conscience—man is not free to do anything, but is free to think anything.

Regarding the state, Grotius followed contract theory, according to which men freely unite into a state in order to defend themselves from perils, transferring sovereignty to one or several men. Only one definition of right can function amongst the great communities of the world, in which all are equal, and the guarantee of this right must be given by the decision of each state to respect conventions. In international relations, peace must be preferred to war but, by virtue of the natural right, states have the right to defend themselves and to use force against force; therefore, in legitimate conditions, states have the right to fight wars. An entirely new conception of the state was outlined during the Renaissance; in the following centuries, international politics operated around these principles.

The competitive state system led to new patterns of diplomacy and new forms of warfare.

Until the Peace of Westphalia (1648), European states confronted the medieval aspirations of the Holy Roman Empire and of the Catholic Church, embodied by the Holy Roman emperor. However, the Thirty Years' War, waged inside the empire between Catholics and Protestants, brought about a new system of international relations. The new nation-states conducted their foreign politics according to the concept of the equilibrium of power. This declared that each time a state increased its power to the point where it became threatening, the other states would form a coalition to counter-balance and undermine the hegemonic ambitions of the powerful state. The equilibrium—which meant a condition of peace—was accomplished by various means, from war to diplomacy. Disequilibrium would quite surely have led to crisis and conflicts. From then on, new patterns of diplomacy and new forms of warfare appeared.

The swearing in of the peace treaty between Spain and the United Provinces

Following the Peace of Westphalia, religion was no longer a cause for warfare among European states; instead, the concept of the balance of power played an important role in structuring diplomatic and military objectives.

The centralized and absolutist monarchies, after overcoming their internal difficulties, sought to expand their power and dominance outside of their historic boundaries. Yet the expansion of one would provoke the resistance of the others who, in order to reestablish equilibrium, made a coalition. Thus, the European political system was constructed based on the principle of the equilibrium of forces, taking into account state interests, and not dynastic or religious motives.

From a political perspective, the Thirty Years' War resulted in the establishment of a new equilibrium in Europe, based on France's supremacy. The Holy Roman Empire finished the war weakened and territorially diminished—to the benefit of both France and Sweden. For the first time in history, at Westphalia, the representatives of most of the European countries gathered in an international congress. The treaty they produced sanctioned the defeat of the Holy Roman Empire, whose decline was accelerated. The main tenets of the Peace of Westphalia were:

- All parties would recognize the Peace of Augsburg of 1555, according to which each prince had the right to determine the religion of his own state, the options being Catholicism, Lutheranism, and, now, Calvinism (the principle of *cuius regio, eius religio*).

- Christians living in principalities where their denomination was *not* the established Church were guaranteed the right to practice their faith in public during allotted hours and in private at their will.

- General recognition was made of the exclusive sovereignty of each party over its lands, people and agents abroad, and responsibility for the warlike acts of any of its citizens or agents. The issuance of unrestricted letters of marque and reprisal to privateers were forbidden.

The Peace represented the first diplomatic encounter at the pan-European level and in it were consecrated the principles of political equilibrium and of state interests. Until the Renaissance, the national interest was generally viewed as secondary to that of religion or morality. After Westphalia, the national interest dominated general European politics and in succeeding centuries states became fiercely competitive. The Thirty Years' War also led to the perfection of military techniques, the disappearance of mercenaries and the formation of national armies.

Advances in military technology (i.e., the military revolution) led to new forms of warfare, including greater reliance on infantry, firearms, mobile cannon and more elaborate fortifications, all financed by heavier taxation and requiring a larger bureaucracy. Technology, tactics and strategies tipped the balance of power. States were able to marshal sufficient resources for the new military environment.

In the 15th century, guns were developed for large sieges. This had an impact on the construction of defensive structures. In order to make artillery less effective, the Italians developed fortifications with thick earth and angled bastions, complete with ditches and entrapments. In the 16th and 17th centuries, these defensive constructions spread throughout the rest of Europe and other significant changes in weaponry and tactics appeared. For centuries, mounted knights and archers had dominated the battlefield, but now they were replaced by musketeers and pikemen.

Illustration of a 17th-century pikeman

By the end of the 16th century, muskets had replaced the bow and arrow. Still, the musket was a large, slow weapon which took two minutes or longer to load. Moreover, the gunpowder necessary to fire a musket was ignited by a match, so it could not be used in wet or windy weather. The slow rate of fire of muskets necessitated that musketeers be defended from sudden cavalry attack by pikemen. Eventually, the invention of the bayonet made each musketeer a potential pikeman. Their tactics depended on maneuvering the various elements of the early-modern army in close coordination. Pikemen could defend against a cavalry attack, but were vulnerable to musket fire.

The Spanish *tercio* was the first successful combination of pikes and muskets. The pikemen were formed in a central square and the musketeers positioned at each corner. *Tercios* were large—about 3,000 men—and difficult to maneuver. The Hapsburg armies of the 17th century were reorganized on a six-rank battalion model that owed more to Gustavus Adolphus than the earlier *tercio* tradition.

On the vast steppes of Eastern Europe, cavalry remained very important. The "winged" horsemen (*Husaria*) of Poland, organized in divisions and supported by artillery, played a key role in warfare. The Polish cavalry showed they could beat the best Western infantry, and they were pivotal in routing the Ottoman forces at the siege of Vienna (1683). Musket fire needed to be concentrated in volleys to be destructive, because the weapons were inaccurate and misfires were common. If all the guns were fired simultaneously, the unit was very vulnerable until the guns were reloaded.

Polish Husaria

The Dutch were the first to effectively overcome this problem: musketeers were drawn up in ranks (generally six)—the front rank fired and then moved back and began to reload, while the rank behind them moved up, fired and repeated the process. The troops had to work together and be thoroughly familiar with their weapons for this tactic to be successful. Maurice of Nassau insisted that soldiers train regularly; in 1597, standard terms of command were introduced throughout the Dutch army to guarantee uniformity. Gustavus Adolphus trained his troops so well that he was able to reduce the number of ranks to three (one kneeling, the second crouching, the third standing) and yet still maintain a continuous fire of volleys. Gustavus Adolphus also reduced the size of tactical units, deploying them in battalions of about 500 men, which made tactical maneuver simpler and more flexible.

The size of armies increased, but problems of logistics and supply still made it very difficult to concentrate large numbers of troops in one location. The problems of moving thousands of tons of flour in addition to large quantities of gunpowder and shot meant that if an army could not "live off the land" it rapidly dispersed or died from hunger. In winter, campaigning was difficult—if not impossible—because of the absence of grass for the horses and livestock to feed on.

The competition of power between monarchs and corporate groups produced different distributions of government authority in European states.

Modern revolutions were the answer to some necessities of general order. They occurred everywhere where the modernization of a society could not take place without an open confrontation against the forces which represented the ancient status quo, especially absolutist monarchs and the conservative nobility. Consequently, regardless of where they took place, the bourgeois revolutions had common features: their premises, general causes, essential objectives, the main participant forces and the idea of reorganizing society based on democratic principles.

The fundamental cause of these revolutions was the necessity of aligning state institutions and legislation with the new production and social groups that developed during the 16th and 17th centuries. The bourgeoisie gradually increased in power, but its ascendancy was not complete until it participated in the political process, either alone or with other social groups. Such a transformation was contrary to the interests of the nobility. This inherent disagreement would eventually lead to a fierce struggle between the old order with medieval values and those who wished to radically change the system.

The monarchy had to face alliances between the bourgeoisie, the inhabitants of towns, the peasants and new categories of nobility, who were all interested in the modern transformation of society. The peasants were still paying heavy taxes either to the nobility or the Church, which kept them in a position of inferiority in relation to the state. In each country where revolutions took place, they had a specific evolution, which was reflected in all of the fields of social life. This reality found its expression in the revolution's particular causes, in the alliances between the forces and in the place that each took during the conflicts and in post-revolution society. All these factors had important consequences on the unequal development of different societies, which is why the transformations occurred at different times and to different degrees.

The first revolution started in the Netherlands (1560s), which had the most flourishing economy in Europe. Mainly Calvinist, the population was condemned as heretical by the Catholic Church. This explains the public's dissatisfaction with the Church and Phillip II of Spain. Soon, the riots evolved into a war for freedom, which led to the independence of the republic of Holland. All of Europe was to be impacted by the radical transformations.

The English Civil War, a conflict between the monarchy, Parliament, and other elites over their respective roles in political structure, exemplified this competition.

In the middle of the 17th century, England was still an agrarian country. Both the bourgeoisie and the new gentry were interested in promoting market activities. The alliance between these two groups was a unique feature of the English revolution. They were hindered by England's political system. The prerogatives of the monarchs were limited, although absolutist tendencies could be seen. The English monarchs received strong support from the Anglican Church; during the Reformation, the king had taken the place of the pope, maintaining the ancient and powerful ecclesiastic hierarchy. The fight against absolutism was to be a fight against the Church.

Another important peculiarity of the English revolution was the fact that its ideology embraced a religious form. The movement which opposed the Anglican Church was Puritanism. The main form of the political conflict before, and in the first phase of, the revolution was the juxtaposition of the king and Parliament. The Parliament used its right to vote against taxes as an important weapon to block absolutist tendencies. Not being able to ensure sufficient income otherwise, the king had to appeal to the Parliament. Yet each new convocation accentuated the dispute. Its anti-absolutist options are clearly expressed in the *Petition of right* (1628). Charles I (1625–1649) tried to rule without the Parliament for a while, but the result was only the accentuation of political opposition. The agitations involved large popular groups which were hostile to absolutism.

The king had to call *The Long Parliament,* so named because it lasted for 13 years. From the beginning, it acted against absolutist institutions and their main supporters, and reduced the monarchy's prerogatives. In order to gain liberty of action, the king left the capital, thereby initiating a civil war. At the beginning of the war, the Parliament's army was supported by most Englishmen; however, the Royalists had a better organized army, which was led by Prince Rupert.

At the beginning of January 1642, a few days after his failure to capture five members of the House of Commons, fearing for the safety of his family and retinue, Charles left the London area for the north of the country. Continuous negotiations, maintained by correspondence between the king and the Long Parliament, proved fruitless. As the summer progressed, cities and towns declared their sympathies for one faction or the other. For example, the garrison of Portsmouth, under the command of Sir George Goring, declared for the king; yet when Charles tried to acquire arms for his cause from Kingston-upon-Hull, Sir John Hotham, the military governor appointed by Parliament in January, refused to let Charles enter Kingston.

Portrait of King Charles I of England

When Charles later returned with more men, Hotham drove them off. Charles issued a warrant for Hotham to be arrested as a traitor but was powerless to enforce it. Throughout the summer months, tensions rose and there was brawling in a number of places, with the first death from the conflict taking place in Manchester. Gradually the Parliament strengthened its forces, the most important role being played by Oliver Cromwell, a representative of the nobility. Cromwell was the leader of parliamentary forces during the civil war and leader of England after it. The king was defeated and executed in 1648, after which the Parliament declared England a Republic. Cromwell assumed the title "Lord Protector of England" until 1658, when he was deposed and executed. Cromwell also led a war against Ireland and passed several laws against Catholicism.

In 1645, Parliament reasserted its determination to fight the war to the end. It passed the Self-denying Ordinance, by which all members of the House of Parliament laid down their commands, and reorganized its main forces into the New Model Army, under the command of Sir Thomas Fairfax, with Cromwell as his second-in-command and Lieutenant-General of Horse. In two decisive engagements—the Battle of Naseby on

June 14th and the Battle of Langport on July 10th—the Parliamentarians effectively destroyed the king's armies.

In the remains of his English kingdom Charles attempted to recover a stable base of support by consolidating the Midlands. He began to form an alliance between Oxford and Newark on Trent in Nottinghamshire. Those towns had become fortresses and showed more reliable loyalty to him than to others. He took Leicester, which lay between them, but found his resources exhausted. Having little opportunity to replenish them, in May 1646 he sought shelter with a Presbyterian Scottish army at Southwell in Nottinghamshire. Charles was eventually handed over to the English Parliament by the Scots and was imprisoned. This marked the end of the First English Civil War.

Charles I tried to negotiate a secret treaty with the Scots, again promising church reform, on December, 28th 1647. Under the agreement, called "the Engagement," the Scots promised to invade England on Charles' behalf and restore him to the throne on condition of the establishment of Presbyterianism within three years. A series of Royalist uprisings throughout England, and a Scottish invasion, took place in the summer of 1648. Forces loyal to Parliament put down most of the uprisings in England after little more than skirmishes, but uprisings in Kent, Essex and Cumberland, the rebellion in Wales and the Scottish invasion all involved the fighting of pitched battles and prolonged sieges.

In the spring of 1648, unpaid Parliamentary troops in Wales changed sides. Colonel Thomas Horton defeated the Royalist rebels at the Battle of St. Fagans (May 8) and the rebel leaders surrendered to Cromwell on July 11th after the protracted two-month siege of Pembroke. Sir Thomas Fairfax defeated a Royalist uprising in Kent at the Battle of Maidstone on June 1. Fairfax, after his success at Maidstone and the pacification of Kent, turned north toward Essex. There, under their ardent, experienced and popular leader Sir Charles Lucas, the Royalists had taken up arms in great numbers. Fairfax soon drove the enemy into Colchester, but his first attack on the town was repelled and he had to settle down for a long siege.

Sir Thomas Fairfax, General during the English Civil War

In the North of England, Major-General John Lambert fought a very successful campaign against a number of Royalist uprisings—the largest being that of Sir Marmaduke Langdale in Cumberland. Thanks to Lambert's successes, the Scottish commander, the Duke of Hamilton, had a chance to take the western route through Carlisle in his pro-Royalist Scottish invasion of England. The Parliamentarians under Cromwell engaged the Scots at the Battle of Preston (August 17th-19th). The battle took place largely at Walton-le-Dale near Preston in Lancashire, and resulted in a victory by Cromwell's troops over the Royalists and Scots, who were commanded by Hamilton. This Parliamentarian victory marked the end of the Second English Civil War.

pardon Almost all the Royalists who had fought in the First Civil War had been granted amnesty due to their agreement not to bear arms against the Parliament, and many of those who received these conditions of amnesty, such as Lord Astley, refused to break their word by taking any part in the second war. Therefore, the victors in the Second Civil War showed little mercy to those who had brought war to the land again. On the evening of the surrender of Colchester, Parliamentarians had Sir Charles Lucas and Sir George Lisle shot. The Parliamentary authorities sentenced the leaders of the Welsh rebels to death, but executed Poyer alone (April 25, 1649), having selected him by lot. Of five prominent Royalist peers who had fallen into the hands of Parliament, three—the Duke of Hamilton, the Earl of Holland and Lord Capel—were beheaded at Westminster on March 9th.

Charles' secret pacts and encouragement of his supporters to break their parole caused Parliament to debate whether to return the king to power at all. Those who still supported Charles' place on the throne, such as the army leader and moderate Fairfax, tried once more to negotiate with him. Furious that Parliament continued to countenance Charles as a ruler, the army marched on Parliament and conducted "Pride's Purge" in December 1648 (named for the commanding officer of the operation, Thomas Pride). Royal troops arrested 45 members of Parliament and kept 146 out of the chamber. They allowed only 75 Members in, and then only at the Army's bidding. This Rump Parliament received orders to set up, in the name of the people of England, a High Court of Justice for the trial of Charles I for treason. Fairfax, a constitutional monarchist and moderate, refused to participate in the trial and resigned as head of the army, allowing Oliver Cromwell to ascend to power.

At the end of the trial, the 59 commissioners (judges) found Charles I guilty of high treason as a "tyrant, traitor, murderer and public enemy." His beheading took place on a scaffold in front of the Banqueting House of the Palace of Whitehall on January 30, 1649. Of the surviving royals not living in exile, nine were executed and most of the rest sentenced to life imprisonment after the Restoration in 1660. Not wanting to take the title of king, as he had recently fought against one, Cromwell preferred the title of Lord Protector. Hence, the new political regime was known as a *protectorate*.

The prerogatives granted to the state leader were very large and Cromwell used them to stop the riots of the peasants, to whom the new nobility refused the right to own land, and of the small bourgeoisie, unsatisfied by the absence of the universal vote. Gradually, the protectorate transformed into an obvious military dictatorship. Its social basis narrowed so that the Stuarts were restored to the throne in 1660, two years after Cromwell's death. In 1660–1685 two monarchs occupied the throne of England, Charles II and James II. From the very beginning, the Restoration was confronted with important difficulties. William of Orange (also known as William the Silent) took the throne in 1688, after swearing to respect the liberties inscribed in the *Declaration of Rights*, an act which consecrated England's transformation into a constitutional monarchy.

Prince of Orange landing at Torbay, a decisive win for the revolution

The monarchy was restored, but only with Parliament's consent; therefore, the civil wars effectively set England and Scotland on course to adopt a constitutional monarchy form of government. As a consequence the future Kingdom of Great Britain, formed in 1707 under the Acts of Union, managed to forestall the kind of often-bloody

---

revolution typical of European republican movements. It was no coincidence that the United Kingdom was spared the wave of revolutions that occurred in Europe in the 1840s. Future monarchs became wary of overruling Parliament too forcefully and Parliament effectively chose the line of royal succession in 1688 with the Glorious Revolution and in the 1701 Act of Settlement. After the Restoration, Parliament's factions became political parties (later becoming the Tories and the Whigs) with competing views and varying abilities to influence the decisions of their monarchs.

Monarchies seeking enhanced power faced challenges from nobles who wished to retain traditional forms of shared governance and regional autonomy.

The absolutist monarchs, who wished to completely control state politics with an iron fist, opposed the nobility and others who desired to participate in government or to keep their privileges or regional autonomy. The *Fronde* (named after a children's game played on the streets of Paris) took place in France between 1648 and 1653. It was a series of conflicts between the nobility and the royalty, caused by the strengthening of royal absolutism and excessive taxation.

The Fronde was meant to break the growing power of the king's authority, but its failure led to Louis XIV's personal absolutist reign. This reaction had started during the ministry of Cardinal Richelieu, who occupied this office between 1624 and 1642 and weakened the power of the nobility and the judicial body. These privileged groups' opposition to the government intensified in 1643 during the rule of Louis XIV's mother, Anna of Austria, and the new chief minister, Richelieu's successor, Cardinal Mazarin.

Parliament refused to approve the government's revenue measures and attempted to put a constitutional limit on them through establishing a forum for the discussion and potential modification of royal decrees. Being at war with Spain, Mazarin reluctantly accepted some of their demands. Nevertheless, the conflict transformed into a war. Parliament was supported by some of the great nobles and by the Parisian leaders, so the king had to conclude the Peace of Rueil (1649), which confirmed concessions to Parliament and ensured amnesty to the rebels.

The second phase of the civil war (1650–1653) was a mixture of rivalries, intrigues, changes of allegiance and treason. Constitutional matters were subordinated to personal ambitions. Mazarin became the target of ceaseless pamphleteers. Conde, the king's cousin and a military leader who helped the royalty in its fights against Parliament, became a rebel after being disappointed in his ambitions for power. He was arrested, but his supporters united and freed him. Conde became dominant for a while after he dismissed Mazarin. Nevertheless, after Anne's intervention, Conde was defeated in a second war (1651–1653) and had to flee. The Fronde ended with a clear victory for Mazarin. Beyond this immediate victory, the Fronde had an impact on France's history because it was one of the most serious challenges to the supremacy of French royalty.

Another example of a monarchy facing serious opposition is the Catalan Revolt, which included a large portion of Catalonia (a Spanish region) in 1640–1659. The main cause was the general discontent provoked by the presence of Castilian troops during the wars between Spain and France. Philip IV's chief minister, Olivares, tried to impose high taxation and civic obligations on the Spanish empire, but his measures resulted in protests across the entire country. Catalonian peasants, compelled to quarter Castilian troops, gathered in an uprising called the *Corpus de Sang* (Bloody Corpus).

Louis XIV of France and Philip IV of Spain discuss the Treaty of the Pyrenees

This riot turned into a political movement and led to the proclamation of a sovereign Catalonian Republic. Olivares, who was occupied by wars he was waging elsewhere, was taken by surprise. Despite some successes (such as the victory against the Spanish army in the Battle of Montjuic in January 1641), the peasants' uprisings became more and more uncontrollable. In 1652, the Spanish army occupied Barcelona and put the

Catalonian capital under Spanish control. Unorganized riots continued in the following years and small fights took place north of the Pyrenees, but from that moment on, the mountains remained the dividing line between French and Spanish territories. The conflict ended with the Treaty of the Pyrenees in 1659.

Period 1: 1450-1648

> ## Key Concept 1.3: Religious pluralism challenged the concept of the unified Europe.

Late medieval reform movements in the Church (including lay piety, mysticism and Christian humanism) created a momentum that propelled a new generation of 16th-century reformers, such as Erasmus and Martin Luther. After 1517, when Luther posted his 95 Theses attacking ecclesiastical abuses and the doctrines that spawned them, Christianity fragmented, even though religious uniformity remained the ideal. Others—notably the Netherlands and lands under Ottoman control, which accepted Jewish refugees—did not.

In central Europe, The Peace of Augsburg (1555) permitted each state of the Holy Roman Empire to be either Catholic or Lutheran at the discretion of the prince. By the late 16th century, northern European countries were generally Protestant and Mediterranean countries were generally Catholic. To re-establish order after a period of religious warfare, France introduced limited toleration of the minority Calvinists within a Catholic kingdom (Edict of Nantes, 1598; revoked in 1685). Jews remained a marginalized minority wherever they lived.

Differing conceptions of salvation and the individual's relationship to the Church were at the heart of the conflicts between Luther, subsequent Protestant reformers, such as Calvin and Anabaptists, and the Roman Catholic Church. The Catholic Church affirmed its traditional theology at the Council of Trent (1545–1563), ruling out any reconciliation with the Protestants and inspiring the resurgence of Catholicism's long–standing political tensions between the monarchies and nobility across Europe, dramatically escalating these conflicts as they spread from the Holy Roman Empire to France, the Netherlands and England.

Economic issues, such as the power to tax and control ecclesiastical resources, further heightened these clashes. All three motivations—religious, political and economic—contributed to the brutal and destructive Thirty Years' War, which was ended by the Peace of Westphalia (1648). The Peace of Westphalia also added Calvinism to Catholicism and Lutheranism as an accepted religion in the Holy Roman Empire, ensuring the permanence of European religious pluralism. However, pluralism did not mean religious freedom; the prince or ruler still controlled the religion of the state, and few were tolerant of dissenters.

The Protestant and Catholic Reformations fundamentally changed theology, religious institutions and culture.

The Protestant Reformation was a 16th century movement for the restructuring of the Roman Catholic Church in Western Europe. The reform was begun by Martin Luther with his *95 Theses*. At the end of October 1517, he posted his theses on the door of Wittenberg Castle church, a location commonly used as a notice board for the university community, and in November he sent them to the different religious authorities.

Luther posts his 95 Theses

The Reformation ended by dividing itself and founding new institutions. The most important four new denominations were Lutheranism, Calvinism, Anabaptism and the Anglican Church. The subsequent Protestant traditions have their roots in these four initial schools. Moreover, the Protestant Reformation led to a Catholic Counter-Reformation, which sought to make changes within the Catholic Church. It led to a variety of new spiritual movements, reorganizations of religious communities, clarification of the Catholic theology and structural changes inside the institution of the Church.

Protestantism, distinguishable from Catholicism and the Orthodox Church by its fundamental principles, desired to return to the roots of Christianity. The Lutheran belief in redemption only through faith is connected with Luther's conception of the complete corruption of man's relationship with God. Lutherans believe that due to the principle of original sin, man is incapable of any personal effort towards redemption; meaning that man's good or bad deeds cannot affect the act of salvation. Concerning predestination, Lutherans affirm that God knows everything and organizes all *a priori*. Protestants prefer the concept of "the invisible Church." They do not accept the Church's infallibility as a depositary of the truth, nor the infallibility of the ecumenical synods. They do not recognize the ecclesiastic hierarchy canonically established on the apostolic succession, but instead believe in universal priesthood.

The reform was a movement for the renewal of religion, which included a triple hypostasis (the Church, faith and ritual). The Reformation movements were recurrent in the Middle Ages. The Church's reaction was cooptation or repression. During the Middle Ages there were numerous heretical movements, like that of the Cathars who believed in dual divinity. Ian Hus, who contested such dogma, was tried and burned at the stake. The reform led to the appearance of new churches and the reorganization of the Catholic Church.

Christian humanism, embodied in the writings of Erasmus, employed Renaissance learning in the service of religious reform.

Erasmus of Rotterdam (approx. 1466–1536) was a Dutch theologian and one of the most important humanists of the Renaissance and Reformation. Since he criticized the Catholic Church, he was considered a precursor of the religious reform movement, although he did not adhere to it and constantly promoted the spirit of religious tolerance. His most important work was *Encomium moriae* ("The Praise of Folly," written in 1509), which was dedicated to Thomas More. It is a satire addressed to scholastic theology and the clergy's immorality, and also includes an apology to the "true Christian," who dedicates his life to faith.

Due to these works, in which he examined the original sources of Christianity, Erasmus is considered a trailblazer of the Protestant Reformation, although he remained a committed Catholic. His attacks against the ecclesiastic authorities' errors resulted in him being labeled a Protestant by the Vatican. Erasmus illustrated his ideological option in *De Libero Arbitrio* (1524), which contains a severe critique of Luther's conception of man's lack of liberty over decision-making, while still admitting the necessity of changes to clergy morality.

From 1517 to 1524, he translated the Greek version of the New Testament into Latin, which Luther in turn used for the transcription of the Bible into German. Erasmus' fight against the traditional belief system was characterized by his humanist opinions, especially by his belief in the necessity of spiritual liberty. Although during the Counter-

Reformation his works were listed in the Index of Forbidden Books, Erasmus had a strong influence on the history of European culture.

Juan Luis Vives was born in Valencia in 1493, to a Jewish family that converted to Christianity, but continued to practice Judaism in a synagogue hidden in the house. This was discovered by the Inquisition and he and his family were brought to trial. His father, grandmother and great-grandfather were executed, while his mother was acquitted but later died of the plague. Juan Luis Vives became a reformer of the European education system and a philosopher, proposing the study of Aristotle in its original language, adapting his books for those who studied Latin and proposing the reform of the Sorbonne. He dedicated the last years of his life to improving the humanist culture.

Sir Thomas More,
English lawyer, writer and politician

Not all humanist thinkers approved the transformation of the foundation of Christianity. Thomas More (1478–1535) was an English lawyer, writer and politician. He gained a reputation for being a proponent of humanism and occupying several public offices, including that of Lord Chancellor. He is famous for his refusal to recognize Henry VIII as the head of England's Church. He was not willing to renounce his principles and the Catholic religion, which ended his political career. He was imprisoned in the Tower of London and executed for high treason.

In 1515, More wrote his most famous and controversial paper, *The Utopia*, in which he opposed the contentious relations of European states in favor of the theory of more ordered and peaceful interactions. In *The Utopia*, private property did not exist and religious tolerance was practiced. The main message of the book is that discipline and order are needed more than liberty. In *The Utopia*, it is suggested that the attempt to discuss public politics outside official forums be punished with death.

More chose the path of literature to envision an imaginary nation and to freely debate controversial political issues. His own attitude regarding the organization he described is a widely debated issue. Although it is hard to believe that More, a faithful Catholic, ever thought of *The Utopia* as a concrete proposal for political reform, some critics noted that More based his book on the Biblical communalism described in the Facts of Apostles. Still, for More, the most important point was the maintenance of the unity of Christendom. The Lutheran Reform, which brought the perils of fragmentation and discord, was, for More, the worst possibility.

Reformers Martin Luther and John Calvin, as well as religious radicals such as the Anabaptists, criticized Catholic abuses and established new interpretations of Christian doctrine and practice.

Martin Luther (1483–1546), a pastor and doctor of theology, was the founder of the Protestant movement. His ideas led to the creation of the Evangelical Lutheran Church. The first Protestant ideas were promulgated by Luther in 1517, in his capacity as a Catholic priest and exegesis teacher at the University of Wittenberg. He was excommunicated from the Catholic Church in 1521. At the advice of his father, Luther had begun to study law in 1505, but later dedicated himself to an ecclesiastical career. The seriousness with which Luther took his religious vocation led to a personal epistemological crisis: how was it possible to reconcile God's laws with man's incapacity to follow them? He found the answer in the New Testament: Jesus did not demand a strict respect for religious obligations, but a faith that relied on love, not fear.

Luther's beliefs led him to engage in a conflict with the Roman Catholic Church in 1517. In order to raise money to build the Basilica of Saint Peter in Rome, Pope Leon X sold indulgencies. Indulgencies ensured purchasers a cancellation of their earthly sins, thereby essentially granting them access to heaven. In October of 1517, Luther published his *95 Theses*, which argued against indulgencies. His theses circulated quickly throughout Germany and were highly controversial.

The pope ordered Luther to appear in Augsburg in front of Cardinal Thomas Cajetan, who demanded that he retract the claims made in the *95 Theses*. Luther replied that he would retract them only if Cajetan could prove that he was wrong based on the Bible. In 1521, an excommunication bull issued by the pope asked Emperor Charles V to execute Luther. The emperor convened an assembly to research Luther's theses, and the Diet declared him "undesirable." However, Luther was saved by his friend, Friedrich III, prince of Saxony. He retreated to Wartburg, where he began to translate the New Testament into German.

Jean Calvin (1509–1564) was a French religious reformer. Along with Martin Luther, he was one of the initiators of the Protestant Reformation. Calvin developed a doctrine, *Calvinism*, which was different from Luther's. It was considered a radicalization of Lutheranism. Calvin recognized only two sacraments: christening and communion. He rejected the dogma of God's real presence in the communion, the invocation of saints, the institution of episcopacy, etc. Preachers were chosen from amongst the faithful and each Calvinist church was spiritually led by a chosen council. Calvin believed in the absolute predestination of chosen ones and of those condemned for eternity; thus, he completely rejected free will.

Calvin's father sent him to the College De la Marche and afterwards to the Sorbonne to study law. His first published paper was a commentary on Seneca's work, *De clementia.* He soon adopted the principles of the Reformation and, in 1532, began spreading them in Paris. Threatened with prison, he took refuge at Nérac under the protection of Margret of Navarre, who had a favorable view of Protestantism. In 1534, subsequent to the persecutions suffered by French Protestants (the Huguenots), he had to flee France. After wande-

John Calvin,
French religious reformer

ring to Basel, Ferrara and back to Paris, in 1536 Calvin established himself for good as a theology teacher in Geneva, where he lived almost half of his life.

The most egregious example of corruption, to Luther, was "indulgences." Indulgences were documents which absolved a person of a past sin, in exchange for a cash payment to the church. The church accumulated a huge amount of money from this chicanery. As a side note, they were only available to the wealthy minority since they were the only ones in a position to pay for them. This looked to Luther like favoritism, when all human beings were supposed to be equal before God. A related practice was called "simony," where a powerful office within the church or a privilege of some kind was purchased with cash.

Nepotism is the promotion of a person to a position of power because of his relationship to the one doing the promoting or because political favors are granted in exchange. For example, the church frequently appointed new Bishops based on payments or because the candidate was an important noble's son. Pluralism is the practice of holding more than one office at the same time. Absenteeism is a situation in which a person does not attend to his or her job. In the context of the Catholic church, Bishops often did not visit their diocese. A major example of absenteeism of the time was that of Thomas Wolsey, the Archbishop of York; Wolsey spent fifteen years without visiting his territory.

The Catholic Reformation, exemplified by the Jesuit Order and the Council of Trent, revived the Church but cemented the division within Christianity.

The Catholic Counter-Reformation, or the Catholic Reformation, was a movement against the spreading of the Protestant Reformation, initiated in 1545 by Pope Paul III with the support of the Catholic monarchs from Spain and the Habsburg Empire. Between 1545 and 1563, several sessions of the Council from Trento took place in Italy, the first one being summoned by Pope Paul III. The pope undertook several severe measures: the condemnation of Protestantism, the renewal of the Roman Catholic Church, the eradication of the abuses and corruption within the Church, instituting a new severe discipline for the Catholic Church, a reorganization of the Inquisition, the prohibition of heretical books and the creation of new religious orders to check Protestantism and promote Catholicism. The actions of the Roman Catholic Church brought Catholicism back to Poland and significant parts of Hungary and Germany. At the same time, religious orders like the Ursulines, the Jesuits and the Piarists appeared. These helped to spread Catholicism in Protestant areas.

The basic principles of the Jesuit order were established in 1534 by a group of students from the University of Paris, led by Ignatius of Loyola. Along with the three usual cenobite promises (obedience, chastity and poverty), the Jesuits introduced a fourth, that of unconditional obedience to the pope. The Jesuits founded educational institutions which were accessible to all social strata. They were the most important disseminators of Counter-Reformation ideas, seeking to reestablish the Catholic faith in Protestant countries such as England, Germany, Holland and Hungary.

The Ursuline nuns (*Ordo Sanctae Ursulae*) were another monastic order promoting Catholicism. The order, whose name is derived from Saint Ursula, was founded in 1535 with the purpose of developing girls' education and caring for the poor and sick. The order was also founded in the context of the Counter-Reformation to improve the level of education and discipline within the clergy and the Catholic faith. For girls, the Ursulines played the same role that the Jesuit order played for boys. Another example of feminine Catholic proselytism was that of Teresa of Ávila, officially named Teresa de Jesús (1515–1582), a Catholic reformer who founded the *Order of the Barefoot Carmelites.*

Saint Teresa of Ávila, Catholic reformer

An instrument used during the Inquisition was the *Index of Forbidden Books*. It was published in 1559 at the Inquisition's initiative, under the papacy of Paul IV and confirmed by the Council of Trento. The Index was a register of the Catholic Church in which all the books the Church considered harmful or heretical were listed. The books from the Index could no longer be read by the Holy See's faithful. Whoever read, owned or took part in the production of a forbidden book was excommunicated. Any good Christian had the obligation to denounce to the authorities anyone who was guilty of breaking this papal order. The Index was renewed periodically and published until 1948, but only in 1966 was a decision issued to suspend its publication. In almost five hundred years, the catalogue had 32 editions, in which were listed many philosophers and scientists like Erasmus of Rotterdam, Blaise Pascal and Jean-Jacques Rousseau.

Religious reform both increased state control of religious institutions and provided justifications for challenging state authority.

The Reformation also had success due to the incompatibility between the modern state, which evolved towards nationalism, and the universality of the Catholic Church, which thought of itself as a supranational organization. The states modernized into absolutist monarchies, monopolizing their authority over their entire territory at the expense of Rome. The privileges and immunities of the Church were no longer tolerated. The monarchs desired to transform the Church into an instrument which could be used in the national interest. At the Concordat of Bologna in 1516, a meeting between Francis I of France and the pope, the kings lost interest in supporting the Reformation. The kings constantly needed money, due to the increase in size of the bureaucratic apparatus and for financing large armies to fight their wars.

The economic-political motivation existed only in the small states, towns and principalities. In different periods and areas of Europe, reformist ideas appeared and crystallized. These included: *sola fide,* the redemption by faith, universal priesthood and *sola scriptura,* meaning that the Bible's authority is the only source of truth.

Monarchs and princes, such as the English rulers Henry VIII and Elizabeth I, initiated religious reform from the top down (magisterial) in an effort to exercise greater control over religious life and morality.

Even before the Reformation, the King of England exerted a considerable influence over the English Church. This explains why the reform in England was initiated not by individual theologians, but by the monarch himself. The reason for the rupture with the papacy was the king's desire to divorce Catherine of Aragon and marry Anne Boleyn, a lady of his court whom he later had beheaded. Pope Clement VII refused to annul Henry's marriage to Catherine. The king decided to break his connection with Rome, which is why the Anglican Church cannot be considered a Protestant church, but instead a Catholic Occidental church that did not submit to Rome. In 1533, Henry VIII prepared the Episcopal consecration of Thomas Cranmer, and in 1536 and 1539 he disbanded about six hundred monasteries and confiscated their holdings.

Elizabeth I of England (1533–1603) proposed a policy for attenuating the conflict between the Catholic and Evangelical faiths. Her compromise was comprised of the *39 Articles*. Elizabeth I's religious opinions have long been debated by researchers. Although Protestant, she kept Catholic symbols, like the crucifix, and minimized the importance of sermons, which were of great importance in the Protestant religion.

Elizabeth I, Queen of England

Elizabeth I was pragmatic in her treatment of religious issues; she searched for a solution which would not annoy the Catholics, but which would satisfy the desires of the English Protestants. She took the title of Supreme Governor of the Church of England because the title of Supreme Leader was not suited for a woman. The new *Act of Supremacy* made all functionaries give an oath to the queen under penalty of losing their jobs. The laws regarding the heresies were canceled in order to avoid a repetition of the persecutions practiced by Mary I. A new *Act of Uniformity* made the use of the 1552 version of the *Book of Common Prayer,* the official religious book of Anglicanism, obligatory; however, the sanctions for those who disrespected it were not excessive.

Throughout Europe, the royalty tried to implement reforms which gave kings greater control over religious affairs. French kings attempted to systematically interfere in ecclesiastical problems. The Concordat of Bologna (1516) gave the king the right to name approximately one hundred bishops and archbishops and nearly five hundred abbots. The king's enormous control, compared to the symbolic authority of the pope, transformed the hierarchy of the French Church into a docile instrument in the king's hands.

In Germany, the princes feared the centralization projects of Emperors Maximilian I and Charles Quint, so they embraced the ideas of the Reformation, which contributed to a strengthening of their authority in prejudice of the Habsburgs. In the Religious Peace of Augsburg (1555) both Catholic and Lutheran confessions were considered equally legitimate.

The *Inquisition,* founded in Spain in 1478 by the Catholic monarchs Ferdinand of Aragon and Isabella of Castile, was the main instrument for maintaining Catholic confession in their kingdom. It was placed directly under the control of the Spanish monarchy. As an ecclesiastical tribunal, the Inquisition only had jurisdiction over baptized Christians. After Jews and Muslims were exiled from Spain, the Inquisition's jurisdiction extended to practically all of the Crown's vassals, becoming a very powerful instrument by which the monarchy controlled religious life.

Some Protestants, including Calvin and the Anabaptists, refused to recognize the subordination of the Church to the state.

The Radical Reformation movement represented a reaction against the symbiosis between ecclesiastic and secular powers, which was present in the Catholic Church and maintained by territorial Protestantism. This direction of the Reformation was considered "radical" because it advocated for a complete overhaul, down to the roots of the Church and the state. The movement was composed of several distinct groups who had many differences and exhibited very little collaboration. The main groups were the Anabaptists, the Spiritualists and the Rationalists.

Spiritualists insisted on interior illumination from the Holy Spirit. They rejected the practices of christening and communion, and believed that, in the church, people were connected only by the common experience endowed by the Holy Spirit. They were widespread in Germany. Their revolutionary wing, led by Thomas Munzer, fought in the Peasant War in 1524–1525, in which over 100,000 peasants were killed by the nobles' army, with the aid of Germany's Catholic and Protestant leaders.

Besieged city during the Peasant War in 1525

Anabaptists represented the most significant part of the radical reform movement. They encountered broad success in areas where medieval dissidence had weakened the pope's power, such as in the Netherlands, Germany, Switzerland and Moravia. They rejected the association between Church and state, the concept of a universal Church, the christening of babies, the bearing of arms and occupation by the magistrates of the civil service. They believed that the Church was the group of the faithful who willingly received christening based on their personal confession of faith. They were known as peaceful men, hardworking and with a high moral purity. The revolutionary Anabaptists, spread throughout Germany and the Netherlands, triggered the revolt from Münster (1535–1536), which announced the instauration of Christ's Kingdom on Earth, with its capital at Münster.

After banishing the Catholic bishop and the opposition, the revolution's leaders allowed a series of excesses. The city fell under the siege of the Episcopal and nobility's armies and all those involved were executed. The revolutionary Anabaptists had nothing in common with the rest of the Anabaptists except for the practice of christening adults. However, this was sufficient for Catholics and Protestants to identify all Anabaptists with the fanatical wing. This deliberate confusion led to numerous waves of persecution against innocent and inoffensive groups. In the beginning, the reformers had been inclined to agree with the Anabaptist positions regarding christening and the sufficiency of the scriptures, but they changed their attitude, fearing they might lose the support of the population and of the secular authorities.

The evangelical Rationalists rejected the doctrine of the Trinity and the Sacrament. They were Christian humanists who tended to reject anything connected to faith that could not be confirmed by reason. They promoted religious liberty and whenever they could they exerted influence over the authorities, obtaining religious liberty for all the subjects in the region. Only towards the middle of the 16th century did they begin to adopt the christening of adults as a symbol of identification with Christ.

Religious conflicts became a basis for challenging the monarchs' control of religious institutions.

The Huguenots were French Calvinists. The term derives from the German word *eidgenosse* which means "confederate." Organized in independent communities, the Huguenots created an administrative and military apparatus by which they became an autonomous corpus in the French Kingdom. The Huguenots were often in conflict with the French monarchy. In 1572, tens of thousands of Huguenots were killed on the Night of Saint Bartholomew.

This massacre of French Protestants in Paris was unleashed by the state during the night. From there, it extended to twenty other cities and lasted over two weeks. Almost 30,000 Huguenots were attacked and killed, and the episode is considered one of the largest massacres of the century. This tragic episode was the result of a series of political, religious and social factors. It was a consequence of the civil and military conflicts between the French Catholic nobility and the Protestant nobility, and resulted in a huge popular reaction.

For a long time, the historical record blamed Catherina Di Medici and Charles IX of France for the slaughter of the Huguenots; however, lacking sources, historians remained unsure about the exact role they played. Today, it is thought that the royal order demanded only the assassination of the Huguenots' leaders. On the morning of August 24th, when Charles IX ordered the killings to cease, the people's wrath could not be stopped. Subsequent to the religious wars that put them in opposition to state officials, the Huguenots managed to obtain freedom of worship, seats in Parliament and about a hundred fortresses (per *The Edict of Nantes,* issued by Henry IV in 1598). The Huguenot military power was abolished by Cardinal Richelieu. Louis the XIV resolved the issue by completely restoring Catholicism, forcing numerous communities of Huguenots to emigrate to Protestant countries.

In England, the monarchs of the Tudor dynasty, Henry VIII and Elizabeth I, had introduced Anglicanism and promoted Protestantism, obtaining enormous benefits from the secularization of ecclesiastical wealth. James I (1603–1625), who inaugurated the dynasty of the Stuarts, cultivated Anglicanism and was very intransigent towards Catholics and Puritans, some of them being forced to flee to America. James I also tried to install the absolute monarchy of divine right, but was blocked by Parliament.

Portrait of King Louis XIV of France

An important characteristic of the English revolution is that its ideology had a religious form. The movement against the Anglican Church is known by the name of Puritanism. The Puritans had as their purpose the "purification" of the Church from the remaining elements of Catholicism, especially the removing of the episcopate and the introduction of Calvinism. Soon, the Puritans divided into two groups: Presbyterians and Independents. The first was more conservative. They favored keeping the Anglican Church organized according to Calvinist principles. The Independents were against any form of organization of the Church. They only recognized the local community as the organizing element, which was not dependent on any superior organism.

The Zebrzydowski Rebellion in Poland pitched the Polish king, Sigismund III against the nobility, in 1606. Sigismund III made attempts to limit the power of both the nobility and the Polish Parliament (the Sejm), triggering the revolt. At the core was also religion: The rebels presented a list of demands to parliament, including the expulsion of Jesuits from Poland and the protection of the Protestant minority there. When these were rejected, conflict broke out. The rebels lost, but they were granted amnesty and the nobles retained their power.

Conflicts among religious groups overlapped with political and economic competition within and among states.

The Protestant Reformation, initiated in 1517 by Martin Luther, divided the greatest part of Occidental Europe into two areas: Catholic and Protestant nations. The war started as a religious conflict, as it had in France and the Netherlands, only this time it had an international dimension for two reasons. First, the Czech Calvinists, who did not want to be led by Germans, formed an affluent group in their country's political and economic spheres and second, the problem of the Baltic Sea emerged. In the region of the Baltics at the beginning of the 17th century, the dominant power was Denmark, which still included Norway. Sweden controlled Finland and Estonia. With its military force, under the rule of the young and brave King Gustav Adolf, it closed Russia's exit to the sea for a hundred years. Gustav Adolf created a powerful state, through legislative and military reforms, by stimulating the economy and culture and by developing a commercial navy.

The northern German states, the Hanseatic cities in Poland, England, Holland and Spain had commercial interests in the Baltics due to its riches, which included grains, fish, wood, iron and copper. The revolt started in 1618 in Prague, when two imperial functionaries were thrown out of a window. It was quashed by Ferdinand II's troops in the Battle of White Mountain (1620), which was followed by a bloody repression, the confiscation of the nobles' fortunes and their forced conversion to Catholicism. Following their plans to weaken the emperor's power, England, Holland and France tried, via money and diplomacy, to provoke a Danish intervention in northern Germany. Gustav Adolf himself died in the battle of Lutzen in 1632.

The Thirty Years' War ended with the Peace of Westphalia in 1648. This document marked the beginning of a European system based on the concept of the nation-state.

Nevertheless, the Holy Roman Empire, although weakened, continued to exist until 1806. In Germany, the appearance of the nation was delayed in comparison to other regions of Western Europe. Under the Habsburg dynasty, which was unable to rule Germany by an absolute monarchy, this statist tendency manifested itself only in Austria and in the other provinces which the Habsburgs governed directly. At this point, the division between Austrian and German history began, and the Protestants received the religious freedom they had fought for. Where the Habsburgs ruled, the most intolerant form of Catholicism endured. The war's destruction brought suffering to Germany and changed its political map. It ensured the Protestant communities the liberty that the Habsburgs had been denying them, but financially, it exhausted the country.

Ambassadors of the Peace of Westphalia

Issues of religious reform exacerbated conflicts between the monarchy and the nobility, as in the French Wars of Religion.

As the reformation spread to many countries and increased to a following of millions, a counter-reformation emerged in Europe. The Protestants became a sizable enough minority in many countries that the more prejudiced Catholics considered them to be a threat. Assaults on Protestants triggered backlashes and full scale wars erupted over the 16th and 17th centuries. One of the leaders who was caught in the middle of these troubles was Catherine Di Medici.

Catherine Di Medici was a member of the extremely powerful bank owning family from Florence who dominated European politics at the time because of their almost monopolistic control of its banking and loans industry. She was the Queen of France under Henry II. After Henry died, leaving no adult heir behind, Catherine ruled on behalf of each of her three young sons; One by one, each son died an untimely death leaving the next brother as a child-king and Catherine as the de facto leader of France until 1589.

Between 1562 and 1598, three wars were fought in France over religious toleration of the Huguenot Protestants. These are known as the wars of religion and cost between two and four million lives. They terminated in a victory for the Protestants with the Edict of Nantes in 1598.

The first of these wars began with an uprising of Protestant nobles in 1562, who seized the city of Orleans. This was a reaction to the slaughter of Protestants who were peacefully worshipping, on March 1st, 1562. Protestants led by a noble named the Prince of Conde seized Orleans on April 2nd. After that, Protestants throughout France followed suit, seizing several other towns. The war ended in a truce, brokered by Catherine Di Medici, Queen of France. The second war took place between 1567 and 1568, ending in little change; the treaty which concluded this one reaffirmed the protection and religious freedom of the Protestants. The final war of religion broke out only months after the end of the second, in 1568. In this one, Conde was killed but Protestants secured legal toleration in France.

In France, the signing of the Treaty of Saint Germain ended the third religious war (1568–1570) between the Catholics and the Protestants. Yet it was a fragile peace, rejected by the intransigent Catholics. The return of the Protestants to the French court outraged the Catholic nobility, but Catherine Di Medici and Charles IX, aware of the kingdom's financial difficulties, decided to maintain peace. To this end, Catherine Di Medici arranged the marriage of her daughter, Margret of Valois, to the Protestant prince, Henry of Navarre. Their marriage, on August 18, 1572, was accepted by neither the King of Spain, Philip II, nor by the pope.

On August 22nd, Admiral Coligny was shot from the window of a house. He was not killed, but the incident led to a crisis: the Protestants demanded revenge. Paris was on the verge of a civil war between the supporters of the Duke of Guise and the Huguenots. To calm the situation, Charles promised Coligny that justice would be done, although he feared he would lose the nobles' support. On the night of August 23rd, at a meeting attended by Catherine Di Medici and the king, the decision was made (historians believe) to assassinate the Huguenot leaders, except for the king's brother-in-law, Henry of Navarra, and Prince Conde.

The gates of Paris were closed and the citizens were given arms in order to prevent a Protestant revolt. The command of the military operations was entrusted to the Duke of Guise and his uncle, the Duke of Aumale. The Huguenots from the Louvre were dragged into the street and killed. Their bodies were gathered in front of the palace, stripped, dragged along the streets of the city and thrown into the River Seine. Admiral Coligny was also killed and thrown out of a window. A wave of violence swept through the entire city. The Parisians started to hunt Protestants and to massacre them without regard for the age or sex of the victim. Trapped inside the city walls, the Protestants had no chance of escape. Those suspected of hiding Huguenots were also in danger of being lynched.

On the morning of August 24th, the king ordered his people to stop the massacres, but they did not comply. He tried to take measures to protect the lives of people who were in danger. The two Huguenot princes, Henry of Navarre (nineteen years old) and Conde (twenty years old) were spared, with the condition that they convert to Catholicism. On August 26th, at a session of the Parliament in Paris, Charles IX tried to take responsibility, on the pretext that the Huguenots had organized a plot against the Crown. The massacres extended to the provinces of Orleans, Meaux, Lyon, Bordeaux, Valence and many other regions. They lasted for three days in Paris and several weeks in the rest of France. The exact number of victims is not known, but one estimate says 3,000 dead in Paris and approximately 30,000 in the rest of France. As historian Jules Michelet asserted, "The Night of Saint Bartholomew did not last a day, but a season."

Prohibition of sermons and arrest of Protestants
in Paris after the revocation of the Edict of Nantes

In Europe, the reactions to this outrageous event were different. The pope was happy that the king managed to escape, organized a *Te Deum* to thank God and ordered Giorgio Vasari to paint three frescos. For Phillip II of Spain, it was the happiest day of his life. Queen Elizabeth I of England wore weeds and kept the French ambassador standing for a couple of hours before pretending she believed the story about the Huguenot's plot. Disgusted, Maximilian II, Charles IX's father in law, described the shameful massacre. Even Tsar Ivan the Terrible was horrified by it. The event changed the rule of Charles IX and the religious politics in France. History traditionally considers Catherine Di Medici the principal antagonist in the massacre of the Protestants.

Aware of the fact that the religious wars between Catholics and Protestants were weakening his kingdom, Henry IV took measures to reconcile the two religions. The international context was also demanding this gesture; France was being threatened by Spain's ambitions. Henry IV issued the Edict of Nantes on April 13, 1598, which temporarily put an end to the religious struggles. It was composed of four separate treaties and granted the Huguenots complete freedom of conscience and of practicing confession in public, but still with substantial restrictions. If the Edict of Nantes set France's religious affairs in order, it happened because that was the king's desire. When the king no longer considered it appropriate to tolerate the Huguenot faith, as was the case with of Louis XIV in 1685, the persecution reappeared with a similar level of brutality.

The efforts of Habsburg rulers failed to restore Catholic unity across Europe.

The Habsburg emperors fought with all their means against the reform and took numerous measures to restore Catholic unity in Europe. Charles Quint (1519–1556) was very famous for his role against the Protestant Reformation. Protestant German princes allied in the Schmalkaldic League, with the purpose of challenging Charles' authority with military force. Charles took measures to contain the spread of Protestantism and convened the Council of Trent, which began the Counter-Reformation. The Society of Jesus, founded by Ignatius of Loyola during Charles' reign, was meant to combat Protestantism; Spain was spared from religious conflict largely by Charles' nonviolent measures. Still, Charles' authority was limited by the German Protestant princes and he decided to take further measures. In 1522, the Inquisition was established, and in 1550 the death penalty was introduced for all cases of heresy.

As Holy Roman Emperor, Charles called Luther to the Diet of Worms in 1521, promising him safe passage if he appeared. Although initially he minimized the importance of Luther's theses, Charles later outlawed Luther and his followers. In 1545, the opening of the Council of Trent began the Counter-Reformation and Charles won to the Catholic cause some of the princes of the Holy Roman Empire. In 1546, he outlawed the Schmalkaldic League (which had occupied the territory of another prince). He drove the League's troops out of southern Germany, and at the Battle of Mühlberg defeated John Frederick, Elector of Saxony, and imprisoned Philip of Hesse in 1547. At the Augsburg Interim in 1548, he created a temporary solution, giving certain allowances to Protestants until the Council of Trent that would restore unity.

Charles' religious politics were continued by his son, Phillip II, whose foreign policy was determined by Catholic and dynastic interests. He considered himself the greatest defender of Catholic Europe, both against the Ottoman Turks and against the Protestant Reformation. He ceaselessly fought against heresy, defended the Catholic religion and limited freedom of worship within his territories, which included the Netherlands, where Protestantism had deep roots. Following the Revolt of the Netherlands in 1568, Philip led a campaign against Dutch heresy and secession, a series of conflicts lasting to the end of his life. Philip's constant involvement in European wars created significant economic difficulties for his state.

In 1588, the English defeated Philip's Spanish Armada, ruining his planned invasion of the country in order to reinstate Catholicism. The war continued for the next sixteen years, in a series of struggles that included France, Ireland and the Netherlands. The most significant victory against the Turks was at Lepanto in 1571, in which the allied fleet of the Holy League turned the tide against Ottoman aggression. Philip also successfully secured his succession to the throne of Portugal.

Under Philip II, Spain reached the peak of its power. However, despite the great quantities of gold and silver coming from the American mines, the riches of the Portuguese spice trade and the enthusiastic support of the Habsburg dominions for the Counter-Reformation, he never succeeded in suppressing Protestantism or defeating the Dutch rebels. The Dutch might have stopped fighting had he not insisted on suppressing Protestantism, but his devotion to Catholicism did not allow him to do so. He was a devout Catholic, and the defeat of Protestantism was ever present in Philip's mind. For a time, he ruled England along with Queen Mary Tudor (known as "Bloody Mary") and there was a reconciliation with the Catholic Church. Heresy trials were reestablished and hundreds of Protestants were burned at the stake.

Philip's greatest mistake was his attempt to completely eradicate Protestantism from the Netherlands, which was a major economic asset for the empire. Under harsh occupation, the Dutch finally rebelled and gained their independence in a war that did a great deal of harm to Philip's empire. His greatest victory was the defeat of the Ottoman fleet at Lepanto, which turned the tide against Turkish aggression. The Habsburg rulers did not manage to restore Catholic unity, and this reality became more and more clear after the Thirty Years' War.

King Philip II of Spain

States exploited religious conflicts to promote political and economic interests.

In the second half of the 16th and the beginning of the 17th century, Europe's international situation was characterized by the rivalry between the great powers and their fight for supremacy. The Italian wars (1494–1516) had led to a weakening of France and to the short period of "Spanish preponderance." The revolution in the Netherlands, the conflicts with England for the supremacy over the seas and civil wars within France all diminished Spanish supremacy. To this end, France allied itself with the Ottoman Empire. During the Thirty Years' War, France continued the alliance system against the Habsburgs, allying with Denmark, Sweden, Holland, Poland and Transylvania.

The Thirty Years' War lasted from 1618 until 1648, and was provoked under religious pretexts. The principal cause was the fight for hegemony in Europe and especially France's desire, led by Cardinal Richelieu, to undermine the Holy Roman Empire's supremacy over Europe. The Holy Roman Empire was the main locus of international tensions, because of the internal conflicts between the Habsburg dynasty and those who adhered to Protestant principles, who did not agree with the idea of restoring the "universal monarchy."

With financial aid and moral support, France encouraged the anti-imperial resentfulness of the German Protestants who, under the guidance of Friedrich IV the Palatine, organized the Protestant Union in 1608. During the war, Germany had military support from France, Holland, Denmark, Sweden (ruled by the great King Gustav Adolf) and Transylvania. On the opposite side, the prince elector Maximilian I of Bavaria organized the coalition named the Pro-Imperial Catholic League in 1609. The Thirty Years' War was the most significant example of international conflict started under the pretext of religious issues. It became one of the longest, most destructive conflicts in European history

A few states, such as France with the Edict of Nantes, allowed religious pluralism in order to maintain domestic peace.

*Admiral Coligny,
Leader of Reformation in France*

The conflict between Catholics and Protestants divided France into two camps that fought for over three decades in the 16th century. The Reformation entered France in the form of Calvinism and found a high number of adherents in the bourgeoisie. The dissatisfied nobility—especially those in the southwest, led by the Bourbon and Conde families and by Admiral Coligny—joined the Huguenots.

The persecutions unleashed by the Catholics, far from annihilating the Reform, made the Huguenots close ranks, defend themselves and counter-attack efficiently. The antagonism between the two groups unfolded with an increasing intensity, leading to no less than eight religious wars between 1562 and 1598. For a while, the tolerance treaties and peace treaties were simply pieces of paper with no real effect.

After the Night of Saint Bartholomew and the ascension to the throne of Prince Henry of Navarre, a Protestant prince who had been compelled to convert to Catholicism, the king issued the Edict of Nantes. This regulated the situation of the reformers, ensuring their social and religious independence. The Huguenots were granted full amnesty and for the future they were granted the liberty of conscience and of practice in all the settlements previously approved by the edicts.

Moreover, they could study at four universities: Montauban, Montpellier, Sedan and Saumur. The Protestants could work in any function, like the Catholics, with whom they now had equal rights. In order to ensure a justice in which they could completely trust, "Houses of the Edict," with Protestant representation, were created in each Parliament. The Edict allowed them to gather in provincial and national synods and obtained a number of fortresses and defended places. All 92 articles were discussed one by one by a commission in which Huguenot delegates were present so as to dispel any suspicions.

The Edict of Nantes, although just in its essential dispositions, dissatisfied the Catholic leaders and the Parliaments tried to oppose it. During Henry IV's lifetime the edict was respected, but under Louis XIII and Louis XIV many privileges were abolished. It was revoked in 1685.

The Netherlands did not have a unified history until the 15th century. In the 14th and 15th centuries, Flanders, Holland, Gelderland and Brabant entered the domination of the powerful dukes of Burgundy, who controlled virtually all the Netherlands. In 1477, Mary of Burgundy restored all the liberties forbidden by her predecessors. Her marriage to Maximilian, the future Maximilian I, brought the Netherlands into the Habsburg Empire.

The ascension of Calvinism fostered the separation of the Netherlands from Catholic Spain. The aristocracy, supported by many for religious and economic reasons, demanded autonomy for the provinces as a reward for removing the Spanish officials. The fight for the independence of the Netherlands (1562–1566) started in Flanders and Brabant, under the leader William, Prince of Orange, who united the regions in the fight against Spain. The fight ended in the Thirty Years' War (1618–1648), when the independence of the United Provinces was recognized in the Peace Treaty of Westphalia. Calvinism was recognized and accepted next to Catholicism and Lutheranism. It was also accepted in the Holy Roman Empire, thus strengthening and ensuring the permanence of religious pluralism in Europe. The Netherlands opened its gates to religious refugees, especially the

Portuguese, the Spanish and the French Huguenots, who all contributed to Holland's prosperity in the 17th century.

Portrait of William I, Prince of Orange

Period 1: 1450-1648

Key Concept 1.4: Europeans explored and settled overseas territories, encountering and interacting with indigenous populations.

From the 15th through 17th centuries, Europeans used their mastery of the seas to extend their power in Africa, Asia and the Americas. In the 15th century, the Portuguese sought direct access by sea to the sources of African gold, ivory and slaves. At the same time, the rise of Ottoman power in the eastern Mediterranean led to Ottoman control of the Mediterranean trade routes and increases in the motivation of Iberians—and then northern Europeans—to explore possible sea routes to the East. The success and consequence of these explorations, and the maritime expansion that followed them, was based on the European adapting Muslim and Chinese navigational technology, as well as advances in military technology and cartography. Political, economic and religious rivalries among Europeans also stimulated maritime expansion. By the 17th century, Europeans had forged a global trade network that gradually edged out Muslim and Chinese dominion in the Indian Ocean and western Pacific.

In Europe, these successes shifted economic power from the Mediterranean to the Atlantic states. In Asia, the Portuguese, Spanish and Dutch competed for control of trade routes and trading stations. In the Americas, the Spanish and Portuguese led in the establishment of colonies, followed by the Dutch, French and English. The pursuit of colonies was sustained by mercantilist economic policies. The creation of maritime empires was also animated by the religious fervor sweeping Europe during the period of the Reformations (Catholic and Protestant).

Global European expansion led to the conversion of indigenous population in South and Central Americas, to an exchange of commodities and crops that enriched European and other civilization that became part of the global trading network and, eventually, to migrations that had profound effects on Europe. The expansion also challenged parochial worldviews in Christian Europe. Yet the Columbian Exchange also unleashed several ecological disasters—notably the death of vast numbers of the Americas' indigenous populations in epidemics of European diseases, such as smallpox and measles, against which the native populations had no defenses. The establishment of the plantation system in the American colonies also led to the vast expansion of the African slave trade, a feature of the new Atlantic trading system.

European nations were driven by commercial and religious motives to explore overseas territories and establish colonies.

The industrial and commercial reprise, which occurred in Europe in the second half of the 15th century, accentuated the lack of exchange instruments, namely gold and silver. Despite the increased activity of the mines in Germany, Slovakia and Transylvania, European production was not able to meet the demands of commerce. The end of the 15th century was a period of scarce and expensive coins and, therefore, of low prices. The need to increase the circulation of metals was a powerful impulse for the exploration of Africa and Asia, where legendary stories told of fabulous treasures of precious metals. At the end of the Middle Ages, Europe imported a lot of precious articles from the Orient: silk tissues, oriental carpets, gems (sapphires and diamonds from India, pearls from Ceylon, etc.), spices from Arabia, colored cloth and medicines from India—the latter playing an important role in medieval pharmacopoeia.

15th century European coins

During this period, salt was the only good known to preserve meat. In the winter, the most important foodstuff was salted meat. Before discovering the rotation of crops and the planting of beets, farmers could keep only a small number of animals during the winter. In order to be sustainable, this severe diet dearly needed condiments, especially given that potatoes and tomatoes were unknown, and vegetables were rarer than they are today. In medieval cities, with their dirty and narrow streets and many disease epidemics, the citizens desired strong, more pleasant aromas to help mask the other terrible smells. They also believed that aromas prevented infection. Aromas were brought to Europe by the Arabs and the Venetians, who sold them for a handsome profit. It would have been very profitable for the Europeans to discover new access roads to the East Indies. The combination of commercial motives and the need for religious proselytism drove European nations to explore overseas territories.

European states sought direct access to gold and spices and luxury goods as a means to enhance personal wealth and state power.

Luxury articles arrived in Europe from Arabia by two routes. The first passed through the Persian Gulf, from where one path led to Damascus and Aleppo (here the merchandise was taken by the Venetians and the Genovese), and another to Trebizond and other ports on the Black Sea (the Russian and Armenian merchants took them to eastern and northern Europe). The second route passed through the Red Sea. From southern India, the ships carried the products of the Orient all the way to Cairo and Alexandria, where Venetian merchants were waiting. Local masters sought to capitalize on these busy routes by instituting many customs and taxes.

For instance, the Sultan of Egypt extracted a tax of one-third of the products which moved through his territory. Merchants also had to pay further taxes at Suez and Cairo. Goods passed through so many hands and were subject to so many taxes, that it is no wonder that spices were sold for three times their price in Venice and five times their price in England. After the Arabs, the Venetians were the main beneficiaries of this commerce. From the 12th century to the 16th century, Venice played the role of an international market for spices and other aromatic oriental goods, especially after the Turks—who conquered Constantinople—closed the ports on the Black Sea and in Syria. Had other roads to the East Indies been discovered, the Arabs and Venetians would have lost their monopoly on trade in luxury goods. The new explorers would thus have enhanced their personal wealth, as well as that of their states.

The rise of mercantilism gave the state a new role in promoting commercial development and the acquisition of colonies overseas.

The first explorations were random and made without method or continuity. They did not end with great discoveries, because they lacked the support of the only two things which could support and pay for such a prolonged effort: a centralized state and economic means. For mercantilist reasons, the maritime states supported the explorers' efforts to free them from the Venetian monopoly on the luxury goods trade and to acquire a rich source of income.

Christianity served as a stimulus for exploration as governments and religious authorities sought to spread the faith and counter Islam, as a justification for the physical and cultural subjugation of indigenous civilizations.

Hernán Cortés, Spanish conquistador

Among the motivations for exploration, historians include religious proselytism as one of the highest priorities. However, it was not the most important reason, and the Portuguese and Spanish explorers had other preoccupations. Christopher Columbus offered to Queen Isabella rich islands, and to the Church, spiritual conquest. Hernán Cortés encouraged his soldiers by reminding them that they were the "champions of the cross" and, if they kept their faith, they would triumph under the sign of the cross. As "champions of the cross," the Spanish conquistadores assumed that their purpose justified any means. The crusaders used Christian propaganda to rationalize an unmerciful war, in which the defeated had to choose between submitting to slavery or being exterminated. The ideal of "disinterested reason" (meaning an attempt to discover the truth of things with no bias or personal agenda) was completely abandoned when Christopher Columbus returned from his voyages with real gold sand. The true purpose of the maritime expeditions was to search for gold and spices.

Advances in navigation, cartography and military technology allowed Europeans to establish overseas colonies and empires.

Geographic explorations were made easier by inventions that perfected the art of navigation. The invention of the stern-post rudder, which was sunk in the water and was easy to maneuver with the aid of a steering wheel, revolutionized the art of navigation and made the Europeans the masters of the seas. The ability to indefinitely increase the steering wheel and the stern-post rudder allowed ship builders to increase vessels' dimensions. In the 15th century, the Portuguese invented the *caravel*. A caravel was a ship with a double system of sails: square sails for the wind from the back and triangular ones against the wind from the face. At the same time, the sunken steering wheel ensured independence from the direction of the winds.

Caravels

In order to determinate the departure point, the direction of travel and the arrival point by measuring the height of stars above the horizon, navigators used the astrolabe, which had been perfected and disseminated by the Arabs; it was later replaced by the sextant. Astrolabes allowed them to calculate latitude, the angle of the horizon with the line drawn by the observer's eye with the North Star. Longitude was determined based on the principle of hourly difference: ship captains observed that the longitude difference between two spots was 15 degrees for each hour. The Chinese had known since ancient times that a magnetic needle shows true north. The navigational compass also became known in Europe in the middle of the 13th century, becoming a practical and easy-to-use tool.

Equipped with the steering wheel, stern-post rudder, compass, quadrant and astrolabe, ships could more effectively sail on the oceans and explore new trade routes. With these vessels, overseas explorers could transport horses, guns and gunpowder, which gave them a tremendous advantage over indigenous populations who had never seen such animals or modern inventions. For instance, although Cortés had smaller military forces, he took advantage of his technological superiority over the Aztecs, which included steel weapons, armor, coifs, cavalry and, most of all, firearms.

Europeans established overseas empires and trade networks through coercion and negotiation.

The reason for Portuguese expeditions was their desire to get rich like the Venetians. They did not think to establish colonies, which they could not populate, but instead they sought to create a commercial monopoly. All of their policies in the Indies were guided by this consideration. International rivalries were the reasons why, in the 16th century, the Portuguese colonial empire expanded well beyond the state's original small territory on the Iberian Peninsula.

The purpose of the first maritime Spanish expeditions was, as in the case of the Portuguese, to get in on the spice trade. However, when the hope of discovering a shorter way to the Indies vanished, the Spanish had to admit that only by organizing agricultural and mine exploitation could they get rich from their discoveries. Therefore, subsequent to their conquest in the Americas, the colonization period began around 1540.

In the Americas, the Spanish found lands which varied according to climate, resources, inhabitants and levels of human civilization. They discovered useful plants, like the potato, cocoa and cotton. The Spanish also acclimatized wheat, rice, fruit trees and animals. The conquest was gradual and was furthered by two means: coercion and negotiation. For their work, Native Americans expected to receive food, clothes and shelter, but these obligations were not respected by the Spanish, who viewed and treated the Native Americans as slaves. Spain's colonial empire became very well organized and changed the shape of the Americas' culture and civilization forever.

The Portuguese established a commercial network along the African coast, in South and East Asia, and in South America.

The era of geographic discovery was opened by the Portuguese when they started to explore the coast of West Africa. Henry the Navigator combined exploration and expeditions with the economic exploitation of the lands he discovered. Compelled by the desire to increase income from commerce of gold, ivory and black slaves, the Portuguese, represented by Bartholomew Diaz, reached the Cape of Good Hope in 1488. Later on, another expedition led to greater familiarity with Africa's southern and eastern shores. These two discoveries enabled the expedition of Vasco da Gama. The expedition he led in 1497 accomplished the main objective of the Europeans—finding a direct route from Europe to India.

Vasco da Gama, Portuguese explorer

After establishing their naval and military supremacy and the commercial domination of India's west shore, the Portuguese began their exploration and conquest of the Malacca Peninsula and Indonesia. The Portuguese Empire was comprised of maritime and provisioning bases; these forts were scattered along western and eastern Africa, at the entrance to the Red Sea and the Persian Gulf, on the west coast of India and in Malacca, Indonesia, China and Japan.

In 1500, the Portuguese began to explore and colonize the Brazilian coast of the Americas. The Portuguese Empire depended directly on the Crown, which exerted a monopoly on maritime explorations and colonial conquests, by means of organizations subordinate to the state. The supreme institution was Casa da India, a maritime and colonial enterprise with its central office in Lisbon. It acquired the necessary funds, organized naval and commerce squadrons, recruited sailors and troops, named functionaries, granted licenses for colonial commerce and calculated the profits of the depositors. The administration of the colonies in Africa, India, Malaysia, Indonesia and Brasilia was conducted by a viceroy of the Indies and by individual governors.

The Spanish established colonies across the Americas, the Caribbean and the Pacific, which made Spain the dominant state in Europe.

As the road towards the east and south was closed by the Portuguese, the Spanish directed their exploration efforts to the west. Christopher Columbus sought to reach Asia from the Iberian Peninsula by crossing the Atlantic Ocean. He estimated a distance which was three times shorter than the real one. He did not suspect the existence of another continent, America, situated between the Atlantic and the Pacific Oceans. His voyage was approved in 1492 by the rulers of Spain, Ferdinand of Aragon and Isabella of Castile. Their reasoning was that, since Spain did not wish to cross the exploration zone which belonged to Portugal, Columbus' route was the only way to discover a maritime route to Asia. Columbus left Spain in August. His expedition reached Isle San Salvador in October.

Later, he discovered many more islands, which he thought were Asia's eastern shores. The discovery had a huge impact—not only for Spain and Europe, but for America as well.

Between the 15th and 16th centuries, the Spanish organized new expeditions to the Caribbean, along the eastern shores of Central America, the Gulf of Mexico and the northern shores of South America. This created favorable conditions for conquering the regions in which the Mayan (Central America), Aztec (Mexico) and Inca (Peru) cultures flourished. The conquest of the Aztec Empire was accomplished under the leadership of Hernán Cortés in two years (1519–1521). In 1534, the Spanish conquered Peru and occupied northwestern South America, afterwards expanding their dominion to Chile and Argentina. In the 16th century, they occupied territory in the Caribbean, Central America, Mexico, Florida and in north, west and southwestern South America, establishing a huge colonial empire in the New World.

Cortés' conquest of Tenochtitlán

The lands were considered the property of the Crown and were owned by the new rulers in the form of territorial concessions. The central organ was the Council of the Indies—created in 1511 and reorganized in 1524—which had the authority to organize and manage the Spanish territories in America. Casa de Contratación was subordinated to the Council of the Indies, had its main offices in Seville and was created to organize and supervise the maritime and commercial connections between Spain and its transoceanic colonies, which were divided into two viceroyalties. One included the territories in Mexico and Central America and the other, those in South America.

The Atlantic nations of France, England and the Netherlands followed by establishing their own colonies and trading networks to compete with Portuguese and Spanish dominance.

The central and southern regions of the Atlantic were dominated by the Portuguese and Spanish. The French, English and Dutch tried to find maritime routes to Asia and India, either through the northwest, rounding North America, or through the northeast, around Asia. The northwestern maritime path was searched for by the French and the English. John Cabot explored the northeastern shores of North America in 1497 and 1498, including Terra Nova (Newfoundland) and Labrador. Martin Frobisher and others explored the region between the west coast of Greenland and Hudson's Bay.

The explorations made on the northeastern shores of North America were carried out at remote latitudes and navigation was hindered by ice; they could not lead to the discovery of a new route to India. The first English and French colonies on the eastern shores of North America appeared in the 17th century. The maritime route towards the northeast was searched for by the English and Dutch. An expedition from 1553 to 1554 entered the White Sea and from there, continued on land to Moscow, establishing English-Russian commercial relations.

When the war started between the United Provinces and Spain, Portugal entered into a dynastic union with Spain. Given these conditions, the Dutch began the gradual conquest of the Portuguese colonial empire in Southeast Asia, which was accomplished due to the maritime and military means offered by the Dutch East India Company. They occupied the Mauritius Islands, east of Madagascar, and established a base at the Cape of Good Hope in 1652. They also conquered the Portuguese colonies in Indonesia, occupying Java, Sumatra, Borneo, Celebes and the southern Malacca Peninsula, which ensured their control over Southeast Asian commerce. The Dutch established commercial relations with India, China and Japan. Holland's maritime and colonial expansion in Southeast Asia was accompanied by new geographical discoveries. In the first half of the 17th century, the Dutch explored the shores of Australia—which they named New Holland—and discovered the islands of Tasmania and New Zeeland (now spelled "New Zealand").

The competition for trade led to conflicts and rivalries among European powers.

The geographical discoveries were followed by an ever increasing struggle for maritime and commercial supremacy between the West European states. Columbus' first expedition created tension between the Spanish and Portuguese, who were searching in opposite directions for a maritime route to India. After fierce disputes, the Treaty of Tordesillas was signed in 1494, demarking both nations' areas of geographic exploration and maritime, commercial and colonial dominion in the world. The Portuguese and Spanish areas were denoted by a line that passed 370 leagues west of the Cape Verde islands—the Portuguese holdings stretching to the east and the Spanish to the west. However, the other European states did not recognize the division of the world between Spain and Portugal, claiming the freedom of participation in maritime, commercial and colonial expansion.

Portugal and Spain's pretentions to solve the dispute over maritime and colonial expansion generated increased opposition from England and Holland. This started parallel to economic and naval development and the fight for maritime domination against the Iberian Empires. The fight intensified in the 16th century, leading to the Spanish-English War. This culminated in the defeat of the Invincible Armada by the English in 1588. It also led to war between Holland, Spain and Portugal, which resulted in the occupation by the Dutch of the Southeast Asian colonies belonging to the Portuguese. A large number of people from Africa, Southeast Asia and the Americas were enslaved. This was the beginning of commerce with black slaves, the eradication of the Native American tribes and the destruction of the indigenous pre-Columbian civilizations.

Destruction of the Spanish Armada

Europe's colonial expansion led to a global exchange of goods, flora, fauna, cultural practices and diseases, resulting in the destruction of some indigenous civilizations, a shift toward European dominance and the expansion of the slave trade.

The discovery and conquest of new territories were followed by an intense process of colonization. The purpose of colonization was the exploitation of new lands, precious metals and local populations. This led to a general exchange of goods and flora and fauna, but also to the spread of diseases, like smallpox, which destroyed whole indigenous civilizations. Black slaves, initially used for gathering pearls, were put to work in mines and on cotton, cocoa and tobacco plantations. Slaves were bought with money or acquired through the exchange of commodities like salt, meat, tobacco and cocoa.

The exchange of goods shifted the center of economic power in Europe from the Mediterranean to the Atlantic states and brought the latter into an expanding world economy.

The geographical discoveries, the novelty and abundance of the products exported to Europe, the influx of a huge quantity of precious metals and the beginning of colonial expansion had multiple consequences on the development of European states. The commerce with the colonies was varied. Spain was selling goods like wine, oil, fabric, iron instruments and weapons, luxury articles and black slaves. The most important good that the colonies exported was precious metals, especially silver and gold. In the first 60 years of colonization, approximately 30,000 kilograms of silver were imported from America, compared to the 59,000 kilograms that were produced in Europe. The annual production of gold was 1,500 kilograms in Europe, 3,260 kilograms in America and 2,400 kilograms in Africa.

The geographic discoveries widened the commercial field considerably. Until the 15th century, this had been limited to relations with Syria and Egypt. The discoveries displaced the commercial routes and centers. The Atlantic displaced the Mediterranean and Baltic Seas as the world's commercial center. The coastal countries—Portugal, Spain, France, England and the Netherlands—became the most important economic and commercial powers. Venice was limited to commerce with the Ottoman Empire and the Hanseatic League lost its supremacy over the Baltic Sea and dissolved.

The Hanseatic League was a confederation of northern European towns and merchant guilds, which organized itself for mutual defense and economic cooperation. The region it occupied included the modern Netherlands, many parts of modern day northern Germany (including the city of Bremen), the Schleswig-Holstein (Southern) part of Denmark and parts of northern Poland. It was an economic common market, that is, it had common laws and taxation.

The exchange of new plants, animals and diseases—the Columbian Exchange—created economic opportunities for Europeans and facilitated European subjugation and destruction of indigenous peoples, particularly in the Americas.

The geographic discoveries revealed the economic possibilities of the Americas. After the conquest, when the Spanish began to valorize the soil of their colonies, they introduced plants like wheat, barley, fruit trees, sugar cane and olives. They also brought animals like the horses, donkeys, oxen, goats and sheep, which were unknown in the New World. At the same time, they sent experts in agriculture and irrigation workers. They brought back to Europe plants and animals that were indigenous to America, such as tobacco, corn, pineapples, tomatoes, potatoes and the turkey. However, during this exchange, communicable diseases were also brought to and from the Americas: the Europeans brought with them to the Americas the devastating diseases of smallpox and measles, and took syphilis back with them.

Europeans exploited the African slave trade due to the establishment of a plantation economy in the Americans and demographic catastrophes among indigenous peoples.

In America, the local population was reduced to servitude and obligations to the colonists, the state and the Church. The Spanish imposed Catholicism on Native Americans and they superimposed their own institutions and structures. In order to ensure the supply of labor the Spanish needed, the indigenous population was forced to do exhausting work on plantations, transportation and in mines. The violent destruction of the social structures and of the traditional way of life, forced labor in the mines, abuses by the Spanish administration and the epidemics provoked by the diseases brought from Europe (smallpox and measles), against which the locals had no immune defense, caused a rapid decline in the Native American population.

Spanish explorers raising a memorial cross in the Americas

This triggered a reaction from some colonists. An important example is the monk Bartholomew Las Casas, who denounced the horrors inflicted by the Spanish against the Native Americans. After these protests, Charles Quint issued the "New Laws" which forbade the enslavement of Native Americans. But the application of these laws was uneven and ineffective because of the colonists' opposition and the continuing abuses of the colonial authorities. The introduction of Native American slavery stimulated the black slave trade, increasingly so, especially in Central America.

Period 1: 1450-1648

> **Key Concept 1.5:** **European society and the experiences of everyday life were increasingly shaped by commercial and agricultural capitalism, notwithstanding the persistence of medieval social and economic structures.**

In the 16th and 17th centuries, Europeans experienced profound economic and social changes. The influx of precious metals from the Americas, and the gradual recovery of Europe's population from the Black Death, caused a significant rise in the cost of goods and services by the 16th century, known as the "price revolution." The new pattern of economic enterprise and investment that arose from these changes would come to be called capitalism. Family-based banking houses were supplanted by broadly integrated capital markets in Genoa, then in Amsterdam and later in London. These and other urban centers became increasingly active consumer markets for a variety of luxury goods and commodities. Rulers soon recognized that capitalist enterprise offered them a revenue source to support state functions, and the competition among states was extended into the economic arena. The drive for economic profit and the increasing scale of commerce stimulated the creation of joint-stock companies to conduct overseas trade and colonization.

Many Europeans found their daily lives altered by these demographic and economic changes. As population increased in the 16th century, the price of grain rose and diets deteriorated, all as monarchs were increasing taxes to support their larger state militaries. All but the wealthy were vulnerable to food shortages, and even the wealthy were not immune to recurrent lethal epidemics. Although hierarchy and privilege continued to define the social structure, the nobility and gentry expanded with the infusion of new blood from the commercial and professional classes. By the mid-17th century, war, economic contraction and slackening population growth contributed to the disintegration of older communal values. Growing numbers of the poor became beggars or vagabonds, straining the traditional systems of charity and social control. In Eastern Europe, commercial development lagged and traditional social patterns persisted; the nobility actually increased its power over the peasantry.

Traditional town governments, dominated by craft guilds and traditional religious institutions, were unable to cope with the burden of rural migrants and growing poverty. The Reformation and the Counter-Reformation stimulated a drive to regulate public morale, leisure activities and the distribution of poor relief. In both town and country, the family remained the dominant unit of production and marriage remained an instrument of families' social and economic strategies. The children of peasants and craft workers often labored alongside their parents. In the lower orders of society, men and women did not occupy separate spheres, although they performed different tasks.

Economics often dictated later marriages (European marriage pattern). However, there were exceptions to this pattern: in the cities of Renaissance Italy, men in their early 30s often married teenaged women and in Eastern Europe, early marriage for both men and women persisted. Despite the growth of the market economy, in which individuals increasingly made their own way, leisure activities tended to be communal, rather than individualistic and consumerist as they are today. Local communities enforced their customs and norms through rituals of public shaming.

Economic change produced new social patterns, while traditions of hierarchy and status persisted.

The period between the 16th century and the middle of the 17th century marks the evolution from feudalism to more advanced modes of economic relations. This process did not happen simultaneously in all countries. It first began in England, the Netherlands and France. In central and eastern Europe, where the old society was still strongly consolidated, the development of the new system occurred later. In Asian countries, the feudal system endured until the modern age. Beginning in the 15th century, and especially during the 16th century, the production capability evolved rapidly, facilitated by the dissemination and improvement of technical achievements from Antiquity and new inventions. One of the most remarkable was the invention of the printing press by Johannes Guttenberg, which established the basis of typographic production.

Johannes Guttenberg with his printing press

Free market relations also developed in those fields in which the technical progress and the demands of the internal and foreign market imposed higher technical and financial demands, a more numerous labor force and a new organization of the production process. Manufacturing became the basic economic goal in the organization of processes of production. Manufacturing accentuated the social divisions and income disparity. Along with dispersed manufacturing, centralized manufacturing, in which the production process took place in buildings and with the means of production belonging to the entrepreneur with capital (i.e., the merchants and bankers), or, in France, to the state, also appeared. Wage workers were employed and the products were destined entirely for exchange.

The appearance of market relations supposed the existence of a large category of workers who were free but, lacking the means of production, had to work as employees. It concentrated the means of production in the hands of the moneyed few. This was the process of the initial phase of capital accumulation, which took place first in England, the Netherlands and France. The methods used to obtain initial capital included expropriation of the peasants' land, increasing feudal rents and ruining small craftsmen. The process of gathering capital began with the concentration of large sums of money in the hands of rich men, who acquired the means of production and the labor force.

The entire economic process had profound consequences on the social structure. New social categories appeared, the most important being the bourgeoisie—bearers of the new relations of production—the laborers, who sold their labor as a means to earn wages in order to provide for their sustenance, bankers and merchants. At the same time, older social structures continued to exist, like the old feudal nobility, which failed to adapt to the new economy. Gradually, a new nobility appeared that was involved in manufacturing and commerce in a way that coincided with the interests of the bourgeoisie. The merchandise-money relationship entered the state economy and began to dominate all aspects of life.

Innovations in banking and finance promoted the growth of urban financial centers and a money economy.

Along with the expansion of internal markets, commercial exchanges between states intensified, leading to the creation of global markets. Commercial companies were created to facilitate economic transactions and banks flourished. Agios appeared, with the purpose of intermediating commercial transactions with high volume and values, especially in the international centers of commerce. Goods were introduced—cereals, wines, spices, etc.—and after negotiations, various commercial and financial transactions were concluded.

Under the Mercantile system, two nations formed government sponsored organizations for the purpose of exploring, establishing colonies and governing manufacturing and trade from those colonies. The British crown established the British East India Company. The Dutch merchants established the Dutch East India Company and the Dutch West India Company. These companies had exclusive licenses from their governments, making them monopolies whose operations were initially funded and directed by their governments. They were financed by investors from their countries' wealthy populations, who expected a return on their investment. Hence, these companies are known as "joint stock companies." They had their own militaries to enforce their will, large shipping and naval fleets and strategic ports abroad.

The Dutch East India Company is considered by some to be the oldest Multinational corporation in the world. (It is often referred to as the "VOC" – the contraction of its name in Dutch.) It was given its charter by the Dutch government in 1602, with the mission of gaining control of the world's spice trade from the Spice Islands in East Asia (present day Maluku Islands of Indonesia). The "VOC" became overwhelmingly the largest company of its type, employing one million Europeans on all levels, over two centuries. It began by establishing a port capital, which is now the capital city of Indonesia, Jakarta. Dutch colonization and spice trade expanded in the region over the next two hundred years. As a result, Indonesia, Malaysia and Australia have Dutch colonial histories (Australia was discovered and surveyed by the VOC before the British colonized it).

The Dutch West India Company was established in 1621. It was smaller in scale than the Dutch East India Company but more significant in human history. It conducted the Dutch component of the slave trade and brought the very first known slaves to America – twenty who were purchased by the Jamestown colony. It settled in what is now New York, although the Dutch colony failed and was taken over by the British. It was responsible for the Dutch operations in the Caribbean.

The British East India was chartered by Queen Elizabeth I in 1600. Its scope of operations was smaller than its Dutch counterpart, but it was much more successful in creating large colonies and wealth, over its three centuries of operations. To wit, it brought the "jewel in the crown" – India – under British hegemony. It opened trade and colonization in every part of the world. For example, it was responsible for creating and managing the Opium trade and the Tea trade in China and wresting control of colonies from the Dutch, such as South Africa and New York.

The Bank of Amsterdam was one of the earliest modern banks and a product of the growth of the money economy during the Renaissance. It was created in 1609. In the beginning, it received both foreign and local coinage at their intrinsic value, deducted a small coinage and management fee and credited clients in its book for the remainder. This credit was known as *bank money*, which was worth more than real coinage. Bank money had the advantage that it was insured against robbery and accidents and that it was backed by the city of Amsterdam. This bank's practices were precursors of those of modern banks.

The Dutch Republic dominated world trade at the end of the 16th century and during the 17th century, conquering a vast colonial empire and operating the largest fleet of merchantmen of any nation. The County of Holland was the wealthiest and most urbanized region in the world. The States General of the United Provinces were in control of the Dutch East India Company and the Dutch West India Company. The free trade spirit of the time received strong augmentation by the development of a modern, effective stock market in the Netherlands. It was the oldest stock exchange in the world, founded in 1602 by the Dutch East India Company.

Engraving of the East India House in Amsterdam

While Rotterdam has the oldest bourse in the Netherlands, the world's first stock exchange – that of the Dutch East India Company—went public in six different cities. Later, a court ruled that the company had to reside legally in a single city, so Amsterdam is recognized as the oldest such institution based on modern trading principles. While the banking system evolved slowly in the Netherlands, the English equivalent was quickly incorporated by the well-connected English, stimulating English economic output. Between 1590 and 1712, the Dutch also possessed one of the strongest and fastest navies in the world. This allowed for conquests, which included breaking the Portuguese sphere of influence on the Indian Ocean and in the Orient, and a lucrative slave trade from Africa and the Pacific.

English traders frequently engaged in hostilities with their Dutch and Portuguese counterparts in the Indian Ocean. The company achieved a major victory over the Portuguese in the Battle of Swally in 1612. The English decided to explore the feasibility of gaining a territorial foothold on mainland India, with the official sanction of the leaders of both India and England (Emperor Nuruddin Jahangir and Queen Elizabeth I), and requested that the Crown launch a diplomatic mission. England eventually came to rule large areas of India with its own private armies, exercising military power and assuming administrative functions.

The growth of commerce produced a new economic elite, which related to traditional elites in different ways in Europe's various geographic regions.

Economic and technical progress, the increase of production and exchange, the intensification of the circulation of money and the disintegration of classical medieval society led to the appearance of new market relations. This process was not constant throughout Europe. It began in England, the Netherlands and France and later expanded to the rest of Europe. The increase of manufacturing production and the ever-growing needs of the urban population led to the flourishing of commerce, the development of markets and trade and of banking activity.

Other Italian banking institutions founded in that period were: *Banca Buonsignori* in Siena, *Casa di San Giorgio* in Genoa and *Sacro Monte della Pietà* in Naples. In 1472, *Banca Monte dei Paschi di Siena* was founded. Today it is the oldest bank in the world still in activity. In Germany, one of the first banking institutions was founded in Hamburg in 1590 by the Dutch brothers Berenberg. In 1619, *The Bank of Hamburg* was founded and in 1621, *The Bank of Nürnberg* was founded. The Italian (Frescobaldi, Strozzi) and German (Fugger, Wesler) financiers made so much profit and were so affluent that they eventually established themselves as the creditors of European monarchs.

The bourgeoisie was composed of enriched citizens (owners of manufacturers, merchants, money-lenders, craftsmen, even some workers who became owners), new intellectuals (jurists, physicians, functionaries) and prosperous countrymen who became farmers. Benefiting from the new conditions of production, it differed from the medieval bourgeoisie, which had been part of the aristocracy. In England, along with the ancient nobility—which did not adapt to the economy of concurrence—a new gentry who were interested in manufacturing and commerce, and who were closer to the bourgeoisie, also appeared. These two social classes became so rich and powerful that soon they did not feel the need for an absolutist regime's protection. The new gentry played an important role in the English Civil War, obtaining, along with the bourgeoisie, new rights and freedoms.

In France, the great nobility became scarce, a consequence of the centralization of the state and of the civil wars. A part of the nobility became nobles of the court. The most influential were the Nobles of the Robe, who worked in administration, justice and in parliament. The nobility was not a closed social group, but an open elite. It often accepted alliances with the bourgeoisie, which increased its economic power and political influence.

Miguel de Cervante,
author of Don Quixote

Los hidalgos were a Spanish social category that could be compared to nobility, but without a title. A hidalgo could also be someone who proved his artistry in the liberal arts and sciences and showed elegant manners. The world's most famous hidalgo was the fictional Don Quijote de la Mancha, the protagonist featured in Miguel de Cervantes' similarly titled novel *Don Quixote*. In 16th and 17th century Spain, the social structure was diverse, formed of nobility, clergy, hidalgos, citizens, bourgeoisie and peasants.

The nobility was stratified into several categories. Those from the oldest and most famous families were the *grands*. At first there were few of them, but later on their numbers grew. Usually a family's first son inherited the greatest part of his father's wealth, while the rest of the sons embraced military or ecclesiastical careers. Then there were the small nobles, *caballeros* and the aforementioned hidalgos, who were rather poor. Across Europe, the new social groups, gaining in wealth due to the profound transformations in the economy, became ever more powerful and began to play an important role in political affairs.

Hierarchy and status continued to define social power and perceptions in rural and urban settings.

The transition from the Middle Ages to modernity is conventionally connected with major events like the Protestant Reformation, which promoted the critical conscience related to religion and church; the discovery of America, which widened perspectives on the world; or humanism, which led to innovations in numerous fields. The Reformation questioned the concept of the Church's absolute power and the Thirty Years' War abolished the concept of "universal empire." British and French colonists occupied the east coast of North America and Spanish conquistadores conquered Central and South America, scattering the entire world with European commercial agencies. Europe was deeply enmeshed in war, revolutions and devastation, but also in extraordinary developments and scientific and artistic progress. Revolutions began in the 17th century. Some of them succeeded and some failed, but the political revolutions showed that many were dissatisfied with the status quo.

The discrepancies within European society deepened. Rich and autocratic kings lived in luxury, while the middle classes—ever more numerous, especially in urban areas—developed and progressed. Society was marked by great transformations; in the cities, bankers constructed profitable businesses, inventors and explorers made new discoveries and merchandise and ideas were spread. The agricultural landscape was modified radically across Europe, especially in England, by the introduction of new and efficient work methods. It was in England that the first Industrial Revolution in textiles, mines, cities, navigable channels and facilities began. The preoccupation with logic and reason led to new, more modern social and political ideas.

The first enlightened absolutists employed both the concepts of Church and state to reach their purpose, which was to ensure the welfare of the state and the people. However, there were also kings and nobles who were not ready to allow their subjects, especially those bourgeoisie who were in full ascension, to take part in political life. The hierarchical medieval social structure continued to exist along with the new social structures.

Still, humanism and the Reformation irreversibly influenced the way in which the middle class thought about themselves and their relation to the burgeoning free market. The riches obtained by these new classes brought them respect and influence. The kings oriented their policies toward the bourgeoisie, in order to counterbalance the power of the princes and the Church. Despite the fact that the bourgeoisie promoted commerce and imposed itself in cultural life, ancient structures of social hierarchy continued to influence society and access to power. From this came a series of conflicts and disputes which led to the "Atlantic revolutions" which, along with *The Declaration of Independence* and the French *Declaration of the Rights of Man and Citizen*, marked the beginning of the bourgeoisie's ascension to power.

Drafting the American Declaration of Independence

Most Europeans derived their livelihood from agriculture and oriented their lives around the seasons, the village or the manor, although economic changes began to alter rural production and power.

In Europe, most of the population continued to be engaged in agricultural production. The appearance of market relations in agriculture in the 16th and 17th centuries took place in the context of technical progress in the agrarian economy, the increase of production and agricultural products in circulation, and the crisis in and decay of feudal social structures. Although mining, manufacturing, commerce, banking and navigation expanded, the agrarian economy and rural population still represented the majority of the populace in Western European economy and society. Generally, the rural population represented 65% to 90% of countries' populations, only reaching 50% in the United Provinces (the Dutch Republic). In order to meet the increased demand for agricultural products, output was increased which, given the limited agricultural surface of arable land in Europe, was achieved through technological progress (e.g., modifications in the cultivated surfaces, cattle run sizes, improvement in crop rotation systems and the restructuring and reorganizing of the agricultural funding method).

The formation of market relations in agriculture was prefaced by familiar societal crisis, including the weakening of the feudal property system and the abolition of the feudal social structures. Bourgeois ownership of land and market relations in agriculture appeared in the context of the domains or fields still in property or in tenure but no longer under feudal control. Largely owned by the nobility, fields began to be worked by employed laborers. However, this process was very slow and, for a long period of time, the feudal structure endured in the agrarian economy. Depending on this process, the genesis of market relations in agriculture took place early and intensively in England, France, Italy, Germany and the Iberian Peninsula.

Subsistence agriculture was the rule in most areas, with three-crop field rotation in the north and two-crop rotation in the Mediterranean; in many cases, farmers paid rent and labor services for their land.

Wheat, barley, rye, millet and corn were planted. Rye dominated the northern regions, and barley and millet dominated the Mediterranean. Land was cultivated repeatedly, which caused its natural potential to be drained. This led to agricultural crisis and famine. In other areas, to avoid the draining of the soil's natural potential, land cultivation was staggered so that no one parcel was over used. For example, biannual crop rotation, a technique used in Antiquity, was a cycle by which land was divided into two parts, one of which was cultivated while the other was left fallow. After a year, the first part was left fallow while the second was cultivated.

Tri-annual crop rotation appeared during the Middle Ages. It divided the land into three parts: spring cereals were planted on the first, autumn cereals on the second and the third was left fallow. A complete cycle lasted three years. The tri-annual crop rotation was the most advantageous method, because it facilitated the restoration of the soil's natural potential and it also diminished the risk of agricultural crisis because of the simultaneous sowing of spring and autumn cereals. The yields were larger, with domestic animals consuming spring cereals and people eating autumn cereals.

The main agricultural trend in the 15th to the 17th centuries was the consolidation of small farm plots into larger ones. The due date of the tenure was shortened, so that the tenure rental was modified in accordance with the price revolution and with the increase of the prices for agricultural products. The farms belonged to the great nobility, the gentry, the yeomanry, rich citizens or the bourgeoisie, who exploited them directly or placed them in tenure. They were worked by salaried agricultural workers with the purpose of obtaining products for the market. For a long period of time, in some regions, farmers continued to pay rent and buy labor services for their land.

The price revolution contributed to the accumulation of capital and the expansion of the market economy through the commercialization of agriculture, which benefited large landowners in Western Europe.

In the 16 and 17th centuries, the following trends created the necessary conditions for an accumulation of capital: technical progress, the evolution of production, the expansion of internal and external markets, the intensification of money circulation, the decline of the feudal system and the appearance of a large labor force, which lacked the means of production and subsistence.

Serfs deliver taxes to their landlords under the feudal system

The economic foundations of the feudal agricultural system began to shift substantially in 16th century Western Europe; the manorial system had broken down by this time and land began to be concentrated in the hands of a few landlords with increasingly large estates. Instead of a serf-based system of labor, workers were increasingly being employed as part of a broader economy based on money. The system put pressure on both landlords and tenants to increase the productivity of agriculture in order to make a profit; the weakened coercive power of the aristocracy to extract peasant surpluses encouraged them to implement new and efficient methods; the tenants also had an incentive to improve their methods, in order to flourish in an increasingly competitive labor market. Terms of rent for the land were increasingly subject to market forces, rather than the previous undeviating system of customs and feudal obligations.

Moreover, Europe profited from the influx of American precious metals in Spain and their redistribution in other European countries. The huge fortunes gathered from the precious metals, and from maritime and colonial commerce, were largely invested in mines, manufacturing, commerce, agriculture and farms organized on a free market basis, thus contributing to the development of market relations in Western Europe. This had one devastating negative side effect however: inflation.

The enclosure movement was an attempt to make farm production more efficient by assigning ownership to specific peasants. In medieval times, land was divided by wealthy land owning nobles but it was farmed in common by many peasants. Enclosure was the process of dividing land into small parcels which were clearly delineated (with a fence or other visible barrier). Historians debate the reasons that this phenomenon occurred but its result was an increase in income for the land lords.

As Western Europe moved toward a free peasantry and commercial agriculture, serfdom was codified in the east, where nobles continued to dominate economic life on large estates.

Eastern Europe continued to function according to the type of feudalism which existed in the Byzantine Empire and the Balkan states. The nobles owed faithful service to the lord, who owned all the land. Nobles were landowners and occupied all the official functions, which is why they took part in the administration of the country. They were relieved from taxation and their lands were attended by serfs or by free peasants who did not own land. Serfs' obligations to the nobles or monasteries were the tithe (one-tenth of their produce), corvée (physical work) and taxes in the form of money. The serfs had many limitations: they were not allowed to leave the land on which they worked, they could not marry without the noble's consent and could only do so on his land, they could not transmit land to their sons without the noble's approval (and then only after paying a tax), their sons had to be serfs, they were not accepted as legal witnesses and they had numerous other limitations imposed on them.

Land was not only a means of subsistence, but also an instrument of domination. It gave nobles economic power because of the crops, taxes and political power it gave them. They had the right to gather taxes from peasants, to judge and arrest them, and in some areas, nobles even had the right to mint coins. Despite the abuse and violence, peasants had no legal recourse for defending themselves. Their dissatisfaction, manifested in riots and revolts, increased in the 15th century and at the beginning of the 16th century spread to Central Europe.

The attempts by landlords to increase their revenues by restricting or abolishing the traditional rights of peasants led to revolt.

The crisis of the 15th century led to a certain social differentiation; it provoked dissatisfaction in rural communities and resulted in the various peasants' revolts. The efforts of the nobles and the monarchy to reduce payments, the desire of land owners to bind their subjects to the land and the impossibility of the poor to take a lot in tenure, led to the appearance of numerous poverty stricken regions. A loan was often the only means of survival for the poor. For these poor men, the only solution was to enter marginalized groups: some became brigands, others gathered into groups (the crackers from Bourgogne, the caimans from Ile-de-France etc.) and spread terror in villages, which they robbed and pillaged. These random acts of violence, born from the desperate need to survive, failed because they did not have a coherent program.

The situation was different for the rural middle class, who managed to take land in tenure and obtain reduced taxes from their superiors. They intended to defend these rights against any modifications which might have harmed them: new taxes, requisitions and, especially, the attempt by the cities, the royal power and even the nobles, to control this class. The foot soldiers of the great peasants' revolts of the 14th and the 15th centuries were made up of this rural middle class. Riots were triggered in Flanders between 1323 and 1328 and in the Scandinavian countries in the first half of the 15th century. The most famous are the Jacquerie revolt in the northern French Beauvaisi region and the revolt of the English peasants in 1381.

This later English peasant revolt had its origins in King Edward III's decision to forbid or to limit the increase in salaries, which was an indirect consequence of the first epidemic of the Black Plague. Disorder occurred when the king tried to impose respect for the law with the intervention of his representatives. These riots lasted for several years and fed an intense agitation in some regions of England. The situation was aggravated in the most populated areas, such as the central and eastern London basin, because of a personal tax which produced a draining of capital.

The Jaquerie take prisoners

The king's decision to impose a tax of one shilling per capita (literally per head) triggered the revolt. In June, led by Wat Tyler, an improvised army composed of peasants entered London and forced the young king to comply with their demands. He abolished serfdom and made all land owners free farmers. Although the revolt was eventually defeated, it established a precedent, and peasants' rights were henceforth a subject of discussion throughout Europe. Concessions were made, which included a guarantee of common law and the recently obtained rights.

Population shifts and growing commerce caused the expansion of cities, which often found their traditional political and social structures stressed by the growth.

The city was, first of all, a dense society concentrated in a small space in the midst of vast, often poorly populated regions. It was, secondly, a center of production and exchange where crafting mingled with commerce, nourished by a monetary economy. The city was also a center of a special system of values, from which sprung the creative and toilsome practice of work, the taste for commerce and money, the predisposition towards luxury and a sense of beauty.

Renaissance cities were modeled on organized plans which included a space enclosed with walls which had scattered defensive towers. The city thus had to be accessed through gates. In these developed cities, human interaction was greatly facilitated by the ease with which one could travel the streets and by the markets. A Renaissance era city was also a social and political organism based on neighborhoods, where the rich were not organized into a hierarchy but formed a group of equals—a unanimous and solitary mass. Time was marked by the regular bells of the church, although the bells in an urban Renaissance society also often rang for calls to riot, to defend the city or to help (e.g., when there was a fire or other emergency).

Prior to the explosion of wealth and population which the Renaissance brought to European cities, these cities had been constructed for a smaller population and much different purposes. Medieval cities were an expansion of the seats of power of feudal landlords. Feudal landlords would establish a stronghold which served as both the elite family's home and a base of defense for their land. Around this, peasants lived and worked the vast areas of land. Markets were held in these areas, after the harvest each year. The most successful of these markets propelled their early medieval sites to grow into extensive market towns. Other cities developed from ports. With the sudden growth of overseas colonization and trade, larger and more sophisticated port facilities were needed, with all of the supporting industries on site. This was the beginning of the growth of relatively small medieval ports into some of Europe's most vast modern cities – London, Rotterdam, St. Petersburg. Other cities developed as villages around early mining sites, to support the small medieval mining operations, and grew with their industries as their products became significant in later centuries.

The new level of growth which came with colonial trade caused logistical and political problems in the emerging cities. Paris is an informative case study. It was the largest northern European city during the Renaissance; a population of about two hundred thousand in the early 16th century. The siege of Paris during the third religious war, which ended in 1598, lasted five years and destroyed the city. But its population had expanded to nearly half a million. King Henri IV addressed this by a campaign of new urban planning. His plan took into consideration new urban problems which developed with the population explosion, such as plague epidemics, transportation and commerce. He conceived of new buildings, not as isolated individual structures as had been done in the past, but as parts of a unified whole which had to interact with each other. Their architecture was interconnected by accessways to facilitate movement and many new buildings were strategically located according to their purpose.

The Place Royale and Place Dauphine were planned to simultaneously be residential and commercial squares, in order to stimulate commerce and manufacturing. Henri IV also commissioned the St. Louis Hospital and had it planned to minimize the spread of plague to the city. His public works also included many modernizations; canal building, drainage and huge areas where the common worker – who was now ubiquitous in the city – could live where they worked and places where they could view art. Henri IV also worked to expand education to less wealthy people.

Henri IV was named "the good king" and is remembered fondly to this day for his benevolence. But his example only shows the best reaction to the strains which a growing and changing population had on European cities. In other cities, medieval systems of government continued in contrast to a rapidly growing merchant and professional middle class populations, who did not fit into the medieval social structure. The monarchs who presided over European cities often continued to build for themselves, as in medieval times, providing nothing to meet the needs of the expanding populations of merchants and manufacturers. Along with a new lifestyle, the new middle class often adopted new ideas, which threatened the social order. This is the origin of many of the rebellions, which Europe experienced in the 17-19th centuries.

Population recovered to its pre-Great Plague level in the 16th century, and continuing population pressures contributed to uneven price increases; agricultural commodities increased more sharply than wages, which reduced living standards for many.

After the Black Plague and a long period of population loss—from 1347 to the end of the 15th century—Europe experienced a strong recovery in the 16th century when the population reached the level it had been at prior to 1347. This fact affected many aspects of public life, from economics to social relations to immigration patterns. At the beginning of the 17th century, the increased population growth leveled off. Plagues and famines still continued in Europe, albeit not at the same level of severity as in the previous centuries. The causes were similar, though in the 16th century some new diseases appeared, such as syphilis (brought by the colonists from the Americas), English "sweat" and the "Moravian plague." The progress made in the medical field allowed for the better diagnosis of the diseases known today as smallpox and measles.

St. Macarius of Ghent Giving Aid to the Plague Victims

Inflation occurred throughout Europe as a result of the changes in the economic realities. The influx of American gold and silver which was brought to Europe from the Spanish colonies was an early and pivotal contributing factor to inflation. The rapid growth of the population was another. The increased frequency and scale of wars in the 16th century put an unprecedented strain on government budgets, causing them to borrow huge amounts of money – money which was now available because of the growth of trade and skilled enterprises. This borrowing and spending also fueled inflation. Agricultural products rose in price, in part because of increased demand from a rising population but also because of the emancipation of peasants in some areas, who could now own their land and sell its products as entrepreneurs, instead of forfeiting it to their landlords.

Major population shifts from rural to urban areas led to the stagnation of countryside populations. The result was that the urban–rural population ratio at the beginning of the 18th century was higher than it had been in the 16th century. Large cities attracted people from the countryside and grew at the expense of regional towns. The immediate impacts were both economic and social. Statistics showed that birth rates in cities declined; it was only because of emigration that their populations increased. Large urban centers like Paris and London were drawing people to markets, to work for a few years or to take up permanent residence. The immigrants tended to be rather young, so cities were crowded with youth looking for work, wanting to marry and generally to flourish; however, they typically did not accumulate much money. This resulted in a decline in the standard of living in cities.

Social dislocation, coupled with the weakening of religious institutions during the Reformation, left city governments with the task of regulating public morals.

Frequent civil and religious wars, social transformations and dislocations made officials and governors of cities determined to take measures against the immoral behaviors which disturbed public life. The Reformation was initiated in a society marked by the Renaissance and the new free market, which exalted man more as an individual than as a member of a collective.

In the 16th century, the Reformation caused a fissure to develop between the Protestant and Catholic citizens of Bern, Switzerland. In this period, playwrights used the opportunity to present anti-Catholic messages during Carnival. Contrasts between Catholics and Protestants were depicted, while others contrasted Jews and gentiles, such as in *Goliath* by Hans von Rüte. Niklaus Manuel was the first writer to present ideas for reform and to belittle the papacy in his plays. In 1522, he wrote two farces about the pope, in which he showed the difference between the pope with his priests and Jesus. Real life events, in particular the Battle of Novara (1513), created the backdrop for Manuel's writings.

In 1520, violent incidents occurred in Bern during Carnival that exemplify the tensions of the Reformation period. In the 1530s, Carnival continued, but the entertainment had a different emphasis than the previous decade. Records show that plays with a serious religious subject matter were put on as early as 1530 in Bern. In *Gideon* (1540), Jews were depicted as losing to their enemies for seven devastating years because they had adopted idolatry and abandoned God. Gideon eventually defeated all the Israelites' enemies but first had to destroy the altar of Ba'al. Although the story, as told in von Rüte's play, was taken from the Book of Judges and was about Jews, Rüte (as with Manuel before him) meant to attack the idolatry of Catholic clerics. The city governors ended the tradition of Carnival theater in an attempt to curtail such critical allegories.

Guillaume Fare,
Religious reformer

Another example of drastic measures enacted to regulate city life are those taken against John Calvin who traveled to Strasbourg and later on through the Swiss cantons. At Geneva, Guillaume Farel asked Calvin to join him in reforming the Church. Guillaume Farel was a French religious reformer who fled France for Switzerland because of the persecution of the Protestants there. Farel was a very active and From 1532 on, Farel lived in Geneva, a city which officially declared its support of the reform movement in 1536. Farel had become the intellectual leader of the French reformers by this time and joined with Jean Calvin to establish a new church in Switzerland. Calvin was invited to reorganize the religious and political structure of the city, but after eighteen months, Farel and Calvin's drastic reforms and interference in state affairs led to their banishment in 1538.

Calvin established an intolerant Protestant theocratic government in Geneva, instituting a severe repression of all the Reformation's adversaries. His punishments went as far as exile and burning at the stake. Women were forced to dress in black clothes and were not allowed to wear makeup. Based on Old Testament texts, he started a campaign against witches and magic, resorting to torture if the accused did not admit his or her guilt. The constitution of the theocratic state of Geneva punished blasphemy, heresy and witchcraft with death. In 1545, over two months, forty-five women were burnt alive in front of the houses which they confessed, under torture, to have bewitched. In cities across Europe, other stringent measures were imposed regulating public morals: laws against prostitution and begging, laws which regularized private life, etc.

The family remained the primary social and economic institution of early modern Europe and took several forms, including the nuclear family.

With the onset of modernity, the family remained the primary social institution. The most common type was the *nuclear family* (also called the *simple family*), composed of husband, wife and minor children who lived and worked together. This combination is considered (by historians) to be the minimal unity of social and economic organization, representing the nucleus for all the other forms of familial structures. The *extended family* (also called the *large family* or the *composed family*) included, along the familial nucleus, other relatives or other generations. In addition to children and their parents, it included grandparents, aunts and uncles (the parents' brothers and sisters and their wives and husbands), cousins and sometimes even great-grandparents. Usually, in an extended family, three generations lived and worked together: children, parents and grandparents.

The Renaissance and Reformation movements raised debates about female roles in the family, society and the Church.

The Renaissance and Reformation roles of women did not change much compared to those of the Middle Ages. Largely, a woman was controlled by her parents from the day she was born until the day she was married, when she was handed directly to her husband. During the Renaissance, women were considered to legally belong to their husbands and were expected to be devote their lives exclusively to taking care of the households, childrearing and church activities. Some formal literacy education was provided to wealthy women and little or no education was available to women of poor families.

Though women were treated as inferior to men, women in different classes had varying roles. Lower class women (the poorest, such as peasants) were expected to be housewives and to take care of every aspects of the daily functioning of the household. The expectation of working class women (those who did manual labor or basic skilled labor for a living) was a little bit different. These women were expected to work for their husbands and help them run their businesses. They would work alongside their husbands, and then go home and take care of the household. Upper class women may have had servants and workers employed by them but were still expected to run the household. It was not strictly illegal for women to work and some women produced hand made goods for sale or did other minor labor sometimes. But rigid social structures and economic realities, left over from the medieval age, prevented them from starting a business or otherwise pursuing their own careers. One had to be a member of a guild in order to learn and do skilled professions, and the guilds never admitted women.

On farms, it was assumed that men would do the majority of the agricultural labor since they are the physically stronger sex. This does not mean that women did not also do agricultural labor at the peak times; they did a lot of it. But as the "weaker" sex, it was assumed that they would have the supporting role, including cooking and producing and mending clothing. Girls were taught that this was their place in the world and formal education – which is the primary ingredient in being able to think independently and perform a trade – was not offered to the lowest classes and offered only in a limited way to the wealthiest women. Neither could they live alone if they were not married. If a woman was single, she was required to move in with a male relative or join a convent and become a nun.

Women were generally barred from roles in the church. During the Protestant Reformation, Convents were shut down. Convents had been a place where women had relative power within the church. Luther expected women to stay at home and be wives and mothers. In terms of teaching or publishing, there are direct references in the Bible which prohibit them from doing so. Reformers and Catholics both invoked these references to prevent women from assuming roles as preachers.

One of the most significant feminine controversies was "La Querelle des Femmes," which took place in the French intellectual environment at the beginning of the 16th century. The controversy was initiated by jurist André Tiraqueau in a debate over the contract of marriage, which formalized the status of woman in society and education. However, while André Tiraqueau asserted that in marriage there must be reciprocal affection, at the same time he stated without any doubt the superiority of man over woman, an attribute that makes the husband the protector of his wife.

André Tiraqueau, French jurist

"La Querelle des Femmes" spread across the boundaries of France, leading to the issue of women's rights being debated in other European countries, increasingly so at the end of the 18th century, especially in France and the United Kingdom with the appearance of feminist writers like Olympe de Gouges and Mary Wollstonecraft.

From the late 16th century forward, Europeans responded to economic and environmental challenges, such as the *Little Ice Age*, by delaying marriage and childbearing, which restrained population growth and ultimately improved the economic conditions of families.

Beginning in the 16th century, the European population had to face environmental changes, such as the *Little Ice Age*, which lasted from the 14th century until the second half of the 19th century. During this period, a sudden decrease in the temperature occurred, especially in the northern hemisphere. The Warm Medieval period which preceded it had been a long period of relatively high temperatures. The beginning of the 13th century marked the expansion of the Small Glacial period, which peaked around 1850, when temperatures began to rise again and the ice retreated. In the middle of the Small Glacial period (1645–1715), solar activity was extremely weak. When volcanic activity on Earth increased, clouds of ash blocked the sun's radiation and brought about a cooling of the climate. These climatic conditions influenced the evolution of society. Low temperatures decrease fertility, so the population stagnated, which had a direct impact on families' economic conditions, which improved significantly.

Scene on the ice

During the Renaissance, there was a major difference in the ages of marriage between Northern and Southern Europe: In the Southern and Eastern countries, marriage normally occurred in the teenaged years and married couples continued to live with their families. In Northern Europe, such as England, France, Germany and Spain, couples started to marry as late as their late twenties. Historians have not conclusively determined why this change happened. What is known is that it slowed population growth by the beginning of the 17th century. In the 17th century, the population of Europe leveled off at about seventy-five million.

Popular culture, leisure activities and rituals reflecting the persistence of old ideas reinforced and sometimes challenged communal ties and norms.

Everyday life of the Medieval and Early Modern periods unfolded in clearly established rituals and observances, in accordance with the Church's calendar. Most of it developed within the limits of a divine determinism. People had vivid and concrete images of religious issues. The sacred world was not separated by an inaccessible abyss. For them, it was natural for the supernatural world to have a direct connection to the world, and for the consequence of their actions to be present in both realms.

The Church continued to manage every moment of life through the use of its sacraments, baptism, marriage and funerals; but mostly by strictly imposing that people respect Sunday, the saints' days both big and small, the postings that announced them and the Ten Commandments. Prayer, the church service, confession and communion continued to guide the moral principles of men. The Church controlled time, the annual calendar and even daily moments: the time for labor and the time for rest, the time to feast, the time for peace and for moments of abstinence. Moreover, it controlled historical time, first of all because it dated time from the moment of Jesus' birth, then because it imposed a certain general perspective upon world history, which began with the Creation and would end with Judgment Day.

Leisure activities continued to be organized according to the religious calendar and the agricultural cycle and remained communal in nature.

In Medieval and Early Modern Europe, the Roman Catholic Church enjoyed exceptional wealth and power. This enabled the Church to not only exercise power over religious matters, but also over social and political affairs. Considering the influence of the Church, it is little surprise that festivals in the Middle Ages had religious origins.

Despite the influence of the Church, it was not able to encourage all Europeans to completely abandon their pagan ancestral beliefs and festivals (usually agricultural celebrations, which were timed to mark the stages of the crop cycle). The Church decided to overcome these pagan influences by holding their own Christian festivals around the same dates as the old pagan festivals. One example of this practice is the ancient pagan festival of Lammas. Held on August 1st as the festival of the "feast of first fruits," Lammas was originally intended to celebrate the completion of the harvest and was traditionally celebrated by burying a loaf of bread in the fields where the crops had grown. With the spread of Christianity, Lammas was transformed into a Christian religious ceremony in which a priest used a loaf of bread made from the harvested crops.

Holidays in Medieval Europe, including Palm Sunday and Easter, were always marked by a cessation of work. Regardless of whether the individual belonged to the noble class or the peasantry, he or she was able to enjoy a day of rest. Holidays were still, however, considered "holy days," and had a strong emphasis on religion. People not only feasted and enjoyed various music and entertainment on holidays, but also attended church and watched plays with religious themes.

Most holidays and festivals were accompanied by feasts. The Church was able to control all areas of people's lives, including festivals and holidays, and it prohibited people from eating meat during the seasons of Lent (the 40th day before Easter) and Advent (the 40th day before Christmas), as well as on Fridays. Feasts were an important part of Medieval European society. Since food was not able to be imported the way it is today, most people in the Middle Ages only ate the food grown in their region.

All Saints' Day, also known as All Hallows Eve, is a Catholic celebration of their saints. It occurs over the evening of October 31st and goes through November 1st. In Britain, it has been celebrated at least since the eighth century.

Blood sports were a common type of entertainment. "Fox Tossing" was a sport practiced by nobles in Europe in the 17th and 18th centuries; a live fox was captured and tossed as high into the air as one could throw it. A sling was usually used; the doomed fox was gerrymandered onto a wide band of cloth which was to be used as a sling, then a person at each end would throw the sling and fox with all their might. This was practiced in Germany, for example.

In Spain, to the present day, bull fighting is a famous national sport. Those who are brave enough fight a live bull in an enclosed arena. Modern Bull Fighting goes back at least to the middle of the 18th century. But it has the elements of Roman gladiatorial fighting; the arena is very reminiscent of the coliseum and the idea of humans combating deadly animals was common to the Roman games as well.

Locals and church authorities continued to enforce communal norms through rituals of public humiliation.

The Catholic Church often used public humiliation to set an example for the populace. It was regularly used as a form of punishment by local authorities and the Church, and is still practiced by different means in the modern era. Public humiliation could take a number of forms. Most often a criminal was placed in the center of town where the locals would inflict some form of "mob justice" on the individual. The punishment of public humiliation could be, among other things, an offender being forced to relate his crime, such as by exaggerated physical parody: a "shame flute" for a bad musician or wearing a giant rosary (Dutch *schandstenen* for "stones of shame") for someone late to church. The offender could alternatively be sentenced to remain exposed in a specific public place, in a restraining device.

In the Netherlands, pillories like the *schandstoel* ("chair of shame") and the *kaak*, or *schandpaal* ("pole of shame"), were used on those who had committed adultery. A scaffolding from which one was thrown into the dirt below, was also employed. Various German-speaking states used *staupenschlag* (whipping or birching, generally on the bare buttocks) as punishment until the 19th century. Corporal punishment was administered in public (in town squares, schools, processions) in order to serve as a deterrent for potential offenders, while enforcing communal norms and routinizing moral life.

Reflecting folk ideas and social and economic upheaval, accusations of witchcraft peaked between 1580 and 1650.

The *witch trials*, also known as *the Great Witch Hunt*, were a period of witch hunts that took place across Europe between the 15th and the 18th centuries. The trials were caused by the belief that Satanic witches were acting as an organized threat against Christianity. Those accused of witchcraft or devil worship were thought to be engaged in such actions as malevolent sorcery at gatherings known as Witches' Sabbaths. Many people, especially women, were accused of being witches, and were put on trial for the crime, with punishments which varied over time and by region.

Preparation for witch burning in 1544

The belief in the reality of magic and the existence of malevolent witches was widespread in Early Modern popular culture, but it was among the educated elite that the idea of witches as Devil-worshippers developed. The Roman Catholic Church had persecuted heretic groups during the Late Middle Ages and in this context the Early Modern witch trials appeared. The climax of the witch hunt was during the religious wars, between 1580 and 1630. The witch hunts diminished in intensity with the coming of the Enlightenment and the spread of rationalist thinking.

During these events, which lasted approximately three centuries, about 40,000 people were executed. Among the most famous trials were the Scottish North Berwick, Swedish Torsakerials, the Trier witch trials (1581–1593), the Fulda witch trials (1603–1606), the Würzburg witch trials (1626–1631) and the Bamberg witch trials (1626–1631). The sociological explanations of the witch-hunts might be found in a complex diversity of factors that marked the period, including the religious sectarianism in the wake of the Reformation and other religious, societal and economic factors.

In 1590, the North Berwick witch trials in Scotland were extraordinary because of the involvement of King James VI. The king had developed a fear that witches were trying to kill him after he had experienced severe storms while traveling to Denmark in order to claim his bride, Anne, earlier that year. On his return to Scotland, the king heard about the trials taking place in North Berwick and ordered the suspects brought to him. He subsequently came to believe that a nobleman, Francis Stewart, was a witch; after the latter fled in fear for his life, he was outlawed as a traitor. Later, the king formed a royal commission to hunt down witches in his kingdom, recommending torture for suspected witches. In 1597 he wrote a book titled *Daemonologie* about the menace that witches were to society.

We want to hear from you

Your feedback is important to us because we strive to provide the highest quality prep materials. If you have any questions, comments or suggestions, email us, so we can incorporate your feedback into future editions.

Customer Satisfaction Guarantee

If you have any concerns about this book, including printing issues, contact us and we will resolve any issues to your satisfaction.

info@sterling-prep.com

Period 2: c. 1648 to c. 1815

Major historical events of the period:

1652-1810:	The Anglo-Dutch Wars
1668:	Portugal regains independence, ending the Iberian Union with Spain
1672-1678:	The Franco-Dutch War
1683:	The Ottoman Empire's expansion is halted with their defeat in the Battle of Vienna
1688-1697:	The Nine Years' War
1689:	British Parliament passes the Bill of Rights
c. 1690:	Liberalism philosophy emerges
1700s:	Russian rulers Peter the Great and his successor Catherine the Great undertake massive reforms of Russian society and politics; Mercantilism is gradually phased out as the dominant economic model throughout Europe
1701-1714:	The War of Spanish Succession
c. 1710:	Nationalism emerges and gradually spreads throughout Europe
c. 1714:	The General Crisis winds down
1715-1789:	The Age of Enlightenment
1740:	The War of Austrian Succession
c. 1750:	The British Agricultural Revolution begins
1755-1764:	The Seven Years' War
c. 1760s:	The Industrial Revolution begins; the Neoclassicism movement begins
c. 1770:	Romanticism movement begins
1772:	The First Partition of Poland divides Polish territory among Russia, Prussia and Austria
1780s:	Utilitarianism philosophy emerges
1789-1799:	The French Revolution
1790s:	Emergence of anarchism
1791:	*The Declaration of the Rights of Man and of the Citizen* is adopted in France
1792-1797:	The War of the First Coalition
1793-1794:	The Reign of Terror in Revolutionary France
1798-1802:	The War of the Second Coalition
1803-1815:	The Napoleonic Wars
1804:	The Napoleonic Code is established under Emperor Napoléon Bonaparte of France
1815:	France's defeat at the Battle of Waterloo and Napoleon's exile to Saint Helena

Period 2: 1648-1815

> ## Key Concept 2.1: Different models of political sovereignty affected the relationship among states and between states and individuals.

Between 1648 and 1815, the sovereign state was consolidated as the principal form of political organization across Europe. Justified and rationalized by theories of political sovereignty, states adopted a variety of methods to acquire the human, fiscal and material resources essential for the promotion of their interests. Although challenged and sometimes effectively resisted by various social groups and institutions, the typical state of the period, best exemplified by the rule of Louis XIV in France, asserted claims to absolute authority within its borders. A few states, most notably England and the Dutch Republic, gradually developed governments in which the authority of the executive came to be restricted by legislative bodies protecting the interests of the landowning and commercial classes.

Between the Peace of Westphalia (1648) and the Congress of Vienna (1814–1815), the European states managed their external affairs within a balance of power system. In this system, diplomacy became a major component of the relations among states. Most of the wars of the period, including conflicts fought outside of Europe, stemmed from attempts either to preserve or disturb the balance of power among Europeans states. While European monarchs continued to view their affairs in dynastic terms, reasons of state increasingly influenced policy.

The French Revolution was the most formidable challenge to traditional politics and diplomacy during this period. Inspired in part by Enlightenment ideas, the revolution introduced mass politics, led to the creation of numerous political and social ideologies and remained the touchstone for those advocating radical reform in subsequent decades. The French Revolution was part of a larger revolutionary movement, which influenced revolutions in Spanish America and the Haitian slave revolt. Napoleon Bonaparte built upon the gains of the revolution and attempted to exploit the resources of the continent in the interests of France and his own dynasty. Napoleon's revolutionary state imposed French hegemony throughout Europe, but eventually a coalition of European powers overthrew French domination and restored, as much as possible, a balance of power within the European state system. At the same time, more conservative powers attempted to suppress the ideologies inspired by the French Revolution.

In much of Europe, absolute monarchy was established over the course of the 17th and 18th centuries.

Absolutism, or Absolutist Monarchy, is an autocratic form of government in which the monarch (emperor, tsar, sultan, king, prince) holds unrestricted political power over the sovereign state and its people. In most cases the throne is inherited, although other means of transmission of power are possible. Absolutist monarchy differs from limited monarchy, in which the ruler's authority is legally bound or restricted by a constitution. Theoretically, the absolute ruler exercises total dominion over the land, but in practice the monarchy is counterbalanced by political groups formed by different social classes and castes of the territory, such as the aristocracy, clergy and the middle and lower classes.

Absolutism created a powerful and visible state apparatus that only had to be answerable to the nobility. It emerged and developed in the period characterized by the disappearance of feudal states and the transformation of the urban middle class into the modern bourgeoisie. The nobility and bourgeoisie used their increasing economic power to promote absolutism and the weakening of the feudal aristocracy, with the purpose of creating an autocratic centralized power.

Queen Elizabeth I of the Tudor dynasty

In most European states, absolute monarchism appeared at the end of the 15th century, reaching its classical forms during the reigns of Elizabeth I (r. 1558–1603) of the Tudor dynasty, Louis XIV (r. 1643–1715) of the Bourbon Dynasty, Peter I the Great (r. 1682–1725) of the Romanov Dynasty, etc. Monarchic absolutism was removed in Western Europe by the bourgeois revolutions in England (the 17th century), the Netherlands (the 16th century) and France (the 18th century). In Central and Eastern Europe, absolutism endured in the form of Enlightened Absolutism (or Enlightened Despotism) which, by means of reforms, extended the survival of absolutist monarchism and slowed the complete abolition of serfdom.

Absolute monarchies limited the nobility's participation in governance but preserved the aristocracy's social position and legal privileges.

As absolute monarchs limited the participation of nobles in government, they kept and increased their own legal privileges. Throughout Europe, the Divine Right of Kings was the theological justification for absolute monarchy. Many European monarchs, such as those in Russia, claimed supreme autocratic power by divine right and their subjects had no right to limit their power. The English aristocracy, including both the old and new nobility, with its modern aspirations, was one of royalty's main allies. James VI of Scotland (later James I of England) and his son Charles I of Scotland and England preserved the nobility's social position and privileges in an attempt to strengthen absolutist institutions. The debate and dissension regarding the monarchy's prerogatives eventually led to the English Civil War.

Spain, in the 16th and 17th centuries, was not a rigidly unified nation, but more of a confederation of semi-autonomous European provinces, with a global colonial network, all under a single king. Its constituent provinces, such as the Spanish Netherlands, Andalusia, Castile and (after 1580) Portugal, had their own cultures, languages, regional assemblies and taxation systems. The government of the whole Spanish Empire was a multi-level structure with a powerful king at the top, several councils directly underneath the king to implement policies, sub-divisions of the councils, called "juntas," and provincial power elites. This complicated system and the nationalism within each province made Spain very difficult to govern effectively. To complicate matters further for the king, the members of the nobility, each with different relative power and loyalty divided between his own province and the king, were always competing for more power. Three kings – Phillip II, Phillip III, and Phillip IV – ruled Spain for a combined total of a century and changed the level of participation of the nobility in government without greatly changing its status in society.

Phillip II of Spain ruled from 1556 to 1598 and Spain's power and wealth reached its zenith during his reign. The name of the Philippines nation is dedicated to him. But his reign was not without disasters as well. The state was financially bankrupt on numerous occasions, due to his extravagant military campaigns and colonial expeditions, resulting in the declaration of independence of the Netherlands from Spain. The surprise defeat of the Spanish navy by England (in 1588) also occurred during his reign. There was not enough of a population base to provide taxes for his military needs and the growing bureaucracy was becoming a threat to his rule. He also faced a parliamentary revolt, which he overcame.

Phillip III of Spain ruled from 1598 to 1621. His model of ruling was a reaction to that of Phillip II and became very unpopular. He changed the power relationships of the nobility greatly. In particular, one man named the Duke of Lerma acquired unprecedented power: The Duke of Lerma became his "Valido" (translation: "Favorite"), effectively a deputy king. Phillip III gave the Duke a great deal of power, even demanding that all business of government be channeled through him first. Lerma's daughter Margaret was a very shrewd politician and had become one of Phillip III's three closest advisors and had used this influence to assist her father's rise to the position of Valido.

Otherwise, Phillip III rearranged the power of the various nobles. Spanish kings ruled through a system of royal councils. For example, there was a council of war and a council of the Inquisition, etc. Phillip III relied on lesser nobles to lead these councils, instead of appointing very powerful noblemen to head them. At the same time, he believed that Phillip II's micro-management of the government had excluded the most powerful nobles too much and had created a complicated system which made decision making and the implementation of policy difficult. (Recall, for example, the growth of the bureaucracy under Phillip II.) While he did not appoint the most powerful nobles to the councils, he subordinated the councils to Lerma. Spain's overseas colonies were at the peak of their size and wealth when Phillip III ascended the throne. He gave the colonial governors greater autonomy to implement policy on their own. Powerful nobles in the colonies were appointed "proconsuls," giving them the power to act very independently from the king. The rise of Lerma, the lesser nobility and the Proconsuls was a major shift in the position of the nobility under Phillip III.

Phillip IV of Spain ruled from 1621 to 1665. His reign was characterized by the themes of unifying and centralizing the sources of power in Spain and improving morality in the public. He attempted to create a unified Spanish military and tax code, which were strongly rejected by the power holders in most of the provinces. He attempted to eliminate inflation and correct the other economic problems which had arisen under Phillip II and III. He closed public brothels and taxed luxury goods (i.e. sin). He supported the further development of juntas, a process which had been started by his father.

Many of his policies were unpopular, which led to an event called the "crisis of the monarchy." This began in 1640 with the revolt of nobles in Catalonia who supported the

French in their invasion of Spain. The same year, Portugal, which had been annexed by Spain in 1580, also rebelled against Spanish Habsburg rule. Portugal became independent in 1668, with the Treaty of Lisbon.

James I of England ruled from 1603 to 1625. He believed in the divine right of kings to rule and had continual conflicts with the English parliament. He wrote *The Law of Free Monarchies* in which he expressed his beliefs about the role and rights of kings and parliaments. He argued for the already prevalent belief that kings rule by divine right. In it, he explained his view of parliament – that it is only a consultative body, not a representative one with real power.

In Brandenburg-Prussia, the concept of absolute monarch took a notable turn with its emphasis on the monarch as the "first servant of the state," but it also echoed many of the important characteristics of Absolutism. Frederick William (r. 1640–1688), known as the Great Elector, used the uncertainties of the final stages of the Thirty Years' War to consolidate his territories into a dominant kingdom in Northern Germany, while increasing his power over his subjects. His actions largely originated the militarist streak of the dominant noble family of the day, the Hohenzollern. In 1653 the Diet of Brandenburg met for the last time and gave Frederick William the power to raise taxes without its consent, a strong indicator of absolutism. Frederick William had support from the nobles, who enabled the Great Elector to undermine the Diet and other representative assemblies. The leading families saw their future in cooperation with the central government and worked to establish absolutist power.

The most significant indicator of the nobles' success was the establishment of two distinct tax rates – one for the cities and another for the countryside – to the great advantage of the latter, which the nobles ruled. Nobles served in the upper levels of the elector's army and bureaucracy, but they also won new prosperity for themselves. The support of the Elector enabled the imposition of serfdom and the consolidation of land holdings into vast estates which provided for their wealth.

By the 19th century, Divine Right was regarded as an obsolete theory in most countries in the Western World, except in Russia where it was still given credit as the official justification for the tsar's power. In Moscow in the 14th and 15th centuries, the boyars retained their influence. However, as the rulers of Moscow consolidated their power, the influence of the boyars gradually eroded, particularly under Ivan III and Ivan IV. Tsar Ivan IV ("Ivan the Terrible") severely restricted the boyars' powers during the 16th century, through the implementation of "conditional land tenure" (*pomestie*). Their ancient right to leave the service of one prince for another was curtailed, as was their right to hold land without giving obligatory service to the tsar.

Ivan the Terrible shows his treasures to the English ambassador

The Boyar Duma, supported by regional councils known as the *"Zemskiy Sobor,"* expanded from around thirty people to around one hundred in the 17th century, and was finally abolished by Tsar Peter the Great in 1711 during his extensive reform of the government and administration. Peter reorganized the government according to the latest Western European models, transforming Russia into an absolutist state. He replaced the Boyar Duma with a senate made of nine members, which had the task of gathering taxes and contributions. As part of the reforms, the Russian Orthodox Church was partially incorporated into the state's administrative structure, transforming it into a tool for governing.

Peter abolished the institution of the patriarch and replaced it with a collective organ, the Holy Synod, under the rule of a secular functionary. During his reign, any vestiges of the local forms of self-government were abolished and, although Peter preserved the nobles' social position, he made them render services to the state. This led to the codification of the "Table of Ranks," which specifically denoted one's position relative to the other state official and nobility.

Louis XIV and his finance minister, Jean-Baptiste Colbert, extended the administrative, financial, military and religious control of the central state over the French population.

Unlike other contemporary kings, Louis XIV was able to choose his policies and ministers without input from Parliament. He could make quick decisions. He didn't need to justify his actions or listen to critics. For 54 years, the Sun King was his own prime minister. Louis XIV took care to implement legal reforms. The Grand Ordinance for Civil Procedure (*La Grande Ordonnance de Procédure Civile*) of 1667, also was also known as the Code Louis, was a uniform civil code, affecting the entire country, and the first of its kind. The Code Louis played an important role in the legal history of France. It formed the basis of the Napoleonic Code, which Napoleon Bonaparte promulgated at the beginning of the 19th century and which was the essential basis of modern constitutional law. Code Louis had the advantage of unifying legislation throughout France, which, until then, had been divided between north and south.

King Louis XIV of France

Louis XIV's rule was characterized by important administrative reforms and by a redistribution of taxes. For centuries, the aristocracy had administered the provinces and cities. During his reign, under the influence of Jean Baptiste Colbert (controller general of finances and secretary of state for the navy), he intervened in local governments. His purpose was to raise more money from taxes. Nothing illustrates the efficiency of Louis XIV's absolutism better than the extraordinary amounts of money raised from taxes, especially toward the end of his reign.

Colbert's successors, using and building upon his techniques, were able to finance extremely costly wars which lasted from 1688 to 1713. Not only did the income increase considerably – beyond the levels already achieved under Richelieu and Mazarin – but the regularity and the relative ease with which these immense sums were gathered are very significant, reflecting the power of absolutism.

The judicial monarchy (in which the king's main role was to make justice) was replaced by an administrative monarchy (the king was the ruler of administration). Finances (at that time overseen by a controller general, Colbert) replaced justice as the council's main concern. The person who was normally responsible for justice, François Michel le Tellier (the Marquis of Louvois) ended by abandoning justice as his main role, dedicating himself instead to the affairs of war. The Council was organized into several smaller councils with different roles and importance. Over time, two managing rival clans developed and were forced to coexist: the Colbert clan took care of the economy, foreign politics, the navy and culture while the Tellier Louvois clan took care of defense. *Divide et impera* ("divide and conquer") was Louis's motto. Having two rival clans, he was sure that none of the ministers would plan a coup d'état.

The army was very important for wielding royal absolutism. Louis XIV commanded his army with professionalism. He gained the respect of his soldiers, from the highest to the lowest ranks, by demonstrating his own ability as a soldier. His authority over army officers was the most important reason for Louis's military successes. Not just the high-ranking officers were chosen by the king, who implemented something like a meritocracy. Louis arrogated to himself the right to promote any officer to colonel. It was a royal army. The king decided who was in command, who was promoted and who was demoted.

The king also had the last word in matters of religion. It was a fact that kings inherited their thrones by divine right – in other words they did not rule by the consent of their subjects, but they were chosen by God. Louis encouraged the habit of calling the king of France "Church's elder son" and "Christian King." He also liked the title he was given at birth – *le dieu-donné* (the gift of God). Conceived by parents of advanced age, Louis was called a wonder-child, sent to save France from spiritual disunion. Therefore, he did not hesitate to intervene personally and decisively in religious affairs.

In the 18th century, a number of states in Eastern and Central Europe experimented with enlightened absolutism.

Wilhelm Roscher, German historian and economist

Enlightened absolutism, or enlightened despotism, represented current political ideas and practices of the second half of the 18th century, especially in Central and Eastern European monarchies. The historical concept was created in 1847 by the German historian Wilhelm Roscher, and is still disputed by academics. The new concept of government entwined the medieval forms of government with the newer ideas of Enlightenment philosophy. Reforms which improved the situation of the people of Central and Eastern Europe resulted from the new type of government. Reformist politics were characterized by an ensemble of measures taken at the royal level in the fields of administration, justice and finance in order to consolidate the feudal state.

In the new conception of government, the status of the monarch appeared to have changed. His power was no longer thought to be divine in nature, but was seen as a delegation of the power of the people; the sovereign no longer appeared as God's chosen envoy, but as a father of his people. Despite the diversity of forms it took, the new conception of government had some common features: a central absolutism, a hierarchy of functionaries and heavy government intervention in the economy, education and religion. It was a unitary conception of governing.

The economic system of the enlightened monarchs was mercantilism. This aimed to achieve an active commercial balance with the monarchy through support of manufacturing and commercial activity. The state intervened in social planning for fiscal and humanitarian reasons. In overseeing the rapport between peasants and nobles, it desired to make an efficient contributor out of each inhabitant. A centralized administrative apparatus was created and was conducted by the sovereign. The nationalist character of the activity of the state made education a government issue.

The importance of the Church was maintained, but it was subordinate to the power of the state, which sought to regularize its activity. Among the most famous enlightened rulers were Maria Theresa and Joseph II (Habsburg Empire), Frederick II (Prussia), Catherine II (Russia) and Constantine Mavrocordat (of the Romanian Principalities). In Prussia, Frederick II, influenced by Voltaire, replaced the old feudal organization of Brandenburg, which was dominated by the Junker aristocracy, with a highly economically developed and urbanized modern state. It had an educational system of the highest quality and was capable of sustaining the country's enormous military efforts.

Joseph II of Austria ruled from 1765 to 1790. He enacted many domestic policies which were extremely progressive for his time: He extended full legal freedom to serfs and reformed the tax system to shift some of the taxation from the serfs to the landed nobility. He made elementary education available to all boys and girls. He reformed the church, in particular he stopped paying the customary tithe to the bishops. While Joseph II enacted apparently humane domestic policies, he was a war hawk. He fought an unsuccessful four year war against the Ottoman Empire and two others against Prussia, both of which also ended in his defeat.

The inability of the Polish monarchy to consolidate its authority over the nobility led to Poland's partition by Prussia, Russia and Austria and its disappearance from the map of Europe.

At the end of the 17th century and the beginning of the 18th, the Polish-Lithuanian Union declined from the status of a great European state to that of a protectorate. The Tsar of Russia actually named the Polish-Lithuanian electors, influencing elections which should have been free and thus deciding the results of all of the debates in Poland's internal affairs.

The first division occurred after the Russian victories against the Ottomans in the Russo-Ottoman War of 1768–1774, which strengthened Russia and endangered the Habsburgs' interests in Central Europe and the Balkans. Having good relations with Russia and Austria, France proposed a series of territorial modifications by which Austria obtained parts of Prussian Silesia, and Prussia got other parts from Poland's fiefdoms. Still, King Frederick II of Prussia didn't have the intention of conceding recently conquered Silesia but was interested in finding a peaceful solution. His alliance with Russia was about to draw him into a war with Austria and the Seven Year' War had weakened Prussia's finances and army. He was also interested in protecting the weakened Ottoman Empire, which could have been a profitable ally had Prussia entered a conflict with Austria or Russia.

Prince Henry of Prussia

Prince Henry, Frederick's brother, spent the winter of 1770–1771 as the representative of the Prussian court in the capital of the Russian Empire, St. Petersburg. As Austria had annexed 13 cities from Spiš in 1769 (thus breaking the Treaty of Lubowla), Catherine II of Russia and her councilor, General Ivan Chernyshyov, suggested to Henry that Prussia could claim some Polish territories, like Ermland. Henry informed Frederick about this proposal and the King suggested a division of Poland's border territories between Austria, Prussia and Russia with the greatest part falling to Austria. Thus, Frederick tried to encourage Russia to direct its expansion toward the weak and dysfunctional Poland, instead of toward the Ottoman Empire. The Austrian politician Wenzel Anton Graf Kaunitz proposed that Prussia take some Polish territories in exchange for ceding Silesia to Austria, but Frederick did not agree.

Although for decades Russia considered Poland a protectorate, Poland had also been devastated by a civil war in which the forces of the Confederation from Bar had tried to draw Poland away from Russian control. The recent restoration of Koliivshchina and other parts of Ukraine had weakened its position even more. Moreover, the Polish King Stanislaus August Poniatowski (Stanislaus I), who was sustained by Russia, was considered too weak and too independent-minded. Eventually the court of the Tsar decided that Poland's utility as a protectorate had diminished.

*Stanislaus August Poniatowski,
King of Poland*

The three powers officially justified their actions as compensation for their efforts to solve the problems of an unstable neighbor and the restoration of order in a country deep in anarchy. In reality, all three of them were interested in territorial conquest.

After Russia occupied the Danubian Principalities, Henry convinced Frederick and the Archduchess Maria Teresa of Austria that the equilibrium of powers would be better maintained by a tripartite splitting of the Polish-Lithuanian Union than by Russia's annexation of protectorates and Ottoman territories.

Under pressure from Prussia, who for a long time had desired to annex the Royal Prussian region of northern Poland, the three powers agreed to the first division of Poland. This was done in light of new possible Austrian-Ottoman alliances, with only small objections on Austria's part, as it desired more territory in the Balkans. The attempt of the confederates from Bar to kidnap King Stanislaus I, on 3rd November 1771, gave the three royal courts a new pretext to point to "Polish anarchy" and the necessity of an intervention to "save" the country and its citizens.

In 1769–1771, both Austria and Prussia had occupied a few frontier territories of the Union and on February 19, 1772, the treaty of partition was signed at Vienna. A previous accord between Prussia and Russia had been signed at St. Petersburg, on February 6, 1772. In the beginning of August, Russian, Prussian and Austrian troops entered the Union's territory and simultaneously occupied the agreed-upon provinces. On August 5th, the three parties each signed the treaty regarding their own territorial conquests at Poland's expense. For the first time, Poland disappeared from the map of Europe.

Peter the Great westernized the Russian state and society, transforming political, religious and cultural institutions; Catherine the Great continued his process.

After a long time at the occidental courts, Peter the Great (1682–1725) returned home with the decision to reform Russian society using the more modern, western model. He cut his boyars' beards and issued a law which forbade all men to have a beard, except for the servants of the Church. Those who desired to keep their beards had to pay a tax. After "the war of the beards," Peter started another one over clothing, saying that if Russia wished to advance faster, it must not insist on its ancient traditions. In 1700, another declaration was made that all boyars, court-men and functionaries had to wear "Western" (non-traditional Orthodox) clothing.

Peter the Great of Russia

The reforms were also extended to the calendar. On December 20, 1699, when there were only a couple of days left until the end of the century, Peter issued a law which established that the counting of years would be done according to the European calendar, starting with the 1st of January, and not the 1st of September, as was the case in Russia at the time. Still, he implemented the Julian calendar, which is offset from the Gregorian calendar by 11 days. The transition to the use of the Gregorian calendar in Russia was made in 1718. In 1703, the first Russian newspaper, *Moskovskie Novosti* ("Moscow News"), appeared in Moscow. It had four pages, which included news about what was going on in Russia and the rest of Europe.

In 1708, Peter created eight enormous territorial divisions (gubernia). Each was led by a governor who was responsible for overseeing public safety, roads, justice and taxes. Due to the necessity of an institution to govern Russia while he was away on campaigns, Peter created the Senate in 1711. In place of the ancient Boyar Duma he named a Council of ministers, to which he added a Justice Chamber and a senate with legislative, juridical and executive authority. The senate answered directly to the Tsar.

Thanks to Peter the Great, Russian industry experienced extraordinary growth. He absolved those who built factories, and their relatives, of state service and paying taxes. He granted them loans with no interest rate and, beginning in 1721, the privilege to buy serfs from landowners, in order to use them in their burgeoning factories. For the aristocracy, he eliminated the old title "boyar" and adopted titles like "count" and "baron."

He encouraged the translation into Russian of manuals with practical subjects like arithmetic and astronomy and founded schools of mathematics, navigation, civil constructions, surgery and mining. Toward the end of his reign, he planned the foundation of the Academy of Sciences. He introduced obligatory education for nobility; starting in 1714, they were not allowed to marry unless they obtained a graduation certificate from an elementary school.

Catherine II ("the Great") (1762–1796) continued the reforms of Peter I. Starting in 1763 she created an orphanage, a settlement for popular hygiene and an institute of education for the nobles' daughters (the famous Smolny Institute). She imported German workers to cultivate the lands of Ukraine and the Volga river basin, hoping that the presence on Russian soil of those honest and active strangers would inspire the Russian peasants. She brought physicians, dentists, architects, engineers and craftsmen to Russia and she founded an Academy of Sciences. During her reign, an epidemic of smallpox devastated the country, which made the Empress determined to find a smallpox vaccination. She encouraged foreign immigrants to settle in Russia, offering them land and sparing them from taxes as an incentive to do so. This led to the creation of an entire German community in the Volga region.

Catherine the Great of Russia

In 1782, she founded a Commission for National Education and a college for teachers' training followed in 1783. The Statute of the National Schools required there be a high school in every city, to ensure free education for boys and girls. Corporal punishment in schools had been common but was forbidden in 1786.

Nakaz, or Instruction for the elaboration of a Code of Laws, was considered by Catherine II to be her greatest accomplishment. In the autumn of 1766, she presented it to the Senate. The Nakaz was strongly inspired by the writings of Enlightenment authors like Montesquieu, Beccaria and Bielfeld, whom Catherine had studied. Subsequent to this initiative, she was called Catherine the Great. The empress desired to make her court the center of Russia's cultural life. She encouraged the translation of foreign works into Russian and in 1783 she established the Russian Academy of Language, which published the first Russian dictionary. She added a court theatre to the Winter Palace and she financed theater presentations. She hired neoclassical architects and bought numerous European paintings.

Challenges to absolutism resulted in alternative political systems.

The fundamental cause of the modern revolutions was the necessity of aligning the organization of production, institutions and legislation with the new productive capacities and social forces that emerged during the 16th and 17th centuries. The purpose of the modern revolutions was to create an adequate environment for the free development and economic initiative of all people.

The Dutch insurrection against their king, illustrated by the oath of abjuration (1581), set a precedent that a king could be overthrown by the populace if it agreed that he no longer fulfilled the responsibilities given to him by God. This questioned the Divine Right of the Kings. It also eventually led to the appearance of the Dutch Republic. The acceptance of a country without a monarchy by other European countries, in 1648, spread throughout Europe, nurturing the resistance to kings' divine powers. Thus, the Dutch Rebellion can be seen as a precursor to the English Civil War (1642–1651) and the French

Revolution (1789–1799), where two monarchs who justified their power by divine right were removed. The Dutch Revolution can also be considered the precursor to liberalism in modern government. The revolutions and civil wars changed the way the population thought and led to changes in the attitudes of the people. Kings were no longer viewed as saints and people began to contemplate their rights. As a result, new political systems began to appear.

The outcome of the English Civil War and the Glorious Revolution protected the rights of the gentry and aristocracy from absolutism through asserting the rights of Parliament.

King Charles I of England

During the English Civil War, James I tried to substantiate absolute monarchy by divine right, but he faced the opposition of Parliament. His son, Charles I (reign: 1625–1649), also encountered opposition from the institution. Parliament opposed King Charles' desire to implement new taxes to fund his wars. In 1628, parliamentarians demanded that the King sign the Petition of Right, which guaranteed people inviolability, recognized the role of the Parliament in establishing taxes and banned martial law in times of peace. The King signed the act, but shortly afterwards he dissolved Parliament. In 1640, confronted with an armed conflict with Scotland, the King convoked Parliament again, hoping it would authorize new taxes. However, Parliament was in opposition once again and was quickly dissolved. This period became known as "The Short Parliament."

As James II Stuart tried to restore monarchic absolutism, the opposition demanded his abdication. The installation of William of Orange (*Wilhelm of Orania*) as regent of England in November 1688, without any kind of incident, became known as the "Glorious Revolution." In 1689, Parliament passed the Bill of Rights, which limited the king's prerogatives: the sovereign could not impose taxes or organize the army without Parliament's consent, the Parliament was to be convoked regularly, the king could not suspend the execution of laws, juridical procedures were to be applied by the jurors, and citizens had the right to choose their representatives. A series of important acts followed in the next years.

The Triennial Act (1694) established the duration of a legislature for 3 years, institutionalizing obligatory periodic elections and ending the right of the king to convoke the Parliament according to his will. After these events, the first parliamentary monarchy in the world was established. The Act of Tolerance (1689) granted relative religious freedom. The Act of Installation (1701) stipulated that the throne could be offered, in absence of direct descendants, to a collateral line of the dynasty, with the condition that the person to whom the throne was offered be of the Protestant faith.

The "Glorious Revolution" consecrated the parliamentary monarchy in which the "king rules but he doesn't govern." The king was the head of the Church, the army and oversaw justice and diplomacy. Executive power belonged to the Cabinet, led by a prime minister, who was responsible to Parliament. The legislative power was entrusted to a bicameral parliament, consisting of a House of Lords and a House of Commons. A system of political parties gradually appeared: the Tories, which supported royal power and mainly represented the nobility, and the Whigs, the party of the Protestants and anti-absolutists, which represented the bourgeoisie, the middle class and those who supported liberalism.

The Dutch Republic developed an oligarchy of urban gentry and rural landholders to promote trade and protect traditional rights.

The ascension of Calvinism helped facilitate the separation of the Netherlands from Catholic Spain. The aristocracy, led by the House of Orange and supported by people for religious and economic reasons. In the Pragmatic Sanction of 1549, King Charles Quintus established The Seventeen Provinces of the Netherlands as an entity separate from France, Burgundy and the Holy Roman Empire. At the time, the Netherlands was one of the most prosperous countries in Europe, and an important center for commerce, finance and the arts.

The independence of the United Provinces was recognized in the Peace Treaty of Westphalia following the end of the Thirty Years' War (1618–1648). While fighting for their independence and involved in the tension between Calvinism and Protestantism, the Dutch established their commercial and colonial empire. The Dutch East India Company was founded in 1602 and the West India Company in 1621. The takeover of Antwerp by the Spanish and the right to control the Scheldt estuary made Dutch ports, especially Amsterdam, busy and profitable trading hubs. Dutch merchants traded on each continent and dominated the exchange market.

A unique political situation emerged in the Netherlands governed by a republican institution, the States General, but a noble position of *stadtholder* dominated by the House Orange-Nassau, also existed. This separation of powers prevented large scale conflicts between nobles and civilians, exemplified by the English Civil War, and encouraged landholders and merchants to promote and protect their newly gained rights.

The Netherlands became a republic upon its independence. There were several levels of rule: The States-General, an urban oligarchy and rural land-lords. The Regenten (Regents) were rulers of individual cities or organizations, and were the leadership of the Netherlands. These were not hereditary leaders but they did gradually consolidate their power through contractual agreements with each other. By the end of the 17th century, they became a class which few outsiders could enter. While the Regenten dominated the cities, rural land holders remained powerful in the country. Over-arching these was the States-General, which was a throw-back to the parliament under the Habsburgs. This body consisted of delegates from each of the seven provinces of the Netherlands and each province had one vote. The House of Orange was the dominant family in this political system, having been the family which led the rebellion against the Spanish for independence.

After 1648, dynastic and state interests, along with Europe's expanding colonial empires, influenced the diplomacy of European states and frequently led to war.

After the Peace of Westphalia, the war of succession for the Spanish throne, in which the powers of Central and Western Europe were engaged, extended the conflict overseas. The stipulations in the treaties of Utrecht and Rastadt had major consequences on diplomatic relations during the 18th century.

Economic, demographic and political factors are hallmarks of a state's evolution. The most notable example was Great Britain which, freed for over a century from its feudal relations, could now act independently, becoming the main beneficiary of the Treaty of Utrecht. Great Britain became the master of the seas, obtained new and rich advantages (especially from South America) and, by occupying Gibraltar, it had the key to the Mediterranean and the possibility of controlling the commercial road toward the western coasts of Africa.

British economic interests outside Europe increased, as England managed to extend its colonial empire. At the same time, two maritime states, Holland and Portugal, which occupied overseas territories dozens of times bigger than their own countries, began to face setbacks due to their need to commit resources to continental military threats. Their maritime power was eventually surpassed by Great Britain's. Spain similarly had to endure an increased English influence in its extra-European territories.

French diplomacy could not forget the numerous political-diplomatic alliances of the past and that the equilibrium principle, used in an attempt to establish a balance of power, had triumphed over Louis XIV's insolvent politics. Louis XV had engaged even more in "luxury wars" (like the war for the succession to the Polish throne or the War of the Austrian Succession, the Seven Years' War). These conflicts had weakened France even more, especially its bourgeoisie which needed peace for its personal competition with the British bourgeoisie. After the peace of Utrecht, there was a greater alliance between Holland and Great Britain because the alliance with London was a guarantee against France and Prussia. During the 18th century Prussia came to increasingly affirm itself in the European arena; it soon started to play a dominant role in continental politics.

Portrait of King Louis XV of France

As a result of the Holy Roman Empire's limitation of sovereignty in the Peace of Westphalia, Prussia rose to power and the Habsburgs, centered in Austria, shifted their empire eastward.

Prince Frederick II was only 28 in 1740 when his father, Frederick Wilhelm I, died and he succeeded to the throne of Prussia. At that time, Prussia was made up of scattered territories, including the duchy of Cleves, the counties Mark and Ravensberg in the west side of the Holy Roman Empire, Brandenburg, Pomerania in the east side of the Empire and the old duchy of Prussia.

Desiring to annex the rich province of Silesia for Prussia, which was poor in raw materials, Frederick refused to recognize the Pragmatic Sanction of 1713, a juridical mechanism which was meant to ensure Maria Teresa's inheritance of Austria. After Charles VI's death, Frederick contested the succession of his 23-year-old daughter, Maria Teresa, and especially her rule over Silesia. Consequently, the War of Austrian Succession began in December 1740, when Frederick invaded and rapidly occupied Silesia.

The treaties of Utrecht (1713) and Rastadt (1714) ended the War of Succession. Austria came under the control of Charles II, who also obtained the Spanish holdings in the Netherlands (Belgium and Luxembourg) and took political control over a great part of Italy, while the throne of Spain went to Philip V, Louis XIV's nephew. Charles II's death in 1740 ended the dynastic line of the Habsburgs. Philip V had been named successor by Charles II, but upon his death, Frederick II ("Frederick the Great") claimed Silesia. In 1740 the War of Austrian Succession began, in which England, Sardinia and Holland were on the Austrian Empire's side, while Prussia was supported by France and Spain.

Frederick the Great of Prussia

Charles II had authored a document, the Pragmatic Sanction, in which he allowed female succession to the leadership in Habsburg-ruled countries. Thus, his daughter Maria Teresa became the Archduchess of Austria and Queen of Hungary. The fights for succession continued, ending in 1748 with the treaty of Aix-la-Chapelle. Austria lost only Silesia, which went to Prussia.

In 1756, the rivalry between the Habsburgs and the Bourbons was ended by the Treaty of Versailles. Disappointed at losing Silesia, Maria Teresa, with the aid of France, Russia, Saxony and Sweden, started a war against Prussia. Also called the Seven Years' War, it was a true worldwide conflict. In the Seven Years' War, the Prussian army entered Sachsen (Saxony) and made an alliance against Prussia with Austria, France and Russia. The strategic skills of the young King led his contemporaries to name him "Frederick the Great." After the War of Austrian Succession, profiting from Austria's weakness at the end of its war with the Ottoman Empire (1739), Prussia became one of the five great European powers. England, Hanover, Portugal and other smaller states entered the war on Prussia's side. After the end of the war, Silesia continued to stay within Prussian boundaries.

After the Austrian defeat of the Turks in 1683 at the Battle of Vienna, the Ottomans ceased their westward expansion.

After centuries of intensive expansion in the Middle East, North Africa, the Caucasus Central Asia, and Eastern and Central Europe, the Ottoman Empire entered a period of decline. After brilliant sultans like Mehmet II, Selim I and Suleiman I, there was a period of stagnation marked by ceaseless wars, especially with the Polish-Lithuanian Union, the Russian Empire and with the Austrian Empire. Russian expansionism was represented by a series of ten wars against the Ottomans in the 17th, 18th and 19th centuries. The Ottoman Empire resisted these attacks (which lasted many years), with the support of those Occidental powers which desired to limit the growth of Russian power.

Eventually, after Polish King Ian III Sobieski defeated Kara Mustafa in the battle of Vienna in 1683, the Turks began to lose their dominant position in Europe. In 1699, after the war with the Holy League, the Ottomans signed the Treaty of Karlowitz. For the first time in their history, the Ottomans had to accept the idea of negotiating with the Austrian Empire from a position of equality. From that moment on, the Austrians began to conquer territories which, for centuries, had stood under Ottoman domination. The defeat of the Russians in the Campaign of Prut (1712) and the Peace of Passarowitz brought a short period of peace between 1718 and 1730. The Ottomans managed to regroup and defeat the Austrians in 1736. The Treaty of Belgrade sanctioned the recovery of some of the territories which had been lost in 1699. Later, during the Crimean War, the Ottoman Empire entered the war against Russia with the British and French as allies.

Drastic changes in Ottoman policy towards Europe began to be seen during this period. The Ottomans began fortifying cities in the Balkans, due to their frontline location next to ascending Central European powers (what would eventually be the German Empire and the Austro-Hungarian Empire). While the Ottomans were experiencing technological stagnation, European development accelerated. In the technological race, the Ottoman Empire couldn't compete with its European rivals – France, the British Empire, Austria and Russia. The Turks began to lose wars and territories to Austria in the Balkans and to Russia in the Caucasus. Ancient possessions like Egypt and Algeria gained their independence from the Ottomans but became dependent on France and England (eventually becoming "protectorates").

Louis XIV's nearly continuous wars, pursuing both dynastic and state interests, provoked a coalition of European powers opposing him.

The European status quo was drastically altered after the death of Philippe IV of Spain in 1665. His son was a minor and quite ill, so Louis XIV made the decision to contest the Spanish inheritance, in his wife's name. His French lawyers made an argument, based on an old Flemish law, according to which when a man was married for the second time, his properties had to be given to the children from his first marriage. Maria Teresa was the daughter of Philip IV's first wife, while Charles was the son of the second. The argument failed because it applied only to private property.

Philippe IV of Spain

In 1672 Louis XIV invaded Holland to punish the Dutch for interfering with the Sun King's actions in occupying the Spanish Netherlands. In April 1672, France declared war on the United Provinces ensuing what became known as the Dutch War. By June, Louis's troops had already conquered 40 Dutch cities and fortresses. On June 22nd, Jan Witt, the Pro-French Dutch ruler, sent emissaries to discuss terms of surrender. The Dutch offered to pay war reparations and to give France the entire Dutch territory south of the river Maas. Louis XIV refused and, as the war was prolonged, Emperor Leopold and the Prince Elector of Brandenburg sent troops to support the Dutch. England also continued to fight on their side, while Sweden, which fought on the French side, was defeated by the Prince Elector of Brandenburg at Fehrbellin (1675). After the peace negotiations, France kept Franche-Comté and the cities of Flanders, and Louis returned his conquests made in the north.

The Nine Years' War (1688–1697) on France was declared by the Dutch in November 1688. After six months, Brandenburg, Spain, England and Bavaria formed a continental coalition. Until 1692, the French fleet dominated the war at sea, but it was eventually defeated by the British navy. The Treaty of Ryswick in May 1697 cost Louis XIV all the conquests recognized in the Peace of Nijmegen and he also had to endure the humiliation of recognizing William of Orange as King of England.

The War of Spanish Succession (1701–1714) ensued when two European royal families had pretensions to the throne of Spain: the Austrian Habsburgs and the French Bourbons. In November 1700, Charles II of Spain died without any heirs. In his will he left the entire empire to Philip of Anjou, Louis XIV's nephew and the second son of the Dauphin, with the condition that the thrones of France and Spain never unite. Both England and Holland recognized Philip V, but Louis XIV made three mistakes. First, at his command, the Parliament of Paris required that Philip V never give up his rights to the French throne. Second, Louis banished the Dutch troops from the barrier fortresses in the Spanish Netherlands. Third, he recognized James II—who was dying and in exile—as James III. As a result, on May 15, 1702, the Great Alliance declared war on France. After the peace treaties of 1713 and 1714, Philip V remained king of Spain but renounced his pretention to the French throne.

Rivalry between Britain and France resulted in world wars fought both in Europe and in the colonies, with Britain supplanting France as the greatest European power.

In 1755, the British navy attacked the French fleet and began a new war. Versailles faced the need to find allies as soon as possible. Lacking other alternatives, France oriented itself toward the Habsburg Empire. In May 1756, at Versailles, the first French-Austrian alliance was signed. The two parties promised each other military support in the form of an army of 24,000 soldiers. Russia denounced the accord with Great Britain and in March 1756 concluded an offensive-defensive alliance with Austria, promising to help them with an army of 80,000 soldiers. All of the great European states were fighting; Great Britain and Prussia on one side, and France, Austria, Russia, Poland and Savoy on the other.

French Ship, Seven Years' War

In spite of the heroic resistance of the French navy, the English maintained their superiority both in the Mediterranean and in the Atlantic and Indian Oceans. In North America, after abandoning Quebec in 1759, France lost Canada (in September Montreal capitulated); in India, the British gained the support of several local sovereigns and in 1716 occupied most of the French possessions in Deccan, Malabar and Bengal. In 1762, the war-weary belligerents desired peace.

In Paris on February 10, 1763, the British and French envoys signed a peace treaty between England and France, thus ending the maritime war and war in the colonies. France lost Canada, but it kept the right to fish in the estuary of the St. Lawrence River and on the coasts of Newfoundland. The islands Saint-Pierre and Miquelon, south of Terra Nova, remained under French domination. The British obtained the coast of Senegal and in India the French retained the five settlements stipulated in the Peace of Aix-la-Chapelle – unfortified places with hinterlands limited strictly to the coastal area. Moreover, France was forced to destroy its fortifications at Dunkerque.

The Seven Years' War represented one of the most important events of European political evolution in the 18th century, and the peace treaties constituted the considerable strengthening of Great Britain and Prussia's power. The Treaty of Paris consecrated the collapse of the first French colonial empire, the rise of Great Britain's maritime power and the extension of its colonial possessions to the detriment of France and Spain.

The French Revolution posed a fundamental challenge to Europe's existing political and social order.

The French Revolution was an important period of social and political insurrections in France that lasted from 1789 until 1799, and was developed further by Napoleon during the subsequent expansion of the French Empire. The Revolution abolished the monarchy, established a republic, involved violent periods of political agitation and culminated in the dictatorship of Napoleon, under which it rapidly brought many of its principles to Western Europe and beyond. Inspired by liberal and radical ideas, the Revolution profoundly altered the course of modern history, triggering the global decline of theocracies and absolute monarchies while replacing them with republics and democracies. The French Revolution unleashed a wave of global conflicts that extended from the Caribbean to the Middle East. Historians widely regard it as one of the most influential events in human history.

The modern era unfolded in the shadow of the French Revolution. Almost all revolutionary movements that followed looked back to the French Revolution as their inspiration. Its central phrases and cultural symbols, such as *La Marseillaise* (the French Revolutionary anthem) and *liberté, égalité, fraternité* ("liberty, equality, brotherhood"), became the clarion call for other major insurrections in modern history, including the Russian Revolution over a century later. The values and institutions of the Revolution dominate French politics to this day.

Globally, the Revolution accelerated the rise of republics and democracies. It became the focal point for the development of all modern political ideologies, leading to the spread of liberalism, nationalism, socialism, feminism and secularism, among many others. The Revolution also announced the birth of total war by organizing the resources of France and the lives of its citizens towards the objective of a military conquest. Some of its central documents, like the Declaration of the Rights of Man, expanded the arena of human rights to include women and abolishing slavery, leading to movements for abolitionism and universal suffrage in the next century.

The French Revolution had a major impact on Europe and the New World. Nationalism was a major outcome of the French Revolution across Europe. The impact on French nationalism was profound. For example, Napoleon became such a heroic symbol of the society that this glory was easily picked up by his nephew, who was elected president (and later became Emperor Napoleon III). The Revolution's influence was great in the hundreds of small German states and elsewhere, where it was either viewed as an inspiring example or was opposed.

Napoleon Crossing the Alps

The French Revolution resulted from a combination of long-term social and political causes, as well as Enlightenment ideas, exacerbated by short-term fiscal and economic crises.

In France the form of government was the absolutist monarchy, in which the power of the king was not limited by representative institutions, like Parliament. The king had to answer only to God. The king could issue laws after consulting his councilors, though he did not need to accept their opinions. The ministers had considerable power, the general controller being the most important because he took care of the king's finances. There wasn't a cabinet in which the ministers could meet, in order to make a common decision. Nor was there an office of the Prime Minster for alternative suggestions to be made regarding royal decrees, for the king accepted no rival to his power. In the provinces, the royal power was represented only by the police, justice and finance intendants, who were named by the king and who reported directly to him. They supervised the gathering of taxes and the practice of religion. They ensured law and order and were responsible for public works, communications, commerce and industry. The popular resentment of the privileges that the aristocracy and clergy enjoyed grew during a financial crisis, subsequent to three very expensive English-French wars and a couple of years with poor crops. The French monarchy didn't receive enough capital from tax revenue to cover its expenses, which is why it had to engage in large scale borrowing during wartime. The payment of the interest became an important component of state expenses. The chaotic manner in which taxes were gathered caused the administration to receive only a part of the entire amount collected.

The provincial and parliamentary states contributed to the administrative confusion which pervaded the Ancient Regime (*Ancien Régime*). While the kings created new structures, they couldn't abolish the older ones so they added different ones to them. In 1789, in France there were 35 provinces, 135 dioceses, 38 military regions, 34 généralités and 13 parliaments. Different juridical systems were active: Roman law in the south and different local laws in the north. France was divided into internal customs areas, so that taxes had to be paid to transport goods from one place to another. There was no uniform administrative system for the entire country.

At the end of the 18th century, the Enlightenment led to the implementation of reforms. "*Les philosophes*," (the Philosophers) like Voltaire, Montesquieu and Rousseau wrote about France's problems and attacked the preconceptions and superstitions of their times. They contributed to the greatest Enlightenment work, *The Encyclopaedia*, whose first volume appeared in 1752 (the last of the 35 volumes came out in 1780). Their purpose was to apply rational analysis in all fields, not being willing to accept tradition or revelation as sufficient reason to believe something. They pleaded for the freedom of the press, of words, of commerce, freedom from arbitrary arrest and for equality. The main targets of their attacks were the Church and the despotic government. They could no longer accept the literal interpretation of the Bible and rejected all that could not be explained by reason, for example, miracles. At the same time, they condemned the Catholic Church for its wealth, corruption and intolerance.

The first, or liberal, phase of the French Revolution established a constitutional monarchy, increased popular participation, nationalized the Catholic Church and abolished hereditary.

Facing general discontent and a severe financial crisis, Luis XVI was forced to convoke the Estates-General, which hadn't gathered since 1614. Shortly after the first session (May 5, 1789), the Third Estate deputies expressed their decision to radically transform the existing situation. Considering that it represented 98 percent of the nation, they transformed the medieval institution of the Estates-General into a modern National Assembly, then into a National Constituent Assembly. Through their actions, France stepped onto the path of revolution.

The essential turning point was when the revolutionary spirit was adopted by a large part of the population. Paris served as the center for the National Guard, which confiscated weapons and ammunition. The Bastille was an old fortress built in the 14th century, which served first as a royal residence and afterwards as a prison where opponents of the regime were locked up without trial. On July 14, 1789, the Bastille was conquered and demolished. The Storming of the Bastille, a symbol of absolutism, gained a symbolic meaning and July 14th became France's National Day.

In August 1789, under pressure from their urban and peasant hosts, the Constituent Assembly decreed the abolition of feudal privileges and adopted the Declaration of the Rights of Man and Citizen (August 26, 1789), which stipulated that the purpose of any society was to ensure man's natural rights, among which were liberty, property and resistance to oppression. The decisions made in August led to a reorganization of France in the first phase of the revolution.

The Storming of the Bastille

The new structure of the country was legislated in the constitution of 1791, according to which France was a constitutional monarchy. It also consecrated the separation of powers, giving to the king a part of the legislative prerogatives, which he shared with a representative assembly. The organization of France into provinces was abolished and France adopted a unitary administration; divided into 83 departments, sub-divided, in turn, into districts, cantons and communes.

After the execution of Louis XVI, the radical Jacobin Republic led by Robespierre responded to opposition at home and war abroad by instituting the Reign of Terror, fixing prices and wages, and pursuing a policy of de-Christianization.

The transformation of France occurred in the context of an intense internal and external conflict. The nobles opposed it with ferocity so the assistance of foreign courts was sought. The King himself tried to flee, but he was captured at Varennes and temporarily suspended from his functions. On January 17, 1793, Louis XVI and some of the members of his family were accused of conspiracy against public liberty and safety, and were executed. Power was then entrusted to a unicameral assembly, the National Convention, which, on September 21, 1792, proclaimed France to be a republic and ruled until October 26, 1795. Several distinct periods ensued. During the first one, the main role was played by the Girondist faction, which consisted of representatives of the bourgeoisie.

They desired to install a republic "of right," which would guarantee property, free trade and citizens' rights. Still, they agreed to Louis XVI's execution, an extreme act which encouraged a powerful counterstrike against the revolution. A coalition of several states gathered against France, threatening a great part of its territory.

The economic situation worsened, along with an accelerating depreciation of the value of French currency. The Revolution itself was threatened. Under these conditions, the Jacobin government was installed and lasted from June 2, 1793 to July 27, 1794. It included representatives of the petty bourgeoisie (*Petite Bourgeoisie*), led by Maximilien Robespierre ("The Incorruptible"), seconded by Louis Antoine de Saint-Just and Jean-Paul Marat. The goals of the Jacobins were stipulated in the Constitution of 1793, and included the idea that "the purpose of society is general happiness." Inspired by Rousseau's ideas, it ensured broad participation by the populace in political affairs, by means of the universal right to vote and plebiscites. Its immediate application was not

Maximilien Robespierre, political leader of the French Revolution and the Reign of Terror

possible, because sixty of the eighty-three departments were under the control of the counter-revolution. Consequently, it was decided that the government would be revolutionary until peace came and it governed with exceptional, dictatorial decisions.

Revolutionary administration came to the institutions. The Committee of Public Salvation had the executive power, the Committee of Public Safety ensured order and the Revolutionary Tribunal judged all the adversaries of the revolution, usually punishing them by sending them to the guillotine. Strict surveillance was introduced in the various jurisdictional areas (*arrondissements*), with the aid of "representatives in mission." On July 13th, Jean-Paul Marat was assassinated by Charlotte Corday, a Girondin, an act which led to the increase of the Jacobin political influence. Georges Danton was removed from the Committee and Robespierre, "the Incorruptible," became its most influential member as it moved to take radical measures against the Revolution's domestic and foreign enemies. In the face of the counter-revolution, the Jacobin dictatorship used terror tactics. This strategy affected not only the former privileged states, but also the supporters of the revolution.

Revolutionary armies, raised by mass conscription, sought to bring the changes initiated in France to the rest of Europe.

The severe measures of the Jacobins ensured the triumph of the revolution, both inside the country and abroad. In the agricultural sector, the feudal organization was abolished completely. The laicization process continued. The republican calendar was introduced, with the months being named after natural phenomena. Facing external danger, general mobilization was imposed. The army was reorganized, with volunteers enlisting in the same units as professional soldiers. The place of noble officers, who were not keen to fight for the triumph of the revolution, was taken by officers chosen from among the ordinary people, some of them even proving to have remarkable military skills: Lazare Hoche, Jean-Baptiste Kleber and Napoleon Bonaparte. The new army managed to defeat the counter-revolutionists and to pass beyond France's boundaries. The opposing camps refused any compromise. Inside the country everyone was suspicious of each other and they often turned on one another. Due to this climate, violence and a lack of stability were widespread.

The Jacobin dictatorship saved France using violent measures and eventually collapsed because of its inner discord. The newly prosperous who supported Danton thought that the Revolution had fulfilled its purpose and had to be ended. On the contrary, the left extremists, led by Hebert, thought that it was necessary to march with the "guillotine head on" until the triumph of universal liberty. The adepts of Robespierre defeated both of these groups and their adherents were sent to the gallows. The "Reign of Terror" practiced by the Jacobins in the last months of their government accentuated the process, chasing away many citizens who thought this regime was guilty of treading on the rights of man.

A new plot by the newly prosperous was successful. On July 27, 1794 (9 Thermidor in the French Republican Calendar), Robespierre and his men were arrested and executed without trial. The Convention entered its Thermidorian phase, during which politics tended towards a normalization of France's internal and external situation. The Jacobin dictatorship exceeded the Revolution's initial objectives. During the Thermidorian Reaction and the Directorate (1795–1799) many of its decisions were revised. But it was their very radicalism which ensured the success of the Revolution.

Women enthusiastically participated in the early phases of the revolution; however, while there were brief improvements in the legal status of women, citizenship in the republic was soon restricted to men.

The French Revolution had a long-term impact on European women, who had no political rights in pre-Revolutionary France. They were considered "passive" citizens, forced to rely on men to determine what was best for them. Feminism emerged in Paris as part of a broader demand for social and political reform. Women demanded equality with men and the end of the patriarchal system of relations. Their main devices for agitation were pamphlets and women's clubs, but the clubs were closed in October 1793 and their leaders were arrested and the movement was crushed.

When the Revolution began, groups of women acted in force, taking advantage of the volatile political climate. Women forced their way into the political sphere and swore oaths of loyalty. Charlotte De Corday d'Armont is an example of such a woman; engaged in the revolutionary political faction of the Girondists, she assassinated Marat, the Jacobin leader. Throughout the Revolution, other women (such as Pauline Léon, of the Society of Revolutionary Republican Women) supported the radical Jacobins, organized demonstrations in the National Assembly and participated in riots.

The Women's March on Versailles is one example of feminist militant activism that occurred during the French Revolution. As they were left out of the movement for increasing the rights of citizens, activists such as Pauline Léon and Théroigne de Méricourt pushed for full citizenship for women. Women were refused the political rights of "active citizenship" (1791) and democratic citizenship (1793). Militant women had a special role in the funeral of Marat, after his murder on July 13, 1793. As part of the funeral, they carried the bathtub in which Marat was assassinated (by Charlotte Corday) and a cloth stained with his blood. On May 20, 1793, women led a crowd that demanded bread and the Constitution of 1793. Their cries remained unnoticed and as a result, the women went on a rampage, sacking shops, seizing grain and kidnapping officials.

Women's March on Versailles

Olympe de Gouges was the author of the Declaration of the Rights of Woman and the Female Citizen in 1791. The Society of Revolutionary Republican Women, a militant group on the extreme left, demanded a law in 1793 that would force all women to wear the tricolor cockade to prove their loyalty to the Republic. They also asked for vigorous price controls to keep bread from becoming too expensive. After the Terror in September of 1793, the Revolutionary Republican Women demanded enforcement, but were countered by market women, former servants, and religious women who forcefully opposed price controls (which would drive them out of business) and resented attacks on the aristocracy and on religion. This hostile environment led to fist fights breaking out in the streets between the two factions of women.

Meanwhile, the men who controlled the Jacobins rejected the Revolutionary Republican Women as dangerous rabble-rousers. At the time, the Jacobins controlled the government; they dissolved the Society of Revolutionary Republican Women and decreed that all women's clubs and associations were illegal. They demanded that women stay home and tend to their families and leave public affairs to men. Organized women were permanently cast out of the French Revolution after October 30, 1793. Most activists were punished for their actions. Many of the women of the Revolution were publicly executed for conspiring against the unity and the indivisibility of the Republic.

A major aspect of the French Revolution was de-Christianization, a movement strongly rejected by the many devout people who remained in France. Especially for women living in rural areas of France, the closing of churches signified a loss of normal status. When the revolutionary changes to the Church were implemented, it triggered a counter-revolutionary movement among women. Although some women embraced the political and social amendments of the Revolution, they opposed the dissolution of the Catholic Church and the formation of revolutionary religions like the Cult of the Supreme Being. These women began to see themselves as the "defenders of the faith" and they took it upon themselves to protect the Church from what they considered a heretical attack on their faith.

Counter-revolutionary women fought against what they saw as the intrusion of the state into their lives. Economically, many peasant women refused to sell their goods for assignats because this form of currency (issued by the National Assembly in 1789-1796) was unstable and was backed by the sale of confiscated Church property. The most important issue to counter-revolutionary women was the passage and the enforcement of the Civil Constitution of the Clergy in 1790. In response to this measure, women in many areas began circulating anti-oath pamphlets and refused to attend masses held by priests who had sworn oaths of loyalty to the Republic. These women continued to adhere to traditional practices such as Christian burials and naming their children after saints - in spite of revolutionary decrees to the contrary.

Revolutionary ideals inspired a slave revolt led by Toussaint L'Ouverture in the French colony of Saint Domingue, which became the independent nation of Haiti in 1804.

At the beginning of the 18th century, the exploitation of the populations of Latin America—given the crisis of the colonial system, the stagnation of economic development and a lack of political rights—generated a powerful wave of national freedom movements. From 1791 to 1803, the insurrection of black slaves on the island of Haiti were led by a former slave, General Pierre-Dominique Toussaint L'Ouverture (1743–1803). Toussaint was, according to his declarations, a descendant of an African leader. The insurrection of the black populace against the less numerous white elite (French and English) was to fight for the abolition of slavery against the British and Spanish troops that were sent to crush them.

The leader of the revolutionaries, François-Dominique Toussaint L'Ouverture, organized an army of slaves (former and current) and, under the slogan "Freedom for all!" banished the Spanish colonizers. In 1795, he concluded a settlement with the French, who

granted him control over the largest part of the island. After the revolution he became governor of Saint-Domingue (now known as Haiti) and, after his death, his compatriot revolutionary, Jean-Jacques Dessalines, banished the French and proclaimed the independence of the Republic of Haiti in 1804.

The colony of Saint-Domingue became one of the richest in Antilles. At the end of the 18th century, the value of its exports surpassed even those of the United States of America. This prosperity was mainly due to the production of sugar and coffee. In 1789, on the eve of the

*Toussaint L'Ouverture,
leader of the Haitian Revolution*

French Revolution, 500,000 black slaves worked in the colony for 32,000 whites and 28,000 free people of mixed race.

While many were inspired by the revolution's emphasis on equality and human rights, others condemned its violence and disregard for traditional authority.

The French Revolution, though it seemed a failure in 1799 and appeared crushed by 1815, had far-reaching results. In France the bourgeois and landowning classes developed as the dominant power. Feudalism was dead; social order and contractual relations were consolidated under the Napoleonic Code. The Revolution unified France and enhanced the power of the nation-state. The Revolutionary and Napoleonic Wars demolished the ancient structure of Europe, hastened the ascension of nationalism, and inaugurated the era of modern, total warfare.

The French Revolution had a major impact on Europe and the New World. The long-term impact on France was profound. It shaped politics, society, religion and ideas, and polarized politics for more than a century. The closer other countries were, the greater and deeper the French impact, bringing liberalism and the end of many feudal or traditional laws and practices. However there were others who criticized its violence and disregard for traditional authority.

Although some historians view the Reign of Terror as an ominous precursor of modern totalitarianism, others argue that this ignores the vital role the Revolution played in establishing the precedents of such democratic institutions as elections, representative government and constitutions. The failed attempts of the urban lower middle classes to secure economic and political gains foreshadowed the class conflicts of the 19th century. While major historical interpretations of the French Revolution differ greatly, nearly all agree that it had an extraordinary influence on the making of the modern world.

Claiming to defend the ideals of the French Revolution, Napoleon Bonaparte imposed French control over much of the European continent that eventually provoked a nationalistic reaction.

Napoleon Bonaparte (born 1769, Ajaccio, Corsica, died 1821, Saint Helen Island), later known as Napoleon I, was a political and military leader of France, whose actions would come to greatly influence all of Europe in the early 19th century. Born on the island of Corsica and serving as an artillery officer in continental France, Bonaparte affirmed himself during the First French Republic and led successful campaigns against the First and Second Coalition against France. In 1799, he organized a coup d'état and proclaimed himself *Prim Consul*; five years later he was crowned Emperor of France. In the first decade of the 19th century, he sent the armies of the French Empire to fight every major European power and dominated continental Europe with a series of military victories. He also maintained France's area of influence by naming members of his family as rulers of other European countries under the form of French clientele states.

The French invasion of Russia in 1812 was a turning point in Napoleon's destiny. His great army suffered devastating losses during the campaign and never recovered completely. In 1813, the Sixth Coalition defeated him at Leipzig. The following year, the Coalition invaded France, forced Napoleon to abdicate and exiled him to an island called Elba. In less than a year he escaped from Elba and returned to power, but he was defeated in the battle of Waterloo in June of 1815. Napoleon spent the last six years of his life under British surveillance on the remote Pacific island of Saint Helena, in order to ensure that he would not escape exile again. An autopsy concluded that he died of stomach cancer, although some scientists maintain that he was poisoned with arsenic.

Napoleon watching Moscow burn

The conflict with the rest of Europe led to a period of total war across the continent. Napoleon's campaigns are studied in military academies throughout the world. Although considered a tyrant by his opponents, he remained a momentous historical figure for creating the Napoleonic Code, which laid the foundations of administrative and juridical legislation in most of the Western European countries.

As first consul and emperor, Napoleon undertook a number of enduring domestic reforms while often curtailing some rights and manipulating popular impulses behind a façade of representative institutions.

With the army's help, on November 8–10, 1799, Napoleon organized a coup d'état against the two chambers which opposed his regime. His political rivals were marginalized, like General Jourdin, the author of the law of obligatory military service. On the ruins of the Directorate was thus built a new regime, the Consulate, led by three consuls, with Napoleon as first-consul. His decrees were stipulated in the Constitution of the Year VIII (Revolutionary Republican calendar) and adopted by referendum towards the end of 1799. The Parliament was made of four chambers. The Legislative body was divided into three parts: the State Council (fifty members named directly by the first consul and who wrote laws), the Legislative Council (which adopted and rejected laws) and the Senate (which verified the law's constitutionality and changes to the constitution).

With his reforms, Napoleon set the basis of today's France. Still, the state needed financial resources to conduct wars. France remained the most populous state after Russia, which was also the richest. Financial reform was implemented, in order to collect taxes and rents owed on property/land holdings (cadaster). Napoleon implemented many enduring reforms to higher education, a tax code and road and sewer systems. He also established the Banque de France (1800), the first central bank in French history, which had a monopoly on issuing currency, the Franc. Napoleon named prefects to the leadership of departments, continuing the centralization of politics. Justice was reformed, with tribunals created at different levels. The most important was the Supreme Court, which was not independent, therefore the principle of the separation of powers was not observed.

Jean-Jacque-Régis de Cambacérès,
author of the Napoleonic Code

The Civil Code, issued in 1804, was based on the respect of individual liberties. It promoted family and the age of twenty-five for majority. Other rights were, still, refused: censorship was introduced and women's rights were limited. The right to primogeniture, or the right for one's first born child to inherit all holdings and titles, was abolished. Napoleon's set of civil laws, the Code Civil, also known as the Napoleonic Code, was prepared by committees of legal experts under the supervision of Jean Jacques Régis de Cambacérès, the Second Consul. Napoleon participated actively in the sessions of the Council of State that revised the drafts. The development of the code was a fundamental change in the nature of the civil legal system, which stressed clearly written and accessible law.

The Five Codes ("*Les cinq codes*") were commissioned by Napoleon to codify criminal and commerce law; a Code of Criminal Instruction was published, which enacted rules of due process. The Napoleonic Code was adopted throughout much of Europe, and remained in force after his defeat. The Code still has importance today in a quarter of the world's jurisdictions, including in Europe, the Americas and Africa. The document spurred the development of bourgeois society in Germany by the extension of the right to own property and accelerated the end of feudalism.

The schism within the French Catholic Church and the need for a united state led Napoleon to negotiate the Concordat of 1801 with the Holy See, which sought to reconcile the mostly Catholic populace to his regime. At the same time, the Organic Articles were presented, which regulated public worship in France. The Pope demanded the resignation of the fractious bishops, the constitutional bishops were demoted and canonical investiture was reinstated.

Napoleon paid great attention to education, emphasizing the university system which prepared imperial personnel. In 1802 the law regarding secondary education was adopted, and in 1806 a law was adopted which laid the foundation for an Imperial University, a management system of the secondary and superior education which established the state's monopoly on education. According to regional data, between 75 and 80 percent of communes had a primary school. This model proliferated in many European countries. The Baccalauréat was established, which instituted a common standard across France for the awarding of a university degree. Many of Napoleon's reforms were implemented during the Consular Period of 1800–1804.

In May 1802, Napoleon instituted the Legion of Honor, a substitute for the old royalist decorations and orders of chivalry, to encourage civilian and military achievements; the order is still the highest decoration in France. Napoleon reorganized the remains of the Holy Roman Empire, made up of more than a thousand entities, into a more streamlined forty-state Confederation of the Rhine; this provided the basis for the German Confederation and the unification of Germany in 1871. Napoleon's sale of the Louisiana Territory to the United States doubled its size and was a major event in American history.

The movement toward national unification in Italy was similarly precipitated by Napoleonic rule. These changes contributed to the development of nationalism and the nation state. Napoleon implemented a wide array of liberal reforms in France and across Europe, especially in Italy and Germany. Napoleon directly overthrew the feudal remains in much of Western Europe. He liberalized property laws, ended seigneurial dues, abolished the guild of merchants and craftsmen to facilitate entrepreneurship, legalized divorce, closed Jewish ghettos and gave the Jews equal rights of citizenship in the French Republic. The Inquisition ended as did the Holy Roman Empire. The power of church courts and religious authority was sharply reduced and equality under the law was proclaimed for all men.

Napoleon's new military tactics allowed him to exert direct or indirect control over much of the European continent, spreading the ideals of the French Revolution across Europe.

In the field of military organization, Napoleon borrowed from previous theorists such as Jacques Antoine Hippolyte, Comte de Guibert and from the reforms of preceding French governments. He continued the policy, which emerged from the Revolution, of promotion based primarily on merit. Corps replaced divisions as the largest army units, mobile artillery was integrated into reserve batteries, the staff system became more fluid and cavalry returned as an important formation in French military doctrine. These methods are now referred to as essential features of Napoleonic warfare. Though he consolidated the practice of

Jacques Antoine Hippolyte, Comte de Guibert, French military theorist

modern conscription introduced by the Directory, one of the restored monarchy's first acts was to end it.

Napoleon's opponents learned from his innovations. The increased importance of artillery after 1807 stemmed from his creation of a highly mobile artillery force, the growth in artillery numbers and changes in artillery practices. As a result of these factors, Napoleon, rather than relying on infantry to wear away the enemy's defenses, now could use massed artillery as a spearhead to pound a break in the enemy's line, which was then exploited by supporting infantry and cavalry. Weapons and other kinds of military technology remained largely static through the Revolutionary and Napoleonic eras, but 18th century operational mobility underwent significant change.

Napoleon's largest influence was in the conduct of warfare. After he was named the commander of the army in Italy, he began to prepare a campaign against it. The Directorate had decided to conduct this war "of diversion" with Piedmont and Lombardy for a very simple reason: to fill the treasury coffers. Napoleon launched a military campaign in Egypt and Syria (1798–1801) under the auspices of protecting French commercial interests, undermining Great Britain's access to India and establishing scientific research projects in the region. This was the main purpose of the campaign in the Mediterranean in 1798, which included a series of naval engagements and the occupation of Malta.

Despite several decisive victories and an initial success in Syria, Napoleon's troops (called L'Armée d'Orient) were forced to retreat because of the conflict in Europe and the defeat of the supporting French fleet. In the naval battle of Abukir, which took place from August 1-2, 1798, the British fleet, led by Admiral Horatio Nelson, defeated Napoleon's French fleet, thereby assuring the dominance of the British fleet in the Mediterranean.

The period of Napoleon's First Consulate was one of the most fruitful in the history of France. The external danger which threatened France was removed by the victory against Austria, at Marengo, in 1800. Napoleon conquered Belgium and Italy and, through the Concordat with the Papacy, Napoleon obtained supremacy over Italy. In 1802, France concluded the Peace of Amiens with England, which stipulated an exchange of possessions: France renounced Egypt and England lost the territories conquered during the previous wars.

Alexander I, Tsar of Russia

Napoleon's rule as an Emperor led to a long series of wars with England and the absolutist monarchies (Russia, Austria, Prussia), caused by the rivalry over economic superiority between the French and English bourgeoisie, the desire of European monarchs to impede Napoleon's ascension and Napoleon's desire to rule the entire world. With a great army, Napoleon managed to obtain several victories against Austria in 1805 and against Prussia in the Battle of Austerlitz in 1806. The only continental power which stood against him was Russia. Napoleon signed a treaty with Russia in 1807 which divided Europe between the emperor of France and the Tsar of Russia, Alexander I. In 1812, Napoleon made a disastrous attempt to invade Russia and was defeated. This was the moment at which Napoleon's fall began. In the Battle of Leipzig in 1813, Napoleon was defeated by a five-nation alliance (Austria, Russia, Prussia, Sweden and Saxony). He received a final and decisive defeat at Waterloo, on June 18, 1815.

Napoleon's expanding empire created nationalist responses throughout Europe.

The nature of nationalism changed dramatically after the French Revolution, with the rise of Napoleon and the reactions for and against, in other nations. Napoleonic nationalism and republicanism were, at first, inspirational to movements in other nations: self-determination and a consciousness of national unity were held to be two of the reasons why France was able to defeat other countries in battle. But as the French Republic became Napoleon's Empire, Napoleon became not the inspiration for nationalism, but the object of its struggle. Napoleon was responsible for spreading the values of the French Revolution to other countries, especially in legal reform and the abolition of serfdom. Napoleon could be considered one of the founders of modern Germany. After dissolving the Holy Roman Empire, he reduced the number of German states from 300 to less than 50, paving the way for German Unification. A byproduct of the French occupation was the strong development of German nationalism.

Under the French Empire (1804–1814), German popular nationalism flourished in the reorganized German states. Due partly to the example of common rule in France, different justifications appeared for the identification of "Germany" with a single state. The experience of German Europe during French domination contributed to a sense of a common cause—to cast off the French invaders and regain control of their own territories. The exigencies of Napoleon's campaigns in Poland, the Iberian Peninsula, Western Germany and the disastrous invasion of Russia in 1812 disillusioned many Germans, both noble and common. The invasion of Russia included almost 125,000 soldiers from the German regions and the loss of that army encouraged many Germans, from all social classes, to imagine a free Central Europe, emancipated from Napoleon's influence.

The disaster in Russia weakened French control over German princes. In 1813 Napoleon initiated a campaign in the German states, with the purpose of bringing them back into the French orbit. The War for Freedom, which culminated with the battle of Leipzig, was also called the Battle of Nations. Over 50,000 soldiers confronted each other over the course of three days. This was the greatest European battle of the 19th century. The struggle concluded with a decisive victory by the coalition of Austria, Russia, Prussia, Sweden and Saxony and ended French domination east of the Rhine. The success encouraged the forces of the coalition to pursue Bonaparte's army across the Rhine. His army and government fell and the victorious coalition imprisoned Napoleon on Elba Island. During the short Napoleonic restoration, also called the 100 Days of 1815, the forces of the Seventh Coalition, including an English-allied army commanded by the Duke of

Wellington and a Prussian army under the command of Gebhard von Blücher, obtained victory in the Battle of Waterloo (June 1815). From the German perspective, Blücher's actions at Waterloo and the combined efforts at Leipzig offered a new reason for national pride and enthusiasm. This became an important point in the discourse among Prussian nationalists in the 19th century.

After the defeat of Napoleon by a coalition of European powers, the Congress of Vienna (1814–1815) attempted to restore the balance of power in Europe and contain the danger of revolutionary or nationalistic upheavals in the future.

The Congress of Vienna (November 1, 1814–June 9, 1815) was a conference of European states which took place at the end of the Napoleonic wars, in order to restore the conservative order in Europe that had existed before the French Revolution. The key words of the Congress were "restoration" and "legitimism." Restoration consisted of the re-enthroning of the dynasties that had been removed by the revolutions, and legitimism was a monarchic theory which considered as a fundamental state principle the right to the throne of the legitimate dynasties and their absolute power. The official sessions started on November 1, 1814. Participating were: the Chancellor Klemens von Metternich of the Austrian Empire; Lord Castlereagh of England; the minister of foreign affairs of France, Talleyrand; Tsar Alexander I of Russia and the Prussian Baron Heinrich Friedrich Karl vom Stein, who was to transform Prussia into a great European power.

Depiction of the Congress of Vienna

The Congress of Vienna ended the Napoleonic Wars and established new boundaries for Europe. Castlereagh, the representative of England, had an important role in the process, as did Nesselrode, the representative of Russia, Hardenberg, representative of Prussia, and Metternich, of Austria. Each delegate sought to win as many advantages for his country as possible through diplomacy and secretly developed agreements.

To that effect, the Austrian chancellor, Metternich, aided by the Austrian secret police, was quite efficient and skillful. During the sessions, the French minister of foreign affairs, Talleyrand, supported by the delegates of small powers, desired to dissolve the English-Austrian-Russian-Prussian alliance and to obtain for his country favorable decisions. The rallying of Napoleon in March 1815, hurried the conclusion of the congressional sessions, the signing of the Final Act and determined the formation of a new anti-French military coalition (Russia, England, Austria and Prussia).

The Congress of Vienna was an important moment in modern international relations, marked by the signing of a declaration regarding the abolition of the black slave trade and the adoption of a regulation concerning the ranks of the diplomatic representatives, which is still in effect today. On June 9, 1815 the Final Act was signed.

Period 2: 1648-1815

> **Key Concept 2.2: The expansion of European commerce accelerated the growth of a worldwide economic network.**

The economic watershed of the 17th and 18th centuries was a historically unique passage from limited resources that made material want inescapable, to self-generating economic growth that dramatically raised levels of physical and material well-being. European societies – first those with access to the Atlantic and gradually those to the east and on the Mediterranean – provided increasing percentages of their populations with a higher standard of living.

The gradual emergence of the new economic structures that made European global influence possible, both presupposed and promoted far-reaching changes in human capital, property rights, financial instruments, technologies and labor systems. These changes included:

> ➤ Availability of labor power both in terms of numbers and in terms of persons with the skills (literacy, ability to understand and manipulate the natural world, physical health sufficient for work) required for efficient production

> ➤ Institutions and practices that supported economic activity and provided incentives for it (new definitions of property rights and protections for them against theft or confiscation and against state taxation)

> ➤ Accumulations of capital for financing enterprises and innovations, as well as for raising the standard of living and the means for turning private savings into investable or "venture" capital

> ➤ Technological innovations in food production, transportation, communication and manufacturing

A major result of these changes was the development of a growing consumer society that benefited from and contributed to the increase in material resources. At the same time, other effects of the economic revolution – increased geographic mobility, transformed employer-worker relations, the decline of domestic manufacturing – eroded traditional community and family solidarities and protections.

European economic strength derived in part from the ability to control and exploit resources (human and material) around the globe. Mercantilism supported the development of European trade and influence around the world. However, the economic, social, demographic and ecological effects of European exploitation on other regions were often devastating. Internally, Europe divided more and more sharply between the societies engaging in overseas trade and undergoing the economic transformations outlined above (primarily countries on the Atlantic) and those (primarily in Central and Eastern Europe) with little such involvement. The Eastern European countries remained in a traditional, principally agrarian economy and maintained the traditional order of society and the state that rested on it.

Early modern Europe developed a market economy that provided the foundation for its global role.

In 1500, there were about 800 widely separated markets in Britain. They were not free markets, but had a regular pattern of operation. Private marketing was the most important development which took place between the 16th century and the middle of the 19th century. In the 19th century, the process of marketing had become widespread and the vast majority of agricultural production was sent to market, as opposed to being kept for use by the farmer and his family. In the 16th century, a market's radius was approximately ten miles and it could support a town of 10,000 inhabitants.

The next step in the evolution of markets was inter-market trade, a process which required merchants, credit transactions and knowledge of the markets and prices and of supply and demand in different markets. Eventually markets became very large, driven by London and other growing towns. By 1700, a national market for wheat had developed.

Legislation regulated registration, controlled weights and measures, fixed prices and regulated the collection of tolls by the government. Market regulations were eased in 1663, when farmers and merchants were allowed self-regulation to hold inventory. But they were still not allowed to withhold goods from the market in an effort to increase prices. In the late 18th century, the idea of "self-regulation" was gaining increasing traction. The absence of internal tariffs, customs barriers and feudal tolls made Britain "the largest coherent market in Europe."

Labor and trade in commodities were increasingly freed from traditional restrictions imposed by governments and corporate entities.

The history of trade unions can be traced back to 18th century Britain, where the rapid expansion of industrial society drew women, children, rural workers and immigrants into the work force in large numbers. This enlarged unskilled and semi-skilled work force was the main reason for the development of trade unions. Trade unions and collective bargaining had been outlawed in the middle of the 14th century, when the Ordinance of Laborers was enacted in the Kingdom of England. As collective bargaining and early worker unions grew at the beginning of the Industrial Revolution, the government began to clamp down on what it saw as the danger of popular unrest at the time of the war.

In 1799, the Combination Act was passed, which banned trade unions and collective bargaining by British workers. Although the unions endured severe repression until 1824, they were already widespread in cities such as London. Workplace militancy had also manifested itself as Luddism and had been prominent in struggles, such as the 1820 uprising in Scotland, in which 60,000 workers went on a strike, which was soon crushed. Sympathy for the plight of workers brought the repeal of the Acts in 1824, although the Combination Act of 1825 severely restricted their activity. By 1810, the first labor organizations bringing together workers of divergent occupations were formed. The first such union was the General Union of Trades, also known as the Philanthropic Society, founded in Manchester in1818. The latter name was to hide the organization's real purpose at a time when trade unions were still illegal.

The Le Chapelier Law (French*: Loi Le Chapelier*), drafted by Isaac René Guy le Chapelier, was a law passed by the National Assembly during the first phase of the French Revolution (June 1791). It banned guilds, the early version of trade unions, as well as compagnonnage (by organizations such as the Compagnons du Tour de France), the right to strike and proclaiming free enterprise. Its promulgation enraged the sans-culottes, who called for an end to the National Constituent Assembly, which still continued through the second phase of the Revolution. The law was annulled on May 25, 1864, through the *Loi Ollivier* which reinstated the right to associate and the right to strike.

Isaac René Guy le Chapelier, author of the Le Chapelier Law

The Combination Act of 1799, entitled An Act to Prevent Unlawful Combinations of Workmen, prohibited trade unions and collective bargaining by British workers. An additional act was passed in 1800. Collectively, these acts were known as the Combination Laws. The 1799 and 1800 acts were passed under the government of William Pitt the Younger out of fear that workers would strike during a conflict to force the government to accede to their demands. The legislation forced labor organizations to continue underground. Sympathy for the plight of workers brought repeal of the acts in 1824. However, in response to the series of strikes that followed, the Combination Act of 1825 was passed, which allowed labor unions but severely restricted their activity.

The Agricultural Revolution raised productivity and increased the supply of food and other agricultural products.

The Agricultural Revolution was the outcome of a complex interaction of economic, social and farming developments. Important processes and innovations occurred, causing a major increase in the food production. The Norfolk four-course crop rotation brought about the implementation of Fodder crops, especially turnips and clover, replacing leaving the land fallow and producing remarkable increases in production. Other agricultural improvements were: the Dutch improvement of the Chinese plough so that it could be pulled with fewer oxen or horses; enclosure, meaning the removal of common rights to establish exclusive ownership of land; higher output of livestock due to more intensive farming with higher labor inputs; development of a national market free of tariffs, tolls and customs barriers; improved transportation infrastructures, such as improved roads, canals and, later, railways; land conversion, land drains and reclamation; increase in farm size and selective breeding. All of these changes resulted in an increase in the food supply.

The putting-out system, or cottage industry, expanded as increasing numbers of laborers in homes or workshops produced for markets through merchant intermediaries or workshop owners.

Historically, the putting-out system was known as the workshop system and the domestic system. In putting-out, work was contracted by a central person to subcontractors who completed it in off-site facilities—either in their own homes or in workshops with multiple craftsmen. It was used in the English and American textile industries, in the shoemaking and lock-making trades and in making parts for small firearms from the Industrial Revolution until the middle of the 19th century. The domestic system was suited to the pre-urban period because workers did not have to travel from home to work, which was quite impracticable due to the state of roads and footpaths, and members of the household spent many hours occupied by farm or household tasks. Early factory owners sometimes had to build dormitories to house workers, especially girls and women. Putting-out workers had some flexibility to balance farm and household chores with putting-out work, this being very important in winter. The development of this trend is often considered to be a form of proto-industrialization, and remained prominent until the Industrial Revolution during the 19th century.

Girls of the putting-out system learning to spin flax

The domestic system was a popular system of cloth production in Europe. It was also used in other industries, including the manufacture of wrought iron ironware such as pins, pots, and pans for ironmongers. It existed in the 15th century, but was most effective in the 17th and 18th centuries and served as a way for capitalists and workers to bypass the guild system, which was considered inflexible. Workers could work from home, manufacturing individual articles from raw materials, then bring them to a central place of business, such as a marketplace or a larger town, to be assembled and sold. The raw materials were often provided by the merchant, who received the finished product, hence the synonymous term "putting-out system." The acquisition of profit largely depended on which part of the putting-out system one was associated with. If one was a worker in the London textiles industry, for example, one had to hire sewing equipment and purchase thread, which often precluded them from eating on a regular basis. Likewise, the fourteen-hour days led to many untimely deaths.

A cottage industry is one where the creation of products and services is home-based, rather than factory-based. While products and services created by a cottage industry are often unique and distinctive, given the fact that they are usually not mass-produced, producers in this sector often face numerous disadvantages when trying to compete with much larger factory-based companies.

A cottage industry is manufacturing activity which includes many producers, working from their homes, part time. The term originally referred to home workers who were engaged in a task such as sewing, lace-making, wall hangings or household manufacturing. Some industries that were usually operated from large, centralized factories had been cottage industries before the Industrial Revolution. Business operators traveled around, bought raw materials, delivered them to people who worked on them at home and then collected the finished goods to sell or ship to another market. One of the factors which allowed the Industrial Revolution to take place in Western Europe was the presence of those business people who had the ability to expand the scale of their operations. Cottage industries were very common at the time when a large proportion of the population was engaged in agriculture, because the farmers often had both the time and the desire to earn additional income during the part of the year (winter) when there was little work to do farming or selling produce by the farm's roadside.

The development of the market economy led to new financial practices and institutions.

By the end of the 16th and during the 17th century, the traditional banking functions of accepting deposits, money lending, money changing and transferring funds were combined with the issuance of bank debt that served as a substitute for gold and silver coins. New banking practices promoted commercial and industrial growth by providing a safe and convenient means of payment and a money supply that was more responsive to commercial needs. Until the end of the 17th century, banking was also important for funding wars, which led to government regulations and the first central banks. The success of the new banking techniques and practices in Amsterdam and London helped spread these concepts and ideas throughout Europe.

The Industrial Revolution and growing international trade increased the number of banks, especially in London. At the same time, new types of financial activities broadened the scope of banking far beyond its origins. The merchant-banking families dealt in everything from underwriting bonds to originating foreign loans. These new "merchant banks" facilitated trade growth, profiting from England's emerging dominance in seaborne shipping. Two immigrant families, the Rothschilds and the Barings, established merchant banking firms in London in the late 18th century and came to dominate world banking in the next century.

A great impetus to country banking came in 1797 when, with England being threatened by war, the Bank of England suspended cash payments. A handful of Frenchmen landed in Pembrokeshire, causing a panic. Shortly after this incident, Parliament authorized the Bank of England and country bankers to issue notes of low denomination. Although the Bank was originally a private institution, by the end of the 18th century it was increasingly regarded as a public authority with civic responsibility toward the upkeep of a healthy financial system.

Bank of England

In Europe, two major factors contributed to the development of private property rights during the Renaissance period: The Protestant movement and the development of global trade. In the Enlightenment period, progressive philosophers challenged the traditional view that ownership was a hereditary and divinely granted privilege and argued instead that it was a natural right and was earned. At first, most harvesting of colonial resources and global trade was done in the Mercantilist system: Instead of earning customers by demonstrating ability in one's industry, in peaceful competition with others, which is how a capitalist system operates, the Mercantilist system worked by an exclusive license being granted to a single party by a monarch, based political reasons rather than merit. In the Mercantilist system, merchants had the right to use force against competitors with the backing of their government and its military, enslave others and deny others the right to explore and settle unexplored territories. While the Mercantilist system denied property rights to the colonial people it exploited as well as to other European entrepreneurs, using deadly force, it did have the positive effect of introducing the concept of property rights into English and European law.

Protestants used biblical arguments to generalize the concept of ownership rights to all individuals. The English Civil War was another milestone in the advancement of property rights, as the anti-monarchy side also used biblical arguments. In particular, the "Levellers" pointed out that one of the biblical commandments is an injunction against stealing. To them, taking the product of someone's labor is a violation of this commandment.

The Enlightenment expanded on this view. In The Second Treatise on Government, John Locke gave a famous argument for property rights which unified biblical and natural evidence. In summary, God provided human beings dominion over the resources of nature and the power to harvest them. The need to survive led to the first claim on private property: taking food from nature. The thing which, in Locke's argument, makes property private and not existential, is the effort of the individual to create it.

The replacement of the Mercantilist system with the Capitalist system during the industrial age caused an explosion of property rights protection legislation in the west, starting in Britain and the Netherlands and then occurring in America. Open competition, with complete freedom of entry into an industry, as opposed to licenses granted by the government, is also a fundamental part of the definition of the capitalist system. This implies respect for property rights: To take from a competitor illegitimately or to use coercive force in business – which is antithetical to the capitalist system – is to steal that competitor's product, labor or means of production. Laws which protect against this are legion in the modern age, as a result of the change away from Mercantilism to free markets and capitalism.

The European-dominated worldwide economic network contributed to the agricultural, industrial and consumer revolutions in Europe.

Colonization was primarily done for economic reasons: to harvest the natural resources of foreign lands (particularly gold) in order to empower the country doing it. Thus at first, the only markets were in Europe and trade was done between each European country and its colonies. The Mercantilist system made the first harvesting of natural resources from the colonized areas economical because it relied on slave- rather than paid labor and on theft rather than on trading with the local people. As colonial empires spread, goods began to be traded not just between Europe and its colonies, but between colonies as well. The growth of permanent large European settlements in the colonies, and indigenous peoples' desire to trade for foreign products, created markets in the colonies. By the 18th century, multi-axis trade patterns had been established, such as the triangular trade system between Europe, northern Africa and the American colonies: Natural resources were shipped from the colonies to Europe, finished products were shipped from Europe to its colonies and millions of slaves were captured and shipped from Africa to the other colonies, to work at the harvesting of the natural resources. Once new markets in the colonies and the global interdependent economic network had developed, revolutions occurred in agriculture, then industry, then in consumption itself.

Trade brought goods to nations which had never had them previously. Goods were made inexpensive by slavery, mass production, technological innovation and the general increase of income. Agricultural revolutions occurred as plants and animals were brought from one continent to another and methods of food production were shared. These agricultural revolutions created population explosions and had both positive and negative side-effects on human diet. Many factors combined to create an industrial revolution, which in turn led to the efficient mass-production of goods: the growth of global trade, including the large scale availability of natural resources; the growth of freedom in Europe, including a new level of freedom to pursue one's chosen profession; changes occurred in the structure of thought during the Enlightenment, in the direction of science, logic and curiosity about natural phenomena; and the rise of new systems of government which were more open to the freedom of the market than any previous ones. A general increase in the purchasing power of the poor majority of Europeans, due to better paying work and the relative drop in the costs of goods, facilitated a culture of consumption which continues to flourish today.

The early modern period was characterized by profound changes in many realms of human life. Among the most important were the development of science as a formalized practice, increasingly rapid technological progress and the establishment of secularized civic politics, law courts and the nation state. Capitalist economies began to develop in their initial form, first in the northern Italian republics, such as Genoa and Venice, and in the cities of the Low Countries (present-day Holland and Belgium), and later in France, Germany and England.

The early modern period also saw the rise to dominance of the economic theory of mercantilism. Therefore, the early modern period is often associated with the decline and eventual disappearance (at least in Europe) of feudalism and serfdom. The Protestant Reformation greatly altered the religious balance of Christendom, creating a formidable new opposition to the dominance of the Catholic Church, especially in Northern Europe. The early modern period also witnessed the circumnavigation of the earth and the establishment of regular European contact with the Americas, India, China, Japan and Southeast Asia. The ensuing rise of global systems of international economic, cultural and intellectual exchange played an important role in the development of capitalism and represents the earliest phase of globalization.

European states followed mercantilist policies by exploiting colonies in the New World and elsewhere.

Mercantilism was the dominant school of economic thought in Europe throughout the late Renaissance and early modern period. Mercantilism encouraged both the many European wars of the period and European expansion and imperialism—both in Europe and throughout the rest of the world—until the 19th century. Examples of mercantilist practices had been seen in early modern Venice, Genoa and Pisa regarding control of the Mediterranean trade of bullion. However, as a codified school, mercantilism's real birth can be attributed to the empiricism of the Renaissance, which first began to quantify large-scale trade accurately.

The Mercantilist system made the first harvesting of natural resources from the colonized areas economical because it relied on slave- rather than paid labor and on theft rather than on trading with the local people. First the Spanish treasure ships and then the East India Companies of the Netherlands and Britain were able to bring natural resources from colonized lands to Europe for the first time in history. Rather than pay for local goods and employ locals for pay to extract resources, as in a capitalist system, Mercantilists did the opposite. This is not to say that honorable trade was never engaged in by Europeans and other people in the initial stages of contact, such as the two-way trade between the French Cours-de-Bois (forest traders) and the Huron Indians in North America. But largely, resources abroad were seen by Europeans as available to whoever would claim them. Usually, the local population could offer little resistance to the Europeans, with their high tech weapons. Thus, Mercantilism enabled an early development of trade and markets, but at the expense of millions of colonial subjects' autonomy and way of life.

England began the first large-scale approach to mercantilism during the Elizabethan Era (1558–1603). An early statement on national balance of trade appeared in *Discourse of the Common Wealth of this Realm of England* in 1581. The period featured various but often disjointed efforts by the court of Queen Elizabeth to develop a naval and merchant fleet able to challenge the Spanish stranglehold on trade and expanding the growth of bullion at home. Queen Elizabeth promoted the Trade and Navigation Acts in Parliament and issued orders to her navy for the protection and promotion of English shipping. A systematic and coherent explanation of balance of trade was made public through Thomas Mun's argument *England's Treasure by Forraign Trade, or the Balance of our Forraign Trade is The Rule of Our Treasure*, written sometime between 1620 and 1630, but published only in 1664.

These efforts organized national resources in the defense of England against the far larger and more powerful Spanish Empire, and in turn established a foundation upon which the British could build an expansive global empire in the 19th century. The authors noted most for establishing the English mercantilist system include Gerard de Malynes and Thomas Mun, who first articulated the Elizabethan system. Numerous French authors helped cement French policy around mercantilism in the 17th century. French mercantilism was best articulated by Jean-Baptiste Colbert (in office, 1665–1683), though the policy was greatly liberalized under Napoleon.

Jean-Baptiste Colbert, French minister of finance

In Europe, the academic belief in mercantilism began to fade towards the end of the 18th century, especially in Britain, in light of the arguments of Adam Smith and the classical economists. The repeal of the Corn Laws by Robert Peel signaled the emergence of free trade as an alternative system. Mercantilism was economic warfare so was well suited to an era of military warfare. Since according to mercantilist theory the level of world trade was seen as fixed, it followed that the only way to increase a nation's trade was to take it from another. A number of wars, most notably the Anglo-Dutch Wars and the Franco-Dutch Wars, can be linked directly to mercantilist theory. Most wars had other causes but they reinforced mercantilism by clearly defining the enemy and justifying damage to the enemy's economy.

Mercantilism fueled the imperialism of the era, as many nations expended significant effort to build new colonies that would be sources of gold (as in Mexico) or sugar (as in the West Indies), as well as becoming exclusive markets. European power spread around the globe, often under the aegis of companies with government-guaranteed monopolies in certain defined geographical regions, such as the Dutch East India Company or the British Hudson Bay Company.

The transatlantic slave-labor system expanded in the 17th and 18th centuries as demand for New World products increased.

The Middle Passage was the stage of the triangular trade in which millions of Africans were shipped to the New World as part of the Atlantic slave trade. Ships departed Europe for African markets with manufactured goods, which were traded for purchased or kidnapped Africans, who were transported across the Atlantic as slaves; the slaves were then sold or traded for raw materials, which would be transported back to Europe to complete the voyage. Voyages on the Middle Passage were large financial undertakings, generally organized by companies or groups of investors rather than individuals.

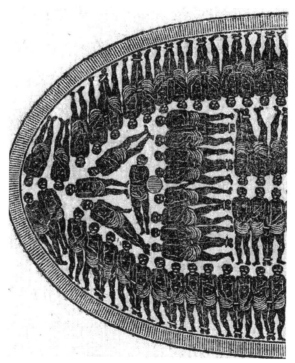

Brutal conditions of the slave ships of the Middle Passage

The Middle Passage was considered the middle stage of enslavement for those being traded from Africa to America. The close quarters and intentional division of pre-established African communities by the ship crews motivated captive Africans to forge bonds of kinship. Traders from the Americas and the Caribbean received the enslaved

Africans. European powers such as Portugal, England, Spain, France, the Netherlands, Denmark, Sweden and Brandenburg, as well as traders from Brazil and North America, took part in this trade. The enslaved Africans came mostly from eight regions: Senegambia, Upper Guinea, the Windward Coast, the Gold Coast, the Bight of Benin, the Bight of Biafra, West Central Africa and Southeastern Africa.

Approximately 15 percent of the Africans died at sea, with mortality rates considerably higher in Africa itself during the process of capturing and transporting indigenous people to the slave ships. The total number of African deaths directly attributable to the Middle Passage voyage is estimated at up to two million; a broader look at African deaths directly attributable to the institution of slavery between 1500 and 1900 indicates up to four million African deaths.

For two hundred years, 1440–1640, Portuguese slavers had a near monopoly on the export of slaves from Africa. During the 18th century, when the slave trade transported about 6 million Africans, British slavers carried almost 2.5 million. The triangular trading system is another term for the transatlantic slave trade, which functioned from the end of the 16th to the beginning of the 19th centuries. It carried slaves, cash crops and manufactured goods between West Africa, the Caribbean, the American colonies and the European colonial powers. The use of African slaves was very important for growing colonial cash crops, which were exported to Europe. European goods, in turn, were used to purchase African slaves, who were then brought by sea from Africa to the Americas. This was the so-called Middle Passage.

The first leg of the triangle was from a European port to Africa. Ships carried supplies for sale and trade, such as copper, cloth, trinkets, slave beads, guns and ammunition. When the ship arrived, its cargo would be sold for slaves. On the second leg, ships made the journey of the Middle Passage from Africa to the New World. Many slaves died of disease in the crowded holds of the slave ships. Once the ship reached the New World, enslaved survivors were sold in the Caribbean or the American colonies. The ships were then thoroughly cleaned, drained and loaded with export goods for a return voyage. This was the third leg, back to their home port. From the West Indies, the main export cargoes were sugar, rum, and molasses; from Virginia, tobacco and hemp. Planters embraced the use of slaves mainly because indentured labor had become expensive. With land widely available, some indentured servants were leaving to start their own farms. Colonists tried to use Native Americans for labor, but they were susceptible to European diseases and died in large numbers. Plantation owners then turned to enslaved Africans for labor. In 1665, there were less than 500 Africans in Virginia, but by 1750, 85 percent of the

235,000 slaves lived in the Southern colonies, Virginia included. Africans made up 50 percent of the South's population.

According to the 1840 United States Census, one out of every four families in Virginia owned slaves. There were over 100 plantation owners who owned over 100 slaves. Less than one-third of Southern families owned slaves at the peak of slavery prior to the Civil War; however, in Mississippi and South Carolina the number of slaves accounted for approximately half of the population. The total number of slave owners was 385,000 (including, in Louisiana, some free African-Americans), amounting to approximately 3.8% of the Southern and border state population. On a plantation with more than 100 slaves, the capital value of the slaves would be greater than the capital value of the land and farming implements.

Overseas products and influences contributed to the development of a consumer culture in Europe.

In the 17-19th centuries, several major changes occurred in Europe which created an unprecedented level of purchasing power for the majority of Europeans: Serfs were freed in European nations and became autonomous workers who could pursue improved incomes. Due to the improvement of types of labor available, surplus income developed in tiers of society which had never had any before. By the 18th century, common laborers in northern Europe and Britain could generally afford metal tools, alcohol, sugared food, tobacco (which had started out as a luxury good for the rich) and foreign cloth.

American plants like corn, potato, tomato, pineapple and tobacco were brought to Europe. Luxury products like sugar, tea, rum and coffee were brought from overseas colonies like America, contributing to an increase in the consumer culture in Europe. The pillaging of the treasures gathered over generations by Amerindians and the intensive exploitation of gold and silver mines, like those from Potosi-Peru or Zacatecas-Mexico, brought a huge influx of precious metals from America to Europe. It also had significant economic and social consequences. Rum, which is produced from sugarcane byproducts and whose origins can be found in ancient China, became a very popular drink in the Caribbean and the American colonies.

Under the Mercantilist system, vast numbers of slaves were forced to plant and harvest sugarcane, throughout Brazil, the Caribbean islands and southern parts of what is now the United States. Sugar plantations became a pivotal part of the British and

Portuguese economies in the 18th centuries and a tremendous demand for refined sugar and sugar products emerged. A major market was for rum, which is produced from sugar.

Sugar plantation in America

Europeans had tasted tea as early as Marco Polo's times. The British developed a general appreciation for tea in the early 18th century. They first experienced it, as far as historical records tell, a hundred years prior to that. By the year 1800, Britain was importing twenty-four million pounds of tea per year and considered it their national drink. This coincided with a boom in sugar importation from the Caribbean plantations. It was the British who introduced tea to India, in an attempt to break the Chinese monopoly on the market.

Silk had been traded to Europeans as early as Roman times, via the Silk Road: Byzantine elites preferred Asian silk for their best clothing. A domestic silk industry developed in Europe in the 17th century and flourished in the late 18th, with technological improvements that made production more efficient. Silk was mainly used for luxury goods like clothing, drapes and decorative things, although it is an extremely sturdy and versatile fabric which can be good for industrial purposes too.

The first permanent British colony in the Americas owed its continued existence to Tobacco and thus the United States does as well. Tobacco leaf was cultivated and refined by North American Indians and noticed by the British colonists. When the Jamestown colony was failing and the British crown had all but abandoned interest in American colonies, the colonists experimented with producing tobacco the way Indians had. The first export of it was very popular among the wealthy in England and smoking soon became a fad. Jamestown survived because of the wealth it gained from tobacco and new colonies were established in North America to try to capitalize further on the arable land and the cash crops it could produce. The end product of British colonization, of course, is the American Revolution. It should also be noted that America now leads the world in education campaigns to de-tobacconize the world and native-born Americans have a lower propensity to smoke than people of any other continent.

Coffee is a product which was discovered by the Spanish when they first made contact with the Aztec. Coffee and chocolate beans and their bi-products became popular in Europe. With colonization expanding to the African continent, coffee beans began to be grown there and eventually became a major crop.

The importation and transplantation of agricultural products from the Americas contributed to an increase in the food supply in Europe.

When Africa, Asia and the Americas were first colonized, the local populations were using their own farming methods, which of course differed from place to place and differed from European methods. Or, they were not agricultural at all. The transplanting of European methods was often disastrous but sometimes an improvement. The worldwide production of food increased greatly from the 17th century on, with good and bad side effects. Ultimately, efficient trade made food from all around the world available to people all around the world. This diversified the human diet and triggered population explosions.

A good case study is the British agricultural revolution, which took place roughly from 1750 to 1900. It was a result of increasing labor productivity and new (non-native) crops. Food production dramatically increased in Britain, enabling that country to cope with the explosion of its population from about ten million to about forty million over this time period. In addition, the diet of the majority of low income people was greatly diversified. One major negative side effect of the transition was the Irish famine of 1844-45; this was a consequence of over-reliance on one of the new foreign crops – the potato. The crop had become so popular that it was almost monolithic in Ireland and Scotland at that time and only one variety dominated. A blight, therefore, was able to devastate the majority of the food supply, resulting in the famine.

Colonists usually forced the indigenous people they conquered to adopt European methods, often without thought to whether the European methods were really superior. Some colonized people did not have an agricultural culture at all, but instead existed quite successfully by hunting game and fishing. Examples of this are the Native American tribes in what is now the northern United States and Canada, and the Xhosa people of South Africa. The Wampanoag Indians of Massachusetts learned that planting multiple plants together, unlike the European method of planting a single plant, succeeded in a healthier crop due to each of the plants enriching each other. Their advanced knowledge of farming was swept away by the early British colonists' insistence of farming the antiquated European way.

After 1492, a global exchange of crops and livestock occurred. Key crops involved in this exchange included maize, potatoes, sweet potatoes and manioc traveling from the New World to the Old, and several varieties of wheat, barley, rice and turnips going from the Old World to the New. There were very few livestock species in the New World, with horses, cattle, sheep and goats being completely unknown before their arrival with Old World settlers. Crops moving in both directions across the Atlantic Ocean caused population growth around the world, and had a lasting effect on many cultures. Maize and cassava were introduced from Brazil into Africa by Portuguese traders in the 16th century.

After its introduction from South America to Spain at the end of the 16th century, the potato became an important crop throughout Europe. The potato allowed farmers to produce more food, and initially added variety to the European diet. The nutrition boost caused by increased potato consumption resulted in lower disease rates, higher birth rates and lower mortality rates, causing a population boom throughout the British Empire, the American colonies and in Europe. The introduction of the potato also brought about the first intensive use of fertilizer, in the form of guano imported to Europe from Peru, and the first artificial pesticide, in the form of an arsenic compound used to fight Colorado potato beetles. Before the adoption of the potato as a major crop, the dependence on grain caused repetitive regional and national famines when the crops failed: 17 major famines occurred in England alone between 1523 and 1623. Although it initially almost eliminated the danger of famine, the resulting dependence on the potato eventually caused the European Potato Failure, a disastrous crop failure caused by blight, which resulted in widespread famine.

Foreign lands provided raw materials, finished goods, laborers and markets for the commercial and industrial enterprises in Europe.

As a wider variety of global luxury commodities entered the European markets by sea, previous European markets for luxury goods stagnated. The Atlantic trade largely supplanted pre-existing Italian and German trading powers who had relied on their Baltic,

Russian and Islamic trade links. The new commodities also caused social change, as sugar, spices, silks and china entered the luxury markets of Europe. The European economic center shifted from the Mediterranean to Western Europe. The city of Antwerp, part of the Duchy of Brabant, became the center of the international economy and the richest city in Europe at the time.

Centered in Antwerp first and then in Amsterdam, the Dutch Golden Age was tightly linked to the Age of Discovery. Portuguese ships laden with pepper and cinnamon unloaded their cargo there. With many foreign merchants residing in the city, which was governed by an oligarchy of banker-aristocrats who were forbidden to engage in trade, the economy of Antwerp was foreigner-controlled, which made the city very international. Merchants and traders from Venice, Ragusa, Spain and Portugal lived there and the city had a tradition of tolerance, which attracted a large Orthodox Jewish community. The city experienced three booms during its golden age, the first based on the pepper market, a second launched by New World silver coming from Seville (ending with the bankruptcy of Spain in 1557) and a third boom, after the 1559 Treaty of Chateau-Cambresis, which was based on the growth of the textiles industry.

Allegorical representation of the Dutch Republic as a ship during the Dutch Golden Age

Despite initial hostilities, by 1549 the Portuguese were sending annual trade missions to Shangchuan Island in China. In 1557, they managed to convince the Ming court to agree to a legal port treaty that would establish Macau as an official Portuguese trade colony. The major Chinese exports were silk and porcelain, which were adapted to meet

European tastes. Porcelain was held in such great esteem in Europe that, in English, china became a common synonym for porcelain. Kraak porcelain (probably named after the Portuguese carracks in which it was transported) was among the first Chinese ware to arrive in Europe in mass quantities. Only the richest people could afford these imports, and Kraak was often featured in Dutch still life paintings. Soon the Dutch East India Company established a lively trade with the East, having imported 6 million porcelain items from China to Europe between 1602 and 1682. The Chinese workmanship impressed many.

Between 1575 and 1587, Medici porcelain from Florence was the first successful attempt to imitate Chinese porcelain. Although Dutch potters did not immediately imitate Chinese porcelain, they began to do so when the supply to Europe was interrupted after the death of Emperor Wanli in 1620. Kraak, mainly the blue and white porcelain, was imitated all over the world by potters in Arita, Japan and Persia— where Dutch merchants turned when the fall of the Ming Dynasty rendered Chinese originals unavailable—and ultimately in Delftware. Dutch and later English Delftware, inspired by Chinese designs, persisted from about 1630 to the middle of the 18th century, alongside European patterns.

In return China imported silver from Peruvian and Mexican mines, which was transported via Manila. Chinese merchants were active in these trading ventures, and many emigrated to places like the Philippines and Borneo to take advantage of the new commercial opportunities.

Spain's increased wealth coincided with a major inflationary cycle, both within Spain and Europe, known as the price revolution. Spain had amassed large quantities of gold and silver from the New World. In 1520, the large scale extraction of silver from Mexico's Guanajuato began. With the opening of the silver mines in Zacatecas and Potosí, Bolivia in 1546, large shipments of silver became a renowned source of wealth. With Europe full of war and religious conflicts, the most powerful European monarchs at the time were the Habsburg rulers, who spent the wealth on wars and art all across Europe. The silver, suddenly spent throughout a previously cash-starved Europe, caused widespread inflation. The inflation was worsened by a growing population with a static production level and low salaries, which damaged local industry. Increasingly, Spain became dependent on the revenues flowing in from its mercantile empire in the Americas, leading to Spain's first national bankruptcy in 1557, due to rising military costs.

Commercial rivalries influenced diplomacy and warfare among European states in the early modern era.

The great geographic discoveries were followed by an increasing struggle between the European powers for maritime and commercial supremacy in their colonial territories. The maritime expeditions of the Portuguese and Spanish were followed by the outbreak of conflict between Portugal and Spain. This was concluded by the treaties of Tordesillas in 1494 and Zaragoza in 1529, which had the purpose of delineating their areas of maritime, colonial and commercial expansion. Portugal and Spain's desire to reserve their exclusive rights to maritime, colonial and commercial expansion generated increased opposition from England and Holland who, due to their economic and naval development, began to contest the maritime dominance of the Iberian Empires. The fight intensified during the 16th century, leading to the Anglo-Spanish War (1585–1604). This culminated in the defeat of the Invincible Armada by the English in 1588, and the Dutch war against Spain and Portugal. Subsequently, in the 17th century, the Dutch occupied the colonies of the Portuguese colonial empire in Southeast Asia. Numerous people from Africa, Southeast Asia and America were enslaved as a result.

English ships and the Spanish Armada

European sea powers vied for Atlantic influence throughout the 18th century.

Following Columbus and the earliest European voyages to the New World and the West African coast, the division of Africa and the Americas between the Spanish Empire and the Portuguese Empire was influenced by the Treaty of Tordesillas. The West Coast of Africa played an important role as it was the source of slave labor. There emerged an elaborate network of economic, geopolitical and cultural exchange—an Atlantic World comparable to the Mediterranean World. It linked the nations and peoples who inhabited the Atlantic littoral of North and South America, Africa and Western Europe.

The main empires that built the Atlantic World were the British, French, Spanish, Portuguese and Dutch; after 1789 entrepreneurs from the United States and Germany played a role as well. Some smaller countries, such as Sweden and Denmark, were also active on a smaller scale. The Atlantic Revolutions were a revolutionary wave in the late 18th and early 19th centuries. They included the United States (1775-1783), France and French-controlled Europe (1789-1814), Haiti (1791-1804), Ireland (1798) and Spanish America (1810-1825). There were also smaller resurrections in Switzerland, Russia and Brazil.

Independence movements in the New World began with the American Revolution (1775-1783), in which France, the Netherlands and Spain assisted the new United States of America as it secured its independence from Britain. Around 1790, the Haitian Revolution broke out. With Spain trapped in European wars, the mainland Spanish colonies were able to secure independence around 1820.

From a long-term perspective, the revolutions were mostly successful. They spread the ideals of republicanism, overthrew aristocracies and kings and established new religions. They emphasized the universal ideals of the Enlightenment, such as the equality of all men, including equal justice under law by disinterested courts, as opposed to particular justice handed down at the whim of a local noble. They showed that the modern notion of revolution, of starting fresh with a radically new government, could actually work in practice.

Portuguese, Dutch, French and British rivalries in Asia culminated in British domination in India and Dutch control of the East Indies.

At the end of the 16th century, England and the United Netherlands began to challenge Portugal's monopoly on trade with Asia, forming private joint-stock companies to finance the voyages of the English East India Company and the Dutch East India

Company, which were chartered in 1600 and 1602 respectively. These companies were intended to carry on the lucrative spice trade, and they focused their efforts on the areas of production—the Indonesian archipelago, the Spice Islands and India—as an important market for the trade. The close proximity of London and Amsterdam across the North Sea, and the intense rivalry between England and the Netherlands, inevitably led to conflict between the two companies. The Dutch gained the upper hand in the Maluku Islands (previously a Portuguese stronghold; present-day Indonesia) after the withdrawal of the English in 1622, but the English enjoyed more success in India, at Surat, after the establishment of a factory there in 1613.

The Netherlands' more advanced financial system and the three Anglo-Dutch Wars of the 17th century made the Dutch the dominant naval and trading power in Asia. Hostilities ceased after the Glorious Revolution of 1688, when the Dutch prince, William of Orange, ascended the English throne, bringing about peace between the Netherlands and England. A deal between the two nations left the more valuable spice trade of the Indonesian archipelago to the Netherlands and India's textile industry to England, but textiles overtook spices in terms of profitability, so by 1720, in terms of sales, the English company had overtaken its Dutch competitor. The English East India Company shifted its focus from Surat—a hub of the spice trade network—to Fort St. George.

English East India Company

Following the Portuguese, English and Dutch, the French also established trading bases in India. Their first such establishment was in 1674 in Pondicherry, located on the Coromandel Coast in Southeastern India. Subsequent French settlements were Chandernagore in Bengal, Northeastern India in 1688, Yanam in Andhra Pradesh in 1723, Mahe in 1725 and Karaikal in 1739. The French were constantly in conflict with the Dutch, and later with the British, in India. At the height of French power in the mid-18th century, the French occupied large areas of Southern India and the area lying in today's Northern Andhra Pradesh and Odisha.

Between 1744 and 1761, the British and the French repeatedly attacked and conquered each other's forts and towns in Southeastern India and in Bengal in the northeast. After some initial French successes, the British decisively defeated the French in Bengal in the Battle of Plassey in 1757 and in the southeast in 1761 in the Battle of Wandiwash. After this, the British East India Company was the supreme military and political power in Southern India as well as in Bengal. In the following decades, it gradually increased the size of the territories under its control.

Period 2: 1648-1815

Key Concept 2.3: The popularization and dissemination of the scientific revolution and the application of its methods to political, social and ethical issues led to an increased, although not unchallenged, emphasis on reason in European culture.

During the 17th and 18th centuries, Europeans applied the methods of the new science—such as empiricism, mathematics and skepticism—to human affairs. During the Enlightenment, intellectuals such as Rousseau, Voltaire and Diderot aimed to replace faith in the divine revelation with faith in human reason and classical values. In economics and politics, liberal theorists such as John Locke and Adam Smith questioned absolutism and mercantilism by arguing for the authority of natural law and the market. Belief in progress, along with improved social and economic conditions, spurred significant gains in literacy and education, as well as the creation of a new culture for the growing educated audience.

Several movements of religious revival occurred during the 18th century, but elite culture embraced skepticism, secularism and atheism for the first time in European history, and popular attitudes began to shift in the same directions. From the beginning of this period, Protestants and Catholics grudgingly tolerated each other after the religious warfare of the previous two centuries. By 1800, most governments had extended tolerance to Christian minorities, and some even to Jews. Religion was viewed increasingly as a matter of private rather than public concern.

The new rationalism did not sweep all before it; in fact, it coexisted with a revival of sentimentalism and emotionalism. Until about 1750, Baroque art and music glorified religious feeling and drama as well as the grandiose pretensions of absolute monarchs. During the French Revolution, romanticism and nationalism implicitly challenged what some saw as the Enlightenment's overemphasis on reason. These Counter-Enlightenment views laid the foundations for new cultural developments during this period and marked a transition in European history to a modern world view in which rationalism, skepticism, scientific investigation and a belief in progress generally dominated, although such views did not completely supplant other world views stemming from religion nationalism and romanticism.

Rational and empirical thought challenged traditional values and ideas.

Rationalism is a philosophical doctrine which asserts that the truth must be determined through reason——not faith or religious dogma. Rationalists maintain that reason is the source of all human knowledge. There is also another, less absolute, form of rationalism which asserts that reason is the main source of the most important type of knowledge. Rationalism has several ideological similarities with humanism and atheism because it offers a frame of reference for philosophical and social problems without religious or supernatural implications. Still, rationalism differs from these ideologies; Humanism concentrates on the superiority of human society and man in the context of nature and its elements. Atheism denies the existence of God, a subject to which rationalism doesn't refer.

Empiricism is the philosophical doctrine that all human knowledge derives from senses and experience, with an emphasis on testing and experimenting. "Empirical" is an adjective often used in reference to the natural and social sciences. It means the use of a hypothesis which may be contradicted by observation and experiment. This new manner of thinking challenged the traditional ways of understanding the world.

Portrait of René Descartes,
French philosopher

Empiricism rejects the hypothesis that humans have ideas with which they were born, or that there can be knowledge without experience. Empiricism contrasts with continental rationalism, which was launched by René Descartes. According to rationalists, thinking must take place through introspection, and not deductive reasoning. Empiricists assert that at birth, the intellect is a "*tabula rasa*" (a blank sheet) and that knowledge can only be gained from experience.

People associated with empiricism include Thomas d'Aquinas, Thomas Hobbes, John Locke (who developed this doctrine in the 17th century and at the beginning of the 18th century) and David Hume. Generally, empiricism is considered the nucleus of the modern scientific method, according to which theories should be based on observation rather than on intuition or faith; in other words, empirical research and *a posteriori* inductive reasoning rather than pure deductive logic.

Intellectuals such as Voltaire and Diderot began to apply the principles of the Scientific Revolution to society and human institutions.

Voltaire, French Enlightenment writer and philosopher

Francois-Marie Voltaire, known by the *nom de plume* Voltaire, was the son of a wealthy lawyer. As such, he was sent to the College of the Jesuit-order Louis-le-Grand, where he was able to read extensively and honed his critical sensibility. Because of his ideas, he was imprisoned in the Bastille for eleven months in 1717. When he was threatened with arrest a second time in France, he left for England. There, he was influenced by John Locke's empiricism and by a new movement called Deism. In his *Lettres Philosophiques*, Voltaire detailed English liberalism (1731).

Voltaire criticized every form of institutional religion. He called himself a Theist, a man with faith in God but who had given up Christianity. When a new warrant was issued against him in 1734, he fled to the semi-autonomous region of Lorraine. There he wrote memoirs, treatises of the natural sciences, history and politics, and also a dramatic and poetic opera. He was introduced by Madame de Pompadour at the royal courts and was accepted into the French Academy. Friedrich the Great, an Enlightened despot, took Voltaire to Potsdam, where he could freely express his anti-clerical beliefs. He was able to work on universal historiography and collaborate with Diderot on the famous *Encyclopédie*. Voltaire's political philosophy was founded on harmony between the monarchs, who hold political power, and the philosophers, who possess wisdom. Along with Jean Jacques Rousseau, Voltaire's doctrine stood as one of the bases of the French Revolution.

Denis Diderot (1713–1784, Paris) was a French philosopher and writer. He was a complex figure of the French Enlightenment, who had a major influence on Rationalism in the 18th century. In 1745, along with Jean-Baptiste D'Alembert, Diderot began to edit the *Encyclopedie*, a famous project, which involved many of the important French Enlightenment writers. He is famous for his philosophical writings Pensées Philosophiques ("Philosophical Thoughts") (1746) and Lettre sur les Aveugles ("Letter to the Blind") (1749). Diderot's vast correspondence describes an objective image of his time. He had a significant influence upon future generations of thinkers in France, Germany and England.

Charles-Louis de Secondat, Baron de La Brède et de Montesquieu (1689–1755), usually known as Montesquieu, was born in a castle in Brède, near Bordeaux, to a family of magistrates belonging to the petite nobility. He was one of the most complex and important figures of the French Enlightenment. He was a counselor in the Bordeaux Parliament, becoming its president after the death of one of his uncles. In 1728, he became a member of the French Academy.

Montesquieu, philosopher, lawyer and writer of the French

Montesquieu's intention for his book, The Spirit of Laws (1748), was to explain human laws and social customs. The book is a comparative study of three types of government (republicanism, monarchism and despotism), influenced by John Locke's ideas. One of the most important ideas presented in the book was that of the separation of the powers of the state in order to ensure the liberty of the individual. The book has the same historical importance even today, as a masterwork which decisively influenced the United States Constitution which, in turn, has influenced many constitutions all over the world.

Locke and Rousseau developed new political models based on the concept of natural rights.

John Locke (1632–1704) was an English philosopher and politician, preoccupied mainly with society and epistemology. Locke is an emblematic figure of the three traditions of thought. In the field of knowledge, he was the founder of empiricism. In politics, Locke condemned absolutism and tyranny and defended liberty and rights, seeing legislative power as the supreme force. He thought that the executive and federative powers should submit to it, for it had the purpose of defending the community against both foreign and internal dangers. If the government broke its mandate, then the people had the right to intervene and exert their sovereignty. Whoever broke the law and the people's rights was actually declaring war on the nation and, in case it was the sovereign, then revolution was an essential mechanism of defense.

Jean Jacques Rousseau, philosopher of the French

Jean Jacques Rousseau (1712–1778) was a French-speaking philosopher born in Geneva. He was a noted writer, composer and one of the most influential thinkers of the Enlightenment. He had a decisive influence, along with Voltaire and Diderot, upon the principles of right and the social conscience of his times. His ideas are extensively found in the changes promoted by the French Revolution in 1789. "The Social Contract," one of Rousseau's most important works, outlines the basis for a legitimate political order within a framework of classical republicanism. Published in 1762, it became one of the most influential works of political philosophy in the Western tradition. It developed some of the ideas mentioned in an earlier work, the article *Economie Politique* (Discourse on Political Economy), featured in Diderot's *Encyclopédie*.

Rousseau claimed that the state of nature was a primitive condition without law or morality, which human beings transcended for the benefits and the necessity of cooperation. As society developed, division of labor and private property required the human race to adopt institutions of law. In the degenerate phase of society, man was prone to frequent competition with his fellow men, while also becoming increasingly dependent on them. This double pressure threatened both his survival and his freedom.

According to Rousseau, by joining together as a civil society through the social contract and abandoning their claim to natural rights, individuals could both preserve themselves and remain free. This was because submission to the authority of the general will of the people as a whole guaranteed individuals against being subordinate to the will of others and also ensured that they themselves obeyed because they were, collectively, the authors of the law.

Although Rousseau argued that sovereignty (or the power to make the laws) should be in the hands of the people, he also made a sharp distinction between the sovereign and the government. The government was composed of magistrates, charged with implementing and enforcing the general will. The "sovereign" was the rule of law, ideally decided on by direct democracy in an assembly. Rousseau opposed the idea that the people should exercise sovereignty via a representative assembly. He approved the kind of republican government of the city-state, for which Geneva provided a model.

Despite the principles of equality espoused by the Enlightenment and the French Revolution, intellectuals such as Rousseau offered new arguments for the exclusion of women from political life, which did not go unchallenged.

Although Rousseau's ideas were more forward thinking than the modern ones of the time in many ways, in one way they were not: he believed in the moral superiority of the patriarchal family in the antique Roman model. In *Émile or About Education*, Sophie, the young woman Émile was destined to marry, represented ideal womanhood and was educated to be governed by her husband, while Émile, represented the ideal man and was educated to be self-governing. That was not an accidental feature of Rousseau's educational and political philosophy; it was essential to his account of the distinction between private and personal relations and the world of political relations. The private environment, as Rousseau imagined it, depended on the submission of women.

Mary Wollstonecraft was a writer and women's rights activist who lived a short but brilliant life, from 1759 to 1797. She wrote *A Vindication of the Rights of Women*, in which she argued against the idea that women were naturally intellectually inferior to men. She wrote many types of works in her 38 year life, but mainly on the education of girls. She drew upon John Locke, the Enlightenment era's pre-eminent advocate of human liberty, who had published an argument about the importance of teaching all children to reason.

Mary Wollstonecraft, 18th century feminist

Rousseau anticipated the modern idea of the bourgeois nuclear family, with the mother at home taking responsibility for the household, childcare and early education. In the late 18th century, beginning with Mary Wollstonecraft in 1792, feminists criticized Rousseau for his confinement of women to the domestic sphere. He has been blamed for so-called modern "child-centered" education. Whether for good or bad, the theories of educators such as Rousseau's near contemporaries Pestalozzi and, later, Maria Montessori and John Dewey, have directly influenced modern educational practices and have significant points in common with Rousseau's.

Olympe de Gouges wrote many plays, short stories and novels. Her publications emphasized that women and men were different, but she said that shouldn't stop them from having equality under the law. In her "Declaration on the Rights of Woman," she insisted that women deserved rights, especially in areas concerning them directly, such as divorce and recognition of illegitimate children. A passionate advocate of human rights, Olympe de Gouges greeted the outbreak of the Revolution with hope and joy, but soon became disenchanted when the revolutionary principle of égalité (equality) was not extended to women. In 1791, she became part of the Society of the Friends of Truth, an association with the goal of obtaining equal political and legal rights for women. Also called the "Social Club," members sometimes gathered at the home of the well-known women's rights advocate, Sophie de Condorcet. It was here that De Gouges expressed, for the first time, her famous statement, "A woman has the right to mount the scaffold. She must possess equally the right to mount the speaker's platform."

That same year, in response to the Declaration of the Rights of Man and of the Citizen, she wrote the *"Declaration des droits de la Femme er de la Citoyenne"* ("Declaration of the Rights of Woman and the Female Citizen"). This was followed by her *"Contrat Social"* ("Social Contract," named after the one of Jean-Jacques Rousseau), which proposed marriage based upon gender equality. She became involved in almost any matter she believed to involve injustice. She opposed the execution of Louis XVI of France, partly out of opposition to capital punishment and partly because she preferred a relatively tame and living king to the possibility of a rebel regency in exile. This earned her the ire of many republicans.

Madame Roland (Manon or Marie Roland) was another important female activist. Madame Roland, born Marie-Jeanne Phlippon, the sole surviving child of eight pregnancies, was born to Gratien Phlippon and Madame Phlippon in March 1754. From her early years she was a successful, enthusiastic and talented student. In her youth she studied literature, music and drawing. From the beginning she was strong willed and frequently challenged her father and instructors as she progressed through an advanced, well-rounded education.

Enthusiastically supporting her education, Jeanne's parents enrolled her in the convent school of the Sisterhood of the Congregation in Paris for one year only. After her convent school education, she pursued her education independently. Several literary figures influenced Roland's philosophy, including Voltaire, Montesquieu, Plutarch and others. Most significantly, Rousseau's literature strongly influenced Roland's understanding of feminine virtue and political philosophy and she came to understand a woman's genius as residing in "a pleasurable loss of self-control."

Roland's political focus was not specifically on women or their liberation. She focused on other aspects of the government, but

Madame Roland, female activist

was a feminist by virtue of the fact that she was a woman working to influence the world. Her personal letters to leaders of the Revolution influenced policy; in addition, she often hosted political gatherings of the Brissotins, a political group which allowed women to join. As she was led to the scaffold, Madame Roland shouted "O liberty! What crimes are committed in thy name!" Most of these female activists were punished for their actions. Many of the women of the Revolution were even publicly executed for "conspiring against the unity and the indivisibility of the Republic."

The Marquis de Condorcet (1743 – 1794) was a French mathematician and philosopher. In the realm of philosophy he strongly advocated for human liberty, including the inter-related liberties of a free market economy and equal rights for women and people of all races. He is most famous for his model of collective judgment, which states that the majority, in politics, is most likely to be correct. Rousseau drew on this theory for proof of his own theory of the general will. There are contradictions in the ideas promoted by Condorcet however. This is best illustrated by the fact that some of them recognize individual rights and equality as sovereign (his promotion of the freedom of the markets and classical liberalism, in which unique individual identities and decisions are implied) while others refer to collectivism (such as his belief that education should be free and equal for all, which depends on (a) someone else paying for the education of the poor and (b) a willingness to ignore the individual differences among students).

New public venues and print media popularized enlightenment ideas.

The increased use of reading materials of all kinds was one of the main features of the "social" Enlightenment. The Industrial Revolution allowed consumer goods to be produced in greater quantities at lower prices, favoring the spread of books, pamphlets, newspapers and journals. The growth of the free market increased the demand for information as it increased the size of the population and the level of urbanization. However, demand for reading material extended beyond business people and the upper and middle classes, as evidenced by the *Bibliothèque Bleue* (the Blue Library), which provided popular reading material for the newly literate classes.

Reading underwent serious transformations in the 18th century. Until 1750, it was done intensively: people owned a small number of books and read them repeatedly, often to a diminishing audience. After 1750, people began to read more extensively, and reading became a more solitary pursuit. The vast majority of the reading public could not afford a personal library. While many of the state-run universal libraries set up in the 17th and 18th centuries were open to the public, they were not the only source of reading material.

On one end of the array was the Bibliothèque Bleue, a collection of cheaply produced books, issued in Troyes, France. Designed for a mainly rural and semi-literate audience, it included almanacs, medieval romances and condensed versions of popular novels. There were some institutions which offered readers access to material without the need to buy anything. Libraries that lent out their material for a small price started to appear, and occasionally bookstores offered a small lending library to their patrons. Coffeehouses offered books, journals and sometimes even popular novels to their customers. *The Tatler* and *The Spectator*, two influential periodicals sold from 1709 to 1714, were closely associated with the coffeehouse culture in London. Both were read and produced in various establishments in the city.

Copy of The Tatler

As Darnton describes in *The Literary Underground of the Old Regime*, it is very difficult to establish what people actually read during the Enlightenment. For example, examining the catalogs of private libraries not only gives an image that is biased in favor of the classes wealthy enough to have had libraries, but it also ignores banned books that were seldom publicly acknowledged. Many works were sold without having any legal trouble at all. Borrowing records from libraries in England, Germany and North America indicate that more than 70 percent of the books lent were novels and less than 1 percent of the books lent were of a religious nature, a fact which supports the general tendency of the time toward declining religiosity.

A variety of institutions, such as salons, explored and disseminated Enlightenment culture.

The history of academies in France during the Enlightenment began with the Academy of Science, which was founded in 1635 in Paris. It was closely tied to the French state, and acted as an extension of a government that was seriously lacking in scientists. It helped to promote and organize new disciplines and train new scientists. It also contributed to the enhancement of scientists' social status and considered them to be the "most useful of all citizens." The academies attest to the rising interest in science, along with its increasing secularization, evidenced by the small number of clerics who were members.

Coffeehouses were especially important to the spread of knowledge during the Enlightenment because they created a unique environment in which people from many different walks of life gathered and shared ideas. Coffeehouse culture was frequently criticized by the nobles, who feared and abhorred the possibility of an environment in which class and its accompanying titles and privileges were disregarded. Such an environment was especially intimidating to monarchs, who derived much of their power from the disparity between classes. If the classes were to join together under the influence of Enlightenment thinking, they might recognize the oppression and abuses of their monarchs and, given their numbers, might be able to carry out successful revolts. Monarchs also resented the idea of their subjects convening as one to discuss political matters—especially those concerning foreign affairs—for rulers thought political affairs to be their business only, which was a result of their supposed divine right to rule.

Although many coffeehouse patrons were scholars, many more were not. Coffeehouse culture attracted a diverse set of people, including not only the educated and wealthy but also the less educated members of the bourgeoisie and even the lower class. While it may seem positive that some patrons were doctors, lawyers and merchants, but with the coffeehouse patrons representing almost all classes, this generated fear in those who sought to preserve the strong class distinctions of the day.

Francesco Procopio dei Coltelli (François Procope) established the first café in Paris, the Café Procope, in 1686; by the 1720s there were around 400 cafés in the city. The Café Procope became a center of Enlightenment, welcoming as patrons such celebrities as Voltaire and Rousseau. The Café Procope was where Diderot and D'Alembert decided to create the Encyclopédie. Robert Darnton in particular has studied Parisian café culture in great detail. He describes how the cafés were one of the various "nerve centers" for *bruits publics*, public noise or rumor. The bruits were a much better source of information than the newspapers.

Philosophers of the French Enlightenment at the Café Procope

Moreover, coffeehouses represented a turning point in history during which people discovered that they could have enjoyable social lives within their communities. The coffeehouses became homes away from home for many who sought, for the first time, to engage in discourse with their neighbors and discuss intriguing and thought-provoking matters, especially those regarding philosophy and politics. Coffeehouses were essential to the Enlightenment, for they were centers of free thinking and self-discovery.

The Debating Societies that rapidly came into existence in 1780 in London present an almost perfect example of the public sphere during the Enlightenment. These societies discussed an extremely wide range of topics. One broad area was women: societies debated over "male and female qualities," courtship, marriage and the role of women in the public sphere. They also discussed political issues, varying from recent events to "the nature and limits of political authority," and the nature of suffrage. Debates on religion were also held. The critical subject matter of these debates did not necessarily translate into opposition to the government; rather the results of the debates quite frequently upheld the status quo.

Historians have long debated the extent to which the secret network of Freemasonry was a central factor in the Enlightenment. Historians agree that the famous leaders of the Enlightenment included Freemasons like Diderot, Montesquieu, Voltaire, Pope, Horace Walpole, Sir Robert Walpole, Mozart, Goethe, Frederick the Great, Benjamin Franklin and George Washington. Freemasonry expanded rapidly during the Age of

Enlightenment, reaching practically every country in Europe. It was especially attractive to powerful aristocrats and politicians, as well as to intellectuals, artists and political activists.

During the Age of Enlightenment, the Freemasons comprised an international network of like-minded men, who met in secret in ritualistic programs at their lodges. They promoted the ideals of the Enlightenment and helped to spread its values across Britain, France and other countries. Freemasonry as a systematic creed with its own myths, values and set of rituals, originated in Scotland around 1600. It spread first to England and then across the Continent in the 18th century. Freemasons created new codes of conduct and a communal understanding of liberty and equality, which was inherited from their guild sociability, "liberty, fraternity, and equality." Scottish Jamesite soldiers held ideals of fraternity which reflected the institutions and ideals of the English Civil War, not the local Scottish customs.

Freemasonry was particularly prevalent in France; by 1789, there were perhaps as many as 100,000 French Masons, making Freemasonry the most popular of all Enlightenment associations. The Freemasons displayed a passion for secrecy and created new degrees and ceremonies. Similar societies, partially imitating Freemasonry, emerged in France, Germany, Sweden and Russia. Masonic lodges created a private model for public affairs. They were a micro-society which constituted a normative model for society as a whole. This was especially true on the Continent: when the first lodges began to appear around 1730, their embodiment of British values was often seen as threatening by state authorities. Furthermore, Freemasons all across Europe explicitly linked themselves to the Enlightenment as a whole.

Another advance which is familiar today was lending libraries. After the modern printing press enabled books to be mass produced and more broadly available (although still expensive), general interest in reading increased throughout Europe. Prior to the end of the 18th century, reading was always done in groups, with one person reading aloud to another. This was partially because books were expensive and the cost could be shared by sharing books. Churches began to make collections of books publically available and – thanks to the surplus income that was becoming available – the wealthy began to provide for the creation of "endowment libraries" in their wills. Some coffee houses also began to offer books for loan in order to draw customers in. The Leeds Library was the first public library in Great Britain, in the modern sense. It opened in 1768.

Despite censorship, increasingly numerous and varied printed material served a growing literate public and led to the development of public.

All across continental Europe, but especially in France, booksellers and publishers had to negotiate censorship laws of varying strictness. The Encyclopédie, for example, narrowly escaped seizure and had to be saved by Guillaume-Chretien Malesherbes, the man in charge of the French censure. Indeed, many publishing companies were conveniently located outside of France so as to avoid overzealous French censors. They would smuggle their merchandise—both pirated copies and condemned works—across the border, where it would then be transported to clandestine booksellers or small-time peddlers.

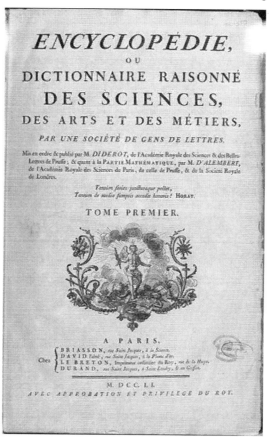

Encyclopédie, edited by Diderot and D'Alembert
during the French Age of Enlightenment

The Enlightenment was not the exclusive domain of illegal literature, as evidenced by the healthy, and mostly legal, publishing industry that existed throughout Europe. ("Mostly legal" because even established publishers and booksellers occasionally ran afoul of the law.) The Encyclopédie, for example, condemned not only by the King but also by Pope Clement XII, nevertheless found its way into print with the help of Malesherbes who knew how to work around French censorship law.

The many scientific and literary journals (predominantly composed of book reviews) that were published during this time are also evidence of the intellectual side of the Enlightenment. From 1680 onwards, scholarly journals influenced European intellectual culture to a greater degree than any other cultural innovation of the time.

The first journal, the Parisian *Journal des Sçavans*, appeared in 1665 but it was not until 1682 that periodicals began to be more widely produced. French and Latin were the dominant languages of publication, but there was also a steady demand for material in German and Dutch. There was generally little demand for English publications on the Continent, which was echoed by England's similar lack of desire for French works. Journals were rarely published in languages commanding less of an international market – such as Danish, Spanish and Portuguese. Although German did have an international quality to it, it was French that slowly took over Latin's status as the lingua franca of the learned circles. This gave precedence to the publishing industry in Holland, where the vast majority of French language periodicals were produced.

Journals were important for their role in shifting attention towards what was new and innovative. They did a lot to promote the enlightened ideals of tolerance and intellectual objectivity, and were an implicit critique of existing notions of universal truth that were monopolized by monarchies, parliaments and religious authorities. The journals suggested new sources of knowledge, science and reason, which undermined these traditional sources of authority.

The modern printing press enabled the mass dissemination of all forms of printed material that we are familiar with today: newspapers, periodicals (journals), books and pamphlets. However, the technology was ahead of the level of freedom when it was introduced in 1454. Europe's political leaders and church leaders still censored anything they did not agree with. Notwithstanding this, provocative writing was often printed and distributed in secrecy. Sometimes, censorship was circumvented by printing it in one country, where it was legal, then bringing the material to the country for distribution.

Pamphlets were among the first form of printed material because they were short. This made them less expensive to print and easier to hide and distribute discreetly, if they contained something provocative. The early Protestants made heavy use of pamphlets, for example, to promote their views at a time when they were a suspect minority.

Books had originally been constructed and copied completely by hand, often in monasteries. Monastic books were simultaneously works of visual art and a tool for making information permanent. Mass-dissemination of information in the modern sense was not a quality of these early books, since they were not mass-produced and were prohibitively expensive for most people. The printing press changed this. Although printed books remained expensive, the collision of modern printing and the achievement of disposable income for the working majority of Europeans (starting in the 18th century) enabled ordinary people to begin to be able to afford their own books. The most notable book to be mass produced was the bible. This enabled the spread of Protestantism, as Catholic services were held in Latin whereas Protestants wanted to make their religion more available to the general public: The union of mass production and being able to read in one's own language made the religion more available to the masses than Catholicism.

Newspapers developed later, as an outgrowth of periodical almanacs. They were widely produced and read by the second half of the 18th century in the American colonies and many European locations. The major difference in their functionality then was that it would take a much longer time to distribute them; the daily newspaper of the twentieth century did not exist. Early newspapers could take days to reach the public, especially in vast regions like the British colonies.

Natural sciences, literature and popular culture increasingly exposed Europeans to representations of people outside Europe.

Scientific literature was another genre of increasing importance at the time. Natural history in particular became increasingly popular among the upper classes. Works of natural history include René-Antoine Ferchault de Réaumur's "*Histoire naturelle des insectes*" (Natural History of Insects) and Jacques Gautier d'Agoty's "*La Myologie complete, ou description de tous les muscles du corps humain*" (The Complete Myology, a description of the muscles in the human body; 1746).

The target audience for natural history was French polite society, indicated more by the specific discourse of the genre than by the generally high prices of its works. Naturalists catered to polite society's desire for erudition – many texts had an explicit instructive purpose. But the idea of taste (le goût) was the real social indicator: to truly be able to categorize nature, one had to have the proper taste, a quality of discretion shared by all members of polite society. In this way, natural history literature spread many of the scientific developments of the time, and also provided a new source of legitimacy for the dominant class.

Outside ancient régime France, natural history was an important part of medicine and industry, as it encompassed the fields of botany, zoology, meteorology, hydrology and mineralogy. Students at Enlightenment universities and academies were taught these subjects to prepare themselves for careers as diverse as medicine and theology. Natural history in this context was a very middle class pursuit and operated as a fertile trading zone for the interdisciplinary exchange of diverse scientific ideas.

The term Republic of Letters was coined by Pierre Bayle in 1664, in his journal *Nouvelles de la Republique des Lettres*. The ideal of the Republic of Letters was the sum of a number of Enlightenment ideals: an egalitarian realm governed by knowledge that could act across political boundaries and rival state power. It was a forum that supported free public examination of questions regarding religion or legislation.

Pierre Bayle,
French philosopher and writer

New political and economic theories challenged absolutism and mercantilism.

Like the French Revolution, the Enlightenment has long been hailed as the foundation of modern Western political and intellectual culture. It has been frequently linked to the French Revolution of 1789. The revolutionaries thought of philosophers like Voltaire and Rousseau as heroes, who could be used to justify their radical break with the Ancient Régime. In any case, the writings of two 19th century historians of the Enlightenment, Hippolyte Taine and Alexis de Tocqueville, emphasized the link between Enlightenment ideas and revolution, as well as the intellectual perception of the Enlightenment itself.

An alternative view is that the philosophy of the consent of the governed, outlined by Locke in Two Treatises of Government (1689), represented a paradigm shift from the old feudal government justification of the divine right of kings. In this view, the revolutions of the 18th century were caused by the fact that the governance paradigm shift often could not be resolved peacefully, with violent revolution the result. Clearly a governance philosophy where the king was never wrong was in direct conflict with one where citizens by natural law had to consent to the acts and rulings of their government.

John Locke was able to root his philosophy of governance in social contract theory, a predominant subject of Enlightenment political thought. Formally, it was the English philosopher Thomas Hobbes who ushered in this new debate with his work Leviathan in 1651. Both John Locke and Jean-Jacques Rousseau developed their own social contract theories in "Two Treatises of Government" and "Discourse on Inequality," respectively. While quite different works, all three argue that a social contract is necessary for man to live peacefully in a civil society. Hobbes said that nature is a state of impoverished anarchic violence in which human life is "solitary, poor, nasty, brutish, and short." He argued that, to counter this, society enters into a social contract to have an all-powerful, absolute leader; that people are willing to give up a few personal liberties in exchange for security and lawfulness.

In contrast, Rousseau's conception of both the state of nature and civil society, and how man moves from one to the other, relied on the supposition that civilized man is corrupt. In his work "Discourse on Inequality," Rousseau argued that natural man is a sentient being who has no want that he cannot fulfill by himself. Once the inequality associated with private property is established, society becomes corrupt and thus perpetuates inequality through the division of labor and, ultimately, power relations. With this in mind, Rousseau wrote "On the Social Contract" to spell out his contract theory. He argued that men join into civil society via the social contract to achieve unity while preserving individual freedom. This is embodied in the sovereignty of the general will, the moral and collective legislative body constituted by citizens.

Political theories such as John Locke's conceived of society as composed of individuals driven by self-interest and argued that the state originated from the consent of the governed (i.e., a social construct) rather than from divine right or tradition.

In 1689 John Locke published his *Two Treatises on Government*. In it, he defined the state of nature as a condition in which humans are rational and follow natural law; in which all men are born equal and with the right to life, liberty and property. However, when one citizen breaks the Law of Nature, both the transgressor and the victim enter into a state of war. Therefore, Locke argued that individuals enter into civil society to protect their natural rights via an "unbiased judge" or common authority, such as the courts.

Both Rousseau's and Locke's social contract theories rest on the presupposition of natural rights. A natural right is not given to man by law or custom. Rather, it is something that all men have in pre-political societies, and is therefore universal and inalienable. The most basic formulation of natural right comes from John Locke in his Second Treatise, in which he introduced his concept of the state of nature. Locke thought that man is perfectly free in the state of nature, within the bounds of the laws of nature and reason. For Locke, civil society was grounded on mutual security, or the idea that one cannot infringe on another's natural rights, as every man is equal and has the same inalienable rights. These natural rights include perfect equality and freedom, and the right to preserve life and property.

Based on his formulation, John Locke argued against slavery on the basis that enslaving yourself goes against the law of nature; you cannot surrender your own rights, your freedom is absolute and no one can take it from you. Additionally, Locke argued that one person cannot enslave another because it is morally reprehensible. Locke did introduce a caveat in his indictment of slavery, he believed slavery was justified during times of war and conflict because it was merely a continuation of the state of war. By "slavery" in this context, Locke meant military servitude, as an aobligation to the society which one has chosen to belong to, once that society is attacked.

Portrait of John Locke,
French philosopher, physician and writer

Locke's theory of natural rights has influenced many political documents, including the French National Constituent Assembly's Declaration of the Rights of Man and of the Citizen and the United States Declaration of Independence.

Mercantilist theory and practice were challenged by new economic ideas, such as Adam Smith's, espousing free trade and a free market.

Physiocracy (from the Greek for "Government of Nature") is an economic theory that was developed by a group of 18th century Enlightenment French economists who believed that the wealth of nations was derived solely from the value of land agriculture or land development, and that agricultural products should be sold at a high price. Physiocracy is perhaps the first well-developed theory of economics. The movement was particularly dominated by François Quesnay (1694–1774) and Anne-Robert-Jacques Turgot (1727–1781). It immediately preceded the first modern school, classical economics, inaugurated by the publication of Adam Smith's "The Wealth of Nations" in 1776.

Adam Smith,
Scottish moral philosopher

Adam Smith (1723–1790) was a Scottish moral philosopher, pioneer of political economics and a key Scottish Enlightenment figure. Smith is best known for two classic works: "The Theory of Moral Sentiments" (1759) and "An Inquiry into the Nature and Causes of the Wealth of Nations" (1776). The latter, commonly known as "The Wealth of Nations," is considered his magnum opus and the first modern work of economics. Smith is cited as the father of modern economics and is still among the most influential thinkers in the field of economics today.

Smith studied social philosophy at the University of Glasgow and at Balliol College in Oxford, where he was one of the first students to benefit from scholarships set up by a fellow Scot, John Snell. After graduating, he delivered a successful series of public lectures at Edinburgh, leading him to collaborate with David Hume during the Scottish Enlightenment. Smith obtained a professorship at Glasgow teaching moral philosophy and during that time he wrote and published "The Theory of Moral Sentiments." In later life, he took a tutoring position that allowed him to travel throughout Europe, where he met other intellectual leaders of his day. "The Wealth of Nations" was a precursor to the modern academic discipline of economics. In this and other works, Smith expounded on how rational self-interest and competition can lead to economic prosperity.

The most significant contribution of the Physiocrats was their emphasis on productive work as the source of national wealth. This is in contrast to earlier schools, in particular mercantilism, which often focused on a ruler's wealth, accumulation of gold and the balance of trade. The Mercantilist school of economics argued that value in the products of society was created at the point of sale, by the seller exchanging his products for more money than the products had previously been worth, while the Physiocratic school of economics was the first to see labor as the sole source of value. The latter thought that only agricultural labor created value in the products of society and all industrial and non-agricultural labor was an unproductive appendage of agricultural labor.

At the time the Physiocrats were formulating their ideas, economies were almost entirely agrarian. That is presumably why the theory considered only agricultural labor to be valuable. Physiocrats viewed the production of goods and services as consumption of the agricultural surplus, since the main source of power was from human or animal muscle and all energy was derived from the surplus from agricultural production. Profit in mercantilist production was really only the rent obtained by the owner of the land on which the agricultural production took place.

Anne Robert Jacques Turgot (1727 – 1781) was a physiocrat and classical liberal who many historians credit with the first reference to "progress." He was an Empiricist and a minister to French King Louis XVI. In his seminal work, *A Philosophical Review of the Successive Advances of the Human Mind* (1750), Turgot argued that the advancement of science would lead to increases in human freedom. Some examples of the veracity of that claim are the first food surplus and the printing press.

Technology has eliminated many of the economic shortages which have greatly inhibited human freedom. The most fundamental such change was the first food surplus, originating from early discoveries about the natural phenomena in food production, which enabled the division of labor. When humans were first able to do more than just subsist, because they could pay others to produce (surplus) food for them, all of their potential was made available to them. The entire progression of human advancement since then would not have been possible without the early scientific discoveries which made surplus food production possible. In more recent times, literacy and education have been enhanced by the printing press. But the printing press is a product of science; Guttenberg first needed to experiment with many combinations of metal until he found that antimony and lead was the correct combination for his printing blocks and he needed to find the right chemical combination for quick-drying ink. Without chemistry, there would have been no printing press; without the printing press, there would have been no education revolution; without education, a human being cannot even conceive of his or her own freedom as a valid concept, let alone do the sophisticated tasks required of a free person. At the beginning of the twenty-first century, science is enabling us to begin to harvest resources from outer space and thus to finally liberate ourselves from our planet.

During the Enlightenment, the rational analysis of religious practices led to natural religion and the demand for religious tolerance.

Enlightenment era religious commentary was a response to the preceding century of religious conflict in Europe, especially the Thirty Years' War. Theologians of the Enlightenment wanted to reform their faith back to its generally non-confrontational roots and to limit the possibility of religious controversy spilling over into politics and warfare, while still maintaining a true faith in God.

For moderate Christians, this meant a return to simple Scripture. John Locke abandoned the corpus of theological commentary in favor of an unprejudiced examination of the Word of God alone. He determined the essence of Christianity to be a belief in Christ the redeemer and recommended avoiding more detailed debate. Thomas Jefferson went further in the Jefferson Bible; he dropped any passages dealing with miracles, visitations of angels and the resurrection of Jesus after his death. He tried to extract the practical Christian moral code of the New Testament. Enlightenment scholars sought to curtail the political power of organized religion in order to prevent another age of intolerant religious war.

Intellectuals, including Voltaire and Diderot, developed new philosophies of deism, skepticism and atheism.

A number of novel religious ideas developed with Enlightened faith, including Deism and atheism. Deism, according to Thomas Paine, was the simple belief in God the Creator, with no reference to the Bible or any other miraculous source. Instead, the Deist relied solely on personal reason to guide his creed, which was eminently agreeable to many thinkers of the time.

Atheism was much discussed but had few proponents. In fact, very few enlightened intellectuals, even when they were vocal critics of Christianity, were true atheists; instead they were critics of orthodox belief. Voltaire and many others thought that without the belief in a God who punishes evil, the moral order of society was undermined. That is, since atheists gave themselves to no Supreme Authority and no law, and had no fear of eternal consequences, they were far more likely to disrupt society. Pierre Bayle (1647–1706) observed that, in his day, prudent persons always maintained an appearance of religion. He believed that even atheists could hold concepts of honor and go beyond their own self-interest to create, and interact in, a society. Locke considered the consequence for mankind if there were no God and no divine law, to be moral anarchy.

The Scottish philosopher David Hume, along with Thomas Hobbes, is cited as a classical compatibilist about the notions of freedom and determinism. The thesis of compatibilism seeks to reconcile human freedom with the mechanist belief that human beings are part of a deterministic universe, whose happenings are governed by physical laws. Hume, to this end, was influenced greatly by the scientific revolution and in particular by Sir Isaac Newton. Hume argued that the dispute about the compatibility of freedom and determinism has been continued over two thousand years by ambiguous terminology.

Portrait of David Hume,
Scottish philosopher

Although he wrote a great deal about religion, Hume's personal views are unclear, and there has been much discussion concerning his religious position. Contemporaries considered him to be an atheist, or at least un-Christian, and the Church of Scotland seriously considered bringing charges of infidelity against him. However, in works such as "Of Superstition and Enthusiasm," Hume specifically seemed to support the standard religious views of his time and place but was nonetheless highly critical of the Catholic Church, dismissing it with the standard Protestant accusations of superstition and idolatry, as well as dismissing as idolatry what his compatriots saw as uncivilized beliefs. He also considered extreme Protestant sects, the members of which he called "enthusiasts," to be corrupters of religion. By contrast, in *The Natural History of Religion*, Hume presented arguments that suggested polytheism had many more positive points, from a philosophical perspective, than did monotheism.

Paul-Henri Thiry, Baron d'Holbach, was a French-German author and philosopher, encyclopedist and a prominent figure in the French Enlightenment. He was born Paul Heinrich Dietrich in Edesheim, near Landau in the Rhenish Palatinate, but lived and worked mainly in Paris, where he maintained a salon. He was well known for his atheism and for his voluminous writings against religion, the most famous of them being "The System of Nature" (1770). Despite his extensive contributions to the Encyclopédie, d'Holbach is better known today for his philosophical writings, all of which were published anonymously or under pseudonyms and printed outside of France, usually in Amsterdam by Marc-Michel Rey. His philosophy was expressly materialistic and atheistic. Today, it is categorized within the philosophical movement called French materialism. In 1761, *Christianisme dévoilé* ("Christianity Unveiled") was published, in which he attacked Christianity and religion in general as an impediment to the moral advancement of humanity. The deistic Voltaire, denying authorship of the work, made known his aversion to d'Holbach's philosophy, writing that the work was entirely opposed to his principles, leading to an atheistic philosophy which he detested.

Religion was viewed increasingly as a matter of private rather that public concern.

The Enlightenment freed human beings from their self-imposed tutelage, which was the incapacity of man to use his own cognitive abilities without being instructed by some "authority." The Enlightenment attacked, in various manners, religious and scientific authority, dogmatism, intolerance, censure and economic and social coercion. The extreme rationalism and skepticism naturally led to deism. The same qualities played an important role in the determination of the later reaction of Romanticism. Reacting to dogmatism, the Enlightenment found a favorable path in a period in which the Church had lost its power to impose upon the social order with the same fervor as it had in the Middle Ages. The philosophers of France, in the middle of the 18th century, transformed the mechanical perspective of the universe into a radically revised variant of Christianity, which they called deism. Faith was no longer a social issue, but a matter of personal choice.

By 1800, most governments had extended tolerance to Christian minorities and, in some states, civil equality to Jews.

During the Enlightenment, politicians and commentators began formulating theories of religious tolerance and basing legal codes on that concept. A distinction began to develop between civil tolerance, concerned with the policy of the state towards religious dissent, and ecclesiastical tolerance, concerned with the degree of diversity tolerated within a particular church. In 1636, Roger Williams and companions, upon the foundation of Rhode Island, entered into a compact binding themselves "to be obedient to the majority only in civil things." In 1663, Charles II of England granted the colony a charter guaranteeing complete religious tolerance.

Roger Williams, founder of Rhode Island

In 1649, Maryland passed the Maryland Toleration Act, also known as the Act Concerning Religion, a law mandating religious tolerance for Trinitarian Christians only (excluding Nontrinitarian faiths). Passed in September 1649 by the assembly of the Maryland colony, it was the first law requiring religious tolerance in the British North American colonies. The Calvert family sought enactment of the law to protect Catholic settlers and some of the other denominations that did not conform to the dominant Anglicanism practiced in England and her colonies. In 1657, New Amsterdam granted religious tolerance to Jews. In 1609, Rudolph II decreed religious tolerance in Bohemia.

The Act of Toleration, adopted by the British Parliament in 1689, allowed freedom of worship to Nonconformists who had pledged the oaths of Allegiance and Supremacy and rejected transubstantiation. ("Transubstantiation" is when the holy bread and wine, used in communion, become the body of Christ.) Nonconformists were Protestants who dissented from the Church of England such as Baptists and Congregationalists. They were allowed their own places of worship and their own teachers, if they accepted certain oaths of allegiance. The Act did not apply to Catholics and non-Trinitarians and continued the existing social and political repression of Dissenters, including their exclusion from political office and also from universities.

The Declaration of the Rights of Man and the Citizen (1789), adopted by the National Constituent Assembly during the French Revolution, stated that no man should be interfered with for his opinions, even his religious ones, provided that they did not disturb the public order as established by law. The First Amendment to the United States Constitution, ratified along with the rest of the Bill of Rights on December 15, 1791, included the following words: "Congress shall make no law respecting an establishment of religion, or prohibiting the free exercise thereof."

The arts moved from the celebration of religious themes and royal power to an emphasis on private life and the public good.

During the Middle Ages and the Renaissance, art had been a privilege of the aristocracy, royalty and the Church. The most famous masterworks of the time depicted kings, popes or nobles and described their realms. Monarchs employed artists to glorify their magnificence and state power. Architectural constructions were designed to intimidate and display absolutist strength. The French Revolution was the event which transferred attention to common individuals and their lives, both inner and outer. Towards the end of the Enlightenment period, the number of paintings and sculptures which reflected private life, the public good and commonplace human emotions increased dramatically. This was largely influenced by the Romantic Movement of the period and the diminishing influence of ecclesiastical art patronage.

Until about 1750, Baroque art and music promoted religious feeling and was employed by monarchs to glorify state power.

The Baroque can be characterized as a period of artistic style in which exaggerated motion and clear, easily interpreted detail was used to produce drama, tension, exuberance and grandeur in sculpture, painting, architecture, literature, dance, theater and music. The style began around 1600 in Rome and spread to most of Europe. The popularity and success of the Baroque style was encouraged by the Catholic Church, which had decided at the time of the Council of Trent, in response to the Protestant Reformation, that the arts should communicate religious themes in direct and emotional involvement. The aristocracy also saw the dramatic style of Baroque architecture and art as a means of impressing visitors and expressing triumph, power and control. Baroque palaces are built around an entrance of courts, grand staircases and reception rooms of sequentially increasing opulence. However, the term "Baroque" extends beyond a simple reduction of either style or period.

Diego Rodríguez de Silva y Velázquez (1599–1660) was a Spanish painter who was the leading artist in the court of King Philip IV and one of the most important painters of the Spanish Golden Age. He was an individualistic artist of the contemporary Baroque period and was an important portrait artist. In addition to numerous renditions of scenes of historical and cultural significance, he painted scores of portraits of the Spanish royal family, other notable European figures and commoners. His masterpiece *Las Meninas* was painted in 1656.

Las Meninas by Diego Velázquez

Johann Sebastian Bach (1685 – 1750) was a German composer. He made a virtue of four part harmony in his compositions. Some of his most well known achievements include: the Brandenburg Concertos, the Goldberg Variations and the Mass in B minor.

Gian Lorenzo Bernini (also Gianlorenzo or Giovanni Lorenzo; 1598-1680) was an Italian artist and prominent architect who worked principally in Rome. During his long career, Bernini received numerous important commissions, many of which were associated with the papacy. At an early age, he came to the attention of the sitting pope's nephew, Cardinal Scipione Borghese, and in 1621, at the age of only twenty-three, he was knighted by Pope Gregory XV. Although he did not fare so well during the reign of Innocent X, under Alexander VII, he once again regained favor and continued to be held in high regard by Clement IX.

Born the same year as Johann Sebastian Bach and Domenico Scarlatti, Handel is regarded as one of the greatest composers of the Baroque era, with works such as Water Music, Music for the Royal Fireworks and Messiah, remaining popular to this day. One of his four Coronation Anthems, Zadok the Priest (1727), composed for the coronation of George II of Great Britain, has been performed at every subsequent British coronation, traditionally during the sovereign's anointing. Handel composed more than forty operas in over thirty years, and since the late 1960s, with the revival of baroque music and historically informed musical performance, interest in Handel's operas has grown.

Artistic movements and literature also reflected the outlook and values of commercial and bourgeois society as well as new Enlightenment ideals of political power and citizenship.

Dutch Golden Age painting followed many of the tendencies that dominated Baroque art in other parts of Europe, such as Caravaggism and naturalism, but was in the vanguard in developing still life, landscape and genre painting. Portraiture was also popular, but historical painting, traditionally the most-elevated genre, struggled to find buyers. Church art was virtually non-existent, and little sculpture of any kind was produced. While art collecting and painting for the open market was also common elsewhere, art historians point to the growing number of wealthy Dutch middle-class and successful mercantile patrons as the driving forces in the popularity of pictorial subjects.

This trend, along with the lack of Counter-Reformation church patronage that dominated the arts in Catholic Europe, resulted in the depiction of a great number of scenes from everyday life, genre paintings and other non-secular pictures. Landscapes and seascapes, for example, reflect the land reclaimed from the sea and the sources of trade and naval power that marked the Republic's Golden Age. One subject that is quite characteristic of Dutch Baroque painting is the large group portrait, especially of civic and militia guilds, such as Rembrandt van Rijn's Night Watch. A special genre of still life was the so-called *pronkstilleven* (Dutch for 'ostentatious still life'). This style of ornate still-life painting was developed in the 1640s in Antwerp by Flemish artists like Frans Snyders, Osias Beert and Adriaen van Utrecht. They painted still lives that emphasized abundance by depicting a diversity of objects, fruit, flowers and dead game, often together with living people and animals. The style was soon adopted by artists from the Dutch Republic.

Today, the best-known painters of the Dutch Golden Age are: the period's most well-known figure, Rembrandt; the master of genre from Delft, Johannes Vermeer; the innovative landscape painter Jacob van Ruisdael; and Frans Hals, who infused new life into portraiture. Some notable artistic styles and trends of the time included: Haarlem Mannerism, Utrecht Caravaggism, the School of Delft and Dutch classicism.

Rembrandt Van Rijn was a Dutch painter who lived and worked during the Golden Age. He is broadly recognized as one of the most talented painters in history. Rembrandt studied the human figure in much the same detail as Leonardo Da Vinci, although for different reasons (artistic more than scientific) and with his own unique style. Some of his (many) notable works are: *The Night Watch, The Anatomy Lesson* and *Bathsheba At Her Bath*.

Neoclassicism is the name given to Western movements in the decorative and visual arts, literature, theatre, music and architecture that draw inspiration from the "classical" art and culture of Ancient Greece or Ancient Rome. The main neoclassical movement coincided with the 18th century Age of Enlightenment and continued into the early 19th century, when it competed with Romanticism.

Daniel Defoe (1660–1731), born Daniel Foe, was an English trader, writer, journalist, pamphleteer and spy, most famous for his novel *Robinson Crusoe*. Defoe is notable for being one of the earliest proponents of the novel, as he helped to popularize the form in Britain. A prolific and versatile writer, he wrote more than five hundred books, pamphlets and journals on various topics (including politics, crime, religion, marriage, psychology and the supernatural). He was also a pioneer of economic journalism.

Daniel Defoe, English writer

Jacques Louis David (1748 – 1825) was a French painter in the neoclassical tradition. His most noted works include *The Death of Marat, Napoleon Crossing the Alps* and *The Pantheon in Paris*; the former commemorated one of the pivotal events of the French Revolution – the assassination of Marat Sade. David was an active supporter of the French Revolution and became a friend of Maximilien Robespierre. During the French Republic, David attacked the Academie Des Artes, which was the governing institution of the visual arts. It was reformed to conform with revolutionary beliefs, under David's lead. David's style of portrait was characterized by serious, intense expressions, yet in his many other paintings had Romantic subject matter and the characters in them were full of motion and energy.

While Enlightenment values dominated the world of European ideas, they were challenged by the revival of public sentiment and feeling.

The transition from the Age of Enlightenment (roughly the 18th century) to the early modern age, was the most pivotal moment in history for everyone who has lived in the aftermath of that moment. Philosophy is the basis of how we humans perceive reality and guides all of the decisions we make. At that moment in history, the very model which western philosophers used to produce new works of philosophy, went through a seminal change: Enlightenment philosophers, such as the rationalists and the Empiricists, focused on logical paths to understanding reality. Post-enlightenment philosophers generally dealt with the question of whether or not humans can understand reality. Their answer was generally "no." Enlightenment philosophers debated the place of individual will and personal autonomy in human society, for the first time in human history. Post-Enlightenment philosophers generally focused on the subject of our obligations to each other.

The philosopher who established the model of modern philosophy and whose work was the transition between Enlightenment and the early modern age, was the German philosopher Immanuel Kant (1724 – 1804). On the question of the pursuit of knowledge, Kant rejected the very validity of the debate between the Rationalists and the Empiricists in *The Critique of Pure Reason* (1781). In it, he proposed that humans cannot know reality and that reality in fact is constructed by humans through interpretation. A modern example of this change in the model of philosophy is the Black Swan problem, which has come into vogue within the most recent generation. Simply stated: Science can never know anything with certainty, because it can never exclude the possibility of an outcome which does not fit a theory. If you watch a thousand swans pass by and they are all white, you would conclude that all swans are white. But this does not rule out the possibility that the 1,001st swan could be black. On the question of free will and the individual nature of human beings, Kant rejected these as valid as well, proposing that peace will only come to human beings through the complete substitution of free will with duty to others. Note the similarities between this and all forms of Statism – Marxist philosophy or Nazi fascism. They are examples of how Kant influenced early modern thought. The vast majority of philosophers since Kant have predicated their assumptions on Kant's basic premises.

Rousseau, a French contemporary of Kant, also rejected the Rationalist-Empiricist debate and postulated that intuition and emotion were the paths to enlightenment. Also dovetailing with Kant, Rousseau's most important work was about the need to educate all human beings for citizenship and how to do so – as opposed to developing a young person's sense of autonomy and independence of mind. In art, the Romantic movement emerged as a reaction to rationalist thinking. It was the artistic expression of the new post-Enlightenment, Kantian, type of thinking: It depicted an escape from reality in the form of ideal scenes and events, drawing greatly on existing myths and the romanticized pseudo-history of great nations (ancient Rome and Greece were popular). The subject matter of Romantic art was retrograde – it was enamored with the imaginary past, not the real present or potential future. In politics, movements like nationalism began to emerge, leading to revolutions. As an example of the practical application of Rousseau's sentiment over reason philosophy, politicians (such as Bismarck and Garibaldi) evoked emotional sentiment about perceived common national identities to inspire their revolutions: In fact, it was their greatest weapon, as it would be for Marxists and fascists world-wide in the twentieth century.

Rousseau questioned the exclusive reliance on reason and emphasized the role of emotions in the moral improvement of self and society.

John Dryden, British poet and playwright

Rousseau believed that the savage stage was not the first stage of human development, but the third stage. Rousseau held that this third savage stage of human societal development was an optimum, between the extreme of the state of brute animals and animal-like ape-men on the one hand, and the extreme of decadent civilized life on the other. This has led some critics to attribute to Rousseau the invention of the idea of the noble savage, an expression which was first used in 1672 by British poet John Dryden in his play *The Conquest of Granada*. Rousseau wrote that morality was not a societal construct, but innate, an outgrowth from man's instinctive disinclination to witness suffering, from which arise the emotions of compassion and empathy.

Contrary to what many detractors have claimed, Rousseau never suggested that humans in the state of nature act morally; in fact, terms such as "justice" or "wickedness" were inapplicable to pre-political society as Rousseau understood it. He thought that in morality proper, or self-restraint, could only develop through careful education in a civil state. Humans "in a state of Nature" could act with all of the ferocity of an animal. They were good only in a negative sense, insofar as they were self-sufficient and thus not subject to the vices of political society. Rousseau asserted that except perhaps for brief moments of balance, at or near its inception, when a relative equality among men prevailed, human civilization has always been artificial, resulting in inequality, envy and unnatural desires.

Rousseau's ideas of human development were highly interconnected with forms of mediation, or the processes that individual humans use to interact with themselves and others while using an alternate perspective or thought process. These include a sense of self, morality, pity and imagination. According to Rousseau, these were developed through the innate perfectibility of humanity.

In Rousseau's philosophy, society's negative influence on men centers on its transformation of *amour de soi*, a positive self-love, into *amour propre*, or pride. *Amour de soi* represents the instinctive human desire for self-preservation, combined with the human power of reason. In contrast, *amour-propre* is artificial and encourages man to compare himself to others, thus creating unwarranted fear and allowing men to take pleasure in the pain or weakness of others. Rousseau was not the first to make this distinction.

In the "Discourse on the Arts and Sciences," Rousseau argued that the arts and sciences had not been beneficial to humankind, because they arose not from authentic human needs but rather as a result of pride and vanity. Moreover, the opportunities they created for idleness and luxury contributed to the corruption of man. He proposed that the progress of knowledge had made governments more powerful and had crushed individual liberty; and he concluded that material progress had actually undermined the possibility of true friendship by replacing it with jealousy, fear, and suspicion. In contrast to the optimistic view of other Enlightenment figures, for Rousseau, progress had been inimical to the well-being of humanity, that is, unless it could be counteracted by the cultivation of civic morality and duty.

Only in civil society could man be ennobled—through the use of reason. The passage from the state of nature to the civil state produced a very remarkable change in man, by substituting justice for instinct in his conduct, and imbuing his actions with the morality they had formerly lacked. Only then, when the voice of duty may override his physical impulses and appetites, did man, who so far had considered only himself, find that himself forced to act on different principles, and to consult his reason before listening to his inclinations. Although in the civil state man forfeited some natural advantages, in return he gained others great enough to stimulate, ennoble and uplift him from the state of an uneducated and unimaginative animal to that of an intelligent being and a man. In his essay *Discourse on Inequality* (1754), which elaborated on the ideas introduced in the *Discourse on the Arts and Sciences*, Rousseau traced man's social evolution from a primitive state of nature to modern society. The earliest solitary humans possessed a basic drive for self-preservation and a natural disposition to compassion or pity. They differed from animals, however, in their capacity for free will and their potential perfectibility. As they began to live in groups and form clans, they also began to experience family love, which Rousseau saw as the source of the greatest happiness known to humanity.

As long as differences in wealth and status among families were minimal, the first societies were accompanied by a fleeting golden age of human flourishing. The development of agriculture, metallurgy, private property and the division of labor with the resulting dependency on one another, however, led to economic inequality and conflict. At the same time, as population pressures forced them to associate more closely, people underwent a psychological transformation: they began to see themselves through the eyes of others and came to value the good opinion of others as essential to their self-esteem.

At the end of the *Discourse on Inequality*, Rousseau explains how the desire to have value in the eyes of others comes to undermine personal integrity and authenticity in a society marked by interdependence and hierarchy. In the last chapter of the social contract, Rousseau asks, "What is to be done?" He answers that all men can do is to cultivate virtue in themselves and submit to their lawful rulers. To his readers, however, the inescapable conclusion was that a new and more equitable social contract was needed. Thus, society corrupted men only insofar as the social contract has not de facto succeeded.

Revolution, war and rebellion demonstrated the emotional power of mass politics and nationalism.

The more precise characterization and specific definition of Romanticism has been the subject of debate in the fields of intellectual history and literary history throughout the 20th century, and a consensus has yet to emerge. That it was part of the Counter-Enlightenment, a reaction against the Age of Enlightenment, is generally accepted. Its relationship to the French Revolution, which began in the very early stages of the period in 1789, is clearly important. But the definition of Romanticism is highly variable from region to region and according to one's individual reaction to it. Most Romantics were broadly progressive in their views. But a considerable number always had, or developed, a wide range of conservative views, and nationalism was strongly associated with Romanticism in many countries.

In philosophy and the history of ideas, Romanticism disrupted the classic Western traditions of rationality for over a century. The idea of moral absolutes and monolithic values led to nationalism, fascism and totalitarianism. In Northern Europe, the Early Romantic visionary optimism and belief that the world was in the process of great change and improvement had largely vanished, and some art became more conventionally political and polemical as its creators engaged polemically with the world as it was. Elsewhere, including in very different ways the United States and Russia, feelings that great change was underway or just about to come were still present. Displays of intense emotion in art remained prominent, as did the exotic and historical settings pioneered by the Romantics. But experimentation with form and technique was generally reduced, often replaced with meticulous technique, as in the poems of Tennyson or in many paintings of the time.

Illustration to Tennyson's poem, "Oenone"

Romanticism emerged as a challenge to Enlightenment rationality.

Romanticism (also known as the Romantic era or the Romantic period) is an artistic, literary and intellectual movement that emerged at the end of the 18th century. In most areas it reached its peak between1800 and 1850. In part, it was a reaction to the Industrial Revolution, the scientific rationalization of nature and the aristocratic, social and political norms of the Enlightenment Age. It was most strongly embodied in the arts, music and literature, though also had a major impact on historiography, education and natural sciences. Romanticism had a significant and complex effect on politics: while it was associated with liberalism and radicalism for much of the Romantic period, its long-term effects on the growth of nationalism were more significant.

The movement emphasized intense emotion as the source of aesthetic experience. It considered folk art and ancient customs to be noble, though also valued spontaneity, as in the musical impromptu. As opposed to the rational and Classicist ideal models, Romanticism revived medieval elements of art in an attempt to escape the effects of industrialism, population growth and urban sprawl.

Example of Romantic art

Although the movement was rooted in the German *"Sturm und Drang"* (Storm and Drive) movement, which preferred intuition and emotion to the rationalism of the Enlightenment, the events and ideologies of the French Revolution were also influences. Romanticism assigned a high value to the achievements of "heroic" individualists and artists, because it was believed that they would elevate the quality of society. It also promoted the individual imagination as a critical authority and allowed it the freedom from classical notions of form in art. There was a strong recourse to historical and natural inevitability, a Zeitgeist, in the representation of its ideas. In the second half of the 19th century, Realism was offered as a polar opposite to Romanticism. The decline of Romanticism during this time was associated with multiple processes, including social and political changes and the spread of nationalism.

Period 2: 1648-1815

Key Concept 2.4: The experiences of everyday life were shaped by demographic, environmental, medical and technological changes.

The legacies of the 16th-century population explosion, which roughly doubled the European population, were social disruptions and demographic disasters that persisted into the 18th century. Volatile weather in the 17th century harmed agricultural production. In some localities, recurring food shortages caused undernourishment that combined with disease to produce periodic spikes in the mortality rate. By the 17th century, the European marriage pattern, which limited family size, became the most important check on population levels, although some couples adopted birth control practices to limit family size. By the middle of the 18th century, better weather, improvements in transportation, new crops and agricultural practices, less epidemic disease and advances in medicine and hygiene allowed much of Europe to escape from the cycle of famines that had caused repeated demographic disaster. By the end of the 18th century, reductions in child mortality and increases in life expectancy constituted the demographic underpinnings of new attitudes toward children and families.

Particularly in western Europe, the demographic revolution, along with the rise in prosperity, produced advances in material well-being that did not stop with the economic: Greater prosperity was associated with increasing literacy, education and rich cultural lives (the growth of publishing and libraries, the founding of schools and the establishment of orchestra, theaters and museums). By the end of the 18th century, it was evident that a high proportion of Europeans were better fed, healthier, lived longer, and were more secure than at any previous time in human history. This relative prosperity was balanced by increasing numbers of the poor throughout Europe, who strained charitable resources and alarmed government officials and local communities.

In the 17th century, small land holdings, low-productivity agricultural practices, poor transportation and adverse weather limited and disrupted the food supply, which caused periodic famines. By the 18th century, Europeans began to escape from the Malthusian imbalance between population and the food supply, which resulted in steady population growth.

The General Crisis of the 17th century in Europe was marked by widespread economic distress, social unrest and population decline. A significant cause of mankind's woes during these times was the climate-induced reduction in agricultural production. Agricultural production and food supply per capita both declined due to changes in temperature. In the five to thirty years after this reduction in food supply there were social disturbances, wars, mass migrations, epidemics and famines; all of which can be directly or indirectly linked back to the change in temperature.

The economic chaos, famine and war led people to emigrate, and Europe saw peak migration overlapping with the time of peak social disturbance. This widespread migration, in conjunction with declining health caused by poor nutrition, facilitated the spread of epidemics. The number of plagues peaked during the period of 1550–1670. As a result of war fatalities and famine, the population declined. In the 18th century, the mild climate improved matters considerably, leading to the speedy recovery of both Europe's economy and its population.

Reverend Thomas Robert Malthus, founder of Malthusianism

Malthusianism is a school of ideas derived from the political/economic thought of the Reverend Thomas Robert Malthus, as laid out in his 1798 work, "An Essay on the Principle of Population," which describes how unchecked population growth is exponential while the growth of the food supply was expected to be arithmetical. Malthus believed there were two types of "checks" that could reduce the population, thereby returning it to a more sustainable level. He believed there were preventive checks, such as moral restraints (abstinence, delayed marriage until finances become balanced) and restricting marriage from persons suffering from poverty and/or defects. Malthus also believed in positive checks, which lead to premature death (disease, starvation, war) and resulted in what is called "a Malthusian catastrophe." The catastrophe would reduce a population to a more sustainable, level. The term has been applied in different ways over the last two hundred years and has been linked to a variety of other political and social movements, but almost always refers to advocates of population control.

By the middle of the 18th century, higher agricultural productivity and improved transportation increased the food supply, allowing populations to grow and reducing the number of demographic crises (a process known as the Agricultural Revolution).

The British Agricultural Revolution was the unprecedented increase in agricultural production in England due to increases in labor and land productivity between the mid-17th and late 19th centuries. Agricultural output grew faster than the population until 1770, and thereafter England's productivity remained among the highest in the world. The increase in the food supply contributed to the rapid growth of population in England and Wales, from 5.5 million people in 1700 to over 9 million people by 1801. Domestic production increasingly gave way to food imports in the 19th century as the population more than tripled to over 32 million people. The rise in productivity accelerated the decline of the agricultural share of the labor force, adding to the urban work force on which industrialization depended: the Agricultural Revolution has therefore been cited as a cause of the Industrial Revolution.

One of the most important innovations of the British Agricultural Revolution was the development of the Norfolk four-course rotation, which greatly increased crop and livestock yields by improving soil fertility and reducing the number of rotations in which a field would be left fallow. The farmers in Flanders (in parts of France and current day Belgium) discovered a still more effective four-field crop rotation system, using turnips and clover (a legume) as forage crops to replace the three-year crop rotation fallow year. Turnips can be grown in winter and are deep rooted, allowing them to gather minerals unavailable to shallow rooted crops. Clover changes nitrogen from the atmosphere into a form of fertilizer. This permit the intensive arable cultivation of light soil on enclosed farms and provided fodder to support increased numbers of livestock, whose manure further added to the soil's fertility.

Turnips first show up in the probate records in England as early as 1638, but were not widely grown until about 1750. Fallow land constituted around 20 percent of the arable area in England in 1700 before turnips and clover were extensively grown. Guano and nitrates from South America were introduced in the mid-19th century and fallow land steadily declined to about 4 percent in 1900. Ideally, wheat, barley, turnips and clover would be planted in that order in each field in successive years. The turnips helped keep the weeds down and were an excellent forage crop—ruminant animals could eat their tops and roots through a large part of the summer and winters. There was no need to let the soil lie fallow as clover would return nitrates (nitrogen-containing salts) back to the soil. The clover made excellent pasture and hay fields, as well as green manure, when it was ploughed under after one or two years. The addition of clover and turnips allowed more animals to be kept through the winter, which in turn produced more milk, cheese, meat and manure, which maintained soil fertility.

John Loudon McAdam, Scottish engineer, pioneer of macadam road construction

High wagon transportation costs made it uneconomical to ship commodities very far outside the market radius via road, generally limiting shipment to less than twenty or thirty miles to a market or to a navigable waterway. Water transport was, and in some cases still is, much more efficient than land transport. In the early 19th century, it cost as much to transport a ton of freight thirty-two miles by wagon over an unimproved road as it did to ship it 3,000 miles across the Atlantic. A horse could pull at most one ton of freight on a macadam road (a multi-layer stone-covered and crowned road with side drainage, invented around 1820). But a single horse could pull a barge weighing over thirty tons.

Commerce was aided by the expansion of roads and inland waterways. Road transport capacity grew exponentially from 1500 to 1700, increasing fourfold over this time period. Railroads would eventually reduce the cost of land transport by over 95 percent; however, they did not become important until after 1850.

In the 18th century, the plague disappeared as a major epidemic disease and inoculation reduced smallpox mortality.

Local outbreaks of the plague are grouped into three plague pandemics: the first plague pandemic from 541 to 750, which spread from Egypt to the Mediterranean (starting with the Plague of Justinian) and Northwestern Europe; the second plague pandemic from 1345 to 1840, which spread from Central Asia to the Mediterranean and Europe (starting with the Black Death), and probably also to China; and the third plague pandemic from 1866 to 1960, which spread from China to various places around the world, notably India and the West Coast of the United States.

The English physician Edward Jenner demonstrated the effectiveness of cowpox to protect humans from smallpox in 1796, after which attempts were made to eliminate smallpox on a regional scale. The vaccine was introduced to the New World in Trinity, Newfoundland in 1800 by Dr. John Clinch, a boyhood friend and medical colleague of Jenner. As early as 1803, the Spanish Crown organized the Balmis expedition to transport the vaccine to the Spanish colonies in the Americas and the Philippines in order to establish mass vaccination programs there.

The U.S. Congress passed the Vaccine Act of 1813 to ensure that a safe smallpox vaccine would be available to the American public. By about 1817, an effective state vaccination program existed in the Dutch East Indies. In British India, a program was launched to propagate smallpox vaccination by Indian vaccinators, under the supervision of European officials. Nevertheless, British vaccination efforts in India, and Burma in particular, were hampered by distrust of vaccination, despite education efforts, tough legislation and improvements in the local efficacy of the vaccine and vaccine preservative.

By 1832, the federal government of the United States established a smallpox vaccination program for Native Americans. In 1842, the United Kingdom banned inoculation, but later progressed to a policy of mandatory vaccination. The British government introduced compulsory smallpox vaccination by an Act of Parliament in 1853. In the United States, between 1843 and 1855, first Massachusetts, and then other states, began to require smallpox vaccination. Although some disliked these mandatory measures, coordinated efforts against smallpox continued, and the disease continued to diminish in wealthy countries. By 1897, smallpox had largely been eliminated from the United States.

The consumer revolution of the 18th century was shaped by a new concern for privacy, encouraged the purchase of new goods for homes and created new venues for leisure activities.

The term consumer revolution refers to the period from approximately 1600 to 1750 in England in which there was a marked increase in the consumption and variety of luxury goods and products by individuals from different economic and social backgrounds. The consumer revolution marked a departure from the traditional mode of life characterized by frugality and scarcity to one of increasing mass consumption in society. The consumer society emerged in the late 17th century and intensified throughout the 18th century. Change was propelled by the growing middle-class, who embraced new ideas about luxury consumption and the growing importance of fashion, rather than necessity, as the arbiter for purchasing.

This revolution encompassed the growth in construction of vast country estates specifically designed to cater to comfort and the increased availability of luxury goods aimed at a growing market. These included sugar, tobacco, tea and coffee, which were increasingly grown on vast plantations in the Caribbean as demand steadily rose. In particular, sugar consumption in Britain during the course of the 18th century increased by a factor of 20. Moreover, the expansion of trade and markets also contributed to the burgeoning consumer revolution, by increasing the variety of goods that could be made available to the affluent portion of society.

This pattern was particularly visible in London, where the gentry and prosperous merchants took up residence and created a culture of luxury and consumption that was slowly extended across the socio-economic divide. Marketplaces expanded as shopping centers appeared, such as the New Exchange which was opened in 1609 by Robert Cecil in the Strand. Shops started to become important places for Londoners to meet and socialize and they became popular destinations alongside the theatre. London also saw the erection of luxury buildings, designed by architects like Nicholas Barbon and Lionel Cranfield, as indicators of social status.

Nicholas Barbon, architect and economist

There was growth in industries like glassmaking and silk manufacturing, and much pamphleteering of the time was devoted to justifying that people's private vice for luxury goods was for the greater public good. Bernard Mandeville's influential work The Fable of the Bees, which was published in 1714, was quite controversial because he argued that a country's prosperity ultimately lay in the self-interest of the consumer. These trends accelerated in the 18th century, as rising prosperity and social mobility increased the number of people with disposable income. Important shifts included the marketing of goods for individuals, as opposed to items for the household, and the marketing of goods as status symbols, related to changes in fashion and the desire for aesthetic appeal, as opposed to just their utility.

The pottery innovator and entrepreneur, Josiah Wedgewood, noticed the way aristocratic fashions, themselves subject to periodic changes in direction, slowly filtered down through society. He pioneered the use of marketing techniques to influence and manipulate the direction of the prevailing tastes and preferences to make his goods appealing to the aristocracy; it was only a matter of time before his goods were being purchased by the newly moneyed middle class as well as his traditional patrons. His business model was followed by producers of a wide range of products, which added to the growth of the post-sustenance consumption economy.

Josiah Wedgewood, potter and businessman

By the 18th century, family and private life reflected new demographic patterns and the effects of the commercial revolution.

With the onset of the Agricultural and Industrial Revolution in the late 18th century, this relationship was finally broken. An unprecedented growth in the urban population took place over the course of the 19th century, both through continued migration from the countryside and the tremendous demographic expansion that occurred at that time. In England, the urban population jumped from 17 percent in 1801 to 72 percent in 1891 (for other countries the figure was: 37 percent in France, 41 percent in Prussia and 28 percent in the United States).

The change leading to this state in Europe was the Agricultural Revolution of the 18th century, which was initially quite slow. The decline in the death rate was due to two factors: first, improvements in the food supply brought about by improved agricultural practices and better transportation prevented death due to starvation and lack of water. Agricultural improvements included crop rotation, selective breeding and seed drill technology. The second stage of significant improvements in public health reduced mortality, particularly that of infants and children. These were not so much medical breakthroughs as they were improvements in water supply, sewerage, food handling and general personal hygiene that stemming from growing scientific knowledge of the causes of disease. This was all aided by an increase in the education of mothers, who were still (largely) viewed as only having a role in the domestic portion of life.

A consequence of the decline in mortality was an increasingly rapid rise in population growth (a "population explosion"), as the gap between deaths and births grew wider. This change in the health of the population occurred in Northwestern Europe during the 19th century due to the Industrial Revolution. Another consequence of declining mortality was a change in the age structure of the population. Previously, the majority of deaths were among children in the first five to ten years of life. Therefore, more than anything else, the decline in death rates entailed the increasing survival of children. Hence, the age structure of the population became increasingly younger and more of these children were able to survive and enter the reproductive cycle of their lives while maintaining the high fertility rates of their parents. The bottom of the "age pyramid" widened first and accelerated population growth.

Although the rate of illegitimate births increased in the 18th century, population growth was limited by the European marriage pattern and, in some areas, by the early practice of birth control.

Birth control became a contested political issue in Britain during the 19th century. The economist Thomas Malthus argued in "An Essay on the Principle of Population" (1798) that population growth generally expanded in times and regions of plenty until the size of the population relative to the primary resources caused distress. He demonstrated that two types of checks hold population within resource limits: positive checks, which raise the death rate, and preventive checks, which lower the birth rate. The positive checks included hunger, disease and war; the preventive checks included abortion, birth control, resort to prostitutes, postponement of marriage and celibacy. Malthus later clarified his view that if society relied on human misery to limit population growth, then sources of misery (e.g., hunger, disease and war) would inevitably afflict society, as would volatile economic cycles. On the other hand, "preventive checks" to population that limited birth rates, such as later marriages, could ensure a higher standard of living for all, while also increasing economic stability.

His ideas came to carry great weight in British political debate in the 19th century, and they heavily influenced the movement toward the adoption of laissez-faire liberal capitalism. Malthusians were in favor of limiting population growth and began actively promoting birth control. The term "voluntary motherhood" was coined by feminists in the 1870s as a political critique of "involuntary motherhood" and as a way to express a desire for women's emancipation. Advocates for voluntary motherhood disapproved of contraception, arguing that women should only engage in sex for the purpose of procreation and advocated periodic or permanent abstinence.

Annie Besant, publisher of Fruits of Philosophy

In contrast, the birth control movement advocated for contraception so as to permit sexual intercourse as desired without the risk of pregnancy. By emphasizing "control," the birth control movement argued that women should have control over whether or not they would reproduce; the movement was closely tied to the emerging feminist movement. The Malthusian League was established in 1877 and promoted the education of the public about the importance of family planning and advocated for the elimination of penalties against the promoters of birth control. It was initially founded during the "Knowlton trial" of Annie Besant and Charles Bradlaugh in July 1877. They were prosecuted for publishing Charles Knowlton's *Fruits of Philosophy* which explained various methods of birth control. The trial of Bradlaugh and Besant counter-productively triggered a wave of public interest in contraception, and sales of Knowlton's book surged. Starting in the 1880s, birth rates began to drop steadily in industrialized countries, as women married later and families in urban living conditions increasingly favored having fewer children.

As infant and child mortality decreased and commercial wealth increased, families dedicated more space and resources to children and child-rearing, as well as private life and comfort.

Economic progress led to an improvement of everyday life and to increased life expectancy. The advantages of the domestic system were that workers could work at their own speed while at home, and children working under this system were better treated than they would have been in the factory system, although the homes were polluted by the toxins from the raw materials. As the woman of a family usually worked at home, someone was often there to look after the children. The domestic system is often cited as one of the causes of the rise of the nuclear family in Europe, as the large profits gained by common people made them less dependent on their extended family. These considerable sums of money also led to a much wealthier peasantry with more furniture, higher-quality food and better clothing than they had previously. The domestic system was largely centered in Western Europe and did not take a strong hold in Eastern Europe.

Cities offered economic opportunities, which attracted increasing migration from rural areas, transforming urban life and creating challenges for new urbanites and their families.

In terms of the social structure, the Industrial Revolution witnessed the triumph of a middle class of industrialists and businessmen over a landed class of nobility and gentry. Ordinary working people found increased opportunities for employment in new mills and factories, but these were often under strict working conditions with long hours of labor dominated by a pace set by machines. As late as the year 1900, most industrial workers in the United States still worked a ten-hour day (twelve hours in the steel industry), while earning from 20 to 40 percent less than the minimum deemed necessary for a decent life. However, harsh working conditions were prevalent long before the Industrial Revolution took place. Pre-industrial society was, in general, very static and often cruel—child labor, dirty living conditions and long working hours were more prevalent than during the Industrial Revolution.

Industrialization led to the creation of the factory. Arguably the first highly mechanized factory was John Lombe's water-powered silk mill in Derby, England, which was operational by 1721. Lombe learned silk thread manufacturing by taking a job in Italy and acting as an industrial spy; however, since the silk industry there was a closely guarded secret, he was unable to acquire the knowledge he needed to reproduce the silk industry on an industrial level in England. Because Lombe's factory was not successful, there were no immediate attempts to follow his path of industrialization. Therefore, the large scale rise of the modern factory began at a later date, when the process of cotton spinning had been mechanized.

The factory system contributed to the growth of urban areas, as large numbers of workers migrated into cities in search of work in factories. Nowhere was this better illustrated than the mills and associated industries of Manchester, nicknamed "Cottonopolis," and the world's first industrial city. Manchester experienced a six-fold increase in its population between 1771 and 1831. Bradford grew by 50 percent every ten years between 1811 and 1851, and by 1851 only 50 percent of the population of Bradford had actually been born there. For much of the 19th century, production was done in small mills, which were typically water-powered and built to serve local needs. Later, each factory had its own steam engine and a chimney to provide an efficient draft through its boiler.

Robert Owen, reformer

The transition to industrialization was not without difficulty. For example, a group of English workers known as Luddites formed to protest industrialization and sometimes sabotaged factories. In other industries the transition to factory production was not so divisive. Some industrialists themselves tried to improve factory and living conditions for their workers. One of the earliest such reformers was Robert Owen, known for his pioneering efforts in improving conditions for workers at the New Lanark mills, and often regarded as one of the key thinkers of the early socialist movement. By 1746, an integrated brass mill was working at Warmley near Bristol. Raw material went in at one end, was smelted into brass and was turned into pans, pins, wire and other goods. Housing was provided for workers on site. Josiah Wedgwood and Matthew Boulton (whose Soho Manufactory was completed in 1766) were other prominent early industrialists who employed the factory system.

The Agricultural Revolution produced more food using fewer workers; as a result, people migrated from rural areas to the cities in search of work.

The process of enclosing property accelerated in the 15th and 16th centuries. The more productive enclosed farms meant that fewer farmers were needed to work the same land, leaving many villagers without land and grazing rights. Many of them moved to cities in search of work in the emerging factories of the Industrial Revolution. Others settled in the English colonies. English Poor Laws were enacted to help these newly poor.

The Industrial Revolution changed a mainly rural society into an urban one; however, this was not always true, as evidenced by the varying levels of urbanization in Northern and Southern Belgium. During the Middle Ages and the Early Modern Period, the lowland region of Flanders (Northern Belgium) had been characterized by the presence of large urban centers. At the beginning of the 19th century, Flanders, with more than 30 percent of the population city-dwellers, was one of the most urbanized regions in the world. By comparison, this proportion reached only 17 percent in Wallonia (southern Belgium), barely 10 percent in most West European countries, 16 percent in France and 25 percent in Britain.

By the 19th century, industrialization did not affect the traditional urban infrastructure, except in Ghent. Also, in Wallonia, the traditional urban network was largely unaffected by the industrialization process, even though the proportion of city-dwellers rose from 17 to 45 percent between 1831 and 1910. Especially in the Haine, Sambre and Meuse valleys, between the Borinage and Liège, where there was large-scale industrial development based on coal-mining and iron-making, urbanization was rapid. During these eighty years the number of municipalities with more than 5,000 inhabitants increased from only 21 to more than 100, concentrating nearly half of the Walloon population in this region.

Nevertheless, industrialization remained quite traditional in the sense that it did not lead to the growth of modern and large urban centers, but to a conurbation of industrial villages and towns developed around a coal-mine or a factory. ("Conurbation" is when municipalities merge because of their growth.) Communication routes between these small centers only became populous later and with a much less dense urban morphology than, for instance, the area around Liège where the old town was there to direct migratory flows.

The growth of cities eroded traditional communal values, and city governments strained to provide protection and a healthy environment.

The 18th century saw the rapid growth in voluntary hospitals in England. The latter part of the century brought the establishment of the basic pattern of improvements in public health over the next two centuries: a social evil was identified, it was brought to the attention of private philanthropists (who were those who had become wealthy in business), and changing public opinion led to government action.

James Lind, Scottish doctor

The practice of vaccination became prevalent around 1800, following the pioneering work of Edward Jenner in treating smallpox. James Lind's discovery of the causes of scurvy amongst sailors and its mitigation via the introduction of fruit on lengthy voyages, was published in 1754 and led to the adoption of this practice by the Royal Navy. Efforts were also made to promulgate health matters to the broader public; in 1752 the British physician Sir John Pringle published "Observations on the Diseases of the Army in Camp and Garrison," in which he advocated for the importance of adequate ventilation in military barracks and the provision of latrines for soldiers.

With the onset of the Industrial Revolution, living standards amongst the working population began to worsen, due to cramped and unsanitary conditions in urban areas. In the first four decades of the 19th century alone, London's population doubled and even greater growth rates were recorded in new industrial towns, such as Leeds and Manchester. This rapid urbanization exacerbated the spread of disease in the large conurbations that built up around workhouses and factories. These settlements were cramped and primitive and had no organized sanitation systems. Disease was inevitable and its incubation in these areas was a concomitant of the unhealthy lifestyle of the inhabitants. The lack of access to housing led to a rapid growth of slums and the per capita death rate began to rise to alarming levels, almost doubling in Birmingham and Liverpool. Thomas Malthus had warned of the dangers of overpopulation in 1798. His ideas, as well as those of Jeremy Bentham, became very influential in government circles in the early years of the 19th century.

The first attempts at sanitary reform and the establishment of public health institutions were made in the 1840s. Thomas Southwood Smith, a physician at the London Fever Hospital, began to write papers on the importance of public health and was one of the first physicians brought in to give evidence before the Poor Law Commission in the 1830s, along with Neil Arnott and James Phillips Kay. Smith advised the government on the importance of quarantine and sanitary improvement in limiting the spread of infectious diseases, such as cholera and yellow fever.

The Poor Law Commission reported in 1838 that the expenditures necessary to the adoption and maintenance of measures of prevention would ultimately amount to less than the cost of the disease that was constantly engendered. It recommended the implementation of large scale government engineering projects to alleviate the conditions that allowed for the propagation of disease. The Health of Towns Association was formed in Exeter on December 11, 1844, and vigorously campaigned for the development of public health in the United Kingdom. Its formation followed the 1843 establishment of the Health of Towns Commission chaired by Sir Edwin Chadwick, which produced a series of reports on the poor and unsanitary conditions in British cities.

These national and local movements led to the Public Health Act, passed in 1848. It aimed to improve the sanitary condition of towns and heavily populated areas in England and Wales, by placing the supply of water, sewerage, drainage, cleansing and paving under a single local body with the General Board of Health as a central authority. The Act was passed by the Liberal government of Lord John Russell, in response to the urging of Edwin Chadwick. Chadwick's seminal report on "The Sanitary Condition of the Labouring Population" was published in 1842 and was followed by a supplementary report a year later.

Vaccination for various diseases was made compulsory in the United Kingdom in 1851, and by 1871 legislation required a comprehensive system of registration run by appointed vaccination officers. Further interventions were made by a series of subsequent Public Health Acts, notably the 1875 Act. Reforms included latrinization (installation of public restrooms), the building of sewers, the regular collection of garbage followed by incineration or disposal in a landfill, the provision of clean water and the draining of standing water to prevent the breeding of mosquitoes. So began the inception of the modern public health movement.

The concentration of the poor in cities led to a greater awareness of poverty, crime and prostitution as social problems, and prompted increased efforts to police marginal groups.

London and other European cities were fast reaching a size unprecedented in world history, due to the onset of the Industrial Revolution. It became clear that the locally maintained system of volunteer constables and "watchmen" was ineffective, both in detecting and preventing crime. A parliamentary committee was appointed to investigate the system of policing in London. Upon his appointment to the position of Home Secretary in 1822, Sir Robert Peel established a second and more effective committee, and acted upon its findings. Royal assent to the Metropolitan Police Act was given, and the Metropolitan Police Service was established in London in September of 1829 as the first modern and professional police force in the world.

Peel, widely regarded as the father of modern policing, was heavily influenced by the social and legal philosophy of Jeremy Bentham, who called for a strong and centralized, but politically neutral, police force that maintained social order, protected people from crime and acted as a visible deterrent to urban crime and disorder. Peel decided to standardize the police force as an official paid profession, to organize it in a civilian fashion and to make it answerable to the public.

Sir Robert Peel, Home Secretary of Great Britain

The 1829 Metropolitan Police Act created a modern police force by limiting the purview of the force and its powers, and envisioning it as merely an organ of the judicial system. Their job was apolitical; to maintain the peace and apprehend criminals for the courts to process according to the law. This was very different from the Continental model of the police force that had developed in France, where the police worked within the parameters of the absolutist state as an extension of the authority of the monarch and functioned as part of the governing state.

In 1863, the Metropolitan Police were issued the distinctive custodian helmet, and in 1884 they began using whistles that could be heard from a distance. The Metropolitan Police became a model for the urban police forces in most countries, such as the United States and most of the British Empire.

This page was intentionally left blank

We want to hear from you

Your feedback is important to us because we strive to provide the highest quality prep materials. If you have any questions, comments or suggestions, email us, so we can incorporate your feedback into future editions.

Customer Satisfaction Guarantee

If you have any concerns about this book, including printing issues, contact us and we will resolve any issues to your satisfaction.

info@sterling-prep.com

Period 3: c. 1815 to c. 1914

Major historical events of the period:

1800s: The Great Divergence begins; Laissez-faire economic thought becomes prominent component of European liberalism

c. 1815-1871: Italian unification process

1815-1914: Congress of Europe balance of power system enforced

c. 1818: Conservatism philosophy emerges

1820s: Greek War of Independence

1825: The Decembrist Revolt in Russia

1830: Second French Revolution of 1830

1830-1831: Polish officers and citizens revolt against Russian rule in The November Uprising

1840s: The European Potato Failure

c. 1847-1848: Marxism political thought emerges

1848: The Revolutions of 1848

c. 1848: Realism art movement begins

1850s: Pan-Slavism nationalist thought develops in Russia; women's suffrage movement emerges in Europe; naturalism literary movement emerges

1850-1900: Political parties develop throughout Europe

1850s-1950s: Growing indigenous resistance in Africa and India against Brittish colonialism

1853-1856: The Crimean War

1860s: Impressionism art movement emerges

1866: The Austro-Prussian War

1870-1871: The Franco-Prussian War

1870s-1914: The New Imperialism movement and The Scramble for Africa

1871: Unification of Germany is accomplished

1873-1896: The Long Depression

1878: Congress of Berlin redraws Balkan political map

1880s: Modernism movement emerges

1890s: Zionism nationalist movement gains traction; primitivism art movement emerges

1890s-1900s: The anti-imperialism movement emerges

1905: The Revolution of 1905 in Russia

1912: Italy annexes Libya and the Dodecanese islands

1912-1913: The First Balkan War

Period 3: 1815-1914

Key Concept 3.1: The industrial revolution spread from Great Britain to the continent, where the state played a greater role in promoting industry.

The transition from an agricultural to an industrial economy began in Britain in the 18th century, spread to France and Germany between 1850 and 1870, and finally to Russia in the 1890s. The governments of those countries actively supported industrialization. In southern and eastern Europe, some pockets of industry developed, surrounded by traditional agrarian economies. Although continental nations sought to borrow from and in some instances imitate the British model—the success of which was demonstrated at the Crystal Palace Exhibition in 1851—each nation's experience of industrialization was shaped by its own matrix of geographic, social and political factors. For example, the legacy of the revolution in France led to a more gradual adoption of mechanization in production, ensuring a more incremental industrialization that was the case in Britain. Despite the creation of a customs union in the 1830s, Germany's lack of political unity hindered its industrial development. However, following unification in 1871, the German Empire quickly came to challenge British dominance in key industries, such as steel, coal and chemicals.

Beginning in the 1870s, the European economy fluctuated widely because of the vagaries of financial markets. Continental states responded by assisting and protecting the development of national industry in a variety of ways, the most important being protective tariffs, military procurements, and colonial conquests. Key economic stakeholders, such as corporations and industrialists, expected governments to promote economic development by subsidizing ports, transportation and new inventions; registering patents and sponsoring education and preventing labor strikes. State intervention reached its culmination in the 20th century, when some governments took over direction of the entire process of industrial development under the pressure of war and depression and/or from ideological commitments.

Great Britain established its industrial dominance through the mechanism of textile production, iron and steel production and new transportation systems.

During the industrial revolution, Great Britain offered many of the necessary foundations for entrepreneurs to be successful. The clearest was due to the peaceful union of England and Scotland which allowed for efficient, barrier-free trade between the once two nations and an extensive coastline and river system to share. Britain's legal factors included a system that allowed for free-market capitalism and joint-stock companies to form, as well as the "rule of law" in which the sanctity of contracts were honored.

Industrial scene from the United Kingdom showing ironworks

The increased liberalization of trade, with an already existing merchant base, allowed Britain to produce and use emerging scientific and technological developments more effectively than countries that maintained an absolutist monarchy as a mode of governance. Britain emerged from the Napoleonic Wars as the only European nation not ravaged by financial plunder and economic collapse of the homeland during the campaign, and having the only merchant fleet of any useful size (European merchant fleets had been destroyed during the war by the Royal Navy). Britain's extensive, export-oriented cottage industries also ensured that markets were readily available for many early forms of manufactured goods. The conflict resulted in most British warfare being conducted overseas, reducing the devastating effects of territorial conquest that affected much of

Europe. This was further aided by Britain's geographical position as an island separated from Continental Europe.

Britain's success in the Industrial Revolution was also due to a confluence of dense natural resources in the North of England, the English Midlands, South Wales and the Scottish Lowlands. This meant that coal, iron, lead, copper, tin, limestone and water power were locally and abundantly available, creating excellent resource conditions in which industries could expand. Additionally, the moist climate of northwest England was ideal for the spinning of cotton, which made it the perfect environment for a textile industry boom.

Great Britain also had a dense population compared to its geological size; a full labor force was ready to meet the new demands of industrial innovation. The above-mentioned political stability that began in 1688, produced a society very receptive to change; most rural resistance to industrialization was quelled by the Enclosure movement, and the landed gentry established commercial interests that lead to the abolition of obstacles against capitalism.

Seventy percent of European urbanization occurred in Britain between 1750 and 1800. Britain's population grew 280 percent from the years 1550 to 1820, while the rest of Western Europe grew only 50 to 80 percent. By 1800, only the Netherlands was more urbanized than Britain. This occurred due to a change in land allocation in which wood grown for homes was replaced by mined brick and slate and as such that land could then be used to feed the population. Additional land would be freed up once chemical fertilizers replaced manure, and once work traditionally done by horses could be mechanized; a workhorse needed three to five acres to graze upon, while even the early steam engines produced four times more mechanical energy than the horse, without needing the maintenance that a living animal requires.

By 1700, five-sixths of coal mined worldwide was in Britain. Despite having Europe's most urbanized, literate, and lowest taxed population, the Netherlands had no coal, and thus failed to industrialize on par with Great Britain. In fact during this time, the Netherlands was the only European country to see its city and population size shrink. By the 1830s, Britain would have run out of suitable river sites to build new mills on; however, it had the power of coal to continue its industrialization.

Britain's ready supplies of coal, iron ore, and other essential raw materials promoted industrial growth.

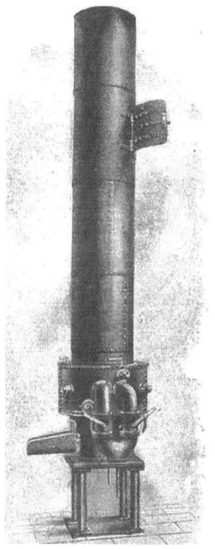

Cupola furnace

During the era of the Industrial Revolution, wood and other bio-fuels were replaced by coal and a great change in the metal industries followed. Smelting with coal had begun before the Industrial Revolution from 1678 on through innovation by Sir Clement Clerke and others who used coal reverberatory furnaces known as *cupolas*. The cupolas worked by using the flames fed by ore and charcoal (from wood) to reduce oxidization of a metal. However, coal required much less manpower to mine than cutting down trees and converting the wood to charcoal. Coal was also more readily available than wood. For any given amount of heat produced, coal was far more labor-effective. Coal also had the advantage that impurities in it do not transfer into the metal when heated by it. This technology was applied to lead (starting in 1678), to copper (from 1687 on) and to iron (in the 1690s).

In Coalbrookdale in 1709, Abraham Darby used innovative blast furnaces fueled by coke. The coke pig iron he created was mostly used to produce cast iron goods such as kettles and pots. Coke pig iron was not used to make bar iron until the mid-1750s, when his son Abraham Darby II built Horsehay and Ketley furnaces. By then, coke pig iron was less expensive than charcoal pig iron. In 1778, Abraham Darby III used the increasingly cheaper and abundant cast iron as a structural material following the construction of the Iron Bridge.

To meet these demands, Britain's natural supply of iron was supplemented by imports, most notably from Sweden in the mid-17th century, and later from Russia to the end of the 1720s. After 1785 however, imports ceased to be necessary as new iron-making technology was developed, and Britain then became an exporter of bar iron and wrought iron goods.

The most influential development of the 1800s was *hot blast* for saving energy during pig iron production; by using the waste exhaust heat to preheat combustion air, the amount of fuel needed to produce a bar of pig iron was cut by one-third using coal and by two-thirds using coke. As the technology improved, these ratios improved even more. Hot blast also increased the capacity of furnaces by raising the operating temperatures.

Due to the increasing efficiency, manufacturers could use less fuel. Using less coal or coke meant that even less impurities would transfer into the finished pig iron product. This gave way to the possibility of using lower quality (less costly) coal or *anthracite* in places where coking coal was not available or too expensive. However, transportation costs dropped tremendously by the end of the 19th century, making this advantage fleeting.

Before the Industrial Revolution, steel was an expensive commodity and only used where iron could not be (i.e., edge cutting tools or springs). However, two decades before the industrial era, an innovation in the production of steel was made. The raw material for steel was *blister steel* which was made during the cementation process.

The advancements and innovations in metallurgy produced inexpensive iron and steel. Suddenly, the ability to make nails, hinges, wires and other hardware boosted a number of other industries. Additionally, the development of machine tools further advanced the working of iron, making it invaluable in the steadily growing machinery and engine industries.

Economic institutions and human capital such as engineers, inventors and capitalists helped Britain lead the process of industrialization, largely through private initiative

During the First Industrial Revolution, the developing capitalist system placed the industrialist as the dominant player instead of the merchant. Industrial capitalism and large industry, when controlled by financiers, gave way to the corporation and financial capitalism. In other words, industrial empires accrued assets that were managed by people who were removed from the actual production, yet were becoming the dominant figures of the industry.

International trade flourished with new and influential advances in the electrical and chemical industries, and the replacement of sailing ships with more efficient and better designed steamships made from an increasingly available supply of cheap iron (and steel, after 1870). Britain had little momentum in comparison to other major powers such as Germany (whose Industrial Revolution would make it an economic equal with Britain).

Through the Victorian era, British business simultaneously saw improvement and was worsened by agreements and alliances of disparate firms and the use of gasoline-powered electric power and internal combustion engines; while previous business leaders in industrialized European countries had benefitted from the greater efficiency and complexity in the manufacturing processes, domestic demand now came to be outstripped by production due to the vastly expanded output as a result of lower manufacturing costs. This was the reality in all industrialized nations, but Britain suffered most acutely. After fifteen years of economic precariousness, the Long Depression occurred in Great Britain from 1873–1896. After 1873, almost every business in every industry had to contend with deflation and low profit margins.

Bank run during the Panic of 1873

In response to an extensive depreciating economic trend, industrializing nations such as the U.S., Germany and especially Britain would become increasingly interested in investment opportunities overseas. Other countries who had made such investments in Britain gained much influence in the realms of British economics and politics. The potential benefits of investing overseas led to the creation of super-corporations and conglomerates founded by competing financiers. By the end of the Victorian era, industries such as banking, shipping and insurance had taken prominence over the manufacturing industry.

London financial houses had gained control of British industry by the 1870s and this worried the legislators who were entwined with foreign governments or their developments (for example, railroads) about the safety of their investments overseas. Britain maintained an official policy in support of overseas investments. Due to the uncertainty around the potential economic and political consequences, however, British businesses continued to pressure the government for stringent policies that would protect the massive number of investments in places all over the world (like Egypt). This pressure on the government continued throughout the years before the Crystal Palace Speech.

Benjamin Disraeli, the British Prime Minister in 1872, was in opposition to the growing liberal movement and in the Crystal Palace Speech he detailed the ways that Britain should be maintaining England's colonies and traditions and called for a refocusing of government priorities.

Britain's parliamentary government promoted commercial and industrial interests because those interests were represented in Parliament.

Economic interventionism is a policy which favors intervention by the government into market processes in order to promote the general welfare by rectifying mistakes. Potential benefits from this policy include the acknowledgement and correction of market mistakes, managing of money supply and interest rates, increasing profits, increasing employment, working towards income equality, reducing or increasing prices, and general economic growth and expansion. Regulation by the British government took many forms but always had the objective of either creating or limiting a right, developing or diminishing a duty or allocating a responsibility.

These objectives could be carried out using market regulation, social regulation, industry self-regulation (for instance, a trade association), binding contractual obligations between various parties, legal restrictions or accreditation. Commonly regulated mandates of the British state were controls on economic segments such as wages, prices, certain individuals' employment in particular industries, development approvals, production standards for specific goods, market entry and the military forces and services.

Following the British example, industrialization took root in continental Europe, sometimes with state sponsorship.

The Industrial Revolution began in Britain in the 1780s, but was not fully felt until the 1830s or 1840s. The Industrial Revolution occurred a little later in Continental Europe than in Great Britain. In many industries, this involved the application of technology developed in Britain in new places. Often the technology was purchased from Britain or British engineers, with British entrepreneurs moving abroad in search of new opportunities. By 1809, part of the Ruhr Valley in Westphalia was called "Miniature England" because of its similarities to the industrial areas of England. The German, Russian and Belgian governments all provided state funding for the development of new industries. In some cases, such as iron, the variance in availability of resources locally meant that only some aspects of British technology were adopted.

France moved toward industrialization at a more gradual pace than Great Britain, with government support and with less dislocation of traditional methods of production

The traditional peasant class of France experienced gradual yet significant change in the late 1800s and into the early 1900s. The French peasantry was living traditionally and was extremely poor until between 1870 and 1914. Rural France was modernized by developments such as republican schooling, the building of railroads and universal military conscription. All students began to learn standardized French in order to promote the central government's goal of a creating a unified city-state based out of Paris.

Led by advocate, poet and politician Alphonse de Lamartine, railroads were utilized in the adoption of modernization in traditional and underdeveloped regions across the nation. France constructed a centralized railroad system which traveled out of Paris, as well as some tracks which went east to west. Centralized in Paris, the new system was meant to promote certain cultural and political objectives, not create the most efficiency. Once some consolidation had been completed, regional monopolies were controlled by six rail

Alphonse de Lamartine, French writer, poet and politician

companies. The government had control over these monopolies in issues of small technical detail, train fares and general finances.

Most of the construction of French railroads, including expert engineering and planning, land acquisition and the building of infrastructure (such as tunnels, bridges and track beds), was overseen by British engineers hired by the French government's Department of Bridges and Roads. This department was also responsible for subsidizing lines along the German border for military purposes. Management infrastructure for the railway system, labor for track-laying, and building and operating stations were provided by private operating companies. Most of the equipment used on these projects was imported from Britain and therefore French infrastructural development did not necessarily lead to growth in the French industrial sector.

By beginning the entire railway system at once, France had a greater reliance on British assistance and expertise and ultimately completion was delayed (although approaching the project this way was politically expedient). To solve the problem of financing, France acquired some funding from the Rothschild family and certain members of the Bourse (the Paris stock exchange). This meant that in comparison to London and New York, France was not developing a flourishing stock exchange. Though the railroads achieved some degree of modernization in parts of rural France, they contributed to the Industrial Revolution by facilitating a national market for imported, manufactured products (cheeses, wines and raw materials), but there were no local industrial centers created from it. Since the creation of the railroads was meant to further military, political and moralistic goals as opposed to economic goals, freight trains were smaller and more lightly loaded than they were in Britain, Germany or Belgium, where rapid industrialization was taking place.

Industrialization in Prussia allowed that state to become the leader of a unified Germany, which subsequently underwent rapid industrialization under government sponsorship.

The 1883 Zollverein treaties were responsible for forming the German Customs Union, or Zollverein, which was officially created in 1834 and was a coalition of German states tasked with the management of economic policies and tariffs within their territories. By 1866, most German states were part of Zollverein. The original agreements between Prussian and Hohenzollern territories were economics based, ensuring that non-contiguous territories of the Hohenzollern family (the ruling family of Prussia) engaged in economic contact. These agreements also sought to bring economic unity to a divided Germany by creating economic growth and exchange with the removal of economic obstacles, such as differing units of weight and measurement in the different German states.

Individual states heavily depended on domestic customs as their primary income source, and this proved to be a problem, restricting and hampering trade and industrial development. State rulers did not want to implement customs duties and give up rent-based income. The impasse between states and the effort of national industrialization was eventually overcome by an external decision—the repeal of the Continental System. This action put the English industry and German tradesmen in direct conflict, causing the united German Trade and Tradesmen's Union to issue demands for tariff protection against English exports.

There was an effort in 1820, led by Württemberg, to create a Customs Union which would include all the middle-sized German states, Württemberg itself, Baden, Bavaria and the two Hessian states. Austria and Prussia were to be intentionally excluded from this Customs Union because there was worry that they, as major German powers, would be too overbearing. Each state did not show equal interest in or prosper the same amount from the Customs Union. In Baden, economic development progressed promisingly; the state had long borders and infrastructure that fostered trade. Economic development in Bavaria, however, was slow and sparse. The Bavarian regime implemented a protective tariff to be enacted on imported goods. This led to an agreement between Baden and Hessen-Darmstadt, which did not last. A second agreement intended to encourage an economic rapport between Bavaria and Württemberg was finalized in Stuttgart in 1825 and created the South German Customs Union.

In response to the activity of the Prussian states, Hesse, Saxony and Hannover, as well as Great Britain, France, the Netherlands and Austria also developed economic

---

agreements. These various states and nations established trade agreements and also vowed that none of them would join the Prussian Union. The Union, seeking to maintain the status quo instead of fixing problems caused by the tariff barriers, eventually drove Baden and Württemberg to join the Prussian Union, later renamed the German Customs Union. The German Customs Union had grown by 1835 and encompassed a majority of the states in the German Confederation, even Württemberg, Thuringia, The Hessen states, Baden, Bavaria and even Saxony. It was successful in maintaining a protectionist tariff system with foreign trade partners, while removing many internal customs battles.

The creation of the customs union was primarily motivated by Prussia. Due to the disapproval of Prince von Metternich and how protected its industry was, Austria was not welcomed into the Zollverein. In 1867, after the founding of the North German Confederation, the Zollverein spanned approximately 425,000 square kilometers and had reached out to non-German states, including Sweden-Norway, to make economic agreements. When the German Empire was formed in 1871, the customs union fell under its control. Though not in the empire, Luxembourg remained in the Zollverein until 1919, but it was not until 1888 that every state within the Empire was part of the Zollverein.

Prince Klemens Wenzel von Metternich of the Austrian Empire

In efforts to equalize shipping rates and lower freight service prices, Prussian railroads were nationalized in the 1880s. However, railroads were used by the government to make profits so rates were not lowered as much as possible; subsequently the railroads became an important source of state revenue. The less industrialized agrarian areas were favored as Prussia nationalized its railroads, which led to slower economic development. Also, an adequate tax system was never developed because the railroad surpluses made the collection of other tax revenue unnecessary.

The development of the "National System" is attributed to Georg Friedrich List (1789-1864), an influential 19th century German-American economist, a forefather of the German historical school of economics. List is known as one of the leading advocates of railroad development and the original thinker for theories of European Unity — the foundation of European Economic Community.

List believed that nations of the temperate zone have all the required and necessary conditions to naturally progress through stages of economic development to their normal economic existence. The stages include: pastoral life, agriculture, agriculture married with manufacturing and finally, the combination of agriculture, manufacturing and commerce. The state has the responsibility to progress the nation through these stages and must create the proper environment for the stages to occur using means such as administrative action or legislation.

List also developed ideas on how to navigate industrial politics. He proposed that all nations should start out having free trade and use this free trade to help stimulate and improve the nation's agriculture. A nation's agriculture will improve through trade with richer and more cultivated nations, the export of raw products and the import of foreign manufactures. Once a nation's economy is advanced enough that it can manufacture for itself, home industries should be given protection so that they can develop and not risk being overpowered by competition from stronger foreign industries which operate in the home market. Once national industries are strong enough not to be threatened by this type of competition then a nation has reached its highest stage of progress. This means that the nation should again adopt free trade as a rule, and the nation will then be officially and completely incorporated into the universal industrial union. A nation will have some losses during the protective period, but will end up gaining much more in productive power in the end. In other words, the initial and temporary expenditure is analogous to that of an individual's education.

A combination of factors, including geography, lack of resources, the dominance of traditional landed elites, the persistence of serfdom in some areas and inadequate government sponsorship, accounted for eastern and southern Europe's lag in industrial development.

Countries on the periphery of European imperialism were often used to produce specialized resources. These peripheral countries would be inhibited overall in their industrial development, although this brought short-term economic benefits. Core countries of European imperialism would advance at faster rates due to trade opportunities with specialized peripheral countries. The core countries would be exposed to cheaper resources and progress both economically and industrially at a pace faster than the rest of the world. Throughout the 19th century, a larger market and quantity of raw materials gave Europe an economic edge. Developing core areas did not have sufficient land and were unable to supply all the necessary resources to continue industrialization, so it was vital that they acquire these resources from less densely populated areas.

Europe traded manufactured goods with the Americas and other colonies in exchange for raw materials. Similar trade situations existed in certain parts of China and Asia, but the West had an advantage that came with their colonization. Normally, as raw material sources started to proto-industrialize, import substitution would occur, which in turn would diminish any market-hegemonic nations had for their manufactured goods. European's control over their colonies also gave them control in preventing a situation like this. When trading textiles from India, import substitution was used in Britain's favor. Industrialization allowed Britain to make domestic cotton production lucrative and eventually to surpass India as the top cotton supplier in the world. Western and Eastern Europe also established profitable trade relations due to the lack of freedom and forced labor in the East which facilitated their progress to proto-industrialization and a massive generation of raw materials.

"A DIVIDED DUTY."

Indian cotton excise duty cartoon (1895)

Samuel Huntington coined the term "The Great Divergence," which refers to how the Western World in the 19th century became the most rich and powerful major civilization in the world. This term encompasses the period of the West's rise despite pre-modern growth constraints and its eclipse of the Ottoman Empire, Mughal India, Qing China and Tokugawa Japan.

The Age of Discovery occurred in tandem with The Great Divergence, along with major events such as the Scientific Revolution, the Industrial Revolution, the Commercial Revolution, the Age of Enlightenment and the rise of colonial empires everywhere. It is important to note that this term has been further developed by other scholars, and there is still an active debate as to what conditions led to this unquestionable divergence in development. Contributing factors may have included lack of government intervention, customary traditions, colonialism or geography.

Core-developed areas prior to the Great Divergence were the Indian subcontinent, East Asia, the Middle East, and Europe. Each of the core areas gained various levels of development due to differences in political and cultural institutions. For instance, at this time India still had access to large swathes of unused resources, whereas Japan, China and Western Europe had developed quickly and to a high level which limited energy and land availability. Western development was aided by shifts in governmental policies from mercantilism to laissez-faire classical liberalism.

In the West, during the Great Divergence, technological advances in areas of agriculture, mining and transportation (e.g., steamboats, railroads) were highly valued and promptly implemented, much more so than in the East. The East and West were increasingly separated by the industrialization brought about by technology and the economic complexities of modernized agriculture, fuel, and trade and resources. When Europe began substituting coal for wood in the mid-19th century, this was the moment when alternative and modern energy production emerged.

During the Second Industrial Revolution (c. 1870-1914), more areas of Europe experienced industrial activity, and industrial processes increased in scale and complexity.

The First Industrial Revolution, beginning in the late 18th century in Britain, spread throughout Western Europe. The Second Industrial Revolution, or the Technological Revolution, followed as a segment of the larger Industrial Revolution and started sometime between 1840 and 1860, lasting until World War I. The Second Industrial Revolution spanned from the time Bessemer steel was introduced to industry in the 1850s until early forms of factory electrification, the development of the production line and resulting mass production. Important aspects of the Second Industrial Revolution were the mass production of steel and iron, the use of machinery in manufacturing becoming commonplace, increasing use of oil and steam power and the beginning of electrical communication and electricity use. The Low Countries (so named because of their location below sea level), Britain, France and primarily Germany all experienced rapid industrial development.

New technologies, such as petroleum, the internal combustion engine, electricity, communication technologies (e.g., telegraph, radio, telephone), new materials and substances (e.g., alloys and chemicals) became extremely important in this period. The First Industrial Revolution saw the development and use of iron, steam engine technology and textiles, while the Second Industrial Revolution was engineering and science oriented and based on petroleum, railroads, steel, chemicals and new electricity technologies.

A system of mutual beneficence developed between iron and steel, railroads and coal at the start of the Second Industrial Revolution. Materials and products could be cheaply transported on railroads, and this led to cheap materials with which to build more rails. Meanwhile, railroads were benefitting from cheap coal which ran their steam locomotives.

Mechanization and the factory system became the predominant modes of production by 1914.

Machine tools were first used at the start of the First Industrial Revolution, but more mechanization called for more varied metal parts. These parts were usually made of cast iron or wrought iron. They were handmade which caused imprecision and made the production of these parts slow and expensive. From these drawbacks came the first machine tools, such as the boring machine created by John Wilkinson. This machine's function was to bore a precise hole, which it did in the first steam engine, created by James Watt in 1774. Henry Maudslay spearheaded the development of machine tool precision, and Joseph Whitworth refined these advancements. Screw threads, created by a screw-cutting lathe making interchangeable V-thread machine screws, became the standard around 1800, when Maudslay made the practical commodity available.

Portrait of industrialist John Wilkinson

A design that Joseph Whitworth created in 1841 was used by many British railroad companies and through this exposure became the world's first national machine tool standard, which was named the British Standard Whitworth. In addition to a variety of company and industry standards, the British Standard Whitworth was used during the 1840s throughout the 1860s in Canada and the United States as well.

The indispensability of machine tools to mass production can be seen in the fact that the Ford Model T was produced using 32,000 almost exclusively electricity-powered machine tools. Henry Ford said that mass production could not have happened without electricity because it allowed equipment and machine tool placement to be ordered along with the work flow.

New technologies and means of communication and transportation – including railroads – resulted in more fully integrated national economies, a higher level of urbanization, and a truly global economic network

From the 1860s onward, steel production increased until it was financially possible for rails to be made from steel. Steel, being a much more durable material, steadily replaced iron as the railroad building standard. Steel's greater strength meant that rails of longer length could be rolled and they would not bend or break as easily. Wrought iron was much softer than steel and could be damaged by hammers or heavy locomotives.

In the year 1857, at Derby Midland railroad station, steel rails were first used instead of iron rails. The old iron rails needed replacements every three to six months, but the steel rails were still in perfect condition six years after they were first laid down, even though 700 trains went over them every day. This set the stage for increased worldwide rail construction in the late 19th century. Steel rails not only lasted ten times longer than iron rails, but were also cheaper, with the cost of steel continuing to fall. Powerful locomotives could be used more frequently, and these carried longer trains and longer rail cars which positively impacted productivity directly. Railroads quickly became the dominant form of transportation with the most infrastructure in the industrialized world. Throughout the rest of the century, the cost of shipping steadily decreased.

The idea of harnessing electrical power was developed theoretically and practically by scientist Michael Faraday. Using his research on a conductor carrying a direct current, which was surrounded by a magnetic field, Faraday developed his ideas on electromagnetic fields in physics. The practical use of technological electricity was based on his invention of electromagnetic rotary devices.

Sir Joseph Swan

Sir Joseph Swan was the inventor of the first usable incandescent light bulb. In 1881, he supplied the Savoy Theatre in London with 1,200 Swan incandescent lamps, which made the Savoy the first building entirely lit up using electricity. In 1879, in what was the first installation of electrical street lighting worldwide, Swan's light bulb was used in Newcastle upon Tyne to light up Mosley Street. Next came the lighting of the home and industry. Holborn Viaduct in London was the first major central distribution supply plant for electrification. This was in January, 1882; the first in North America followed in September of 1882, located at the Pearl Street Station in New York.

The National Academy of Engineering called electrification "the most important engineering achievement of the 20th century." Electric lighting offered improvement in working conditions in numerous ways: the heat and pollution from gas lighting was eliminated and fire hazards were reduced to the point where electrical costs were far less than fire insurance premiums. Three years after Frank J. Sprague invented the first DC motor in 1886, 110 electric street railroads were either using his equipment or implementing the technology. By 1920, the emergence of the electric street railroad as major infrastructure occurred. In city households, electrification was not common before the 1920s. The 1939 World's Fair saw the first commercial introduction of fluorescent lighting. Inexpensive production of chemicals, such as magnesium, sodium hydroxide, aluminum and chlorine, became possible after electrification.

In 1848, both the production and refining industries of petroleum began in Scotland with the first oil works. In the same year, a chemist called James Young set up a small business refining crude oil and discovered that he could procure a variety of useful substances from slowly distilling the oil. He named one of the substances he obtained "paraffin oil" because it resembled a paraffin wax after congealing at lower temperatures. Paraffin wouldn't be sold for fuel or as a solid until 1856, but Young created the first purely commercial oil works and refinery in the world in 1856 at Bathgate. He manufactured lubricating oils and naphtha using oil extracted from locally mined turbinate, shale and bituminous coal.

Ancient Chinese well drilling techniques and technology, such as cable tool drilling used for drilling brine wells, was introduced in Europe in 1828. Some wells produced salt domes which also held natural gas and these were sometimes used for evaporation of the brine.

The first "modern oil well" is thought to have existed near Titusville, Pennsylvania in 1859, where Edwin Drake's attempt – one out of many in the mid-19th century – at creating an oil well actually worked, beginning a major boom in oil production in the United States. Chinese laborers taught Drake about cable tool drilling. The first production from the well was used as kerosene for heaters and lamps. The European market was fed with similar developments from Baku (present-day Azerbaijan).

The efficiency of kerosene lighting surpassed vegetable oils, tallow and whale oil, and proved to be less expensive. Before the gas mantle and despite the availability of town gas lighting, kerosene was used because of the brighter light it produced. The gas mantle and kerosene were both replaced by electricity (in the 1890s for street lighting and in the 1920s for household lighting).   No use was found for the unwanted byproduct of oil refining (gasoline) until the mass production of automobiles began after 1914 and World War I brought gas shortages. Shortages were alleviated with the creation of the Burton process, which induced thermal cracking to effectively double the yield of gasoline.

An English chemist, William Henry Perkin, discovered synthetic dye in 1856. The state of the field of chemistry at that time could be considered primitive; the chemical industry had barely begun and the arrangement of the elements in compounds was still a difficult quandary. Synthetic dye was accidentally discovered when Perkin realized that a crude mixture created from aniline produced a substance with an intense purple color after being extracted with alcohol. He called the substance "mauveine" and marketed it as the first synthetic dye in the world.

The discovery of mauveine triggered the creation of many new aniline dyes and factories producing them quickly sprang up across Europe. Though the research was begun by Perkin along with other British companies, the German chemical industry had outstripped the work of the British by the end of the century. The chemical industry became increasingly dominant throughout this time.

Charles Goodyear, co-inventor of vulcanized rubber

An American named Charles Goodyear and a Briton named Thomas Hancock discovered the vulcanization of rubber in the 1840s and paved the way for the boom of the rubber industry, including the manufacturing of rubber tires. In 1887 in South Belfast, John Boyd Dunlop was responsible for the invention of the first practical pneumatic tire, which happened at a critical time in road development. Late 1890 saw the commercial production of the pneumatic tire.

Though the first safety bicycle to become a commercial success was designed by John Kemp Starley, the modern bicycle was invented by an English engineer named Harry John Lawson in 1876. There was a "bike boom" in the 1890s due to the popularity of the designs.

As the popularity of the bicycle grew, the quality and extent of road networks improved. Most were improved using a method created by John Loudon McAdam, a Scottish engineer, called the Macadam method. During the 1890s bike craze, roads began to be constructed with hard surfaces, and the invention of modern tarmac by British civil engineer Edgar Purnell followed in 1901.

The first automobile was patented in 1886 by the German inventor Karl Benz. Features of this vehicle included wire wheels, as opposed to wooden wheels seen on carriages, a very advanced coil ignition connecting to an engine between the rear wheels (designed by Benz himself) and evaporative cooling instead of a radiator. Twin roller chains to the rear axle transmitted power. Instead of simply being motorized, like the motorized stage coach or horse carriage that was already available, this first automobile was designed so the vehicle could generate its own power. The Benz Patent Motorwagen, as Benz called it, made history in 1886 as the first commercially available automobile.

Henry Ford, a pioneer in the automobile industry, created his first car in 1896. His colleagues were other individuals who would go on to build their own companies and in 1903 Ford founded the Ford Motor Company. Ford had a vision of every average worker owning a car and strove to make production reach a scale of affordability. To meet this production scale demand, a new system of production, called the assembly line, was implemented. On the assembly line, all tools and work were within easy reach or on a conveyor belt to avoid any human movement that was unnecessary. The process of manufacturing using the assembly line was called mass production.

A telegraph system was installed commercially for the first time by Charles Wheatstone and Sir William Fothergill between Camden Town in London and the Euston railroad station in May of 1837. Telegraph networks proceeded to expand rapidly throughout the century, an underwater cable was even built between England and France by John Watkins Brett. In 1866 the Atlantic Telegraph Company was formed in London in order to handle construction of a cross-Atlantic commercial telegraph cable. The project was carried out by Captain Sir James Anderson and the cable-laying ship *SS Great Eastern*, successfully completed after on July 18th, 1866 after many mishaps.

Between the 1850s and 1911, the worldwide communication system was ruled by cable systems laid by British submarines. This was due to an accomplished strategic goal of connecting the British Empire by telegraph, referred to as the All Red Line or the All Red Route. Similar to the early telegraph, the telephone (patented by Alexander Graham Bell in 1876) was initially used primarily to more efficiently conduct business transactions. Maxwell's electromagnetic theory proved to be one of the most valuable and significant advancements in science; it dealt with the unification of magnetism, light and electricity. New development of more efficient transformers, motors, and electric generators only became possible with a scientific understanding of electricity. In his electromagnetic theory, Maxwell predicted the phenomenon of electromagnetic waves and these predictions were demonstrated and proven correct by the work of Heinrich Hertz and David Edward Hughes.

Radio was successfully commercialized by Guglielmo Marconi, an Italian inventor, by the end of the 1800s. In 1897, Marconi founded the Wireless Telegraph & Signal Company in Britain and succeeded in sending Morse code across Salisbury Plain, as well as in transmitting a wireless communication over open sea for the first time. In 1901, the first transatlantic transmission was made from Poldhu, Cornwall to Signal Hall, Newfoundland. In 1904, Marconi began a commercial service which transmitted nightly news to ships via powerful stations on either side of the Atlantic.

Guglielmo Marconi, Italian inventor

The advances in radio broadcasting and modern electronics were underpinned by the further progress in developing the technology of the vacuum tube done in 1904 by Sir John Ambrose Fleming. The invention of the triode followed, thanks to Lee DeForest, who invented a tube which allowed electronic signals to be amplified. This invention would set the stage for the emergence of 1920s radio broadcasting.

Due to previously mentioned advances in communication and transportation, Western powers' dependence on their colonies grew. Much of the simple goods and raw resources needed to fuel the industry of the Western powers were provided by the colonies. Trade of goods was also booming due to increased production capabilities and colonialism was assisting in breaking down old economic systems. Also, colonized people became dependent on the presence of the industrial powers for their livelihoods. In later stages of the colonial age, colonizing nations recognized their dependence on colonized people by attempting to work with their colonies in different ways, such as allowing members of the colonized people to be included in their own governments.

The integration of economies was possible because of standardization and specialization. *Standardization* referred to different countries being able to connect their industries. For instance, in continental Europe, the most effective method of transporting goods that were mass produced was by railroad, which became the standard method of transportation. Railroads not only crossed borders, but could function identically in each country. Standardization helped to create predictability in industry. America and Britain, since their machinery was all steam-driven and functioned on the same fuel, could export their technology anywhere in the world with confidence that the machinery would work using coal from anywhere it went. *Specialization* shaped different countries' economies in different ways, as each nation had certain goods that it could produce more efficiently due to certain advantages in natural resources, infrastructure and labor force.

Volatile business cycles in the last quarter of the 19th century led corporations and governments to try to manage the market through monopolies, banking practices and tariffs.

Railroads were essential in the creation of the enterprise of modern business. Before the use of railroads, businesses were individually owned or managed by partners. These owners often had very limited day-to-day hands on responsibilities. When new kinds of industry called for knowledge in engineering or mechanics, managers with the necessary expertise were hired.

Railroads were complex businesses that required vast amounts of capital to build and maintain. Initially, this was financed by what later became known as the "railway mania" of the 1840s, whereby thousands of the middling gentry and the newly literate middle class began to invest in British railway development. This unprecedented boom in investment in one sector inevitably led to a bubble, which promptly burst when it was realized that there was an inevitable need for practices of standardization to be brought into the sector. As a result, many individuals found that their investments had fallen prey to poor financial management, unnecessary or redundant construction, and/or outright fraud. Due to this, both the government and private citizens realized that there was a greater need for regulation and consolidation in the railway sector.

A further push factor increasing demand for regulation occurred after a collision on the Great Western Railroad in Britain in 1841. The Sonning Cutting collision in December 1841, which killed eight people, led to recommendations that passenger cars and cargo cars be separated. This is just one example of how fatal accidents, which increased as the railway network grew, led to the reform of railway safety practices. These disastrous accidents led to the reorganization of railroads into different departments with clear lines of management authority. When the telegraph became available, telegraph lines were built along the railroads.

At the same time, both the British government and private citizens became aware of the fact that they needed better ways to keep track of costs. For example, rates could only be calculated if the cost of a ton-mile of freight or the number of cars was known. From these needs, a practice called "railroad accounting" was developed. It would later be used by steel and other major industries and developed, over time, into what is modern accounting.

A necessary condition for all of the above-mentioned improvements was a push towards monopolization due to the cannibalistic and redundant nature of newly developing industries. These changes began to occur throughout the industrialized world, most notably in the United States. During this period of rapid industrialization there were two main types of monopolization taking place: through vertical integration, where as many possible components from raw materials to transport to market are controlled by one company; and through horizontal integration, where one organization pushes to control a market share of all industrial output in one sector. These concepts were developed in the United States, though the practices gradually began to be adopted in Europe.

Frederick Winslow Taylor created the concept of "scientific management," another development imported into American business practices. In work such as bricklaying or shoveling, scientific management was at first concentrated on reducing the number of steps needed to complete a task by analyzing studies of time and motion. As the concept evolved and was applied to such areas as industrial engineering, manufacturing engineering and business management, it helped restructure factory operations completely, and later would be used in restructuring portions of the larger economy.

Frederick Winslow Taylor,
American mechanic engineer

This growth in private sector innovation of business practices led to a growth in specialization, which often led to certain countries having a monopoly in a specific sector. As a result, and so as to not become overly dependent on outside nations for essential products, nations began to implement high tariffs as a means to encourage domestic industry to produce essential goods. This was met with limited success and often led to wasting capital; but it was an understandable response on the part of European countries now finding themselves reliant on nations with whom they had been at war less than fifty years earlier.

Period 3: 1815-1914

> **Key Concept 3.2: The experiences of everyday life were shaped by industrialization, depending on the level of industrial development in a particular location.**

Industrialization promoted the development of new socioeconomic classes between 1815 and 1914. In highly industrialized areas, such as western and northern Europe, the new economy created new social divisions, leading for the first time to the development of self-conscious economic classes, especially the proletariat and the bourgeoisie. In addition, the economic changes led to the rise of trade and industrial unions, benevolent associations, sport clubs, and distinctive class-based cultures of dress, speech, values and customs.

Europe also experienced rapid population growth and urbanization that resulted in benefits as well as social dislocations. The increased populations created an enlarged labor force, but in some areas migration from the countryside to the towns and cities led to overcrowding and significant emigration overseas. Industrialization and urbanization changed the structure and relations of bourgeois and working class families to varying degrees. Birth control became increasingly common across Europe, and childhood experience changed with the advent of protective legislation, universal schooling and smaller families. The growth of a cult of domesticity established new models of gender behavior for men and women. Gender roles became more clearly defined as middle-class women withdrew from the workforce. At the same time, working-class women increasingly participated as wage-laborers, although the middle class criticized them for neglecting their families.

Industrialization and urbanization also changed people's conception of time; in particular, work and leisure were increasingly differentiated by means of the imposition of strict work schedules and the separation of the workplace from the home. Increasingly, trade unions assumed responsibility for the social welfare of working-class families, fighting for improved working conditions and shorter hours. Increasing leisure time spurred the development of leisure activities and spaces for bourgeois families. Overall, although inequality and poverty remained significant social problems, the quality of material life improved. For most social groups, the standard of living rose; the availability of consumer products grew; and sanitary standards, medical care and life expectancy improved.

Industrialization promoted the development of new classes in the industrial regions of Europe.

The Industrial Revolution did not presuppose change only in the economic sphere, it also affected the social structure by motivating a middle class triumph—businessmen and industrialists over aristocrats, nobility and gentry. There were increased opportunities for average working people to become employed with new factories and mills. Unfortunately, these opportunities required long hours at a pace set by a machine and generally strict working conditions. Even into the 1900s, a majority of American industrial workers continued to make 20 to 40 percent less than the minimum deemed acceptable to maintain a decent living standard and they were still working ten-hour days. However, before the Industrial Revolution, harsh working conditions were extremely prevalent. In pre-industrial society, long hours, child labor and dirty living conditions were commonplace and society was generally cruel and static.

Enterprise Cotton mill, North Carolina 1897

Over the years, "middle class" has meant different, sometimes very different concepts. Those who did not fit into either the nobility or the peasantry of Europe were at one point referred to as the middle class. This group neither owned land like the nobility nor worked the land like the peasantry, but instead were "bourgeoisie" (literally translates to town-dweller) who engaged in the mercantile functions of the city. For the French during the French Revolution, the middle class was helpful in giving the Revolution its legs. Within capitalism, members of the middle class were seen as those with so much capital they were capable of challenging nobles. From the capitalist perspective, being a millionaire who owned capital was basically the criteria for being "middle class" during the Industrial Revolution.

The capitalist middle class began as referring to the bourgeoisie and the world of the petit bourgeois. Yet much of the petit bourgeois world became impoverished or proletarian and the growth of finance capitalism led to the middle class being recognized as white collar workers, professionals and labor aristocracy. A middle class' size depends on its definition: is it defined by manners, values, environment of upbringing, social network, wealth or education?

In industrialized areas of Europe (i.e., western and northern Europe), socioeconomic changes created divisions of labor that led to the development of self-conscious classes, such as the proletariat and the bourgeoisie.

During the time of feudal order, under the Law of Privilege, nobles autonomously exercised claims of rule by divine right. The bourgeoisie represented a social class of political progressives in support of natural rights and constitutional government. A desire of the bourgeoisie to be free of the royal encroachments and feudal trammels upon personal liberty, property ownership and commercial rights was a huge motivator of uprisings and wars such as the French Revolution, the English Civil War and the American War of Independence. During the 19th century, the class of the bourgeoisie gained political rights as a liberal class promoting civil liberties and religious rights for the lower classes. The bourgeoisie established itself as a progressive political and philosophical force in modern societies of the West.

The bourgeoisie class, which had grown quite expansive by the middle of the 19th century in the wake of the Industrial Revolution, began to stratify by economic function and business activity. The haute bourgeoisie were the bankers and industrialists, and the petite bourgeoisie were white-collar workers and tradesmen. Towards the end of the 19th century, the capitalists who had been the original bourgeoisie were now part of the upper class and working-class men and women found themselves ascending to the lower strata of the bourgeoisie due to developments of technical and technological occupations. The shifts in the makeup of classes, however were entirely incidental.

Wage-earners are a class whose ability to work, or labor-power, is their only possession of material significance. In Marxist language, this group (especially industrial workers) is referred to as the proletariat. One who belongs to this group or class is a proletarian. This class does not retain ownership of the means of production; they can only subsist by selling their labor power. Proletarians are wage-workers, while those individuals who earn a salary (payments for periods of work time, as opposed to hourly wage, for example) may be referred to as the salariat. However, Marx asserts that a "wage-laborer" may not make a wage per se. The proletariat and the bourgeoisie or capitalist class, according to Marx, are constantly in opposing positions because workers will always want the highest wages possible, and owners or employers always want wages or costs kept as low as possible.

Karl Marx, German philosopher

Marxism asserts that capitalism is a system basically existing on the bourgeoisie's exploitation of the proletariat. This exploitation occurs when workers, who alone have no means of production, must use means of production owned by others to be able to produce and therefore earn a living. Instead of the workers obtaining their own means of production, they have to get hired by and work for capitalists to produce goods and services. Whatever they produce is the property of the capitalist or employer who sells the product at the market.

From the wealth produced by selling the product at the market, a portion pays the variable costs (i.e., the wages of the workers), another portion pays constant costs (costs to renew the means of production), some portion pays for rents, taxes, interest, etc., and a surplus value is the capitalist's profits. Surplus value on the proletariat level is the difference between the wealth a worker produces by doing their work and the wealth consumed in order to provide labor to capitalist companies and survive. Some of the surplus value gets used to increase or renew the means of production, either in quantity or quality; this is called capitalized surplus value. The capitalist class consumes whatever is left.

In some of the less industrialized areas of Europe, the dominance of agricultural elites persisted into the 20th century.

International trade and shipping industries boomed during the Industrial Revolution. There was more need for raw materials due to increased production and European merchants purchased a majority of the goods. Between 1750 and 1914, internationally traded goods increased five times in value, and between 1800 and 1900 annual shipping increased from 4 million tons to 30 million tons. The second half of the 19th century saw expanded trade into markets such as food and wool. The Corn Laws were repealed in 1846 and England began trading large amounts of industrial products in exchange for wheat from places all over the world. World trade was further revolutionized by the vast expansion of railroads following the invention of the steam engine. Since goods could be more easily traded across vast distances, this especially included the Americas and East Asia. When heat processing and refrigeration went through a similar revolution in the 19th century, meat could be shipped long distances without spoiling. This effort was spearheaded by tropical countries like Australia and the South American republics.

Horse-drawn machinery of the mid-1800s, like the McCormick reaper, were revolutionary to the harvesting process, and large amounts of crops were able to be processed after the invention of the cotton gin. Steam-powered threshers and tractors came into use around this time period as well, though they were expensive and often a dangerous fire hazard. The first successful development of a gasoline-powered tractor was around 1900. The Fordson, the John Deere and the International Harvester Farmall companies were beginning to replace draft animals (horses in particular) with portable and mechanized power by the 1920s. Other farm equipment, such as self-propelled mechanical harvesters, trans-planters and planters, have been invented since then, transforming agriculture into an almost entirely mechanized process. The previously impossible speed and scale these inventions allowed lead to significantly higher production quality.

Experimentation with fertilizer, from a scientific perspective, was first undertaken by John Bennet Lawes at the Rothamsted Experimental Station in 1843. By obtaining phosphate from sulfuric acid containing dissolved coprolites, Lawes discovered the first commercial process for fertilizer production. In 1909, a major breakthrough allowing crop yields to reach unprecedented levels was demonstrated by the Haber Bosch method, which synthesized ammonium nitrate. This was revolutionary, and in sync with the increasing world population post-World War II, the use of synthetic fertilizer was increasingly adopted all over the world.

Drawing of John Bennet Lawes, English entrepreneur and agricultural scientist

In the 19th century, in numerous different European nations, various types of relationships between agriculturalists and industrialists emerged. A nation's political system and the extent to which it industrialized could be determining factors in the relationships that developed. England and Germany are two examples of nations which differ from many other European nations in these respects.

In Germany, "Junkers" was the name of a unique land-owning class with significant power in the political realm. Before the unification of Germany in 1871, this class was the land-owning nobility residing in the Principate, which eventually merged into Germany. After unification, these nobles no longer had the same status, but those who became Junkers managed to survive the creation of the Republic as well as industrialization by adapting. Instead of crops, which were less profitable, they began raising animals and they modernized. Due to their savvy adaptation, inherited wealth and the fact that they were the educated elite, these families remained among the most powerful in Germany.

The extent to which England had historically relied on trade and its incredible rate of industrialization were two things that set England apart. In comparison to most other

European countries, England is resource-poor due the combination of high population density and small geographical size. That being said, the industrialization of England came earlier and was much more thorough than that of any other European nation. In the 19th century, England's survival was linked to business operations overseas which were already dependent on methods of modern transportation. Industrialists gained power quickly and land-owners lost political influence and importance to them. However, similar to the situation of the Junkers in Germany, land-owners remained distinct in the British social structure, entrenched in their own rigid tier.

Political modernization and industrialization did not proceed as quickly in other parts of Europe. There were of course national differences as well (although overwhelmingly elites of the agricultural industry maintained their power by being quick to modernize their systems in varying degrees). The power of landowners is as old as civilization, as land is needed for agriculture and food is essential for survival. However, due to the desire on the part of the land-owning classes to keep possession of their lands in the hands of their offspring, systems of inheritance were designed whereby land could remain in the same family's possession for centuries. This meant that even through the growth of mercantilism and the rise of the new industrialists, many of the wealthiest and most powerful members of British society were the land-owning gentry.

Class identity developed and was reinforced through participation in philanthropic, political and social associations among the middle classes, and in mutual aid societies and trade unions among the working classes.

During the 18th and 19th centuries, social assistance was provided to increase the general welfare of the working population. Benefits included efforts to combat sickness and unemployment. In defense of their rights, workers joined together in organizations called trade unions or labor unions. Unions could work to achieve any number of common goals including better working conditions, achieving better benefits like health care and retirement, achieving higher pay, improving workplace safety standards, increasing how many employees are assigned to complete certain work, and protecting the integrity of the trade. Maintaining or improving conditions of employment or in the workplace were usually the most common purposes of union organizations. More specifically, these goals could entail negotiation of wages and benefits, work rules, workplace safety and policies, complaint procedures and rules governing the hiring, firing and promotion of workers.

Trade unions first originated in Great Britain, though the practice spread to other countries throughout the period of the Industrial Revolution. Any actor in the workforce could participate in a trade union – individual employees, professionals, apprentices, students, past workers and/or the unemployed. People first began to try setting up a nation-wide general union in the 1820s and 30s.

John Doherty first attempted to create a national presence with his association entitled the National Union of Cotton-Spinners. However, when that organization did not gain traction, he created the National Association for the Protection of Labor in 1830. In a short time, the association had 150 unions, including organizations mostly for textile workers, but also for mechanics and blacksmiths under its umbrella. Between 10,000 and 20,000 members existed within the five counties of Cheshire, Nottinghamshire, Leicestershire, Derbyshire and Lancashire. In the union's weekly publication, *Voice of the People*, it aimed to establish legitimacy and awareness and stated the desire "to unite the productive classes of the community in one common bond of union."

The trade unions created in the 1850s were permanent and better resourced, but often less radical. Though 1860 saw the establishment of the London Trades Council, the Sheffield Outrages created the necessity of establishing the Trades Union Congress which was done in 1868 and proved to be the first national trade union center which enjoyed any longevity. By this point, the liberal middle class had begun to accept the existence and requests of the trade unions.

Members of the Irish Women Workers' Union

Educated Europeans also created and joined numerous social groups as their freedom and wealth increased with the Industrial Revolution. Women's rights groups began to gain momentum in all of the industrializing nations. Though these were primarily political groups with the goal of obtaining political equality for women, they also supported many moral causes, such as anti-alcohol movements, aiding the poor and improvements in the education and welfare of children. Academic societies were established, such as the Royal Historical Society in London. Membership in these societies was by invitation only to ensure that they were accessible exclusively to individuals of the desired social categories.

Europe experienced rapid population growth and urbanization, leading to social dislocations.

From ancient civilization up until the 18th century, society had been composed of small town centers where pockets of the population conducted economic activity primarily consisting of trading at markets and small scale manufacturing; the majority of the populace worked as subsistence farmers in some capacity and in rural environments. Both urban and rural populations remained in equilibrium and at unchanging ratios to one another due to the primitiveness and stasis of agriculture during this time.

Finally, the equilibrium was upset in the late 18th century by the onset of the Industrial and Agricultural Revolutions. Over the course of the 19th century, an unprecedented growth in urban population occurred due to massive amounts of demographic expansion and the continual migration of rural inhabitants into urban environments. The urban population in England increased from 17 percent in 1801 to 72 percent in 1891.

Along with better harvests caused in part by the commercialization of agriculture, industrialization promoted population growth, longer life expectancy, and lowered infant mortality.

During the Industrial Revolution, the life expectancy for both children and adults increased dramatically. In Europe, those changes started slowly and were originally prompted by the Agricultural Revolution of the 18th century. Improved food supply from higher agricultural yields and better transportation contributed to the lowed death rates. In turn, the decline in mortality rates corresponded to a sharp increase in population. It is important to note that it was increased life expectancy, not increase in birth rates, that brought about this population change. Countries that experienced significant population changes during the late 19th century as a result of the Industrial Revolution were those in northwestern Europe.

Agricultural productivity reached an unprecedented high, due to the advances of the Industrial Revolution. As a result, cities such as Birmingham and Manchester experienced major improvements and expansions of their trade, industry and commerce as workers who were no longer needed to work the land flocked into the cities. Worldwide trade continued to grow and it became possible to trade cereal from North America and import refrigerated meat from South America and Australasia. Public transportation systems also contributed to urban expansion by making it possible for the working class to live farther away from the center of the city.

After 1740, the population of England and Wales, stagnant for the past forty years, rose dramatically, more than doubling, from 8.3 million in 1801 to 16.8 million in 1850, based largely on improvements in conditions. Another fifty years saw the population double again to 30.5 million. Overall, in two centuries (from 1700 to 1900) Europe's population increased from 100 million to 400 million. Per capita income and population increased simultaneously during the Industrial Revolution for the first time in history.

With migration from rural to urban areas in industrialized regions, cities experienced overcrowding, while affected rural areas suffered declines in available labor as well as weakened communities.

The biggest contributing factor to over-urbanization was rural-to-urban migration and factors associated with it. Lower death rates, which resulted from the demographic transitions brought about by the Agricultural and Industrial Revolutions, led to less available land and work opportunities for rural residents. The larger process of urbanization was influenced by various economic factors that "pushed" migrants away from their homes and "pulled" them towards new, most often urban, areas.

During the Middle Ages and the Early Modern Period, Flanders was characterized by the presence of large urban centers. At the beginning of the 19th century Flanders, now more than 30 per cent urban, remained one of the most urbanized in the world. By comparison, this proportion reached only 17 per cent in Wallonia, barely 10 per cent in most West European countries, 16 per cent in France and 25 per cent in Britain. 19th century industrialization largely did not affect the traditional urban infrastructure.

Post-industrialization, farm workers migrated to the city in droves in search of better work opportunities and higher pay. Consequently, rural areas suffered from a decline in the labor force. Due to wide-spread mechanization of the agricultural industry, the lack of workers was not a significant issue. In fact, few workers could keep up with the new levels of production required by mechanization. Some countries' agricultural industries were under less pressure because greater amounts of food could be imported from nations' colonies or other countries. Another response to the shift in labor was for landowners (such as the Junkers in Germany, or farmers in Scotland and Ireland) to switch to raising different products such as cattle or potato farming, in which workers could be better used and mechanization was not feasible.

The book and newspaper publishing industry experienced massive expansion with the application of the new technology of steam power to industrial printing processes. The increased amount of reading material stimulated higher rates of literacy and mass political participation. Of the world population in 1800, only 3 percent lived in cities, while today close to 50 percent live in cities. This upswing can be attributed to modern industry fueling massive urbanization and the rise of new major cities, often populated by large numbers of migrants moving from rural to urban areas.

STEAM BOOK AND JOB PRINTING ESTABLISHMENT.

BROWNLOW, HAWS & CO.,
BOOK AND FANCY JOB PRINTERS,
Machine Rulers, &c., &c.,
KNOXVILLE, TENN.

Advertisement in the Knoxville Whig
for a steam printing service operated by the paper's publisher

Over time, the Industrial Revolution altered the family structure and relations for bourgeois and working-class families.

During the pre-industrial period, the available technology was limited and stagnant. Economic activity was relegated mostly to the household, and customs and traditions were foundational to processes of production and distribution. Harsh living conditions were universally accepted; high mortality rates and short life spans were common in both rural and town living conditions and productivity of farms was low. Due to the Hobbesian nature of existence in pre-industrial and nascent industrial societies, there was a need for strong family units, as this was often the only way to shelter oneself from the "brutish, short and nasty." Though a family's social and economic status was determined by local custom, birth and legacy, a family would only survive if it proved to be a strong, productive unit.

A family gathered around a harpsichord in the 18th century

As an economic unity, a family in the pre-Industrial era was dependent on each family member conducting specialized labor. Typically, a family unit was multi-generational with older members providing land and acquired capital and assets, while the younger generation provided the labor. The production of goods not only supplied the family's household needs, but were also used to trade in the market. Family units could also produce manufacturing goods and provide services instead of focusing on agricultural production. Throughout the pre-industrial era, labor provided by family members was vital in sustaining a viable family economy, operating a farm or business and providing support for elder generations. Education was usually viewed as unnecessary and too costly in families where the fertility rate was high and every child was expected to continue working for the family.

Eventually, the population moved towards stability through a decline in birth rates, with several factors contributing to this decline. In rural areas, childhood death rates continued to decline and at some point parents realized they did not need too many children to be born to provide enough workers for the land and ensure comfort in old age. At the same time, increased urbanization changed the traditional value placed upon fertility and the value of children in rural society. For urban citizens, limited living space and increased cost of living contributed significantly to high costs of having many dependent children in a family.

The role of the family as an economic unit shifted post-industrialization; the family, which was once a productive unit, became a consumptive unit. The new technology developed in the Industrial Revolution made large-scale farming possible using fewer people. Children were viewed as liabilities more than economic assets or necessities. The family economy continued to be phased out as industrialization of the capitalist market led to increased and large-scale production at farms, factories and mines. Family units no longer worked together; as wage labor became common, they used earned wages to buy goods for the entire family unit to consume.

The European model of family economy was common in other parts of the world, though there were differences depending on culture and customs. Non-European countries, however, felt the effects of industrialization differently than European counties. Indigenous societies, including their traditional family organization, were often viewed by their colonizers as inferior to that of European society. In the wake of the new technologies and the need for resources and cheap labor brought about by industrialization; this belief was often used to justify exploitation of both the people and the resources in the European powers' extraterritorial holdings.

Bourgeois families became focused on the nuclear family and the cult of domesticity, with distinct gender roles for men and women.

The family structure that is most normalized is the nuclear family, although there are many other common forms of family structure. A nuclear family is an adult couple and their children. It usually focuses on a married couple and this couple can have any number of children. The definition of nuclear family is somewhat fluid and has continually expanded throughout history. Some definitions recognize only biological children and full-blood siblings, while others say that a nuclear family may contain stepparents, step- and half-siblings and adopted children. The early 20th century saw the first use of the term "nuclear family."

The nuclear family structure was present during the 17th century in Western Europe and New England, largely due to theocratic governments or a strong religious influence in the society. The nuclear family became a social unit of financial viability with the development of industrial technologies and early capitalism.

There was a significant shift in gender roles in the late 18th and early 19th centuries that is widely believed to have caused an emergence of "separate spheres" in the 19th century. This concept included the increasing influence of evangelical ideology which emphasized female religious virtue and domesticity. Women were confined to the domestic sphere and did not work outside the household, whereas men led a public life and were able to work. Sexual desire was seen as sinful and society started to think differently about the female body. Women were no longer considered the more "lustful" sex, but were seen as vessels to carry out the function of motherhood. When women deviated from the prescribed domestic role, they were ostracized and labeled dangerous sexual beings.

Kitchen still life with female figure

Though women were excluded from the bulk of professional roles, they carved out niches for themselves doing work such as teaching and charity work. Although available work was limited for women, working-class women still managed to gain employment in textile trades; much of the work could be done from home. The workforce for women began to expand towards the end of the 19th century and women started to become shop assistants, clerks and typists. Even so, the notion of the male "breadwinner," the head of a family who was financially responsible for the entire family, was increasingly engrained in society. Though women were able to get more jobs than before, they were still expected to leave those jobs when they got married. Gender roles were further reinforced by the 1890s persecution of homosexuals; the expectations of men to display sexual attraction towards women, "masculine" traits (such as physical strength, assertiveness and chivalry) increased. Women and men still lived side by side, but with accentuated gender distinctions; the realms of their existences were often very separate, even by the end of the 19th century.

By the end of the century, wages and the quality of life for the working class improved because of laws restricting the labor of children and women, social welfare programs, improved diet, and the use of birth control.

During the Victorian era, young children were routinely employed in mines, factories and as chimney sweeps. From the beginning of the Industrial Revolution, child labor was a significant portion of the labor force. Children as young as four were employed in factories with dangerous and working conditions. Also prevalent during this period was the employment of child labor in the new industrial centers of Europe.

In working class and poor families, it was often expected that children would work to help with family expenses. Children frequently worked at dangerous jobs for long hours. They were paid low wages, usually earning 10 to 20 percent of an adult male's wage. Many children in 19th century Great Britain lived in single-parent households, due to death or abandonment. The remaining parent was usually the mother, who struggled with finances because women were only allowed certain job opportunities and made very little money. These circumstances caused many children to enter the workforce at a young age to help make ends meet for their family. Children worked in coal mines because they were small enough to wriggle through tunnels that were too low and narrow for adults. Children were also able to get work as shoeblacks, crossing sweepers, errand boys or selling cheap goods such as matches or flowers. Some children took apprenticeships in trades such as construction or domestic service.

The first regulation of industrial employment and child labor in the United Kingdom was with the passing of the Factory Acts in 1833. The Factory Acts made it illegal for children under the age of nine to work in factories, and imposed requirements on industrial workplaces to increase sanitation, ventilation and safeguards in connection with machinery. The Factory Acts subsequently led to the introduction of a ten-hour workday for women and children through the Ten Hours Act in 1847. Those opposed to these regulations had predicted severe economic consequences, yet the ten-hour workday was a success and helped to combat objections to other ideas about factory legislation. After the 1860s, more industries were incorporated into the Factory Act. For example, the 1842 Mines Act passed in Great Britain made it illegal to employ any children under the age of ten in underground mines.

Leisure time centered increasingly on the family or small groups, concurrent with the development of activities and spaces to use that time.

Developments outside of industry that occurred during the Industrial Revolution included parks and museums. Parks in urban environments became areas which preserved a sense of nature in cities and were used for sporting activity and events. Particularly beautiful areas were made into national parks so that the natural beauty would be preserved and remain safe from development. Western culture is believed to be where organized sports first developed, with the Industrial Revolution and the resulting mass production allowing more leisure time. Sports were a non-elitist form of entertainment and there were many types of sports to play, observe or wager on. Advances in global communication and mass media allowed for sports to become a professional industry.

Early museums were called "public" but were actually only open to the middle and upper classes. With the 1759 opening of the British Museum came the idea that appreciation of the artifacts on display could be ruined by large crowds. Only small groups, made up of visitors who had previously applied for admission in writing, were admitted into the galleries each day. The popularity of the British Museum increased in the 19th century and was found to appeal to all age groups. People especially enjoyed visiting the museum during national holidays.

Some consider the Ashmolean Museum to be the first modern public museum. It was founded in 1677 in the University of Oxford and consisted of Elias Ashmole's personal collection, including books, engravings, antique coins, geological specimens and zoological specimens (including a taxidermy dodo, the last such to be seen in Europe).

British Museum in London

During the French Revolution, in 1793, the Louvre, the first public museum in France, opened in Paris. This allowed unprecedented free access to view the former French royal collections, regardless of one's status or station. Artworks collected by the French monarchy throughout history were displayed to the public part-time. The task of organizing the Louvre as the center for a hypothetical national system of museums fell to the *Conservatoire du Muséum National des Arts*. This task became even larger and more complicated as Napoleon I conquered European cities and collected art as he went. Some of these artworks were returned to their owners after Napoleon was defeated in 1815, but many never were. Though the national museum system was never completed during his rule, Napoleon's ideas about museums promoting nationalistic zeal were influential throughout Europe, especially in Britain.

A heightened consumerism developed as a result of the Second Industrial Revolution.

The term "consumerism" can refer to the excessive purchase of goods and consumption of material. Consumer culture first began to be recognized in the late 17th century and became more noticeable throughout the 18th century. Consumerism may have been accelerated by an expanding middle-class who were beginning to purchase goods based on ideas of luxury and fashion, as opposed to survival. From a political and economic perspective, consumerism can be seen as a necessity for the continuation of competition in capitalist markets for profits. Another factor in the rise of consumerism could be the growing political strength of working class organizations around the world, while a simultaneous expansion in technological development led to an increase in productivity and a decline in enforced scarcity. This was a precondition for the rise of the consumer culture developing around therapeutic entertainment, debt and home ownership.

Luxury for the middle class was more accessible with the rise of consumer culture and this shift created an increase in the building of large country estates designed for comfort. In the Caribbean, sugar, tobacco, tea and coffee were grown on huge plantations and these luxury items were marketed to the middle-class who developed an increasing demand for them.

Critics of consumerism claim it was propelled by colonialism, and maintain that its expansion was due to supply and not demand. European populations were also consuming ever-increasing masses of exotic goods in addition to domestic goods. The equation of consumption of material goods with success or even freedom did not exist before mass production and colonial imports. It was a notion that was strategically constructed and provided later, with the goal of increasing domestic consumption.

Industrialization and mass marketing increased both the production and demand for a new range of consumer goods – including clothing, processed foods, and labor-saving devices – and created more leisure opportunities.

The availability of consumer goods dramatically increased after the Industrial Revolution despite the main focus on the capital goods sector and industrial infrastructure, such as oil, steel, mining, communications networks, industrial cities, transportation networks and financial centers. The experience of shopping changed with the introduction of department stores; customers had a massive array of goods in one place for the first time. This helped promote shopping as a leisure activity. There was an abundance of resources in the wake of the Industrial Era, whereas before scarcity had been the norm. Products and resources were available in huge quantities and at low prices; therefore, anyone in the industrialized West had access to these goods. By the early 1900s, however, the average consumer in Western Europe spent 80 to 90 percent of his income on necessities, primarily food.

There has always been intentionality in consumerism, it did not simply develop from capitalism. Marketing was not acknowledged as a distinct field of expertise in the pre-modern era due to the predominance of small business. The study of marketing emerged in the 19th century in response to changing intensity and patterns of activity in the economy, and the study of economics as a science. During the Industrial Revolution, national and international economies employed purposeful retailing and advertising, which eventually developed into systemized marketing. Marketing was recognized as a technical field and an area of study by the late 19th century.

Thomas J. Barratt, a British man who has been referred to as "the father of modern advertising," created an advertising campaign for Pears Soap involving targeted slogans, images and phrases. He innovated the practice of public endorsements by recruiting celebrities and scientists willing to speak on behalf of the product. One of these celebrities was Lille Langtry, a singer and actress with a famously flawless complexion. She became the first woman to endorse a commercial product for compensation when she gave a testimonial for Pears Soap.

Thomas J. Barratt, English advertiser

Many of the ideas and practices, still basic to marketing today, were conceived and introduced by Barratt. Throughout the 19th century, as the economy expanded globally, so did advertising. A French newspaper, *La Presse*, was the first to print paid advertising in June 1836. Using this new technique, the paper could lower its price, expand its readership and increase profitability. Soon, every paper would be employing this business strategy.

New efficient methods of transportation and other innovations created new industries, improved the distribution of goods, increased consumerism, and enhanced the quality of life.

Unimproved roads were extremely slow, costly for transport and dangerous. In the 18th century the use of layer gravel became increasingly prevalent, with the three-layer Macadam road paving system coming into use in the early 19th century. Roads were repaired so they would shed water and ditches that facilitated drainage were installed. A layer of stones smoothed the surface and allowed horse's hooves and wagon wheels to pass over more readily without sinking into the mud. It cost a lot to improve and repair roads and though they made land travel cheaper, travel by railroad soon became the primary transportation infrastructure.

A View in Whitechapel Road (caricature, 1831)

Land transportation became much less costly with the spread of railroads. From the 1890s into the 20th century, electric street railroads, including trams, trolleys and streetcars were developed. After 1920, cars and buses began to replace street railroads. The mechanization of overland transportation was complete with the introduction of internal combustion powered vehicles traveling on highways. Prices of transporting farm goods to train stations or markets dropped when trucks became available, and this type of motorized transportation via highway also reduced inventories.

Pipelines were first used in the second half of the 19th century, became major infrastructure throughout the 20th century and are recognized as the most energy efficient means of transportation. Liquids and natural gas are most efficiently pumped using centrifugal compressors and pumps.

During this period, as automobiles gained popularity, advances such as improved steering, multi-speed transmissions and hand brakes were developed. The most important form of modern automotive propulsion was invented by Nikolaus Otto, consisting of the four-stroke gasoline internal combustion engine. A similarly structured diesel engine was created by Rudolf Diesel. Though automobiles were successful in providing faster mass transit, there was some effort to regulate new automobiles with the Locomotive Act of 1865. This act required any self-propelled vehicle to not exceed two miles per hour and be manned by a crew of three, including a man who had to jog in front of the vehicle waving a red flag of warning and blowing a signal horn.

Because of the persistence of primitive agricultural practices and land-owning patterns, some areas of Europe lagged in industrialization while facing famine, debt, and land shortages.

During the mid-1840s, in Northern Europe there was a food crisis referred to as the European Potato Failure. Potato blight was a potato disease that destroyed potato crops across Europe in the 1840s and caused widespread famine. Ireland was hit particularly hard because a particular variety of potatoes, the Irish Lumper, were the majority grown in Ireland and those crops were devastated by the potato disease. This period has been referred to as the "Hungry Forties." The Scottish Highlands and Ireland suffered most during this crisis. There was widespread starvation because other staple food sources were unavailable.

The period of mass starvation and disease in Ireland, along with the concomitant emigration from the area between 1845 and 1852 is known as the Great Famine or the Great Hunger. Two-fifths of the population relied completely on cheap potato crops to survive so this crisis has also been called the Irish Potato Famine (mostly outside Ireland). The island's population decreased by 20-25% during this period, due to migration and to death from starvation and disease.

Women and her children starving from the potato famine in 19th-century Ireland

Many of these immigrants eventually found their way to the United States, and now account for a large portion of the population of the Northeastern part of the country. The famine was both devastating and bolstering to the Irish people. Its effect on Ireland's political, cultural and demographic landscape was irreversible. This historical event became part of folk memory and a rallying point for those in the resulting diaspora and those who remained to fight for the Irish Home Rule and United Ireland movements.

Famine added further strain to the relations between the Anglo-Saxon British Crown and the Celtic Irish. Irish republicanism gained popularity, culminating with the Irish achieving independence in the 20th century. The history of the Irish is often viewed as divided by the famine into pre- and post-famine history.

In 1816, 1817 and 1819, serfdom was abolished in Estland (present-day Estonia), Courland (parts of present-day Latvia), and Livonia (present-day Lithuania). However, all the land remained in the hands of the nobility and labor-based rent extraction lasted till 1868. This system was eventually replaced by the working of the land by landless laborers and/or sharecropping. Landless workers had to ask permission to leave an estate, as the conditions of their employment were something akin to indentured servitude. The nobility did not have enough power to muster real opposition to the freeing of the serfs. The noble class was scattered, suffering from a lack of primogeniture and there was much mobility and turnover of families from one estate to another.

Grand Duchess Elena Pavlovna was the Tsar's aunt. She was an important power behind the scenes from 1855 to 1861. Through the close relationship she had with the Alexander II, she helped garner interest from powerful supporters about a plan for emancipation. Alexander II led a major agrarian reform in 1861 during which he freed the serfs, earning him the popular nickname Tsar Liberator.

Grand Duchess Elena Pavlovna of Russia

However, the abolition of serfdom was not universally beneficial to the serfs themselves; in most Russian provinces there was very little access to land for the newly freed serfs. This led to their need to seek employment, which essentially amounted to something akin to indentured servitude. Further, the landowners who were relatively sophisticated compared to the newly freed serfs, often took advantage of the latter's naivety. Landowners charged extremely high rates for suboptimal land and extracted a price from the serfs that was untenable. Many advisors in the Russian Empire had advised that this was inevitable and advocated a policy of state purchase of serfs, who would then gradually be retrained and relocated so as to make the transition to "freedom" as smooth as possible. However, individuals like Grand Duchess Elena Pavlovna, won out, which led to the creation of conditions that made a revolution in Russia inevitable, as some have argued.

Key Concept 3.3: The problems of industrialization provoked a range of ideological, governmental and collective responses.

The French Revolution and the Industrial Revolution triggered dramatic political and social consequences and new theories to deal with them. The ideologies engendered by these 19th century revolutions – conservatism, liberalism, socialism, nationalism and even romanticism – provided their adherents with coherent views of the world and differing blueprints for change. For example, utopian socialists experimented with communal living as a social and economic response to change. The responses to socioeconomic changes reached a culmination in the revolutions of 1848, but the failure of these uprisings left the issues raised by the economic, political and social transformations unresolved well into the 20th century.

In the second half of the 19th century, labor leaders in many countries created unions and syndicates to provide the working classes with a collective voice, and these organizations used collective action such as strikes and movements for men's universal suffrage to reinforce their demands. Feminists and suffragists petitioned and staged public protests to press their demands for similar rights for women. The international movements for socialism, workers' rights and women's rights were important examples of a trend toward international cooperation in a variety of causes, including the abolitionist (antislavery) and peace movements. Finally, political parties emerged as sophisticated vehicles for advocating reform or reacting to changing conditions in the political arena.

Nationalism acted as one of the most powerful engines of political change, inspiring revolutions as well as campaigns by states for national unity or a higher degree of centralization. Early nationalism emphasized shared historical and cultural experiences that often threatened traditional elites. Over the course of the 19th century, leaders recognized the need to promote national unity through economic development and expanding state functions to meet the challenges posed by industry.

Ideologies developed and took root throughout society as a response to industrial and political revolutions.

The term "ideology" was conceived during the contentious philosophical and political debates and fights of the French Revolution. It was devised in 1796 by Antoine Destutt de Tracy, who combined the words "idea" and "logos" in reference to one feature of his "science of ideas" (to the study itself, as opposed to the focus of the study). He isolated three aspects: ideology (the subject), general grammar (the means) and logic (the reason) and argued that among these aspects, ideology was the most general term, because the science of ideas also encompassed the study of their expression and deduction.

Antoine Destutt de Tracy, French Enlightenment philosopher

Napoleon Bonaparte used the word "ideologues" to refer to his intellectual opponents with scorn. Over time, the word "ideology" has lost some of its negative connotation and it is now a neutral term used in the analysis of contradictory political opinions and views held by different social groups.

Liberals emphasized popular sovereignty, individual rights and enlightened self-interest, but debated the extent to which all groups in society should actively participate in its governance.

Liberalism emerged among European philosophers and economists during the Enlightenment. It is a political philosophy or worldview to which the ideas of liberty and equality are central. Classical liberalism champions liberty while social liberalism is more focused on equality. Liberals typically promote ideals and programs in connection with freedom of speech, freedom of the press, freedom of religion, free markets, civil rights, democratic societies, secular governments and international cooperation. John Locke, a philosopher during the 17th century, is often credited with establishing liberalism as a distinct philosophical tradition. He promoted the idea that everyone has a natural right to life, liberty and property, which should not be trampled on by the government.

Classical liberalism is a belief in unmitigated human liberty, with the implication that humans are unique autonomous individuals who trade their labor to one another for the sake of personal gain. (This is distinct from Marxism, which groups human beings into collectives and assumes that humans must produce for the benefit of society at large, as the aforementioned organization of labor leads to the exploitation of the many at the hands of the few.) It is a reaction to monarchy and statist economic control. The arguments for human liberty and autonomy originate with John Locke's *Second Treatise* on government, which was a direct criticism of the encroaching despotic rule which Locke witnessed in England during the 17th century.

Roughly one hundred years after Locke, another English philosopher, Adam Smith, undertook a seminal investigation of the nature of human economic interaction on the part of free individuals. His findings became the basic principles of classical economics on which Liberalism is predicated, and the beginning of the modern field of study called "economics." They were published in 1776, the year of the American Declaration of Independence, as *An Inquiry Into the Nature and Causes of The Wealth Of Nations –* usually referred to as *The Wealth of Nations* today.

In his seminal text, Smith argues that the advancement of society necessitates division of labor and specialization. Smith explains this in the manufacturing of pins, whereby the process is made altogether more efficient by one worker focusing on the head, another worker focusing on the shaft, and another worker focusing on the assembly of the constituent pieces into the whole. Through this, the output of these three workers together could be far greater than if the same three individuals had to construct the whole pin themselves. This notion of specialization eventually led to the adoption of manufacturing lines and drastically improved the efficiency of factories in the era of industrialization.

Emile Durkheim, a German scholar who lived a century after Smith, expanded on the key idea Smith had espoused: that free markets increase people's living standards because of the greater specialization of labor that leads to more efficient production. This was the argument in Durkheim's doctoral thesis, published in 1896 under the title *The*

Division of Labor in Society. His most important finding was that as a country matures, specialization requires its system of government to shift from despotism to popular government and its justice system to move from a focus on criminal law and retribution to civil law and the peaceful resolution of conflicts in the civil courts.

Emile Durkheim, German scholar

Liberalism has existed in Europe since the 17th century. It is often referred to as either the English or French version, with English liberalism promoting the increase of democratic values and constitutional reform and French liberalism focusing on the elimination of authoritarian political and economic structures in addition to nation-building. John Stuart Mill (1806 – 1873) was a British philosopher, political economist and civil servant. He made significant contributions to social and political theory and the political economy and has been referred to as the most influential English-speaking philosopher of the 19th century. Mill promoted individual liberty as more important than state control. He said that an individual's drive to improve himself and his circumstances is the only source of pure freedom.

By promoting that "individual efforts to improve" have value, Mill showed how people could pursue self-improvement without causing harm to others. Mill promoted utilitarianism, an ethical theory that had been established by Jeremy Bentham, who posits that society should be organized in such a way that the greatest amount of good can be spread among the greatest number of people. Mill worked extensively on the theory of the scientific method and was a great proponent of the use of empiricism to combat the long-held myths that governed society. Mill also served as a Member of Parliament in addition to being an important figure in liberal political philosophy.

Jeremy Bentham (1748 – 1832), who is considered to be the creator of modern utilitarianism, was a philosopher, jurist and social reformer from Britain. He became an important scholar of the Anglo-American philosophy of law. His radical political ideas eventually had an impact on the establishment of welfarism. Bentham promoted individual and economic liberty, the separation of church and state, freedom of expression, women's rights, the right to divorce, animal rights and the decriminalizing of homosexual acts. He also advocated for the abolition of slavery, the outlawing of the death penalty and the abolition of physical punishment, including that of children. Though Bentham staunchly supported the extension of legal rights to individuals, he rejected the concept of natural law and natural rights. Among his students were his secretary and colleague James Mill, John Stuart Mill (James Mill's son), the legal philosopher John Austin and Robert Owen, who was one of the founders of the utopian socialist experiment at New Lanark Mills. Other important adherents of liberalism and radical liberalism were Henri de Saint-Simon, Charles Fourier, August Bebel and Clara Zetkin.

Radicals in Britain and republicans on the continent demanded universal male suffrage and full citizenship without regard to wealth and property ownership; some argued that such rights should be extended to women.

The radical liberal movement began in England during the 1790s and focused on parliamentary and electoral reform by stressing the concepts of natural rights and popular sovereignty. Radical liberalists rejected any form of privilege, including the monarchy and aristocracy, and attempted to rally the masses in favor of democratic reform. In 1832, the Reform Act was passed as a response to the public pressure that had been instigated by radical liberalists. The middle class was enfranchised by the Reform Act, but the act failed to fulfill further radical requests.

Chartism was a British working-class protest movement beginning with the People's Charter in 1838 and continuing until 1858, which sought political reform in order to improve the status of working class people. Chartists largely employed petitions and mass meetings in order to pressure politicians to enact universal suffrage for working class people. Flora Tristan (1803 – 1844) was a socialist writer, activist and one of the founders of modern feminism. She was also the painter Paul Gauguin's grandmother. Tristan produced numerous works, most notably *Peregrinations of a Pariah* and *The Workers' Union*, her last essay, which solidified the public's perception of her as a political activist.

Flora Tristan, feminist

The Workers' Union promoted ideas similar to those of Utopian Socialists like Charles Fourier (whom Tristan knew personally) and the French Socialists – the Saint Simonians – whose works Tristan had studied. While she paid homage to the ideas of previous socialists, Tristan was the first to note the link between working class freedom and women's rights. She expressed the need for the liberation of women in order to fulfill the emancipation of the working class, which would in turn unite society. Flora Tristan died in 1844. During her life, she enlarged on her colleagues' and mentors' socialist concepts and established a sensible program that working class people could realistically pursue. She took a new approach to seeking working class rights, including women's rights as an important component of that struggle.

Conservatives developed a new ideology in support of traditional political and religious authority, based on the idea that human nature was not perfectible.

The political and social philosophy of conservatism advocates the continuation of or return to traditional social institutions. The term conservatism was coined by François-René de Chateaubriand in 1818, during the Bourbon Restoration, which sought to reverse the new policies that were enacted as a result of the French Revolution. Though the term has often been used to refer to right-wing politics, it encompasses a wide range of views. There are no policies that are universally thought of as conservative, because the definition of conservatism depends on what is considered traditional in a given place and time. Thus, conservatives from different areas can be in opposition. Edmund Burke was an 18th century politician who opposed the French Revolution but was in favor of the American

Revolution and is recognized as one of the main theorists of conservatism in Great Britain during the 1790s.

Anarchists asserted that all forms of governmental authority were unnecessary and should be overthrown and replaced with a society based on voluntary cooperation.

The political philosophy of anarchism promotes freedom from controlling forces, including state government, which anarchists see as needless and destructive. Modern anarchism stemmed from secular or religious Enlightenment thought, principally Jean-Jacques Rousseau's promotion of the moral centrality of liberty. The 1790s were characterized by the political unrest that stemmed from the French Revolution. Amidst this chaos, William Godwin, often thought of as the initiator of philosophical anarchy, devised the initial concepts of political and economic anarchy, though he did not use the term at the time.

In his work *Political Justice* (1793), Godwin professed that society is negatively impacted by government because the latter has an interest in maintaining the subservience and ignorance of the former. He believed that people, when left to their own accord, would use their powers of reasoning to create a harmonious society. Godwin rejected anything that could be seen as "mentally enslaving" people, including laws, property ownership and marriage, and hypothesized that if citizens improved their education en masse, then government would become superfluous. Thus, he believed that a process of natural evolution, not force, would remove the government from power.

Pierre-Joseph Proudhon was a French philosopher who is considered the first person to identify himself as an anarchist, a description he assumed in his pioneering work *What is Property?* (published in 1840). He devised the theory of spontaneous order in society, in which structure develops without the intervention or imposition of an overarching organization, like a government.

One of the most important figures of anarchism was Mikhail Alexandrovich Bakunin (1814 – 1876), a Russian revolutionary anarchist and founder of collectivist anarchism and the social anarchist tradition. Bakunin was a famous activist and ideologue, which helped him achieve significant influence on radicals in Russia and Europe.

Georges Eugène Sorel (1847 – 1922) was a French philosopher and theorist of revolutionary syndicalism. The term "sorelianism" generally refers to the anti-individualist, anti-liberal, anti-materialist, anti-positivist, anti-rationalist, spiritualist syndicalism Sorel endorsed. Sorelians rejected bourgeois democracy, the innovations of the 18th century, the secular spirit and the French Revolution in favor of classical tradition. Sorel thought that the working class would only achieve victory in the class struggle using myth and a general strike. He believed class conflict would result in the renewal of the bourgeoisie, in addition to the proletariat. At first, Sorel subscribed to a revised version of Marxism; however, in 1910, he rejected socialist literature and in 1914, claimed socialism to be dead because of pervasive misconceptions about Marxism.

In 1909, Sorel became enamored with Maurrassian integral nationalism, which had a great influence on his works. Sorelianism is considered to be a precursor of fascism, though this is often the case with radical philosophers when the interpretation of their ideas is left to the individual interpreting them. Sorel's idea of the power of myth in people's lives inspired both Marxists and Fascists and, coupled with his defense of violence, is the contribution for which he is most often remembered.

Georges Eugène Sorel, French philosopher and syndicalism theorist

Nationalists encouraged loyalty to the nation in a variety of ways, including romantic idealism, liberal reform, political unification, racialism with a concomitant anti-Semitism and chauvinism justifying national aggrandizement.

Nationalism refers to a common group sentiment that can be expressed as a belief or political ideology of identifying with, or becoming attached to, a country. Historically, nationalism has developed in countries when influential groups within a society have sought to remedy the widespread dissatisfaction with traditional identities that had arisen. This often leads to revisionism and the deification of an idealized past or a glowing future. Nationalism was arguably the most influential notion in the 19th and early 20th century. It would eventually become a main motivational factor in the crumbling of the Austro-Hungarian Empire, the German Empire and the Ottoman Empire. Further, nationalism would eventually lead to the onset of two world wars and the implementation of mass genocides all around the world.

Johann Gottlieb Fichte (1762–1814) was a German philosopher and one of the founders of German idealism, a philosophical movement stemming from Immanuel Kant's theories and ethical ideas. Fichte contributed to the field of political philosophy and is considered to be one of the founders of nationalism in Germany.

The Brothers Grimm (Jacob 1785–1863 and Wilhelm Grimm 1786–1859), were German academics, linguists, cultural researchers, lexicographers and writers, most widely known for the folk tales they published during the 19th century. In 1812, their first collection of stories, *Children's and Household Tales*, was published. It was revised and republished several times between 1812 and 1857 and grew from the 86 stories that had been included in the original collection to 200 tales.

The Brothers Grimm, German writers

The Grimm brothers grew up in Hanau, Germany. When they were still young, their father died and the Grimm family subsequently experienced significant poverty. Both brothers attended the University of Marburg, where they acquired an interest in German folklore, which they saw as a way to preserve and promote Germany's traditional literature and culture. This pastime eventually developed into the lifelong pursuit of collecting

German folk tales. Their goal was to produce a scholarly work on folk tales and in the process they devised a way of collecting and recording stories that served as the foundation for folklore studies. The Grimm brothers also authored collections of German and Scandinavian mythologies, which were well-received, and began to compile a complete German dictionary in 1838.

In 1894, a political scandal known as the "Dreyfus affair" developed in France and continued to divide that country until 1906. A major role was played by the press and public opinion. This event can be seen as a starting point for the virulent anti-Semitism that would take root across Europe in the succeeding fifty years. It began in December 1894, when Captain Alfred Dreyfus, a Jew, was convicted of treason and received a sentence of life in prison for allegedly releasing secret French military information to the German Embassy in Paris.

Two years later, in 1896, evidence relieving Dreyfus of guilt and identifying the real culprit as French Army major Ferdinand Walsin Esterhazy came to light. However, this new evidence was suppressed by high-ranking military officials and Esterhazy was acquitted after a two-day trial. Furthermore, the army falsified documents which were used to make added charges against Dreyfus. In 1899, Dreyfus returned to France from Devil's Island in French Guiana, where he had been imprisoned, for a second trial. An intense political and judicial conflict arose between "Dreyfusards," French citizens who were mostly anticlerical, pro-republican and believed in Dreyfus' innocence, and anti-Dreyfusards, French citizens who were mostly pro-army, Catholic and believed Dreyfus was guilty.

The new trial concluded with Dreyfus being convicted and sentenced to 10 more years in prison; however, he was pardoned and freed. Eventually, it was proved that the charges against Alfred Dreyfus were false and in 1906, the army reinstated him as a major. Dreyfus served throughout World War I, working his way up to the rank of lieutenant-colonel. He died in 1935.

A further expression of nationalist anti-Semitism occurred in Vienna under the reign of Mayor Karl Lueger (1897-1910). It would be a mischaracterization to call him an outright German nationalist, however, due to his populist tendencies and the general popularity of nationalism in the German-speaking world at the time, he pragmatically adopted nationalist rhetoric as a means to maintain control of his city. While Lueger's nationalism was pragmatic, his anti-Semitism was not. He truly thought that the Jews were responsible for many of the maladies of contemporary Germanic society and that they were a poison to its progress towards its true potential.

While Mayor Karl Lueger mistreated Jews during his term in office, the narrative of anti-Semitism that he set in motion was only fully expressed later – after Versailles – when the people of Germany and Austria were looking for a scapegoat. The young, Vienna-born Adolf Hitler was greatly influenced by the thinking of the late mayor who had already put forth narratives of anti-Semitism that the Nazi Party could later exploit. Hitler was further influenced by Leuger's belief that a capital city needs to be functional, grand and green. To a large extent this is why Hitler employed many architects during the war, and shortly after conquering a territory would initiate grandiose construction projects to project the power of the German Reich.

Pan-Slavism was a nationalist sentiment that developed in Russia in the mid-19th century. A nascent sentiment for the unification of the Slavic lands had always existed in the Russian Orthodox Church, who saw it as their duty as "the Third Rome" to unite all Slavic peoples. The Russian *Imperator* (Emperor) governed the country under the slogan of *Pravoslaviye, Samoderzhaviye, Narodnost* (Orthodoxy, Autocracy, Nationality). In the wake to Russia's pivotal role in the rescuing of Europe from Napoleon, an ideology of Russian exceptionalism began to take hold. The Russians began to think that the Slavic peoples, mainly manifested in the Russian state, had a unique position as the saviors of decadent Europe and the protectors of the true Christian faith. This led to the promotion of increased agitation of the Slavic peoples under the control of the Ottoman Empire (Serbs, Slovenians and Bulgarians).

Eventually, the Russo-Turkish War broke out, which was won by the Russians. Many of the pan-Slavists had rallied behind the war effort because they believed a Russian victory would lead to the liberation of these Slavic peoples and eventually to the establishment of a Slavic Union with Russia's Emperor as the leader. However, the *realpolitik* of the era meant that complete liberation of these territories was impossible, with part of Bulgaria remaining under direct Ottoman control. This was met with widespread criticism by the pan-Slavists, some of whom would go on to form the ultra-nationalist group *Narodnaya Volya* (the People's Will), a group that eventually assassinated Tsar Alexander II in 1881.

Giuseppe Mazzini was a noted proponent of nationalism in this era and is largely credited with creating the narrative that led to the unification of Italy. Though Mazzini was opposed to the House of Savoy's unification of the Italian state under King Victtorio

Emanuele, his ideas on unification and how to keep the state together were extremely influential. He was an advocate of the governing philosophy of Republicanism and vehemently opposed Marxism, rationalism and atheism. Further, he was an early proponent of the idea of creating a "United States of Europe," and is seen as one of the forefathers of today's European Union.

Giuseppe Mazzini, Italian statesman

A form of Jewish nationalism, Zionism, developed in the late 19th century as a response to growing anti-Semitism in both Western and Eastern Europe.

Zionism is a nationalist and political movement of Jews calling for the re-establishment of a Jewish homeland in Israel. Zionism arose in Central and Eastern Europe in the late 19th century where it was referred to as Hovevei Tziyon. At the time, leaders of the movement were pursuing the goal of establishing a Jewish homeland in Palestine, which was under the control of the Ottoman Empire. Until 1948, Zionism's chief concerns were re-establishing Jewish sovereignty in the Land of Israel, gathering up Jewish refugees and eliminating antisemitism.

Theodor Herzl (1860–1904), who was born Benjamin Ze'ev Herzl, was an Austro-Hungarian journalist, playwright, political activist and writer, and one of the founders of modern political Zionism. He created the World Zionist Organization and advocated for Jews around the world to migrate to Palestine in support of the effort to establish a Jewish nation (Israel). While he was a reporter for the *Neue Freie Presse* in Paris, Herzl covered the aforementioned Dreyfus affair and witnessed the mass rallies that followed the trial, at which chants of "Death to the Jews!" were common.

Herzl had originally advocated Jewish emancipation and assimilation, but later came to believe that Jews should leave Europe and establish a nation of their own. He thought Dreyfus had been wrongly convicted and this may have been a factor in Herzl's adoption of the Zionist cause and decision to relocate to Britain in 1896. The *Neue Freie Presse* had declined to print Herzl's Zionist political writings. According to Henry Wickhamsteed, he was "fanatically devoted to the propagation of Jewish-German 'Liberal' assimilationist doctrine."

Theodor Herzl, a founder of modern political Zionism

In late 1895, Herzl wrote *Der Judenstaat* (The Jewish State), which was published in February 1896 and received both praise and condemnation. The book promoted the idea that Jewish people should abandon Europe for Argentina or preferably Palestine, the historic homeland of the Jews. Herzl argued that Jews already had a nationality, they were just in need of a nation, which would protect them from anti-Semitism and allow for the free expression of Jewish culture and religious practice. These ideas quickly circulated among Jews around the globe and received international attention from others as well. Hovevei Zion and other Zionist movements supported Herzel's ideas, but he was rejected by the Jewish establishment who believed him to be an obstacle to their assimilation efforts.

Governments responded to the problems created or exacerbated by industrialization by expanding their functions and creating modern bureaucratic states.

Over the course of the 18th century, a modern bureaucracy emerged as the Department of Excise in the United Kingdom grew. The bureaucracy was relatively efficient and professional, which enabled the government to impose significant taxes in order to raise the massive amount of money they needed to fund wars. By the late 18th century, the ratio of fiscal bureaucracy to population in Britain was about 1 to 1300, which was nearly four times greater than that ratio in France, which also employed a large bureaucracy. The ancient Chinese Imperial Examination was the inspiration for the Northcote-Trevelyan Report of 1854, which recommended that recruitment into the bureaucracy should be based on merit, which could be determined via an examination. It was believed that bureaucrats should enter with a certain level of education and then be promoted based on their performance rather than by "preferment, patronage or purchase."

While they were still exempt from paying taxes under Louis XIV of France, the old nobility did not possess power or political influence. They made comparisons between the former absolute monarchies and the current monarchies using bureaucracy to enforce their agendas. France also experienced explosive government expansion during the 18th century, accompanied by the rise of the French civil service, in which complex bureaucratic systems were established, a phenomenon that became known as "bureau-mania." When Confucian texts were translated during the Enlightenment, Western philosophers became exposed to the idea of meritocracy and began to see this as an alternative to the traditional ancient European regimes. In the early 19th century, Napoleon sought to adopt a meritocratic system by reforming France's bureaucracies and other territories by instituting a standardized Napoleonic Code; however, ironically the effort resulted in the expansion of bureaucracy in France.

By the mid-19th century, bureaucratic administration was being used widely in the industrialized world. Philosophers like John Stuart Mill and Karl Marx offered theories about the economic functions and power structures of bureaucracy in contemporary life. Max Weber provided the initial endorsement of bureaucracy as a necessary component of a modern nation, and by the late 19th century bureaucratic systems had been installed in other large institutions, in addition to governments.

Liberalism shifted from laissez-faire to interventionist economic and social policies on behalf of the less privileged; the policies were based on a rational approach to reform that addressed the impact of the Industrial Revolution on the individual.

The laissez-faire movement in Europe was initially promoted by the physiocrats, a group founded by Vincent de Gournay, a successful merchant. De Gournay believed government should permit natural laws to coordinate economic activity and the state should become involved only to safeguard people's rights to life, liberty and property.

Laissez-faire ideas became an important component of European liberalism during the 19th century. Many of the physiocrats' ideas spread around Europe and were embraced to some degree in Sweden, Tuscany, Spain and the United States. In 1843, *The Economist* newspaper, which developed into a powerful proponent of laissez-faire capitalism, was founded in Britain. The rise of oil companies and other British companies seeking governmental support for their international operations led to a diminishing of the laissez-faire economic practices that had previously prevailed in the British Empire.

In the West, those who championed the ideas of scientific social planning, such as the sociologist Auguste Comte and the social researcher Charles Booth, influenced the appearance of social policy in countries after the Industrial Revolution. Investigations that uncovered the brutal conditions in the urban slums of Victorian Britain resulted in changes, such as the eventual abolition of the "Poor Laws" and liberal welfare reforms. Germany also developed the Bismarckian welfare state in the 19th century. The contraction and ultimate abolition of the Poor Laws occurred in England and Wales about 1870.

Portrait of Auguste Comte, sociologist

Government reforms transformed unhealthy and overcrowded cities by modernizing infrastructure, regulating public health, reforming prisons and establishing modern police forces.

Voluntary hospitals grew rapidly throughout the 18th century in England. Towards the end of that century, a system emerged for the improvement of public health concerns. It operated by the initial identification of a concern, the application of private philanthropy in addressing the concern, and the resulting change in public opinion about the concern influencing government action related to the concern. Some examples of this system in practice are the prevalence of the practice of vaccination that emerged in the 1800s, following the groundbreaking work of Edward Jenner in treating smallpox and the introduction of fruit on lengthy voyages after the publication of James Lind's work in 1754, which identified what causes scurvy. Efforts were also made to provide public health education to the wider public. In 1752, the British physician Sir John Pringle published *Observations on the Diseases of the Army in Camp and Garrison*, which promoted the provision of outhouses for soldiers' use and the necessity for proper ventilation in military barracks.

Though working class living standards were upgraded in conjunction with the start of the Industrial Revolution, downsides to development, including the overcrowding and unsanitary conditions that resulted from mass migration to urban areas, also occurred. Between 1800 and 1840, London's population doubled and newly industrial towns, such as Leeds and Manchester, experienced even greater rates of growth as people flocked to cities in search of better jobs and economic prosperity. Cities were unprepared for such a large influx of people and did not have the means to house them and did not provide organized sanitation services. Hence, the spread of disease was inevitable. The per capita death rate rose significantly, almost doubling in Birmingham and Liverpool. In 1798, Thomas Malthus began to warn of the dangers of overpopulation. His ideas, along with those of Jeremy Bentham, came to influence government policy in the early 19th century.

Urban areas began to be transformed. Crime rates decreased with the organization of modern police forces responsible for protecting public safety, overcrowding was ameliorated and streetlights appeared. On November 12, 1884, Lviv (a city in what was then the Temesvár in the Kingdom of Hungary) became the first Continental European urban area to install public electric lighting.

Thomas Malthus, English cleric and scholar

Governments promoted compulsory public education to advance the goals of public order, nationalism and economic growth.

In the late 19th century, much of Western, Central and parts of Eastern Europe began to administer elementary education in reading, writing and arithmetic because politicians believed that in order to fulfill the duties of citizenship, an individual must have a basic educational foundation. As literacy rates increased, people became aware that secondary education was limited to those who could pay for it. By the onset of World War I, governments that had originally invested in primary education services began to also give attention to secondary education. In 1884, a trailblazing conference on education took place at the International Health Exhibition in London and was attended by education specialists from across Europe.

The Elementary Education Act of 1880 made school attendance mandatory for children between the ages of five and ten. This requirement was difficult for poorer families to meet because they were often tempted to send their children to work instead of to school, in order to bring in more money for food, clothing and other basic necessities. Truancy Officers were dispatched to the homes of students who failed to attend school, but this was ineffective in improving their attendance. Employed children below the age of thirteen were required to prove they had met the minimum educational requirements. Employers of children who weren't able to show this proof to the government risked being penalized. In 1893, the Elementary Education (School Attendance) Act increased the age of compulsory school attendance to eleven years. Later that year, the requirement was expanded to include blind and deaf children, who had no means of acquiring education up to that point. In 1899, the act was further amended increasing the age of compulsory school attendance to twelve years.

Under the 1891 Elementary Education Act, the state paid school fees of up to ten shillings per pupil. The Voluntary Schools Act of 1897 also provided grants to public elementary schools that were not funded by school boards (typically schools run by the Church).

Political movements and social organizations responded to the problems of industrialization.

After the conclusion of the French Revolution in 1789, European powers sought to restore conditions to their previous existence. At the Congress of Vienna in 1815, the European empires managed to design a balance of power that they could all accept, known as the Metternich system. However, their attempts to maintain peace were not able to quell the spread of revolutionary movements between 1815 and 1871, inspired by industrialization and the French Revolution. The working class and certain philosophers promoted socialist, communist and anarchistic ideas. The middle class and merchants advocated for liberalism, unrestricted trade and capitalism. The rise of nationalism in Germany, Italy, Poland, Hungary and elsewhere led those countries to seek freedom from foreign rule.

Congress of Vienna, 1815

Greece was able to successfully overthrow its Ottoman rulers in the 1820s. The conflict was viewed in a romantic light by European diplomats and intellectuals who saw in the Greeks a shared "European" history and began to largely see the Ottomans as a distinct "other." In many ways this was indicative of the nationalism that would grow and flourish in this era. There was a search for a common enemy, be it external or internal, that could be characterized as the "other" as a means to unite the nation under a common goal.

Mass-based political parties emerged as sophisticated vehicles for social, economic and political reform.

A political party is a group of people with common goals who seek to gain and exert power in political systems in hopes of achieving their shared goals. There is some similarity in how political parties operate around the world, but there are also major differences.

The first distinct political parties emerged in England out of the disorder that occurred when many different factions of Whigs arose after the old Whigs lost power. One such group was known as the "Rockingham Whigs," led by Charles Watson-Wentworth. The Rockingham Whigs also received intellectual guidance from the conservative political philosopher Edmund Burke, who outlined the basic structure of a political party as a group of men bonded together by shared principles which they seek to promote on a national level.

The modern day Conservative Party stemmed from the early 19th century "Pittite" Tories – who took their name from the leader of the group William Pitt the Younger. In the late 1820s, disputes over political reform fractured the Pittite Tories and the Duke of Wellington's government dissolved. In the wake of this disruption, Robert Peel began to put together a new alliance. In 1834, he issued the Tamworth Manifesto, which laid out the basic ideas of Conservatism. In 1859, the Whigs, free trade Tory followers of Robert Peel, and independent Radicals created the Liberal Party under Lord Palmerston. Over time, under the lengthy leadership of William Ewart Gladstone, the Liberal Party developed into a party which represented the concerns of the expanding urban middle-class.

In the second half of the 19th century, political parties were developed in countries throughout Europe. The 1848 Revolutions in Germany, France, Austria and other countries ignited liberal sentiment and led to the creation of representative groups and political parties. Large socialist parties were established in Europe at the end of the 19th century. Some of them adhered to Marxism while others advocated social democracy, which called for the use of reformism and gradualism.

Workers established labor unions and movements promoting social and economic reforms that also developed into political parties.

Political parties were often created in conjunction with labor unions, which made it easier for workers to foster social and economic change. On May 23, 1863, Ferdinand Lassalle founded the Social Democratic Party in Germany. In 1869, the Social Democratic Workers' Party (SDAP) of Germany, merged with the ADAV at a conference held in Gotha in 1875, taking the name Socialist Workers' Party of Germany (SAPD). In 1878, Otto von Bismarck used the Anti-Socialist Laws to abolish the party on account of its pro-revolution, anti-monarchy stance; however, in 1890, it was legalized once again and renamed itself the Social Democratic Party (SDP).

Ferdinand Lassalle, philosopher and political activist

In the Landtag (state parliament), the SDP was occasionally able to exert influence on issues like education and social policy. In Hesse, the SDP successfully advocated to separately list church taxes in assessments and for improvements in judicial procedure. The SDP was also sometimes successful at raising wages and bettering municipal laborers' working conditions. For example, in the late 19th century, thanks to SDP pressure in the Reichstag, the factory inspection system was improved. The SDP also secured an allowance for the families of military reservists who were called up for training or maneuvers. In the 1880s, the SDP argued for and achieved the implementation of improved safety measures for miners and improved oversight of the mines in the coal-rich region of Saxony.

The United Kingdom's Labour Party is a center-left political party that emerged from the 19th century trade union movement and socialist political parties and is composed of a diverse array of ideologies, from staunchly socialist to more moderately social democratic. The Russian Social Democratic Labor Party (RSDRP), also known as the Russian Social Democratic Workers' Party or the Russian Social Democratic Party, was a revolutionary socialist political party established in Minsk in 1898 in order to unify the Russian Empire's disparate groups under a single party. The RSDLP eventually split into Majority (*Bolsheviki*) and Minority (*Mensheviki*) divisions, with the former developing into the Communist Party of the Soviet Union. The RSDLP platform was based on an idea promulgated by Marx and Engels: Russia's revolutionary potential was strongest in its industrial working class, as opposed to its more numerous rural farmers. Prior to the Second Congress, the intellectual Vladimir Ilyich Ulyanov, better known by his *nom de guerre* Vladimir Lenin, joined the revolutionary movement. In 1902, Lenin published *What is to be Done?*, which stated his view of the party's purpose: to create "the vanguard of the proletariat." He called for a disciplined, centralized party composed of committed activists in order to achieve that purpose.

Feminists pressed for legal, economic and political rights for women as well as improved working conditions.

The modern Western feminist movement occurred in three waves, each of which addressed differing facets of the same issues raised by feminists. The first wave occurred during the 19th and early 20th centuries and was focused on women's suffrage. In England, it also included the promotion of equal contract, marriage, parental and property rights for women. By the late 19th century, feminist activists were focusing mostly on gaining political power and suffrage, though additionally some feminists were lobbying for women's sexual, reproductive and economic rights.

At the close of the 19th century and beginning of the 20th century, women's suffrage was first achieved in Britain's Australasian territories. The self-governing colonies of New Zealand granted women the right to vote in 1893. South Australia granted female suffrage (both the right to vote and run for parliamentary office) two years later, in 1895 and Australia approved female suffrage in 1902. Britain took a bit longer to concede female suffrage. The Women's Social and Political Union (WSPU), headed by Emmeline Pankhurst and her two daughters, Christabel and Sylvia, aggressively advocated for women's suffrage in Britain between 1903 and 1917.

Members of the WSPU adopted the slogan "deeds, not words" and thus went on hunger strikes, destroyed property at significant buildings and set fires in empty houses and churches. Founders of the WSPU also established a women-only organization that was allied with the independent Labour Party to advocate for social reform and women's suffrage. Norah Dacre Fox (later Norah Elam), a passionately militant feminist, was made General Secretary of the WSPU by 1913. She was an especially effective propagandist and orator who also wrote speeches for Christabel Pankhurt. Other significant figures of the feminist movement in Britain during this time were Flora Tristan and Barbara Smith Bodichon. Finally, in 1918, the Representation of the People Act extended suffrage to women over thirty years of age who owned houses and in 1928, suffrage was granted to any woman over the age of twenty-one.

Emmeline Pankhurst, feminist

Various private, nongovernmental reform movements sought to lift up the deserving poor and end serfdom and slavery (e.g. young prostitutes, children, women, the elderly)

During this time, other social movements concerned with less fortunate members of society (including children, those living in poverty, women and prostitutes) emerged. Compulsory education did not exist in England during the 18th century. Rowland Hill established the first Sunday school at Surrey Chapel in London. By 1831, about a quarter of the British population attended Sunday schools, which offered basic literacy and religious instruction each week. In industrial cities, Sunday schools were complemented by "ragged schools," which provided charity to the poor in industrial areas and eventually by educational opportunities that were publicly funded by the school boards of the late 19th century.

While drunkenness was frowned upon, abstaining from drinking alcohol was rarely encouraged or practiced prior to the temperance movement that emerged in the early part of the 19th century. During the 1830s, there was a surge in the number of temperance groups in England, the United States and the British colonies, particularly New Zealand and Australia. Josephine Elizabeth Butler (1828–1906) was a British feminist and social reform advocate during the Victorian era. She was passionately religious and identified as an evangelical Anglican. Butler was particularly involved in issues related to the welfare of prostitutes. From 1869 to 1886, she led an effort to repeal the Contagious Diseases Acts (both in Britain and internationally), which allowed for the unjust imprisonment of women suspected of engaging in prostitution.

Period 3: 1815-1914

Key Concept 3.4: European states struggled to maintain international stability in an age of nationalism and revolutions.

Following a quarter-century of revolutionary upheaval and war spurred by Napoleon's imperial ambitions, the Great Powers met in Vienna in 1814-1815 to re-establish a workable balance of power and suppress the liberal and nationalist movements for change. Austrian Foreign Minister Klemens von Metternich led the way in creating an informal security arrangement to resolve international disputes and stem revolution through common action among the Great Powers. Nonetheless, revolutions aimed at liberalization of the political system and national self-determination defined the period from 1815 to 1848.

The revolutions that swept Europe in 1848 were triggered by poor economic conditions, frustration at the slow pace of political change and unfulfilled nationalist aspirations. At first, revolutionary forces succeeded in establishing regimes dedicated to change or to gaining independence from great-power domination. However, conservative forces, which still controlled the military and bureaucracy, reasserted control. Although the revolutions of 1848 were, as George Macaulay Trevelyan quipped, a "turning point at which modern history failed to turn" they set the stage for a subsequent sea change in European diplomacy.

A new breed of conservative leader, exemplified by Napoleon III of France, co-opted nationalism as a top-down force for the advancement of state power and authoritarian rule in the name of "the people." Further, the Crimean War (1853-1856), promoted by the decline of the Ottoman Empire, shattered the Concert of Europe established in 1815 and opened the door for the unifications of both Italy and Germany. Using the methods of Realpolitik, Cavour in Italy and Bismarck in Germany succeeded in unifying their nations after centuries of disunity. Their policies of war, diplomatic intrigue and, at Bismarck's insistence, manipulation of democratic mechanisms created states with the potential for upsetting the balance of power, particularly in the case of Germany.

Following the Crimean War, Russia undertook a series of internal reforms aimed at achieving industrial modernization. The reforms succeeded in establishing an industrial economy and emboldened Russia's aspirations in the Balkans. They also led to an active revolutionary movement, which employed political violence and assassinations and was one of the driving forces behind the 1905 Russian Revolution.

After the new German Emperor Wilhelm II dismissed Chancellor Bismarck in 1890, Germany's diplomatic approach altered significantly, leading to a shift in the alliance system and increased tensions in European diplomacy. Imperial antagonisms, growing nationalism, militarism and other factors resulted in the development of a rigid system of alliances. The Great Powers militarized their societies and built up army and naval forces to unprecedented levels (enabled by the industrial and technological advances), while at the same time developing elaborate plans for the next war. The long-anticipated war finally came in the summer of 1914. The assassination of the heir to the Austrian throne in Sarajevo forced the political leaders of the Great Powers, locked in the rigid structure of the Triple Entente versus the Triple Alliance, to implement war plans that virtually required the escalation of the hostilities. The ensuing Great War revealed the flaws in the diplomatic order established after the unifications of Germany and Italy, but more importantly, it produced an even more challenging diplomatic situation than that faced by the diplomats in 1814-1815.

The Concert of Europe (or Congress System) sought to maintain the status quo through collective action and adherence to conservatism.

The Concert of Europe, also known as the Congress System (after the Congress of Vienna), represented the status quo balance of power that loosely existed in Europe from the end of the Napoleonic Wars (1815) until the outbreak of World War I (1914). It was founded by Austria, Prussia, the Russian Empire and the United Kingdom, who were the members of the Quadruple Alliance that had toppled Napoleon's First French Empire. France later became the fifth member of the Concert of Europe.

Lord Castlereagh,
British Foreign Secretary

At first the Concert was led by the British foreign secretary Lord Castlereagh, Austrian Chancellor Klemens von Metternich and Tsar Alexander I of Russia. Charles Maurice de Talleyrand-Périgord of France was largely responsible for quickly restoring France to her former glory as a stalwart of international diplomacy.

The Concert's time period is referred to as the Age of Metternich (because of the influence of the Austrian chancellor's conservatism and the impact Austria had on the German Confederation) or as the European Restoration (after the Congress of Vienna's efforts to restore Europe to its pre-French Revolution state).

The Concert of Europe attempted to maintain the balance of power in Europe during the 19th century, hoping that this would ensure the solidification of peaceful relations on the continent. Their efforts were overwhelmingly successful in avoiding a large conflict involving many European countries for nearly a hundred years – until the outbreak of World War I. Britain and France were the two foremost powers in Europe during the first half of the 19th century, but by the 1850s Russia and Prussia were beginning to catch up. The Crimean War of 1854–1855 and the Italian War of 1859 destabilized the peaceful relations among the superpowers in Europe and the emergence of the German Empire as a power also contributed to the restructuring of the balance of power in Europe. Over a twenty-year period, Otto von Bismarck, the German Chancellor, employed treaties and alliances among European countries, such as the Triple Alliance, to maintain the balance of power in Europe.

While there were no official rules or institutions adopted by the Concert of Europe, any member nation could call for a conference in a time of crisis. The growth of nationalism, the 1848 Revolutions, the Crimean War, the unification of Germany and the Risorgimento in Italy and the Eastern Question all contributed to the erosion of the Concert of Europe's effectiveness.

Metternich, architect of the Concert of Europe, used it to suppress nationalist and liberal revolutions.

Prince Klemens Wenzel von Metternich (1773 – 1859) was an Austrian politician and statesman and an important diplomat who was the Austrian Empire's Foreign Minister from 1809 and Chancellor from 1821 until the revolutions of 1848 forced him to resign. One of Metternich's first undertakings was to seek peace with France through the marriage of Napoleon and the Austrian Archduchess Marie Louise. He also oversaw Austria's entry into the War of the Sixth Coalition on the Allied side, signed the Treaty of Fontainebleau, exiling Napoleon, and commanded the Austrian delegation at the Congress of Vienna (which partitioned Europe amongst the major powers following the fall of Napoleon). Metternich was given the title of Prince of the Austrian Empire in October of 1813.

Austrian Archduchess Marie Louise says goodbye to her family

Under his rule, the "Metternich system" of international congresses continued for ten more years during which Austria aligned itself with Russia and also somewhat with Prussia. This period was the peak of Austria's diplomatic power. Metternich was a traditional conservative who was eager to maintain the balance of power in Europe, especially by checking Russia's desire to increase its territorial holdings in Central Europe and the Ottoman Empire. He disapproved of liberalism and sought to avoid the fragmentation of the Austrian Empire, through activities like suppressing the nationalist revolts in Austrian North Italy and the German states, and employing censorship and spies to quell discontent in Austria.

Conservatives re-established control in many European states and attempted to suppress movements for change and, in some areas, to strengthen adherence to religious authorities.

The goals of conservative political parties differ greatly between nations. Conservative and classical liberal parties often prefer private property rights, while communist, socialist and green parties support the communal ownership of land or measures mandating socially responsible action by property owners. (Note that in this context, "liberal" refers to classical liberalism; political parties referred to as "liberal" in the 21st century are much different from classical liberalism, often leaning toward socialist ideology.) Social issues are what conservatives and liberals primarily disagree upon. Conservatives generally oppose behavior that does not adhere to social norms. Modern conservative parties often define themselves by their rejection of liberal or labor parties.

In Europe, Belgium, Denmark, Iceland, Finland, France, Greece, Iceland, Luxembourg, the Netherlands, Norway, Sweden, Switzerland and the UK all had relatively successful conservative political parties into the 1980s. Around the world, in Australia, Germany, Israel, Italy, Japan, Malta, New Zealand, Spain and the U.S., no conservative parties existed—though Christian Democrats or liberals existed as major right-wing parties. Ireland and Portugal both had right-wing political parties that were hard to classify: the Fine Gael and Progressive Democrats in Ireland and the Social Democratic Party in Portugal. Over the years, the Swiss People's Party has drifted to the extreme right and is no longer considered to be a conservative party. In Italy, which was united by liberals and radicals (the Risorgimento), liberals, not conservatives, emerged as the party of the Right. In 1980, in the Netherlands, conservatives morphed into a new Christian democratic party.

In Austria, Germany, Portugal and Spain, conservatism was swallowed up by fascism or the far right.

A wave of revolutions occurred in Europe during the first half of the 19th century, driven by increased nationalism, the hope for national unification and freedom, the desire to abolish slavery in many states and the liberalizing of political systems. Militaries and governments were mostly controlled by conservatives, who reasserted their power by crushing political movements and often by strengthening dependence on religious authorities.

In the first half of the 19th century, revolutionaries attempted to destroy the status quo.

The Revolutions of 1820 were part of a revolutionary wave occurring in Europe, which included revolutions to institute constitutional monarchies in Spain, Portugal, Russia and Italy. There was also a revolution in Greece in order to gain independence from the Ottoman Empire. Unlike the revolutionary wave in the 1830s, these uprisings tended to take place on the European periphery. The Revolutions of 1830, which followed those of the previous decade, were a revolutionary wave in Europe that included two romantic nationalist revolutions: the Belgian Revolution in the United Kingdom of the Netherlands and the July Revolution in France. During this time, there were also revolutions in Congress Poland (still unofficially controlled by Russia) and Switzerland.

The Greek War of Independence between Greek revolutionaries and the Ottoman Empire lasted from 1821 to 1832 and resulted in Greek independence. The Russian Empire, Great Britain, France and many other European powers provided support to the Greeks, while the Ottomans received assistance from their vassals — the Vilayet of Egypt and the Beylik of Tunis. In 1814, a secret group known as the Filiki Eteria had been established with the goal of liberating Greece from the Ottoman Empire. The Filiki Eteria planned to stage uprisings in the Peloponnese, the Danubian Principalities and in and around Constantinople. The first revolt, which was quickly crushed by the Ottomans, was initiated on March 6, 1821 in the Danubian Principalities. This inspired Greeks in the Peloponnese to act, which they did on March 17, 1821, when the Maniots declared war on the Ottomans. This declaration inspired a wave of revolts against the Ottoman Empire by other territories subject to its control.

Man takes an oath for entrance into the Filiki Eteria

After much negotiation, three of Europe's superpowers — Russia, Britain and France — decided to intervene and each sent naval support to Greece, which ultimately helped in the destruction of the Ottoman-Egyptian fleet. With the further assistance of a French expeditionary force, the Greeks were able to expel the Turks from the Peloponnese and regain part of Central Greece by 1828. Greece was finally recognized as an independent country four years later in May of 1832. Today, Greece celebrates its independence as a national holiday each year on March 25th.

The Decembrist revolt in Russia occurred on December 26, 1825 when Russian army officers led approximately 3,000 troops in an uprising in opposition to Nicholas I's assumption of the throne following his elder brother Constantine removing himself from the line of succession. Many of the soldiers, including officers who took part in this uprising, were strongly influenced by the revolutionary spirit of France, which they had returned from after occupying. The educated officers from the middling gentry began to see that they had more in common with the upper-class French than they did with the peasants in their own country. Further, they were able to see what peasants are capable of when they themselves are given access to an education and released from the bonds of servitude.

Upon their return to Russia, they sought to petition for similar reforms in their homeland; however, they were met with claims from the monarchy and its defenders that the only way to keep Russia in one piece was through the rule of an autocratic Tsar. The uprising was quickly quelled by those loyal to the Tsar, and many of the belligerents were killed or exiled to Siberia. The exiled soldiers did not see this as a lost cause, and though they no longer asked for reforms from the Tsar, they began to improve the conditions of living for those in the countryside, most notably through providing them with basic education.

The November Uprising (1830-31), also known as the Polish–Russian War or the Cadet Revolution, was a militant revolt against the Russian Empire that took place in Poland. It was initiated in Warsaw on November 29, 1830 by young Polish officers from Congress Poland's military academy. Many Polish citizens joined the officers, and the rebellion extended to the territories of Lithuania, Western Belarus and the right-bank Ukraine. The Imperial Russian Army was eventually able to quell the revolt due to its greater size. Following the revolt, Tsar Nicholas I declared that Poland would continue to be part of Russia, with Russian military barracks in Warsaw.

Louis Philippe I, Duke of Orléans

The French Revolution of 1830, also called the July Revolution or Second French Revolution, overthrew King Charles X, the French Bourbon monarch. Following Charles' expulsion, his cousin Louis-Philippe, Duke of Orléans, assumed the throne in France, marking a shift in power from the House of Bourbon to the House of Orléans and the substitution of the principle of hereditary right for popular sovereignty. Supporters of the Bourbons were known as Legitimists and supporters of Louis Philippe were referred to as Orléanists.

The revolutions in 1848 challenged the conservative order and led to the breakdown of the Concert of Europe.

The Revolutions of 1848 were a series of political upheavals throughout Europe in the spring of 1848. The revolutions encompassed the largest revolutionary wave in European history. It should be noted that when one reads of a "spring" in relation to an uprising ("the Prague Spring," "the Arab Spring," etc.) this is inspired by the events of 1848. The revolutions typically lasted less than a year as countries were able to bring them under control relatively quickly.

The revolutions were fundamentally democratic and sought to topple the historical feudal structures and establish independent nation-states. The revolutionary wave emerged in France in February of 1848, and swiftly inspired other revolutions in Europe and Latin America. More than 50 nations were affected by revolutions during this time. There were six main factors around which the uprisings were concentrated. First, widespread dissatisfaction with the political leadership of the day. Second, dissatisfaction with the level of participation in government available to citizens. Third, dissatisfaction with the lack of freedom of the press. Fourth, dissatisfaction with the treatment of the working classes. Fifth, the growth of consciousness of nationality and the desire to organize on this basis. And sixth, the regrouping of the reactionary forces whose base was the royalty, the aristocracy, the army, the Church and the peasantry.

The revolts were conducted by loose, unorganized and informal groups of middle class citizens and workers who were not able to develop the cohesion they needed to overcome the stronger, better organized governmental forces they sought to oust. Tens of thousands of people died as a result of the conflicts, with many being forced into exile. Solid reforms were achieved in some countries, including the abolition of serfdom in Austria and Hungary, the end of absolute monarchy in Denmark, the establishment of a parliamentary democracy in the Netherlands and the end of the Capetian monarchy in France. The revolutions were most intense in France, the Netherlands, Germany, Poland, Italy and the Austrian Empire. Russia, Sweden, Great Britain and much of Southern Europe remained free from revolts during this period.

In 1818, the British had decided not to intervene in European issues that did not directly impact Britain. They opposed Alexander I's plan to suppress future uprisings. The Concert of Europe had become less powerful as the shared aims of the European superpowers were slowly supplanted by increasing political and economic disputes. The European revolutionary upheavals of 1848 sought a restructuring of the Congress of Vienna's frontiers along national lines, which further eroded the power of the Concert of Europe.

The breakdown of the Concert of Europe opened the door for movements of national unification in Italy and Germany as well as liberal reforms elsewhere.

The Concert of Europe officially unraveled in the second half of the 19th century due to wars between its members, such as the Crimean War (1853–56), the Italian War of Independence (1859), the Austro-Prussian War (1866) and the Franco-Prussian War (1870–71). While the Congress System was again used during the Congress of Berlin (1878), which redrew the political map of the Balkans, the former balance of power in Europe had been replaced by a series of shifting alliances.

The Risorgimento (Italian unification) is the name for the political and social movement that unified the various states of the Italian peninsula into the single Kingdom of Italy in the 19th century. There is no consensus on the precise dates for the beginning and end of Italian unification, but most scholars agree that it began in 1815 with the Congress of Vienna and the end of Napoleonic rule, and ended in 1871 when Rome became the capital of the Kingdom of Italy. With the unification of Italy there was a push for maximizing territorial gains in the new Italian state, known as Terre Irredente. This movement sought control of the areas that make up modern Italy in addition to the Dalmatian Coast of Croatia, parts of Slovenia, Nice and large portions of southern Switzerland. Due to Italy's loss in World War I, these territorial gains were not granted in the Treaty of Saint-Germaine; however, Italy was given the strategic city of Trieste and large portions of the Venetia-Giuli regions at the base of the Alps, the border of present-day Slovenia.

Austria emerged as a dominant power in Central Europe following the Congress in Vienna, which took place in 1814-1815 following the Napoleonic Wars. At the time, it was not foreseen that Prussia would eventually gain enough power to compete with Austria. The German dualism that emerged presented two solutions to the issue of Germany's unification: the "Greater German solution" (unification of all German-speaking populations into one nation) and the "Lesser German solution" (unification of northern German states without Austria). There were factors besides the strength of Bismarck's *Realpolitik* which shifted Germany's political, economic, military and diplomatic relations with other countries during the 19th century. Reaction to nationalism in Denmark and France provided a focus for the expression of German unity. Military successes, particularly those of Prussia in three regional wars, resulted in widespread excitement and pride that politicians harnessed to encourage nationalism and support for unification. When a unified Germany (without Austria) was established in 1871, the problem of dualism was resolved — at least temporarily.

The Crimean War demonstrated the weakness of the Ottoman Empire and contributed to the breakdown of the Concert of Europe, thereby creating the conditions in which Italy and Germany could be unified after centuries of fragmentation.

The Crimean War (1853–56) was fought between Russia, who ultimately lost the conflict, and an alliance of Great Britain, France, Sardinia and the Ottoman Empire. In 1851, Napoleon III forced the Sublime Porte (the Ottoman government) to accept France as the guardian of Christian sites in the Holy Land. Russia rejected this designation, asserting its status as guardian of all Eastern Orthodox Christians in the Ottoman Empire. In response, France sent naval forces to the Black Sea, which Russia answered with its own display of force: in 1851, Russia sent soldiers to the Ottoman provinces of Moldavia and Wallachia. Britain, now fearing for the security of the Ottoman Empire, sent a fleet to join the French with the expectation that this would cause the Russians to deescalate.

Scene from the Crimean War

When diplomacy was unsuccessful in resolving the conflict, the Sultan declared war on Russia in October of 1851. After the Ottomans experienced a naval disaster that November, Britain and France declared war on Russia. The Crimean Peninsula, which was the location of a majority of the conflict's battles, was captured by the Allies. Britain was surprised to discover that France and Russia had been secretly planning to enter into a postwar alliance in order to dominate Europe. In light of this, Britain abandoned its plans to attack St. Petersburg and instead signed a one-sided settlement with Russia that achieved virtually none of Britain's war goals, the major one being to wrestle the strategic city of Sevastopol from Russian hands.

The Crimean War was ended by the Treaty of Paris on March 30, 1856. Upon its conclusion, the Ottoman Empire became a member of the European Concert, and the other European superpowers pledged to respect its independence and borders. Russia relinquished a small amount of its territory and its claim to guardianship of Christians in the Ottoman Empire. International commission was established to promote free travel and trade on the Danube River. Moldavia and Wallachia remained under nominal Ottoman rule, but were allowed to have independent constitutions and create national assemblies.

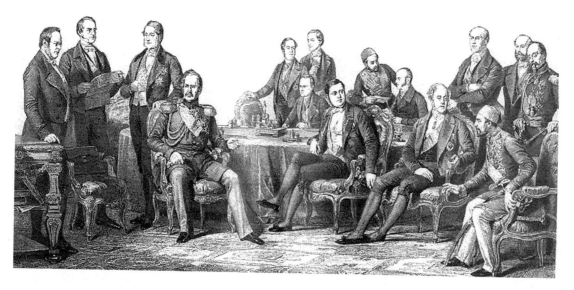

Treaty of Paris, 1856

At this time, new rules of wartime commerce were established in order to enable the relatively smooth functioning of the burgeoning global economy in the event of a war. Privateering (piracy) was made illegal, but ships sailing under a neutral flag were left unmolested as long as they were not carrying war materials. Ships flying under an enemy flag were subject to blockade; if they were found not to be carrying war material, they were allowed to pass without seizing their cargo. The Crimean War introduced many innovations and new technologies, such as railroads, the telegraph and new methods of nursing. The Crimean War was also a turning point in Russian domestic and foreign policy as Russian intellectuals advocated for fundamental reforms to government and social systems following Russia's defeat. The conflict served to decrease the power of both Russia and Austria, so that neither country could continue to promote stability in Europe. This paved the way for Napoleon III of France, Cavour of Italy and Otto von Bismarck of Germany to launch wars in the 1860s that reshaped Europe.

A new breed of conservative leaders, including Napoleon III, Cavour and Bismarck, co-opted the agenda of nationalists for the purposes of creating or strengthening the state.

Conservative leaders sought to increase the power of their countries and reestablish their dominance of European politics and equilibrium. Louis-Napoléon Bonaparte (1808-1873), the nephew and heir of Napoleon I, was the only president of the French Second Republic and eventually became known as Napoleon III, when he assumed the role of Emperor of the Second French Empire. Napoleon was the first president of France to be elected by a direct popular referendum. Both the French Constitution and the French Parliament prevented him from seeking a second term, so he staged a coup d'état in 1851, seizing the throne as Napoleon III on December 2, 1852 – the forty-eighth anniversary of the coronation of Napoleon I.

Early on, Napoleon's government employed censorship and other harsh forms of repression in order to oppress his opponents. Around six thousand people were sent to prison or penal colonies until 1859. Thousands more, including France's greatest novelist of the period Victor Hugo, went into voluntary exile during this time. Napoleon III's foreign policy goals sought to reaffirm France's power in Europe and internationally. He advocated for both popular sovereignty and nationalism in France. Beginning in 1866, when Chancellor Otto von Bismarck was pursuing German unification, Napoleon began to face mounting pressure from Prussia. In July of 1870, Napoleon entered the Franco-Prussian War with an inferior military and with no allies. The French army was quickly defeated and Napoleon III was captured during the Battle of Sedan. As a result, the Third Republic came to be formed in Paris and Napoleon was exiled to England, where he died in 1873.

Camillo Paolo Filippo Giulio Benso, Count of Cavour, Isolabella and Leri (1810 – 1861), commonly known as Cavour, was an Italian political figure instrumental in the movement for Italian unification. He founded the original Liberal Party and created for himself the position of Prime Minister of the Kingdom of Piedmont-Sardinia, which he maintained throughout the Second Italian War of Independence and Garibaldi's efforts to unify Italy. Following the unification of the Kingdom of Italy, Cavour became the first Prime Minister of Italy. After serving for just three months he died and did not live to see Venetia or Rome incorporated into Italy.

In his early years as a politician, Cavour ushered in many economic reforms in his native region of Piedmont and created a political newspaper known as *Il Risorgimento*. Following his election to the Chamber of Deputies, Cavour swiftly climbed the ladder of

Camillo Paolo Filippo Giulio Benso, Italian politician

the Piedmontese government, eventually gaining control of the Chamber of Deputies byfostering a union between left-center and right-center politicians. Cavour eventually became prime minister of Italy in 1852. As prime minister, Cavour successfully negotiated Piedmont's interests throughout the Crimean War, the Second Italian War of Independence and Garibaldi's expeditions. He managed to make Piedmont a new European superpower because at this point Italy was almost completely united and was now five times bigger than Piedmont had been prior to Cavour becoming prime minister.

Otto Eduard Leopold, Prince of Bismarck (1815 – 1898), known as Otto von Bismarck, was a conservative Prussian politician who greatly influenced German and European affairs between 1860 and 1890. In the 1860s, he oversaw a series of wars that by 1871 had unified the German states (with the exception of Austria) into an influential empire under Prussian leadership. Following Germany's unification, Bismarck skillfully employed balance-of-power negotiations to maintain Germany's status as a European superpower. In 1862, King Wilhelm I made Bismarck Minister President of Prussia, a position he retained until 1890. Bismarck started three swift but decisive wars against Denmark, Austria and France, in which he employed the smaller German states to provide support to Prussia in order to defeat France, Germany's chief rival. Bismarck's *Realpolitik* approach to diplomacy and strict rule of Germany earned him the nickname the "Iron Chancellor." German unification and economic growth were Bismarck's foremost goals. While he did not favor colonialism, he did build an overseas empire in response to demands by both the elites and the masses. A skilled diplomat, Bismarck employed his skills of negotiation to safeguard Germany's status as a superpower and maintain peace in Europe until the 1880s.

The creation of the dual monarchy of Austria-Hungary, which recognized the political power of the largest ethnic minority, was an attempt to stabilize the state by reconfiguring the national unity.

Austria was eventually overtaken by Prussia as the dominant German power in Europe following the Austro-Prussian War, also known as the German War (1866). The Austro-Hungarian Compromise of 1867 replaced the empire's former single Austrian

Empire (1804-1867) with a dual structure. The fact that Hungarians were not happy with Vienna's leadership and the rise of nationalism in different areas of the Austrian Empire also led to the adoption of this dual structure. Hungarian dissatisfaction with Vienna's leadership arose in part from Austria's suppression, with Russian assistance, of the liberal Hungarian Revolution of 1848–49. By the late 1850s, many Hungarians who had been in favor of the 1848–1849 revolution were willing to accept the Hapsburg monarchy. Their rationale was that while Hungary had the right to complete internal independence, under the Pragmatic Sanction of 1713, foreign affairs and defense were to be shared between Austria and Hungary.

After the Austrians were defeated at Königgrätz, the government sought reconciliation with Hungary in order to recover its superpower status. The new foreign minister wanted to end the stalled negotiations with the Hungarians. In order to preserve the monarchy, Emperor Franz Joseph began negotiating a compromise with the Hungarian nobility. Hungarian leaders demanded and were granted the Emperor's coronation as King of Hungary and the restoration of a separate parliament in Budapest with the power to enact legislation for the Holy Crown of Hungary.

Following the reforms of 1867, the Austrian and Hungarian states enjoyed equal power. The Compromise needed to be renewed regularly, as did the customs union between Austria and Hungary. Issues having to do with foreign affairs and the military were overseen by both countries, but all other governmental issues were left to each individual state to deal with. At the time, Austria-Hungary was one of the world's great superpowers.

In Russia, autocratic leaders pushed through a program of reform and modernization, which gave rise to revolutionary movements and eventually to the Revolution of 1905.

Four issues in Russian society led to the Russian Revolution: the agrarian problem, the nationality problem, the labor problem and the educated class problem. Individually, these issues may not have impacted the course of Russian history, but in combination they led to a revolution. The government eventually became aware of these widespread issues, although it did not effectively address them. In 1903, the Russian Minister of the Interior, Plehve, said that after the agrarian problem, the most serious issues afflicting Russia were the Jews, the state of the schools and the workers. The Russian economy was enmeshed in European finances so the contraction of Western markets in 1899-1900 hurled Russian industry into a crisis which continued beyond the dip in European industrial production that occurred as a result of the market contraction and led to great social unrest in the years leading up to the revolution of 1905.

In January 1905, an event that came to be known as "Bloody Sunday" took place when Father Gapon led a massive crowd to the Winter Palace in St. Petersburg to present a petition to the Tsar. When the crowd reached the palace, Cossacks opened fire and killed hundreds of people. The Russian people were outraged by the massacre and declared a general strike, demanding a democratic republic, marking the start of the Russian Revolution of 1905. Soviets, the Russian word for councils, were founded in cities throughout the country.

Construction of barricades during Bloody Sunday

In September 1905, there was an uprising that began on the battleship *Potemkin* stationed at the naval base on Kronstadt Island off the coast of St. Petersburg. These sailors eventually formed a revolutionary party, demanding better working conditions for the people of St. Petersburg and the empire as a whole. As a reaction to "Bloody Sunday" and the Kronstadt Rebellion, in October of 1905, Nicholas grudgingly issued his well-known October Manifesto, which conceded the immediate establishment of a national Duma (Parliament). Suffrage was expanded and no legislation was allowed to be enacted without the Duma's approval. Moderates were satisfied by these measures, but socialists dismissed the concessions as insufficient and attempted to carry out further strikes.

By the end of 1905, there was chaos among the reformers and the Tsar's position was strengthened for the time being. The author of the October Manifesto was Count Sergei Yulyevich Witte, an influential policymaker, who oversaw extensive industrialization across the Russian Empire and served under the last two emperors of Russia. He was also a pioneer of Russia's first constitution and Chairman of the Council of Ministers (Prime Minister) of the Russian Empire.

Count Sergei Yulyevich Witte, policymaker of Russia

The unification of Italy and Germany transformed the European balance of power and led to efforts to construct a new diplomatic order.

After 1848, the European landscape was different. The revolutions were over and most liberals and nationalists now sought to cooperate with their governments rather than attempt to overthrow them. Many governments were pleasantly surprised to find that they could strengthen their countries by agreeing to certain liberal reforms and adopting some of the nationalists' demands. In the second half of the 19th century, Europe was largely influenced by a select few powerful nation-states. These powers were different than the ones that had reshaped Europe during the Congress of Vienna; therefore, the balance of power in Europe, which had prevented war between 1815 and 1854, was upset. The emergence of two new countries with the unifications of both Germany and Italy, increasing international tension, armed conflict and the formation of two hostile alliances led to World War I, the largest and most horrific war the world had yet experienced.

Cavour's Realpolitik strategies, combined with the popular Garibaldi's military campaigns, led to the unification of Italy.

The Second War of Italian Independence started in April of 1859 when the Sardinian Prime Minister, Camillo Benso, Conte de Cavour, made an alliance with Napoleon III. In 1856, the Sardinians had sent troops to support the British and French in the Crimean War. Cavour and Napoleon III signed a Treaty of Defensive Alliance to safeguard themselves against the Austrians, who were provoked by the treaty.

Cavour and Napoleon agreed that Savoy and Nice would be ceded to France, while Tuscany and Emilia would be ceded to Piedmont. Referendums were held in all those provinces and the annexations were overwhelmingly approved. Cavour had been able to persuade most people that the unification of Italy would outweigh the territorial losses of Savoy and Nice. It was then left to Garibaldi, an Italian general and politician, to depose the Bourbon Kingdom of the Two Sicilies and bring southern Italy under the jurisdiction of Piedmont. Garibaldi was outraged that Nice, which was his birthplace, had been surrendered to France. He originally wanted to regain it, but a popular revolt in Palermo redirected him to the south. Cavour denied Garibaldi the brigade of Piedmontese that he wanted in order to capture Sicily, causing Garibaldi to recruit a thousand redshirt volunteers. They landed at Marsala in Sicily and won battles at Calatafimi and Milazzo, which gave them control of Sicily. Cavour tried to appropriate Sicily for Piedmont, but Garibaldi and his colleague Francesco Crispi refused.

Though he really wanted an invasion to occur, Cavour convinced Victor Emmanuel to write to Garibaldi asking him to refrain from invading the mainland. He composed a second letter telling Garibaldi to go ahead with the invasion, but it was apparently never sent. Cavour tried to conjure a liberal revolution in Naples, but people were not receptive to the idea. Garibaldi invaded and tried to make it to Naples before Cavour was able to check his advance. On September 7, he made it into Naples, the largest Italian city at the time, and declared Victor Emmanuel to be King of Italy. Garibaldi became the military dictator of Southern Italy and Sicily. He imposed the Piedmontese constitution but called for Cavour's removal.

Garibaldi refused to abandon his plans and sought to conduct an invasion of the Papal States. Cavour was worried that in the event of Papal States invasion, France would declare war in order to defend the Pope and would successfully prevent Garibaldi from commencing an attack. Garibaldi's forces had been diminished by the Battle of Volturno, so Cavour swiftly invaded the Papal regions of Umbriaand Marche. This linked the territories captured by Piedmont with those that had been secured by Garibaldi. The King and Garibaldi met and, as a result, Garibaldi ceded his control of Southern Italy and Sicily, which united Italy.

Bismarck employed diplomacy and industrialized warfare and weaponry and the manipulation of democratic mechanisms to unify Germany.

Otto von Bismark, First Chancellor of Prussia

Otto von Bismarck, the First Chancellor (1862–1890) to Wilhelm I of the Kingdom of Prussia, was the most well-known German advocate of *Realpolitik*. Bismarck employed *Realpolitik* during his mission to secure Prussian dominance in Germany. He affected political issues, including the Schleswig-Holstein Question and the Hohenzollern candidature, to rile other nations and ultimately to cause wars if they were seen as necessary to achieve his goals. Another example of the utilization of *Realpolitik* principles was in Prussia's outwardly irrational decision not to demand territory when it defeated Austria (the decision later led to the unification of Germany). Bismarck masterfully presided over the complex political landscape in Germany. He established the first modern welfare state in order to gain the support of the working class, which might otherwise favor his socialist opponents.

In the 1870s, Bismarck allied himself with the Liberals in a culture war with the Catholic Church. He ended up losing the culture war because the Catholics responded to his hostility by creating a powerful Center party and, because of the universal male suffrage, were able to gain a bloc of seats. In response, Bismarck reversed himself, ended the culture war, broke with the Liberals, imposed taxes and established an alliance with the new Center party in order to oppose Socialists. Bismarck was a staunch Lutheran and was loyal to the king, who offered Bismarck his full support, against the counsel of his wife and his heir. While Germany's parliament was elected by Germans, in practice it did not enjoy real control of the government. Bismarck was suspicious of democracy and ruled via a strong, well-trained bureaucracy where power was in the hands of a traditional Junker elite made up of the landed nobility of the East. Under Wilhelm I, Bismarck largely influenced both domestic and foreign affairs until 1890, when he was deposed by young Kaiser Wilhelm II.

As the head of revolutionary conservatism, Bismarck became a hero for German nationalists. He is usually portrayed favorably by historians as a moderate politician who assisted with the unification of Germany and helped maintain the balance of power and peaceful relations in Europe.

After 1871, Bismarck attempted to maintain the balance of power through a complex system of alliances directed at isolating France.

Once Germany had been unified, Bismarck turned his attention to using his diplomatic skills to assist with the maintenance of peace in Europe. He was forced to contend with French revanchism, particularly with France's desire to regain the territorial losses of the Franco-Prussian War. As a result, Bismarck employed a diplomatic policy that sought to isolate France, while maintaining positive relationships with the rest of Europe. For example, Bismarck had little desire to engage in naval or colonial skirmishes so he actively avoided conflict with Great Britain. Historians emphasize that Bismark did not desire further territorial expansion on the European continent, and his maneuvering to form interlinking and cross-sectional alliances was his attempt to prevent Europe from descending into pan-European conflict.

Emperor Franz Joseph of Austria-Hungary

Bismarck was cognizant of the fact that other European nations were wary of the powerful new Reich (Empire) he had created, so he focused on maintaining peace in Europe based on a balance of power that would promote the growth of the German economy. Bismarck was afraid that if Austria, France and Russia formed an alliance, they would be able to conquer Germany. Bismarck knew that if two of those three countries formed an alliance, then the third could likely be persuaded to ally with Germany if Germany was willing to make significant concessions. His solution to the problem was to form an alliance with two of the three nations. In 1873, he established the

League of the Three Emperors, an alliance between Wilhelm of Germany, Czar Alexander II of Russia and Emperor Francis Joseph of Austria-Hungary. Together those three countries would control Eastern Europe and ensure that restless ethnic groups, such as the Poles, were kept under control. The issue of the Balkans was the more serious and Bismarck's solution to the problem was to extend power to Austria in the Western Balkan areas and to Russia in the Eastern Balkan areas. The Three Emperors alliance eventually dissolved in 1887.

Following the dissolution of the League of the Three Emperors, Bismarck negotiated the Dual Alliance with Austria-Hungary, in which each country promised to support the other in the event of a Russian attack. Austria-Hungary, Italy and Germany also entered the Triple Alliance, negotiated by Bismarck in 1882. Britain was brought into the "Mediterranean Agreement" with Italy and Austria-Hungary. Any reconciliation achieved between Russia and Germany did not last; though the Three Emperors' League was reformed in 1881, it quickly disintegrated, ending the varying forms of solidarity the three empires had shown one another since 1813. The 1887 Reinsurance Treaty negotiated by Bismarck between Germany and Russia, was intended to stop any Franco-Russian alliance that would threaten Germany. Unless Russia attacked Austria-Hungary, both sides agreed to remain neutral towards each other. However, when Wilhelm II succeeded Bismarck in 1890, he did not renew the Reinsurance Treaty and this created the potential for serious issues for Germany if there were to be a war.

Bismarck's dismissal in 1890 eventually led to a system of mutually antagonistic alliances and heightened international tensions.

In the 19th century, the major European powers had gone to great lengths to maintain a pan-European balance of power, resulting in a complex network of political and military alliances throughout the continent by 1900. These alliances first began in 1815 when Prussia, Russia and Austria had entered the Holy Alliance. The League of the Three Emperors was negotiated by German Chancellor Otto von Bismarck in October of 1873, and attempted to unite the monarchies of Germany, Austria-Hungary and Russia. The agreement was unsuccessful, however, because Russia and Austria-Hungary could not come to terms with Russia regarding Balkan policy. Ultimately, the Dual Alliance of 1879 was formed between Germany and Austria-Hungary. The Ottoman Empire continued to weaken and this agreement was an attempt to combat Russian encroachment in the Balkans. Italy was included in the expanded Triple Alliance in 1882.

Bismarck had led an effort to keep Russia as Germany's ally; in the event that war broke out, Bismarck wanted to avoid having to fight two powers, France and Russia, at once. Bismarck's efforts were somewhat forgotten once he retired from power and Wilhelm II took power as Kaiser (German Emperor). The Kaiser, for instance, never renewed the Reinsurance Treaty with Russia in 1890. Two years later, in opposition to the power of the Triple Alliance, the Franco-Russian Alliance was signed. A series of agreements, called the Entente Cordiale, were signed between Britain and France in 1904, and in 1907 the Anglo-Russian

Convention was signed by Britain and Russia. Britain was not formally allied with France of Russian as a result of these treaties, but they made it likely that Britain would back France or Russia in any conflict they entered. The interlocking bilateral agreements which grew from this became known as the Triple Entente.

Nationalist tensions in the Balkans drew the Great Powers into a Series of crises, leading up to World War I

In the second half of the 19th century, much of the competition between the major powers of Europe was focused on the Balkans. Russia's interest in the region was ideological and with the hope that the Balkans could serve as a unifier for pan-Slavism, thereby aiding Russia's desire to have greater control of the Mediterranean, while Britain only wanted to thwart Russia's plans. Meanwhile Austria-Hungary, due to the Italian-German unification, was unable to expand its power to the southwest. It fell to Germany to mediate the competition over the Balkan territories because it had no direct interest in the region, and after the 1871 Franco-Prussian War was now the most powerful continental nation.

Russia and Austria-Hungary, both allied with Germany in the League of the Three Emperors, were also the two powers most intent upon controlling the Balkans. Due to this tension, the Congress of Berlin basically mediated disputes based on conflicting goals between nations that were supposedly allies. German Chancellor Bismarck, on behalf of the German Empire, was arbiter of the debate and ultimately had to choose which ally to support. Consequences of the decision were to have direct effects on European geopolitics in the future.

The Congress of Berlin was a month-long meeting, which took place from June 13th to July 13th, 1878. Germany, Russia, Great Britain, Austria-Hungary, France and Italy, the Great Powers, had representatives present, as did the Balkan States (Greece, Romania, Montenegro and Serbia) and the Ottoman Empire. The goal of the Congress was to determine the territories of the Balkan Peninsula states in the aftermath of the Russo-Turkish War (1877-1878). Signing the Treaty of Berlin brought the Congress to an end and replaced the original and preliminary treaty signed three months before between the Russians and the Ottoman Empire, called the Treaty of San Stefano.

Austria-Hungary had occupied Bosnia and Herzegovina since 1878, but sparked the 1908-1909 Bosnian Crisis by annexing the former Ottoman territory. The fracturing Ottoman Empire and the Balkan League fought the First Balkan War in 1912 and 1913. An independent Albanian State as well as increased territorial holdings in Greece, Serbia, Bulgaria and Montenegro resulted from the Treaty of London which further reduced the

Ottoman Empire. Most of Macedonia was taken from Bulgaria in its June 16th, 1913 attack on Serbia and Greece, and then Bulgaria lost Southern Dobruja in the Second Balkan War to Romania.

Berlin Congress, 1878

To a large extent the conflagrations over this period in the Balkans precipitated the onset of World War I in 1914. The intermingling web of alliances, the rise of nationalist sentiments and the competition for control of economic resources created conditions whereby all that was needed to begin a pan-European war was a small spark. It was no coincidence that this spark eventually came in the form of a Serbian nationalist named Gavrilo Princip, associated with the loosely Russian-supported "Black Hand," who assassinated the Austro-Hungarian Archduke Franz Ferdinand in the Bosnian capital of Sarejevo. This triggered a series of compulsory declarations of war due to the intertwined web of alliances that had been established in the 19th and early 20th centuries.

Period 3: 1815-1914

> **Key Concept 3.5: A variety of motives and methods led to the intensification of European global control and increased tensions among the great powers.**

The European imperial outreach of the 19th century was in some ways a continuation of three centuries of colonization, but it also resulted from the economic pressures and necessities of a maturing industrial economy. The new technologies and imperatives of the Second Industrial Revolution (1870 -1914) led many European nations to view overseas territories as sources of raw materials and consumer markets.

While European colonial empires in the Western hemisphere diminished in size in this period as former colonies gained independence, the colonized countries remained dependent on Europe and Southern Asia in the early 19th century, and a combination of forces created the conditions for a new wave of imperialism there and in Africa later in the century. Moreover, European national rivalries accelerated the expansion of colonialism as governments recognized that actual control of these societies offered economic and strategic advantages. Notions of global destiny and racial superiority fed the drive for empire, and innovations such as antimalarial drugs, machineguns and gunboats made it feasible. Non-European societies without these modern advantages could not effectively resist European imperial momentum.

The "new imperialism" of the late 19th and early 20th centuries was promoted in European nations by interest groups that included politicians, military officials and soldiers, missionaries, explorers, journalists and intellectuals. As an example of a new complex phase of imperial diplomacy, the Berlin Conference in 1884-1885 outlined the procedures that Europeans should use in the partition of the African continent. By 1914, most of Africa and Asia were under the domination of Great Britain, France, Portugal, Germany, Belgium, and the Netherlands. Notwithstanding the power of colonial administrations, some groups in the colonial societies resisted European imperialism, and by 1914, anticolonial movements had taken root within the non-European world and in Europe itself.

Imperialism exposed Europeans to foreign societies and introduced "exotic" influences into European art culture. At the same time, millions of Europeans carried their culture abroad, to the Americas and elsewhere, through emigration, resulting in the creation of a variety of mixed cultures around to world.

European nations were driven by economic, political and cultural motivation in their new imperial ventures in Asia and Africa.

Many European statesmen and industrialists pushed for expanding European holdings in Africa, which would eventually be called "the scramble for Africa." Bismarck pushed for a policy of *Weltpolitik* (World Politic), which mandated colonization as a necessity for the emerging German power. Bismarck knew that the only way that Germany would be taken seriously in European politics was through entering into the game of colonization. In this vein, Germany established colonies in Togoland, Samoa, southwest Africa and New Guinea for commercial purposes, while they established control over East Africa and China for political reasons.

Great Britain itself had used the East Africa Company to exert control over what are now Kenya and Uganda, but it wasn't until 1895 that Britain formally took over and renamed the land "the East Africa Protectorate." From 1885 to 1908, Leopold II of Belgium owned the Congo Free State, while the Dutch retained possession of the Dutch East Indies.

King Leopold II of Belgium

Around this time, Italy obtained new lands, including Somaliland, Eritrea and modern-day Libya through the 1911 Treaty of Lausanne. The colonial empires of Portugal and Spain were much smaller; during the Latin American revolutions at the beginning of the 19th century, most of those colonies had fought for and won their freedom from them.

In the mid-to-late 19th century, before the Industrial Revolution, silk, spices, tea and other goods from Asia were the primary motives behind European imperialism. Excluding the British East India Company, the European presence in Asia consisted mostly in the form of trading stations or tactical outposts that were investments in protecting important trade routes.

As the Industrial Age took hold, European demand for raw materials in Asia markedly increased. The Long Depression of the 1870s drove Europe to seek new markets in Africa, the Americas, Eastern Europe and Asia for their industrial products and financial services. During this same time, there was a shift in the attitude toward colonial expansion called "the New Imperialism." Previously colonies had been indirectly ruled through trade with their mother countries; now the emphasis shifted to formal colonial control. From the 1870s to 1914 (the beginning of World War I), the already established colonial holdings in Asia by the UK, France and the Netherlands were vastly expanded by colonizing in the Middle East, on the Indian Subcontinent, and in Southeast Asia.

Other concurrently emerging imperial powers were Japan (after the Meiji Restoration), Germany (at the end of the Franco-Prussian War in 1871), Tsarist Russia, and the United States (after the Spanish-American War in 1898).

European national rivalries and strategic concerns fostered imperial expansion and competition for colonies.

Colonial expansion between the 1870s and WWI (1914) was dominated by the idea of "the New Imperialism" or "empire for empire's sake." It was a time of aggressive and never before seen pursuit of overseas conquest and territorial expansion, this lead to the colonizers developing theories of racial superiority, defining the indigenous population ("the natives") as unfit to govern themselves.

During this time, Europe's collective empires acquired nearly 8,880,000 square miles (23,000,000 km²) to add to their foreign colonial properties. In what is known as "the Scramble for Africa," the unoccupied until that time continent became the focus of the new imperialist expansion. At the same time, that some of this scrambling for territories also took place other areas of the world, specifically in Southeast Asia and the East Asian seaboard, as Japan became interested in the potential for territory as well.

Commentary on the Fashoda Incident: cartoon of John Bull, unfazed by reports that France is to make a power moved in Sudan

From 1884-1885, the Berlin Conference defined "effective occupation" (direct rule and organization usually via armed conquest) as the measure of international recognition of a colonial claim made by a European power, thus mediating imperial competition amongst Britain, France and Germany. In 1898, however, conflicting imperial interests would almost send France and Britain to war with one another in the Fashoda Incident. The fear of war led to the signing of the 1904 *Entente Cordiale* between the two. It was this same spirit of imperial competition between the European powers that led to the outbreak of World War I in 1914. The Pan-Germanic League was formed as a merging of pan-Germanism and imperialism in Germany; it was thought that Britain's global presence gave them unequal opportunities to explore the international markets, and so Germany's potential for economic progress (and therefore its security) was threatened.

The search for raw materials and markets for manufactured goods, as well as strategic and nationalistic considerations, drove Europeans to colonize Africa and Asia, even as European colonies in the Americas broke free politically, if not economically.

Europe's ruling class also had their eyes on Sub-Saharan Africa for both political and economic reasons. As was the case in most other industrial countries, Great Britain's balance of trade had been unfavorable for some time, with the continental market growing increasingly wary due to the Long Depression of 1873 to 1896. Fortunately, the deficit could be increasingly offset from the money brought in from the overseas investments. It was no surprise then that Africa seemed so attractive; it would offer Britain, France, Germany and others a vast new market which would bolster their own economies.

Surplus capital would then garner the greatest profits overseas, where goods were less expensive, raw materials — abundant and competition — less intense. Many of those raw materials, like copper, cotton, rubber, palm oil, cocoa, diamonds, tea and tin were not available in Europe, adding to the list of imperial causes. Britain had enterprises on the southern and eastern coasts of Africa due to their need for coaling stations, drydocks and areas for the buying of supplies in order for the empire to maintain its maritime dominance and keep order in its worldwide colonial holdings.

Compared to other colonized continents, however, the investments made in Africa were minor; the companies involved in African trade were all small, except for Cecil Rhodes's De Beers Mining Company in Rhodesia (now, Republic of Zimbabwe). Léopold II of Belgium would later violently abuse the Congo Free State, arguing that protecting overseas African markets would raise the issues of low prices and over-production.

Europeans justified imperialism though an ideology of cultural and racial superiority.

The English-speaking academic works of the time allow scholars to understand imperialism through the British experience. In the late 1870s, the term "imperialism" was brought into English by those opposed to the imperial policies of British Prime Minister Benjamin Disraeli, but briefly taken up by those in support of imperialism, such as Joseph Chamberlain. To some people, imperialism was something of a philanthropic ideal ("the white man's burden"), others argued that it was laden with political self-interests, and still others simply connected it to commercial greed.

Chamberlain was a keen imperialist and supporter of a stronger British Empire. He wanted to expand the Empire's influence in Asia, Africa and Americas. Chamberlain envisioned new closer relationships between Britain and her colonies through trade and resources. In 1895, he became a Colonial Officer, gaining international recognition as European nations competed for territories. Chamberlain governed over 10 million square miles of colonial territories with a combined population of 450 million people. He believed that positive government actions, such as investment in infrastructure and treatment of diseases, would make the populations more loyal to their metropole, creating what he called "constructive imperialism."

Joseph Chamberlain, British imperialist

Liberal John A. Hobson and Marxist Vladimir Lenin added to the definition of the term "imperialist," giving it a macroeconomic dimension. Marxist understandings of imperialism would be greatly influenced by Lenin, particularly through his book *Imperialism, the Highest Stage of Capitalism*. In this work, Lenin explained that imperialism was the natural course of capitalism, in so far as a capitalist nation must continuously seek investments, resources and a labor force, and thus would constantly require new colonies. Imperialism has been, and continues to be, understood as the end game of capitalism by later Marxist theoreticians.

The belief that an individual's behaviors were determined by their environment was used to rationalize colonization by many Westerners. The idea was that people who lived in a tropical environment were effectively "less civilized," thus domination through colonial expansion into such regions was seen as a civilizing mission. From out of the three waves of European colonialism, first in the Americas, then in Asia and finally in Africa, *environmental determinism* was used to place native populations in a racial hierarchy.

Climate was also proposed to be a factor, Where the Northern Europe and Mid-Atlantic weather was believed to foster a hard-working and morally upright individual, the Mediterranean climate was thought to result in lazy, immoral and sexually promiscuous populace, while the Sub-Saharan African environments were thought to produce naive and backward cultures that needed the direction and interference of Europeans to help them govern themselves.

Industrial and technological developments (i.e., the Second Industrial Revolution) facilitated European control of global empires.

There are many who believe that industrialism and the resultant growth in technology made imperial expansion inevitable. Due to the relative variance in development between the core (Europe) and the periphery (areas colonized in Asia, Latin America, and Africa) the expansion of territorial holdings was both relatively easy and essential for growth. Expansion was easy due to the fact that the European powers had weapons, modes of transportation and scientific knowledge that made their defeat of indigenous populations a *fait accompli*. Their expansion was necessary as the European powers' need for natural resources extended far beyond that which they could find domestically. Due to the combination of these two factors, imperialism grew on the periphery as a means to exploit the resource-rich but technologically poor indigenous peoples.

The motive for imperialism did not end with the need for resources. They also sought to expand as a means to broaden the markets in which they could sell the goods they produced. As the European market was finite, there was a need to find ever new markets in order to expand the revenue streams of European countries and companies. The areas which would come under imperial control provided the perfect means to achieve this goal. Even though they could very rarely pay for the goods they received from Europe in currency, they could easily pay in natural resources, which were received by the Europeans at a cost considerably lower than market. This would legitimize the exploitation of the newly held lands as they were purportedly "compensated" for the theft of their natural resources.

The development of advanced weaponry invariable ensured the military superiority of the Europeans over colonized areas.

During the modern era, weapons advanced significantly. It was the stable cause insuring the superiority of the colonial powers of the native population. A few examples of weaponry to come out of this time are the Minié ball, breech-loading fire arms, self-contained cartridges and automatic weapons.

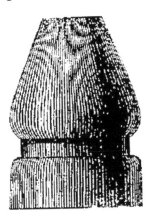 

Minié balls

The Minié ball was a cone-shaped, soft lead bullet that was slightly smaller than the barrel of a firearm with four grease-filled grooves on the outside and a cone-shaped hollow in its base. The bullet was made to swell under the pressure and increase muzzle speed. When the rifle was shot, the expanding gas pushed on the base of the bullet, distorting it to engage the rifling, and giving it spin for accuracy, a better seal for reliable speed and longer range, and rid the barrel of debris. This design allowed for the quick loading of rifles, which in turn expanded the use of rifles, rather than the smoothbore musket, as a mass battlefield weapon.

When ammunition can be quickly put into an opening in the weapon while the shooter is holding it, differing from the time-consuming method of pouring gunpowder into the muzzle, it is called *breech-loading. Muzzle-loading* can take up to a minute just to make one shot possible, as opposed to breech-loading, which allows for a near-instant reload while not requiring the shooter to take his weapon off the target. Breech-loading technology had been around since the late 14th century in Burgundy; however, after the 19th century, new advances were made to breech-loading weapons with greater success rates, and this was finally applied to artillery by 1875. One-shot breech-loading weapons were employed throughout the second half of the 19th century, but would be gradually replaced by repeat-firing designs by the American Civil War. These manual breech-loading arms would then be replaced by manual magazine feeds, and then later by self-loading weapons.

In connection with the French gunsmith François Prélat, Jean Samuel Pauly developed the first self-contained cartridges in Paris in 1808. These cartridges used a round bullet, a paper casing, and a copper base with mercury fulminate primer powder. Pauly's cartridge was loaded into the breech and fired with a needle. The first completely metallic cartridge (containing powder in a metallic shell) would be developed and patented by another Parisian gunsmith, Benjamin Houllier in 1846.

New rapid-fire weapons capable of multi-shot fire (mostly volley guns) appeared in the early to middle 19th century. Machineguns at this time were air-cooled and recoil-operated, but with the development of the Gatling gun with multiple barrels, they became much more widely used. However, Gatling guns were very heavy, complex and costly, and the lighter and less expensive recoil-operated machineguns provided an invaluable supplement to them on the battlefield. Additionally, recoil-operated machineguns could be used from a lower position and be carried though difficult terrain by just one man. The multi-barrel design, with its high firing rates, would only be employed again as automatic aircraft cannons and mini-guns about 150 years later.

Colonial soldiers benefited from the advances in weaponry in several ways, including, an increase in accuracy, range and rate of fire. Additionally, these new weapons could be mass-produced, making the cost dramatically lower.

These benefits played out in the two examples of the Amritsar Massacre in India during the British Raj and the New Zealand colony against the native Maori peoples. The massacres made possible by these advances in weaponry resulted in a burgeoning Indian non-cooperation movement with their colonial rulers that eventually led to India's independence.

The New Zealand government appealed to the Colonial Office for additional soldiers to defend Auckland in 1860. Because this petition was not successful, the government then asked Britain for more modern weaponry in 1861, including the Calisher and Terry carbine (which used breech-loading mechanics). Britain filled the order by providing 3,000 to 4,000 carbines to New Zealand a few years later.

Communication and transportation technologies allowed for the creation of European empires.

During the 19th century, travel and communications changed greatly through new innovations. Internal commerce and exporting was revolutionized because of Britain's development of the steam engine; shipping times were reduced, larger amounts of goods could be sent with less expense, and shipments became more predictable to track. Also, once the steamship entered the picture, previously impassable routes became sailable; a river that hitherto had only carried goods in one direction could now be navigated in both directions.

As the benefits of steam engine trade took hold, new routes like the Suez Canal were developed. Trade changed all across the Near East as well, and saw a dramatic rise over the course of the 19th century. By 1900, sailboats visiting Istanbul were around five percent of all ships to come into port (though this was a greater percent than any year of the 1800's). Larger ships prompted port cities to build deeper harbors. Of the trade ships operating in Ottoman waters, Europeans owned 90 percent of them. This rerouting changed the dynamics of trade in Iran, Iraq and Arabia, as the customary routes through Istanbul, Aleppo and Beirut were no longer as heavily trafficked, leading to a loss of profits for those cities.

Land transport was changed with the advent of railroads, which shortened travel times, altered rural and urban relationships, and prompted population shifts. Bulk goods were given inexpensive and reliable transport by railroad, thus opening up the fertile, rural (inner) regions of lands to be accessible for the first time. Agriculture advanced rapidly once these railroads were in place; thousands of tons of cereals were soon being shipped along these routes. The Anatolian 1,488-mile line served 7 million passengers, and the Balkan 1,054-mile line served 8 million. By 1911, over 13,000 people were employed by railroads. Most of the financing for railroads came from European bankers and investors, thus giving them significant political power.

Advances in medicine supported European control of Africa and Asia by saving European lives.

Innovations in chemistry and laboratory procedures and equipment transformed medicine in the 19th century. Virology and bacteriology replaced outdated theories of infectious disease epidemiology. New methods developed by physicians and rapid progress in science changed the entire practice of medicine.

With his research beginning in 1857, the Frenchman Louis Pasteur put his professional reputation behind the theory that yeast is a microorganism, and that might infer how diseases are spread. A further advancement in pathology and the germ theory of disease was when German physician Robert Koch discovered spores, vaccinated lab animals with them and reproduced anthrax. Koch went on to publish his paper on the bacterial pathology of wounds in 1878, and Pasteur examined the role that spores had in natural settings. The germ theory was reinforced though Koch's identification of the "tubercle bacillus" in 1881. Pasteur and Koch both sent out medical missions to Alexandria, Egypt during the cholera outbreak, but it was Koch's group that

Louis Pasteur, French chemist and microbiologist

discovered the cholera pathogen. After losing this rivalry over the Alexandrian outbreak to Koch, Pasteur went on to develop the rabies vaccine, which was his third vaccine.

Robert Koch, German physician and microbiologist

Koch's bacteriologists and Pasteur's group brought medicine into the era of "scientific medicine." In 1888, the world's first biomedical institute, the Pasteur Institute, opened and received donations from all around the world. Koch was awarded the Nobel Prize in medicine in 1905, and is still thought of as the founder of medical microbiology.

The 20th century saw great innovations in surgery and pharmacology as the scientific method was applied to medical research. Methodical study and diagnosis came to be employed by hospital physicians studying patients' symptoms. New procedures were available through anesthesia and the improvement of operating rooms to make them aseptic. Vaccinations against endemic infectious diseases, such as the flu, were developed, thus preventing influenza epidemics. However, it should be noted that even more so than medical innovations, the death toll from many fatal illnesses of the 20th century was reduced because of advances in nutrition and sanitation.

Imperial endeavors significantly affected society, diplomacy and culture in Europe and created resistance to foreign control abroad.

From 1870-1914, Europe was much more stabilized than it had been in previous points in its history. Political reforms in established states like Austria and Britain, as well as the formation of new states like Italy and Germany, greatly contributed to this. The booming technological innovations of the Industrial Revolution, coupled with this internal stability, led European states to have both the ability and will to attempt to seize political power outside of their own countries.

Although imperialism was not a new concept for 19th century Europe (e.g., Spain, Portugal and the Netherlands had long ago expanded into large overseas empires), the new technologies of the 19th century encouraged even more imperial growth. For example, the invention of the telegraph gave states the ability to monitor their imperial properties from vast distances; the discovery of a treatment for malaria called quinine allowed troops to journey into the inlands of Africa and conquer it. In this new era of imperialism, European states took over large areas of Africa and Asia.

Imperialism created diplomatic tensions among Europeans states that strained alliance systems.

Germany took part in the race for African colonies as well, which made both Great Britain and France very nervous. As a means of quelling potential conflicts, Kind Leopold II was able to convince Germany and France that a common trade in Africa was in the best interests of all three countries. At the initiative of Portugal and with the support of Great Britain, Otto von Bismarck of Germany invited representatives from many European states, the U.S. and the Ottoman Empire to participate in the Berlin Conference of 1884-1885.

The Berlin Conference (also known as the *Congo Conference* or the *West Africa Conference*) provided a structure for the European colonization of and commerce in Africa during the era of the New Imperialism, and coincided with Germany's rise as an imperial actor. The Berlin Conference was meant to foster joint policy with regards to Africa. It produced the *General Act of the Berlin Conference*, which can be understood as the ratification of the Scramble for Africa; the conference paved the way for increased European colonial expansion into African lands, which destroyed most existing forms of African independence or self-governance.

Berlin Conference

The pinnacle of imperialist disputes over territory was between Britain and France in Eastern Africa, known as *The Fashoda Crisis of 1898*. A French mission to Fashoda along the White Nile River was undertaken with the intention of taking over the Upper Nile River basin, thus preventing Britain from expanding in Sudan. When the two armies met, no fighting ensued. However, on the mainland, Great Britain and France were on the verge of war over the issue. The French eventually withdrew their army, reinforcing Anglo-Egyptian governorship over the region. To help maintain stability, an agreement between the two states was arrived at, recognizing Britain's dominance over Egypt, while France maintained its rule over Morocco.

The Moroccan crises (1905–06 and 1911) were two separate international disputes centered on France's efforts to dominate Morocco and Germany's simultaneous efforts to curtail France's power. France had made agreements with Great Britain not to resist its hold over Egypt in exchange for free reign over Morocco in 1904. Concurrently, France had negotiated a clandestine treaty with Spain apportioning Morocco. However, Germany — not a party to either agreement — asserted that Morocco was a fair economic claim. Emperor William II visited Tangier and professed to be for Morocco's self-governance. The subsequent interstate alarm — *the First Moroccan Crisis* — was stabilized in January–April 1906 at the Algeciras Conference, when Germany's and other nations' economic rights were endorsed and both France and Spain were delegated the monitoring of Morocco.

The Second Moroccan Crisis (1911) was caused when the German gunboat *Panther* was sent to Agadir in 1911, supposedly to defend German interests during an indigenous uprising in Morocco, but really sent to intimidate France. During the summer and fall of that year, this "Agadir Incident" ignited talks of war. However, international dialogue continued and the crisis dwindled until its resolution when France was given rights of protectorate over Morocco. In exchange, Germany got pieces of land from the French Congo. These agreements from 1911-1912 led to internationalizing the Tangier zone (Tangier and its surrounding areas) in 1923.

Imperial encounters with non-European peoples influenced the styles and subject matter of artists and writers and provoked debate over the acquisition of colonies.

In discussions of political science and international relations, "anti-imperialism" is a term used largely by members of nationalist movements who want to gain independence from an empire or other colonial power. The term can also refer to a specific theory in opposition to capitalism in Marxist-Leninist discourse. The latter definition can be seen in Vladimir Lenin's work *Imperialism, the Highest Stage of Capitalism*. Anti-imperialism was a self-conscious political movement originating in the late 1800s and early 1900s in Europe. It was formed in opposition to increasing colonial possessions of Europe and the U.S. colonization of the Philippines after 1898.

Vladimir Lenin, Russian communist revolutionary

European imperial missions overseas and the resultant encounters with other cultures acutely influenced the literature and art of the time.

Jules Verne (1828 – 1905) was a French novelist, poet, and playwright and is most notable for his adventure books and his impact on the science fiction literary genre. His partnership with publisher Pierre-Jules Hetzel led to the establishment of the Voyages Extraordinaires, a carefully researched and widely read series of adventure novels (e.g., *Journey to the Center of the Earth, Twenty Thousand Leagues Under the Sea, Around the World in Eighty Days*).

Jules Verne, French writer

Verne is understood to be a major literary figure in France and much of Europe, where he had a great impact on the literary avant-garde and on surrealism. In English-speaking countries, he is thought of as a writer of science fiction (or children's adventure books) due to the much abridged and poorly translated versions in which his books were published.

Primitivism was a Western art movement that took visuals from non-Western or tribal populations. An example would be Paul Gauguin's insertion of Tahitian themes in paintings and ceramics. In an effort to escape from European civilization, Gauguin lived in the French colony of Tahiti and assumed a simplistic existence that he believed more natural than the way he had lived before. In 19th century Europe, during a time when sexual freedom was limited, Gauguin's exploration of the primitive could be interpreted as a yearning for more open sexuality.

"Femmes de Tahiti ou Sur la plage" by Paul Gauguin (1891)

This desire can be seen in Gauguin's paintings, such as *Cruel Tales* and *The Spirit of the Dead Keeps Watch,* depicting Tahiti as an oasis of temperate weather, free love and beautiful young women. These paintings have similarities to classic pastorals which have played a significant role for millennia in creating Western ideas of rural life. The Beaux Arts schools' academic pastoral tradition had been based on sculpture figures of the Ancient Greeks and Gauguin's work extended this tradition to distinctly non-European models. Gauguin thought of his work as a celebration of Tahiti and its society, and that he was defending the Tahitians from European colonialism.

African, Micronesian and Native American art began to be widely viewed and appreciated by the European elites in the early 20th century. Artists, such as Pablo Picasso and Henri Matisse, drew inspiration from these works, especially the starkness and simplicity of other cultures' styles. Along with Gauguin's work, primitivism, Iberian sculpture, African art and tribal masks were different styles of art that artists like Picasso, Matisse and Andre Derain drew inspiration from. In fact, Gauguin achieved much acclaim in Parisian avant-garde circles and his posthumous retrospective exhibitions in Paris in 1903 and 1906 had a strong influence on Picasso's work.

Picasso's work between 1906 and 1909 delved into primitivism, looking at its impact through African tribal masks and sculpture, Iberian sculpture and El Greco's mannerist paintings, and resulted in his important work *Les Demoiselles D'Avignon* and the invention of cubism.

As non-Europeans became educated in the Western values, they challenged European imperialism through nationalist movements and/or by modernizing their own economies and societies.

The idea of anti-imperialism was most popular with and gained most support from the colonized peoples themselves. There were many national liberation movements founded on anti-imperialism during the mid-20th century and onward. The de-colonization processes that occurred in the 1950s and 1960s, when most Asian and African European colonies achieved independence, was possible due to the national liberation movements that arose out of anti-imperialism sentiments.

Some important anti-imperialist movements were the Zulu Resistance, the Sepoy Mutiny in India, the Meiji Restoration in Japan, and the Boxer Rebellion in China.

Zulu were a southern African tribe of strong military organization and skill. Under their acclaimed leader Shaka, they acquired vast lands throughout southern Africa. In the 1830s, Boers – descendants of the original Dutch settlers – migrated into the South Africa's interior, initiating conflicts with Zulu. These conflicts continued well into the late 1800s, however, they never really threatened Zulu's sovereignty.

A Natal Zulu Chief

Eventually, as Zulu expanded their control over southern Africa, they came into the conflict with the British army, which invaded their homeland. Despite some early Zulu victories, they were eventually defeated by the superior British technology and vast resources. Soon, all of southern Africa would come under British rule. In 1906, the Zulu people revolted against British rule and taxation, which became known as the Bambatha uprising.

The Indian Rebellion of 1857 (also known as the Sepoy Mutiny, among many names) broke out in as a reaction to the rule of the British East India Company. The rebellion began as a mutiny of sepoys (i.e., Indian soldiers) of the East India Company's army in the town of Meerut, and soon escalated into other mutinies and civilian rebellions in northern and central India. Other Company-controlled regions, such as Bengal, the Bombay Presidency and the Madras Presidency, remained generally calm. The rebellion considerably diminished the East India Company's influence in the region and ultimately led to the dissolution of the East India Company in 1858. It also prompted the British to reorganize their military, the financial system and the administration of India. The country was thereafter governed directly by the Empire's new British Raj.

Sepoy Mutiny, 1857

In 1885, the Indian National Congress (known simply as the Congress) is a political party founded by members of the Theosophical Society, which included both Indian and British individuals. From the late 19th to mid-20th century, the Congress played a pivotal role in the Indian Independence Movement. Its original goal was to get more educated Indians into government to create more political dialogue between them and the British Raj. Facing opposition from the British government, the demands of the party became more radical within the next few years and the party started to speak out for the independence of India, since the new political regime would likely make them a majority party. Mahatma Gandhi returned to India from South Africa in 1915 and became president of the Congress. After WWI, the party became firmly associated with his name, as Gandhi remained its unofficial spiritual leader. Gandhi's popularity and the prevailing nationalism of that time, along with polices aimed at eliminating caste inequalities, poverty, ethnic and religious divides, made the Congress a dominant political force. Till this day, the Congress is one of two major political parties in India and is one of the oldest and largest democratically run political parties in the world.

The Meiji Restoration was a sequence of events that led to restoration of the imperial rule in Japan in 1868 under Emperor Meiji. Even though there were emperors in Japan prior to that, Meiji Restoration consolidated the political system under the Emperor of Japan and returned the actual power to the Emperor. This process, which spanned the late Edo period (i.e., the Late Tokugawa shogunate) and the beginning of the Meiji period, led to radical changes in Japan's political and social structure. During this time frame of 1868-1912, the Restoration resulted in the emergence of Japan as a modernized nation in the early 20th century.

The New fighting the Old in early Meiji Japan circa 1870

The word "meiji" means "enlightened rule" and the goal of the movement was to merge modern technology with the traditional Japanese culture. When Commodore Matthew Perry arrived in Japan to try to open up its ports for commerce, the Japanese, seeing the large, armed, technologically advanced fleet, became aware of their technological inferiority compared to the western world. The leaders of the Meiji Restoration acted to restore the imperial rule in order to strengthen Japan against the colonial powers, ending the era known as *sakoku*. *Sakoku* was a policy that lasted 250 years and prescribed the death penalty for foreigners entering Japan or Japanese nationals attempting to leave the country.

By the end of the 19th century, the western powers and Japan had forced China's ruling Qing dynasty to accept broad foreign control over the country's economy. In the Opium Wars (1839-1842 and 1856-1860), popular rebellions and the Sino-Japanese War (1894-1895), China resisted the foreigners, but due to the lack of modern military technology, it suffered defeats and millions of casualties. In 1900, a Chinese secret organization called the Society of the Righteous and Harmonious Fists led an uprising in northern China against the spread of Western and Japanese influence there. This uprising became known as the Boxer Rebellion because the rebels were referred to by westerners as "boxers" for their physical exercises. The Boxers conducted killings of foreigners and Chinese Christians and destroyed foreign property. From June to August of 1900, they besieged the foreign district of Beijing (then called Peking), China's capital, until an international force that included American troops subdued the uprising.

The rebellion officially ended with the signing of the Boxer Protocol on September 7, 1901. The terms of the agreement provided that forts surrounding Beijing were to be destroyed, Boxer and Chinese government officials involved in the uprising were to be punished, foreign nations were permitted to station troops in Beijing for their defense, China was prohibited from importing arms for two years and had to pay over $330 million in reparations to the foreign nations harmed by the rebellion. The United States actually returned the money it received from China on the condition that it would be used to fund the creation of a university in Beijing. Other countries also later returned their shares of the reparations. The Qing dynasty, established in 1644, was considerably weakened by the Boxer Rebellion, and, following an uprising in 1911, the dynasty came to an end and China became a republic in 1912.

An attack on Beijing Castle during the Boxer Rebellion

Period 3: 1815-1914

Key Concept 3.6: European ideas and culture expressed a tension between objectivity and scientific realism on one hand, and subjectivity and individual expression on the other.

The romantic movement of the early 19th century set the stage for later cultural perspectives by encouraging individuals to cultivate their uniqueness and to trust intuition and emotion as much as reason. Partly in reaction to the Enlightenment, romanticism affirmed the value of sensitivity, imagination and creativity and thereby provided a climate for artistic experimentation. Later artistic movements such as Impressionism, Expressionism, and Cubism, which relied on subjective interpretations of reality by the individual artist or writer, arose from the attitudes fostered by romanticism. The sensitivity of artists to non-European traditions that imperialism was responsible for bringing to their attention also can be traced to the romantics' emphasis on the primacy of culture in defining the character of the individuals and groups.

In science, Darwin's evolutionary theory raised questions about human nature and physicists began to challenge the uniformity and regularity of the Newtonian universe. In 1905, Einstein's theory of relativity underscored the position of the observer in defining reality, while the quantum principles of randomness and probability called the objectivity of Newtonian mechanics into question. The emergence of psychology as an independent discipline separate from philosophy and neurology led to investigations of human behavior that revealed the need for more subtle methods of analysis than those provided by the physical and biological sciences. Freud's investigations into the human psyche suggested the power of irrational motivations and unconscious drives.

Many writers of the period saw humans as governed by spontaneous, irrational forces and believed the intuition and will were as important as reason and science in the search for truth. In art, literature and science, traditional notions of objective, universal truths and values increasingly shared the stage with a commitment to and recognition of subjectivity, skepticism and cultural relativism.

Romanticism broke with neoclassical forms of artistic representation and with rationalism, placing more emphasis on intuition and emotion.

Romanticism, also referred to as the Romantic Period or Romantic Era, originated in Europe at the end of the 18th century and was a literary, artistic and intellectual movement. Romanticism, with its heyday between 1800 and 1850, was a reaction to a number of things including the scientific rationalization of nature, the Industrial Revolution and the aristocratic social and political norms during the Age of Enlightenment. The results of the Romantic Era are mostly seen in the visual arts, literature and music, but can be said to have also greatly affected the natural sciences, historiography and education. Romanticism also affected politics in complex ways; it was associated with radicalism and liberalism, and had a significant impact on the long-term growth of nationalism.

"Erlkönig" by Moritz von Schwind, example of Romantic art

The movement approached legitimate aesthetic experience as emanating from intense emotion and placed new importance on feelings associated with horror and terror, apprehensiveness and awe at the sublimity and beauty of nature. Within Romanticism, ancient customs and folk culture were considered noble, yet spontaneity was highly valued, as with the emergence of impromptu music. Romanticism rejected the Rational and Classicist ideal models and instead looked to elements of medieval imagery and lifestyle as a psychological escape from crowding, urban sprawl and pollution.

Romantic artists and composers broke from classical artistic forms to emphasize emotion, nature, individuality, intuition, the supernatural and national histories in their works.

Artists' personal styles reflected the Romantic Era, though there was still a concentration on historical painting that usually had a political message. *The Charging Chasseur* was the first artistic success of Théodore Géricault (1791–1824) when it was displayed at the Paris Salon in 1812. His next major work, named *The Raft of the Medusa* and completed in 1821, contained intense anti-government sentiments, and is widely regarded as one of most important and greatest paintings of the Romantic era.

"The Charging Chasseur" by Théodore Géricault

Eugène Delacroix (1798–1863) was an artist who also produced works made famous in the Paris Salon. These famous pieces included *The Barque of Dante, The Massacre at Chios* and *Death of Sardanapalus*. The second painting, completed in 1824, depicted an actual massacre during the Greek War of Independence. Lord Byron (an incredibly influential writer during the Romantic Era) died that year, and the third of these paintings was inspired by one of Lord Byron's plays. Byron and Shakespeare were the two main literary sources of inspiration for Delacroix. He also spent much time in North Africa where he painted numerous colorful scenes of Arab warriors upon their mounts.

After Géricault's *The Raft of the Medusa*, Delacroix's *Liberty Leading the People* (1830) is one of the best-known paintings of French Romanticism. Both are depictions of historical events, or "story painting" (a phrase from the Italian Renaissance referring to the depiction of a number of people caught up in some event, long considered the most advanced and difficult form of art).

Francisco Goya was an incredibly important Spanish artist of the late 18th and early 19th centuries, arguably grouped with the Romantic artists. He was incredibly successful and is often referred to as "the last of the old masters" and "the first of the moderns." Goya became a court painter to the Spanish Crown in 1786 and the early portion of his career is known for his portraits of the Spanish aristocracy and royalty, as well as the Rococo style tapestries for the royal palace. After 1793, his works became darker and more pessimistic. His later art appears to communicate a bleak outlook on social, political and personal levels, which contradicts his apparent social ascend.

The predominant Romantic musicians were German, including Haydn, Mozart and Beethoven, considered masters of instrumental romantic compositions. Musicology was a new discipline emerging at the end of the 19th century and it suggested a distinction between the Viennese Romantic and Classical periods. Guido Adler was an important figure in this study and determined that Schubert and Beethoven as transitional but essentially classical composers. It wasn't until the post-Beethoven generation, with the emergence of composers such as Frédéric Chopin, Robert Schumann, Hector Berlioz and Franz Liszt, that musical Romanticism can be said to have reached full maturity.

Romantic writers expressed similar themes while responding to the Industrial Revolution and to various political revolutions.

Romantic literature tended to evoke or criticize the past, contained a theme of the cult of sensibility, emphasizing women and children, an isolated narrator or artist and to revere nature. Some Romantic authors focused on themes of human psychology and the supernatural or occult, such as Nathaniel Hawthorne and Edgar Allan Poe. Satire was generally regarded as trivial and unimportant during the Romantic era.

Edgar Allan Poe,
writer of the Romantic era

Romanticism in English poetry is predicated on figures who were writing in the mid-18th century such as the Warton brothers, Thomas and Joseph. Joseph believed that to be a good poet one needed imagination and invention. It is widely agreed that Thomas Chatterton was the first Romantic poet to write in English. James Macpherson was a Scottish poet who would later influence both the young Walter Scott and Goethe, and who influenced early Romanticism by writing his Ossian cycles of poetry, published in 1762, which turned out to be an international success.

The first Gothic novel was said to be Horace Walpole's *The Castle of Otranto*. This book delighted in horror and threat, took place in exotic and picturesque settings and was an important precursor to a certain brand of Romanticism. Another strain of Romanticism was Laurence Sterne's *Tristram Shandy*, which brought his unique whimsical version of the sentimental and emotion-based novel to the English reading public.

Following the revolutions of 1848, Europe turned toward a realist and materialist worldview.

The artistic movement called realism began after the 1848 Revolution in France. The Realist movement was a response to Romanticism and History painting; realists disavowed the inflated emotionality and exotic subjects of Romanticism, which since the late 18th century dominated French literature and art. Rather than the drama of Romanticism, Realism sought to depict real and representative people and conditions truthfully, making no attempt to gloss over the depressing or repugnant parts of life. Characters of all different classes were portrayed in realist works. Common situations from ordinary life were depicted; as such, they often represented the many transformations occurring during the Industrial and Commercial Revolutions. After the advent of photography, a new visual medium which fostered an interest in "real" depictions, such realistic works increased in popularity.

Some of the leading figures of the Realist movement were Gustave Courbet, Jean-François Millet, Honoré Daumier and Jean-Baptiste-Camille Corot. They painted ordinary people and events in a contemporary manner and made an effort to portray members of all social classes in a similar fashion. Courbet was Realism's principal advocate, rejecting the popular history painting promoted by the state-sponsored art academy. His seminal paintings *A Burial at Ornans* and *The Stonebreakers* depicted commoners from his native region. The paintings were done on large canvases that were usually used for history paintings.

Artistic Realism was a complement to the naturalist literature of Émile Zola, Honoré de Balzac and Gustave Flaubert. Social realism in art involves the depiction of working class people in a way that grants them the same respectful interest given to higher-class people as subjects to be painted. Another goal of realism was to depict human relations and emotions sincerely. Thus, depicting subjects heroically or sentimentally was rejected in favor of depictions of the mundane lives of common laborers and other ordinary people in everyday settings, engaging in their routine activities.

Positivism, or the philosophy that science alone provides knowledge, emphasized the rational and scientific analysis of nature and human affairs.

Positivism is the scientific philosophy which argues that information gained from sensory experience, interpreted via rational or logical and mathematical treatments, is the only true source of authoritative knowledge. Data that has been received from the senses and verified (also known as positive facts) is referred to as empirical evidence. Hence, positivism is based on empiricism. Positivism also maintains that society, similar to the physical world, operates according to general laws and rejects introspective and "intuitive" knowledge, metaphysics and theology. Positivism has been a persistent theme in the history of Western philosophy, but its modern form was devised in the early 19th century by Auguste Comte, a French philosopher and one of the founders of sociology.

Comte was inspired by the utopian socialist, Henri Saint-Simon, to develop positivism in an effort to overcome the social malaise that came with the French Revolution by promoting a new social doctrine that was based on science. Comte's work had a great influence on 19th-century authors, such as Karl Marx, John Stuart Mill and George Eliot. His ideas about sociology and social evolutionism were a jumping off point for early social theorists and anthropologists like Herbert Spencer and eventually evolved into modern academic sociology, which was presented by Émile Durkheim as practical and objective social research. Comte's social theories culminated in

Auguste Comte,
French philosopher

his work, *The Religion of Humanity*, which led to the establishment of religious humanist and secular humanist groups during the 19th century.

Charles Darwin provided a rational and material account of biological change and the development of human beings as a species, and inadvertently a justification for racialist theories known as Social Darwinism.

Charles Robert Darwin, (1809-1882) was an English naturalist and geologist who is most well-known for his contributions to evolutionary theory, namely that all living species have descended over time from shared predecessors. In his 1859 book, *On the Origin of Species*, Darwin provided compelling evidence in support of his scientific theory of natural selection, which says that the struggle for existence has a similar effect to the artificial selection involved in selective breeding.

While previous concepts of the transmutation of species had been rejected by scientists, by the 1870s, the scientific community, along with much of the general public, had accepted evolution as a fact. Darwin's fascination with the natural world led him to abandon his medical education at the University of Edinburgh in favor of helping to study marine invertebrates. His studies at the University of Cambridge stimulated his passion for natural science and a five-year stint on the *HMS Beagle* established him as a distinguished geologist. Darwin was puzzled by the geographical distribution of wildlife and fossils he

collected during his voyage and launched a detailed study of them, which led to the development of his theory of natural selection in 1838. Darwin's work established evolutionary descent with modification over time as the foremost scientific explanation for the diversification that exists in nature. In 1871, he explored the evolution of humans and sexual selection in *The Descent of Man* and *Selection in Relation to Sex*, which were followed by *The Expression of the Emotions in Man and Animals*. The studies Darwin had conducted about plant life were published in a number of books and in his final book, he explored earth worms and their impact on soil.

Charles Darwin, English naturalist

Darwin's renown meant that he was occasionally associated with ideas and movements that were indirectly or not at all related to his theories. Thomas Malthus had promoted the theory that God intended population growth beyond the available resources to support it in order to motivate humans to work productively and practice reproductive restraint. This theory came to be employed in the 1830s as a justification for workhouses and laissez-faire economics.

Soon after Darwin's *On the Origin of Species* was published, critics labeled his description of a struggle for existence as a Malthusian defense of the English industrial capitalism of the time. Other philosophers and scientists would go on to apply Darwin's name and terms to their own work, including Spencer's use of the term "survival of the fittest" to describe free-market progress and Ernst Haeckel's racist ideas about human development. Since Darwin's time, some thinkers have employed his idea of natural selection to argue for various ideologies, such as racism, warfare, colonialism and imperialism, all of them unrelated to Darwin's theory.

After the 1880s, a eugenics movement emerged that was based on ideas about biological inheritance. This movement sought to justify its ideas using certain Darwinian concepts. In Britain, most people shared Darwin's wariness about voluntary improvement and wanted to encourage those with positive characteristics in "positive eugenics." During the "Eclipse of Darwinism," a scientific foundation for eugenics was provided by Mendelian genetics. Negative eugenics, which sought to justify removing the "feebleminded," was popular in America, Canada and Australia.

In the United States, eugenics introduced mandatory sterilization laws, as did several other countries in succession. The practices used by the Nazis eventually brought the field of eugenics into disrepute. Negative eugenics flourished in statist systems like Nazi Germany, while the free market encouraged the improvement of psychological knowledge and methods. Beginning in the 1890s, the term "Social Darwinism" was infrequently employed, but it became popular during the 1940s when it was used as a derogatory term by Richard Hofstadter to criticize the laissez-faire conservatism of people like William Graham Sumner, who opposed reform and socialism. Since then, "Social Darwinism" has been used as a term of derision by some people.

Marx's scientific socialism provided a systematic critique of capitalism and a deterministic analysis of society and historical evolution.

Karl Marx (1818 – 1883) was a philosopher, economist, sociologist, journalist and revolutionary socialist. He was born in Germany, but eventually became stateless and spent a lot of his life in London and the United Kingdom. Marx's economic theory was one of the numerous competing theories of the nature of labor and its relation to capital. He published many books and pamphlets throughout his life, the two most prominent being *The Communist Manifesto* and *Das Kapital*. Marxism, the term that encompasses his theories about society, economics and politics, promotes the idea that struggle is what moves a society forward. This mode of thinking was formed by Marx's application of the dialectical materialist theory of history postulated by G. F. W. Hegel.

Karl Marx, German philosopher and socialist

Through application of the Hegelian dialectic, history can be seen to progress through various "stages," where new ideas arise to combat entrenched ideas, eventually leading to a synthesis of the two competing ideas. Hegel believed that this process would lead to the establishment of a Universal (Christian) monarchy, while Marx saw this process leading to the eventual creation of a Communist World State.

Marx believed that states at their very core were merely organizations designed in the interest of the ruling class, while at the same time purporting to represent the population over which they governed. Marx predicted that, as in previous socioeconomic systems, the internal contradictions of the capitalist system would eventually lead to it being replaced with ever more progressive forms of governance. He said that the fight between the bourgeoisie and proletariat classes would culminate in the working class gaining political power and eventually creating a classless society, known as a communist society, which would be overseen by a free association of worker-producers. Marx actively sought the implementation of communism by promoting organized revolutionary action by the working class to overthrow capitalism and bring about socio-economic change, thereby speeding up the process of "history."

Marx has been labeled as one of the most significant people in human history. His ideas have inspired intellectuals, labor unions and political parties around the world, and many variations on Marxism have cropped up as a result. Friedrich Engels first used the term "scientific socialism" to describe the ideas of Marxism because, unlike utopian socialism, Marxism is based on the scientific method; its theories are held to an empirical standard with observations a key component of its development. These can result in changes to and/or falsification of elements of the theory.

Marx was the first to distinguish between utopian and scientific socialism by criticizing the utopian features of French socialism and English and Scottish political economics. Marx believed that Utopian Socialism was flawed because of its epistemological position; he believed that the Utopian Socialists were too idealistic in their interpretation of how a real socialist society can be established.

Hegel's historical dialectic provided the scientific impetus for Marx's theory on how a state of communism could be achieved. He felt that through understanding history as a step-by-step process moving towards the goal of universal communism, a mode of observation could be established whereby it was possible to both see how close a society was moving towards communism, and providing supporters a framework in which they could agitate as a means to speed up the process of "history." From his perspective, the Utopian Socialists were idealistic dreamers in their beliefs about how one could establish a communist society.

Realist and materialist themes and attitudes influenced art and literature as painters and writers depicted the lives of ordinary people and drew attention to social problems.

Artistic realism, also known as naturalism, sought to represent subject matter realistically, without artificiality, artistic conventions or implausible, exotic and supernatural elements. Realism existed in the arts throughout history and was largely a matter of technique, training and avoiding stylization. In the visual arts, illusionistic realism refers to the precise depiction of life forms, perspective and details like light and color. Realist art, especially the styles of social realism, regionalism and "kitchen sink" realism, may highlight the ugly or sordid. Historically, there have been various artistic realism movements, such as the opera style of verismo, literary realism, theatrical realism and Italian neorealist cinema.

Honoré de Balzac, realist writer

Honoré de Balzac was a key figure in the realism movement in fiction writing. His main contribution was *The Human Comedy*, which sought to expose the many contradictions of the human condition in a series of over 100 novels. Like many realist writers, Balzac had trouble thriving in the society in which he found himself. He was neither an outright Royalist nor an outright proponent of revolutionary change. Owing to his centrist position, he was often misrepresented by both sides of the French governmental debate. However, through works such as *The Human Comedy*, he was able to accurately represent the inherent contradictions in French society. His work would go on to greatly influence one of the central French authors of the modern period, Alexandre Dumas.

Arguably the most well-known writer to express realism in his work was Charles Dickens. Much of his work was inspired by his experiences living and working in Industrial-era London. When Dickens was twelve, he had to work in a blacking factory, because his family was incarcerated in debtors' prison. He would later go on to write novels about the conditions of child workers in the era. His writings on the conditions of the working class in Britain during the Industrial Revolution were crucial in informing the literate classes, who had not been exposed to the working conditions of those toiling in factories about the horrors of London's workhouses.

Due to his work as a journalist, Dickens knew that the way to expose the population to the horrors of Industrial-era Britain was through developing characters to which readers could relate. In doing this he was one of the first to realize that through creating a character in which the reader could see some of himself, he would grow to have more sympathy for those in a station below him. This was a revolutionary idea for the time, as many still believed that the state one found himself in was ascribed to Divine Will. Through creating characters that showed aspects of humanity to which all members of society could relate, Dickens began to chip away at the façade of the institution of rigid class systems.

Charles Dickens, English writer

Another central figure in the realist literary movement was the Russian writer Fyodor Dostoevsky. His works centered on the divine in an era when questioning the infallibility of Christian institutions was becoming ever more acceptable. His work is a prime example of the use of allegory, with his characters representing differing sets of ideas. While the use of allegory in fictional writing was by no means a new phenomenon, Dostoevsky was able to use this literary device to great effect in most of his writing. Of his many noted works, *The Idiot* is still considered to be one of the greatest works of allegory of the 19th century. This work depicts the fictional Prince Myshkin returning from a Swiss clinic, finding a country that he does not understand and a people to whom he has trouble relating. Many have argued that the protagonist of this novel is meant to be Christ and, given the state of the world in the 19th century, if he were to be sent by God down to Earth, he would not recognize the horrible misrepresentation of a society purportedly organized around the values he preached.

A new relativism in values and the loss of confidence in the objectivity of knowledge led to modernism in intellectual and cultural life.

The huge changes that occurred in Western society during the late 19th and early 20th centuries, led to the emergence of the philosophy of Modernism, which was shaped by industrialization, urbanization and the devastation of the First World War. Modernism rejected the conviction of Enlightenment philosophy and many modernists also rejected religious belief.

Modernists generally thought that traditional forms of art, philosophy and science were becoming outdated due to the innovations that stemmed from industrialization. The poet Ezra Pound's 1934 call to "Make it new!" was the benchmark of Modernism's approach towards what it saw as the now archaic culture of the past. Consciousness of the self was a prominent characteristic of Modernism that led to experiments with form. Modernism openly rejected Realism and made inventive and often irreverent use of the works of the past.

Philosophy largely moved from rational interpretations of nature and human society to an emphasis on irrationality and impulse, a view that contributed to the belief that conflict and struggles led to progress.

The 19th century saw an explosion in the prevalence of philosophy that sought to expose the impulsive nature of humankind. This work was largely influenced by the Deist movement and the German idealist movement, as seen in the works of Emmanuel Kant. These philosophical movements were central in beginning to challenge the normative structure of philosophy as it had existed up until this point and laid the crucial foundations for the works of authors, such as Friedrich Nietzsche, Georges Sorel and Henri Bergson.

Before expanding on the ideas of the aforementioned philosophers, it is essential to first understand the work of G. F. W. Hegel. Hegel's dialectical approach to understanding history, expressed in his seminal work *The Phenomenology of Spirit*, was a precursor to the writings of the philosophers referenced later in this section. The dialectic interpretation of history posits that ideas develop through the ongoing stages of thesis, antithesis, synthesis – all moving towards the true realization of human potential.

The thesis is the reigning set of ideas that form the consensus ideology of the day. These notions are inevitably challenged by new and radical ideas about the flaws of the established ideology of the day and an antithesis is formed. These ideas then both inform each other and a new synthesis is formed when the consensus ideology of the day is ready to accept and incorporate some of the notions in the antithesis, developing a new thesis. In Hegel's view, this process is always ongoing until humans finally are able to reach their full potential. While this dialectical approach to history was not universally accepted by the authors mention further, the promulgation of this notion was a necessary condition for the development of their ideas.

Georg Wilhelm Friedrich Hegel, German philosopher

The best known of the authors to challenge the status quo interpretation of the manner in which society was organized was the German philosopher Friedrich Nietzsche. His most influential ideas centered on the shift from good-versus-bad to good-versus-evil. To Nietzsche, humanity had strayed from proper examination of the human condition with the creation of notions of good versus evil, as evil is not a fixed point and can be shifted to suit the narrative of the status quo of those in power. He observed that this good-versus-evil narrative was employed as a means to justify any number of objectively "bad" acts, as those who had a monopoly on the notions of good-versus-evil could twist their meaning to suit their ends.

The above notion was represented by what he called the "Slave Mentality" of God-fearing Christians who essentially acted as the serfs of the ruling class, while being content with their position due to their Christian faith. This led to his most infamous notion of the "death of God." This notion is often misrepresented in our contemporary understanding due to the hyperbolic nature of his claim. However, what Nietzsche was saying was that God, as interpreted by his contemporaries, was created by man as a means to legitimize and perpetuate a master-slave relationship.

Friedrich Nietzsche's philosophy also challenged the notion of objective truth and presupposed that all observable facts are subject to the conditions in which they exist. His belief in the conditionality of truth is still debated to this day and is seen as one of the focal points in the split in European philosophy between the Anglo-American and Continental schools of thought, Nietzsche and the philosophers that follow belonging to the latter.

Henri-Louis Bergson,
French philosopher

A seminal figure in the growth of philosophy that questioned strictly "rational" observation of the human condition was Henri-Louis Bergson. The main contribution Bergson made to the study of the human condition was to present a justification for the notion of free will. He contested the Kantian notion that free will can only exist outside time and space. In Bergson's theory of "Duration," he posited that it is impossible to measure free will as time is ever expanding and moving, whereas the observation of that time must be fixed, thereby rendering observation of its existence extremely difficult. This challenged the perceived wisdom of the day in that most philosophers and scientists strictly interpreted the condition of man in an empirical manner. To Bergson, this would lead to a misrepresentation, as there are only select pictures of the thing under observation that are taken as representing the whole.

Another prominent philosopher who questioned the strictly rational/empirical approach to understanding society was Georges Sorel. Sorel was an anarcho-syndicalist who could loosely be described as adhering to the Marxist tradition. He believed strongly in the organization of the working classes into syndicates who would fight, violently if necessary, to overturn the exploitative system of the day. Further, Sorel was deeply skeptical of the growing deification of science. He believed that science was not a universal recipe by which any problem could be solved. He recognized that society is not organized in such a manner and attempting to find solutions through scientific means would not work.

Georges Sorel, French philosopher and sociologist

Freudian psychology provided a new account of human nature that emphasized the role of the irrational and the struggle between the conscious and subconscious.

Sigmund Freud (1856-1939), known today as the father of psychoanalysis, was an Austrian neurologist. He earned his medical degree at the University of Vienna in 1881 and subsequently embarked on research into cerebral palsy, aphasia and microscopic neuroanatomy at the Vienna General Hospital. In creating psychoanalysis, a clinical way to treat psychopathology via dialogue between a patient and a psychoanalyst, Freud established therapeutic practices, such as free association, and discovered the principle of transference and its important function in the process of psychoanalysis. Freud redefined sexuality to include its infantile stages and formulated the Oedipus complex as the key idea of psychoanalytical theory.

Freud thought that dreams were related to wish-fulfillments, which provided him with models for the clinical analysis of the formation of symptoms and the mechanisms of repression, in addition to the elaboration of his theory of the unconscious as an agency disruptive of conscious states of mind. Freud hypothesized the existence of libido (an energy invested with mental processes and structures, which produces erotic attachments) and a death drive (the source of repetition, hate, aggression and neurotic guilt). In his later work, Freud promoted an inclusive interpretation and critique of both religion and culture.

Psychoanalysis remains influential within the discipline of psychotherapy, within some areas of psychiatry and across the humanities. It continues to produce widespread and heated debate about its effectiveness, its scientific status and whether it helped or hurt feminism. Though it was not the first methodology in the practice of individual verbal psychotherapy, Freud's psychoanalytical approach came to dominate the field of psychoanalysis in the early 20th century and formed the basis of many later variants.

Developments in the natural sciences, such as quantum mechanics and Einstein's theory of relativity, undermined the primacy of Newtonian physics as an objective description of nature.

In the 17th and 18th centuries, scientific inquiry into light waves emerged, when scientists like Robert Hooke promoted a wave theory of light that was based on experimental observations. In 1803, the English polymath Thomas Young carried out the famed and influential double-slit experiment, which he later detailed in his paper *On The Nature Of Light and Colors*. Cathode rays were discovered by Michael Faraday in 1838. These studies were followed by Gustav Kirchhoff's 1859 identification of the black-body radiation problem, Ludwig Boltzmann's 1877 proposal that the energy states of a physical system can be distinct and Max Planck's 1900 quantum hypothesis that energy is radiated and absorbed in distinct "quanta."

Planck's work supported the observed patterns of black-body radiation from Kirchhoff's earlier work. In 1896, Wilhelm Wien empirically demonstrated a distribution law of black-body radiation, known as "Wien's law." Ludwig Boltzmann also achieved this result independently by using Maxwell's equations; however, it was only valid at high frequencies and underestimated the radiance at low frequencies. Later, Planck used Boltzmann's statistical interpretation of thermodynamics to correct this model and proposed what is now known as Planck's law, leading to the development of quantum mechanics. Robert A. Millikan studied the photoelectric effect, for which Albert Einstein eventually developed a theory.

Albert Einstein, theoretical physicist

Albert Einstein (1879-1955) was a German theoretical physicist who came up with the general theory of relativity, which, along with quantum mechanics, is one of the two foundations of modern physics. His work also influenced scientific philosophy. Einstein is famous in popular culture for the mass–energy equivalence formula he developed: $E = mc^2$. In 1921, he was awarded the Nobel Prize in Physics for his contributions to theoretical physics, in particular, his discovery of the law of the photoelectric effect, an important advance in the development of quantum theory.

Early on, Einstein thought that Newtonian mechanics was no longer sufficient to reconcile the laws of classical mechanics with the laws of the electromagnetic field. This led him to develop his special theory of relativity. Einstein also realized that the principle of relativity could be applied to gravitational fields, and published a paper on general relativity after developing his theory of gravitation in 1916. He continued to grapple with the issues of statistical mechanics and quantum theory, which led to his explanations of particle theory and molecular motion. He also studied the thermal properties of light, which served as a base for the photon theory of light. In 1917, Einstein used the general theory of relativity to model the large-scale structure of the universe.

Modern art, including Impressionism, Post-Impressionism and Cubism, moved beyond the representational to the subjective, abstract and expressive, and often provoked antagonism from those who believed that art should reflect shared and idealized values, such as beauty and patriotism.

Impressionism was a 19th century artistic movement that was promoted by a group of artists in Paris and achieved prominence through the independent exhibitions held there throughout the 1870s and 1880s. Impressionist painting is characterized by delicate yet visible brush strokes, open composition, an emphasis on the precise depiction of light, ordinary subject matter, the depiction of movement and the use of uncommon visual angles. At the time, the conventional art community within France rejected the impressionist style. The term "impressionism" is derived from the title of a Claude Monet painting, *Impression, Soleil Levant* ("Impression, Sunrise"), which provoked the critic Louis Leroy to employ the term in a satirical review published in the Parisian newspaper *Le Charivari*.

"Impression, Soleil Levant" by Claude Monet

Post-Impressionism was an artistic movement that predominantly took place in France from 1886 to 1905. It developed as a reaction in opposition to the Impressionists' focus on naturalism with regard to light and color. Post-Impressionism places a broad emphasis on abstraction or symbolic content, and encompasses the schools of Neo-

Impressionism, Symbolism and Synthetism, in addition to some later Impressionists' work. Key artists of the Post-Impressionist movement are Paul Cézanne, Paul Gauguin, Vincent van Gogh and Georges Seurat.

The term Post-Impressionism originated in 1910 with the British artist and art critic Roger Fry. Fry used the term to refer to the development of French art in the time period since Manet, when he organized an exhibition called "Manet and the Post-Impressionists." Post-Impressionism developed from Impressionism while abandoning its limiting features. Vivid colors were still used, paint often continued to be applied thickly and subject matter remained realistic; however, greater emphasis was placed on geometric forms, the subjects were often imaginatively distorted and unnatural or arbitrary colors were used.

European painting and sculpture were revolutionized in the 20th century by the innovative art movement known as Cubism, considered the most influential style of the 20th century that inspired similar avant-garde movements in music, literature and architecture. The label of Cubism is broadly used to encompass a wide variety of art that was produced in Paris in the 1910s and 1920s. Cubism was pioneered by Georges Braque and Pablo Picasso, who were influenced by works of Paul Cézanne. In Cubist artwork, objects are examined, taken apart and put back together in an abstract form. In Cubism, instead of depicting an object from a single point of view, the artist depicts the subject from many overlapping points of view in order to represent it in its larger context.

This page was intentionally lefy blank

We want to hear from you

Your feedback is important to us because we strive to provide the highest quality prep materials. If you have any questions, comments or suggestions, email us, so we can incorporate your feedback into future editions.

Customer Satisfaction Guarantee

If you have any concerns about this book, including printing issues, contact us and we will resolve any issues to your satisfaction.

info@sterling-prep.com

Period 4: c. 1914 to the Present

Major historical events of the period:

1914-1918:   World War I

1916:   Britain fosters the Arab Revolt of 1916 in Ottoman territories

1917:   Russian Revolution; Finland declares independence from Russia

1917-1925:   Russian Civil War

1918-1920:   The Hungarian-Romanian War

1919-1923:   The Turkish War of Independence

1920:   The League of Nations is formed

1922:   Germany defaults on Treaty of Versailles reparation payments; Benito Mussolini becomes Italian Fascist leader

1933:   Adolf Hitler and the Nazi Party come to power in Germany

1936-1939:   The Spanish Civil War

1938:   Nazi Germany annex Austria and Sudetenland region of Czechoslovakia

1939:   Nazi Germany invades Czechoslovakia, annexes Bohemia and Moravia, establishes puppet Slovak Republic, cedes portions of former Czechoslovakia to Hungary

1939:   World War II begins

1941:   Nazi Germany invades the Soviet Union; Japanese attack Pearl Harbor

1945:   World War II ends

1947-1991:   The Cold War

1948-1952:   The Marshall Plan bolsters economic recovery in Western Europe

1949:   The North Atlantic Treaty Organization (NATO) is created

1954-1962:   The Algerian War of Independence from France

1955:   The Warsaw Pact is signed

1957:   The Hungarian Revolution of 1956 against Communist-Russian domination

1958:   The Treaty of Rome (a proto-European Union treaty) is signed

1968:   Soviet forces invade Czechoslovakia following the Prague Spring movement of political liberalization

1989:   Overthrow of communism in Poland, Hungary, Czechoslovakia, East Germany, Romania and Bulgaria

1990:   German unification is achieved

1991:   Comecon, the Warsaw Pact and the Soviet Union disbanded

1992-1995:   The Bosnian War

1993:   Czechoslovakia splits into the Czech Republic and Slovakia

1994-1996:   The First Chechen War

1999-2009:   The Second Chechen War

> **Key Concept 4.1: Total war and political instability in the first half of the 20th century gave way to a polarized state order during the Cold War and eventually to efforts at transnational union.**

European politics and diplomacy in the 20th century were defined by total war and its consequences. World War I destroyed the balance of power. The Treaty of Versailles ended the war, but created unstable conditions in which extremist ideologies emerged that challenged liberal democracy and the postwar settlement. In Russia, hardships during World War I gave rise to a revolution in 1917. The newly established, postwar democracies in central and Eastern Europe were too weak to provide stability either internally or in the European state system, especially during the Great Depression of the 1930s.

The League of Nations was established after the war to employ collective security in the interest of peace, but could not manage the international tensions unleashed by World War I. The breakdown of the settlement led to World War II, a conflict even more violent than World War I. During this second Great War, the combatants engaged in wholesale destruction of cities, deliberate attacks on civilians and the systematic destruction of their enemies' industrial complexes. The Nazi government in Germany undertook the annihilation of Jews from the whole continent (the Holocaust), as well as the murder of other targeted groups of Europeans. At the end of the war, the economic and political devastation left a power vacuum that facilitated the Cold War division of Europe.

During the 20th century, European imperialism, power and sense of superiority reached both its apogee and its nadir. In the first half of the century, nations extended their control and influence over most of the non-Western world, often through League of Nations' mandates. The idea of decolonization was born early in the century with the formation of movements seeking rights for indigenous peoples; the material and moral destruction of World War II made the idea a reality. After the war, regions colonized and dominated by European nations moved from resistance to independence at differing rates and with differing consequences. Yet even after decolonization, neocolonial dependency persisted, and millions of people migrated to Europe as its economy recovered from the war. This immigration created large populations of poor and isolated minorities, which occasionally rioted because of discrimination and economic deprivation. As European governments tried to solve these problems, the apparently permanent presence of the immigrants challenged the traditional notions of Europe's identity.

The uneasy alliance between Soviet Russia and the West during World War II gave way after 1945 to diplomatic, political and economic confrontation between the democratic, capitalist states of Western Europe allied with the United States and the communist bloc of Eastern Europe dominated by the Soviet Union (also known as the Union of Soviet Socialist Republics, or USSR). During the ensuing confrontation between East and West, called the Cold War, relations between the two blocs fluctuated, but one consequence of the conflict was that European nations could no longer act autonomously in international affairs; the superpowers—the Soviet Union and the United States—controlled international relations in Europe.

Nonetheless, the Cold War promoted political and economic unity in Western Europe, leading to the establishment of a succession of ever-more comprehensive organizations for economic cooperation. In 1957, six countries formed the Common Market, which soon began to expand its membership to include other European states. The success of the Common Market inspired Europeans to work toward a closer political and economic unity, which was to include a European executive body and Parliament.

The founding of the European Union in 1991 at Maastricht included the agreement to establish the euro as a common currency for qualifying member states. Following a series of largely peaceful revolutions in 1989, culminating in the collapse of the Soviet Union in 1991, the formerly communist states of Eastern Europe moved toward democracy and capitalist economies, and over time some of these states joined the European Union. One unforeseen consequence of the end of the Cold War was the re-emergence of nationalist political parties in Western Europe.

World War I, caused by a complex interaction of long- and short-term factors, resulted in immense losses and disruptions for both victors and vanquished.

The *First World War*, or World War I, was the first global war of the modern/mechanized era. It began on July 28, 1914 and ended November 11, 1918. Other than the Mongol conquests, which were not sustained and lasted over generations, World War I was the deadliest conflict up to this point in human history. The war resulted in the death of approximately 9 million combatants and 7 million civilians, with many more psychologically maimed by the sheer brutality of 20th century weaponry being employed against 18th century battle tactics. This extraordinary death toll can be attributed to more sophisticated methods of warfare, both technological and industrial, and the unwillingness on the part of old-school military tacticians to update their strategies in the face of new technological realities. World War I would also set the stage for the Second World War, shape the Middle East into the countries seen today and result in the establishment of the Soviet Union.

American soldiers wounded in France during World War I

All of the world's economic powerhouses were involved in this unprecedented war; the Allies, an alliance of nations formed around the nucleus of the *Triple Entente* (a 1907 agreement of friendship and understanding between major European countries, including the Russian Empire, France and the UK), were in opposition to Germany and Austria-Hungary, which were the *Central Powers*. Italy, which was originally aligned with

Germany and Austria-Hungary as a member of the Triple Alliance, felt that Austria-Hungary had violated the terms of the Triple Alliance by taking the offensive and refusing to give support to the Central Powers. More nations became involved as conflict progressed. The Allies gained Italian, Japanese and the United States' support and the Bulgaria and the Ottoman Empire joined the Central Powers.

Many historians consider the onset of the First World War inevitable. The intertwining alliances that were put in place to prevent such a global confrontation did not take into account the awakening national consciousness of the many peoples who found themselves ruled by a great empire in which they felt they had no stake. Therefore, it is no surprise that the event that sparked the First World War was the assassination of Franz Ferdinand, the heir apparent to the Austro-Hungarian throne, by a Serbian nationalist.

Archduke Franz Ferdinand of Austria

Franz Ferdinand was in Sarajevo (present day capital of Bosnia-Herzegovina) when a member of the "Black Hand" Serbian nationalist group, Gavrilo Princip, lobbed a bomb into the Archduke's carriage on June 28th, 1914. The assassination prompted Austria-Hungary to issue the Kingdom of Serbia an ultimatum and call upon complicated international alliances for support. On July 28, 1914 Austria-Hungary declared war on Serbia and invaded, prompting conflicts involving all the major world powers which spread across the world.

Russia entered the fray, backing the fellow Slavic Orthodox Kingdom of Serbia, while Germany invaded Luxembourg and Belgium (both neutral nations) and then set its sights on France. Britain, who had signed a treaty to "protect with arms the neutral position of Belgium," mobilized against Germany. The battles which occurred in the Lowlands and Northern France became known as the Western Front, and the battles that took place on this front are often conflated with the war itself.

However, the war was worldwide and often the battles on the other fronts were far more brutal that the Western Front, where there was at least a remaining vestige of the civil code that governed the quickly passing age of "gallant" warfare.

Russia defeated Austria-Hungary on the Eastern Front, but was unsuccessful in an attempted invasion of East Prussia due to the fact that this area was guarded by the far better trained and equipped German Army. The Central Powers officially gained support from the Ottoman Empire in November 1914, specifically in the Caucasus, Mesopotamia and Sinai regions; though the Ottoman Army, owing the vast numbers of German's serving in its ranks, was already a *de facto* ally of the Central Powers. In 1915, Italy joined the Allies and Bulgaria joined the Central Powers. Romania and the United States gave allegiance to the Allies in 1916 and 1917, respectively.

In March of 1917, Russia suffered from a governmental collapse and a revolution the following November led to Russia agreeing to terms with the Central Powers. The terms, laid out in the *Treaty of Brest Litovsk*, signified a significant win for Germany until they were nullified following the ultimate victory of the Western allies in 1918. The German offensive during the spring of 1918 along the Western front was impressive, but it was met with a strong response from the Allied forces, who were able to subdue the Germans. Germany, contending with internal revolutionary backlash, agreed to an armistice with the Austro-Hungarian Empire, effectively ending the war in a victory for the Allies on November 11th, 1918.

The end of World War I saw the essential ruin of the European empires including the Ottoman, Russian, Austro-Hungarian and German empires. Land was redistributed and borders were redrawn and mapped out. There was an effort to restore or recreate some independent nations and Germany's colonies were divided among the victors. A peace conference in Paris was held in 1919 during which major powers such as Britain, France, the U.S. and Italy deliberated terms of new treaties. *The League of Nations* was created in the hope of averting another war such as World War I.

A variety of factors – including nationalism, military plans, the alliance system, and imperial competition – turned a regional dispute in the Balkans into World War I.

By 1900, throughout the European continent, there existed a complex web of military and political alliances put in place as an attempt to regain and retain a power balance. The formation of these alliances had begun in 1815 when Prussia, Russia and Austria entered into the Holy Alliance. *The League of the Three Emperors* was an agreement negotiated by the German Chancellor Otto von Bismarck between Germany, Russia and Austria-Hungary in October of 1873; it failed when Russia and Austria-

Hungary could not agree over policy in the Balkans. This led to the 1879 Dual Alliance between Germany and Austria-Hungary which was formed with the intention of opposing the influence of Russia in the Balkans as the Ottoman Empire became increasingly weaker. The Dual Alliance expanded into the Triple Alliance with the inclusion of Italy into the agreement in 1879.

Chancellor Otto von Bismarck

Chancellor Bismarck was especially interested in avoiding wars with France and Russia at the same time and worked to keep Russia aligned with German interests. Bismarck retired when Wilhelm II took the throne as German Emperor (Kaiser) and the alliances Bismarck had supported were decreasingly prioritized. In 1890, for example, the new Kaiser refused a renewal of Germany's *Reinsurance Treaty* with Russia and two years later Russia had entered into the Franco-Russian Alliance. This alliance was formed to counter the power of the Triple Alliance.

Numerous agreements between Britain and France in 1904 were known as the Entente Cordiale. 1907 saw the signing of the Anglo-Russian Convention that steadied British-Russian relations, which had been relatively icy since the end of the Crimean War. Though these agreements never officially allied Britain with France or Russia, they created a likelihood of British backing in any conflict in which France or Russia became involved. These complicated bilateral agreements became known as the Triple Entente. An overview of the extensive treatises and alliances, which intertwined European nations, provides an important foundational perspective when examining specific events that triggered the start of World War I and the way events unfolded throughout the war.

In October 1908, Austria-Hungary added to escalating tension in what came to be called the Bosnian Crisis (1908-1909) by annexing the territories of Bosnia and Herzegovina–former Ottoman land that had been occupied by Austria-Hungary since 1878. This outraged the Serbian Kingdom, due to the large numbers of ethnic Serbs living in Bosnia and Herzegovina. Russia was also enraged as she saw herself as the legitimate protector of all Orthodox Slavs who had previously been under the Ottoman yoke. Political maneuverings by Russia led to a destabilization of certain peace agreements. This region, already known as the "powder keg of Europe," was fraught with a high level of tension and

Russia's actions exacerbated the fracturing accords. The First Balkan War, fought between the Balkan League and a divided and crumbling Ottoman Empire, lasted from 1912-1913. It ended in the *Treaty of London,* which left the Ottoman Empire smaller and more powerless than ever, allowed for the creation of an independent Albanian state and increased the land holdings of Serbia, Bulgaria, Greece and Montenegro.

The Second Balkan War commenced on June 16, 1913 when Bulgaria attacked Serbia and Greece and lasted thirty-three days. This war resulted in Bulgaria losing the majority of Macedonia to Serbia and Greece, and forfeiting Southern Dobruja to Romania. These battles contributed to destabilization of the region and further primed circumstances which would lead to World War I.

Illustration of Serbian volunteers of the Second Balkan War

The concept of military strategizing was significant in terms of the death toll of the First World War although it is impossible to determine whether the pre-existence of battle plans increased casualties in this war, whether the slaughter would have been worse without them or if they had no effect. As a fact, the most aggressive nations had developed comprehensive battle plans prior to the declarations of war (the notable exception being the United States). France had been planning as early as 1913 to recapture the territory of Alsace-Lorraine, which it had lost to Germany in 1871. Germany had also developed the

"Schlieffen Plan," which called for the conquering of France from the north through Belgium. This move is often studied in war studies departments as it is the perfect example of hitting an enemy where they least expect it; however, it had the unintended consequence of breaching Belgian neutrality, which brought Britain into the war.

Furthermore, the Austro-Hungarian Empire had long set its sights on fully conquering the Balkans and bringing the region decisively under their control. Finally, the Russians also had plans for what they wanted to gain from the war, with their main prize being the Ottoman capital of Constantinople. They viewed its capture and renaming it Tsargrad (City of the Tsar) as their main goal in the war. The Tsar sought to reestablish the Russian Orthodox Church's claim as the legitimate protector of Eastern Christianity in the ancient Byzantine capital.

New technologies confounded traditional military strategies and led to massive troop losses.

Though World War I was largely fought by employing 18th century military tactics, it was carried out using technology of the 20th century, which led to unprecedented numbers of casualties. Major military forces, which in some cases were numbering in the millions, began using modernized technology by late 1917, including wireless communication and telephones, armored cars, tanks and aircraft. Also, there was a revamping of artillery and infantry formations; by 1914, cannons were placed in the front line to be shot at targets, and by 1917, it was typical to employ indirect fire with guns, and even machineguns and mortars. New techniques for ranging and spotting, using aircraft and sometimes field telephones were developed. In response, counter-battery and sound detection tactics became commonplace. The Allies struggled to catch up to and neutralize Germany, who employed use of heavy indirect fire.

Trench warfare was a common form of combat and very deadly, often resulting in hundreds of lives lost in order to gain a yard of territory. There was a bitter saying on the Western Front that thousands of men would be sacrificed in order for the commanding officer to move his whiskey cabinet one foot closer to Berlin. Some of the deadliest battles in world history took place during World War I, including Ypres (Belgium), the Marne (France), the Somme (France), Verdun (France), and Gallipoli (Ottoman Empire). Despite the British naval blockade, Germany was able to retain a constant gunpowder supply by using nitrogen fixation, known as the Haber process. Chemical weapons such as tear gas and mustard gas first had large scale use in World War I, although artillery was the weapon which used the largest amounts of explosives and accounted for the most casualties. Steel helmets were developed for protection due to the vast number of head wounds from exploding shells.

French soldier with his horse, Battle of the Marne, World War I

Unrestricted naval warfare was also undertaken, initially by Germany, using U-boats (submarines) in 1917. Kaiserliche Marine ordered the U-boats to prevent the British Isles from receiving necessary supplies. The Italians, dropping grenades in Libya in October of 1911 during the Italo-Turkish War, were the first to use fixed-wing aircraft for military endeavors. By 1914, the military utility of aircraft (not only for attacking, but also for gathering reconnaissance) was being expanded with the development of fighter aircraft, aircraft weaponry and anti-aircraft guns. The Germans used Zeppelins and, along with the British, created strategic bomber aircraft.

Unmoving reconnaissance stations in the form of manned balloons which floated high above the trenches were used to report enemy movements and to accurately aim artillery assaults. Typically, each balloon had a two-person crew with parachutes in the case of an air assault by the enemy. Though observation balloon crews were equipped with parachutes, parachutes were not provided to aircraft pilots because the large parachutes of the time were too heavy for small planes with only a small power capacity, and British authorities thought that having a parachute might be an inducement to cowardice.

Observation balloons offered vital military advantage and therefore they were high-priority targets for enemy assaults. Armies protected and defended their observation balloons using friendly aircraft patrol and anti-aircraft guns; the balloons led to the development of unusual weapons, such as the air-to-air rocket. Due to the fact that observation balloons allowed for the conduct of wide-spread reconnaissance, their use in warfare led to the development of air combat, as well as stalemate in trench warfare, because troops could not move without being detected. Throughout 1915 and 1916, Germany used air warfare technology to carry out air raids on England, hoping that British morale would be affected and that British troops would respond by diverting their aircraft from the front lines to combat the German air raids.

Automatic fire weapons were first introduced in the middle of the nineteenth century and used with devastating effect in the Crimean War and the American Civil War. But the truly modern machinegun was introduced in World War I, with machineguns becoming standard infantry weapons. Machineguns, which could fire ten rounds per second, and mass charges of entire battalions of soldiers were a deadly combination. The death toll from any single method in World War I cannot be accurately counted, but machineguns accounted for a significant portion of the thirty million soldiers killed or wounded in battle.

The most notorious and insidious weapon, the first thing which most people think of when they think of combat in World War I, was poison gas. This was arguably the first use of a weapon of mass destruction in modern times. It not only killed huge numbers of soldiers, it created a new type of apocalyptic injury: acidic burns, which were much more difficult to treat than bullet and shrapnel wounds, scarred the bodies and lungs of thousands of soldiers.

The battle tank was invented and first employed during World War I. Initial successes were questionable, as its extremely slow speed made it a sitting duck for artillery fire and infantry, and combat strategies had not been developed for the use of this unprecedented new tool. Whether the tank caused more casualties or lowered the death toll in the war is debatable; one possibility is that far fewer infantry were killed in similar battles with the tank than in previous battles without. But the Germans quickly developed counter-measures to the tank as well as their own tanks.

One of the complicating factors in attacking an enemy's trench was the presence of barbed wire. After running across "no man's land" a typical distance of five hundred yards, while being shelled by mortars and raked with machinegun fire, the advancing enemy often needed to scale barbed wire while still under fire. A huge number of additional deaths were caused by the delay in scaling the wire.

The effects of military stalemate and total war led to protest and insurrection in the belligerent nations and eventually to revolutions that changed the international balance of power.

A series of peace treaties developed at the Paris Peace Conference were imposed upon the Central Powers in order to officially end the war, though it had ceased in 1918. In the *Treaty of Versailles*, the state of war between Germany and the Allied Powers was officially ended, and this segued into the formation of the League of Nations on June 28, 1919. The Peace Conference recognized nations newly liberated from Germany's rule and demanded that the defeated countries pay reparation to those nations whose civilian populations had been harmed. Because of the collapsed economies and financial difficulties in many parts of Europe in the aftermath of the war, the majority of these reparations became the responsibility of Germany, who still retained a functioning economy.

Painting of a Paris Peace Conference session, 1919

As outlined in the *Treaty of Saint-Germain* and the *Treaty of Trianon*, Austria-Hungary was sectioned into the four successor states of Austria, Hungary, Czechoslovakia and Yugoslavia which loosely followed ethnic divisions. Transylvania became a part of Greater Romania instead of Hungary. Over 3.3 million Hungarians ended up under foreign rule based on stipulations made by the Treaty of Trianon. In the pre-war Kingdom of Hungary, 54% of the population was Hungarian, yet Hungary was only allotted 32% of the former territory of the Hungarian Kingdom. In the span of four years (between 1920 and

1924) 354,000 Hungarians fled former Hungarian territories which had been partitioned off to Romania, Czechoslovakia and Yugoslavia.

The Russian Empire withdrew from World War I following the October Revolution of 1917, and subsequently lost territory on its western front, most notably in Estonia, Finland, Latvia and Eastern Poland. Bessarabia was unified with Romania in April 1918. As the Ottoman Empire dissolved, many swathes of land that were non-Anatolian territory were portioned as protectorates to the Allied powers. The Turkish presence in the Anatolia territory formed the Republic of Turkey. The 1920 *Treaty of Sèvres* was supposed to section off the Ottoman Empire, except it was never signed by the Sultan and the Turkish National Movement rejected it outright. The Turkish War of Independence followed, and in 1923 the *Treaty of Lausanne*, which was far less exacting, was signed.

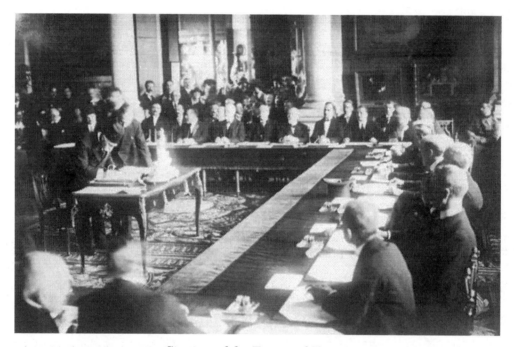

Signing of the Treaty of Sèvres

In the aftermath of the war, Poland, who had not been recognized as an independent nation, reemerged after over a century. The Serbian Kingdom, despite having suffered the most causalities per capita as a "minor Entente nation" during the war, gained prominence as the core of a new multinational state which incorporated the Kingdom of Serbs, Croats and Slovenes and was later named Yugoslavia. A combination of the Kingdom of Bohemia, or the Czech Kingdom, and the Kingdom of Hungary was renamed Czechoslovakia. Russia, now stripped of Finland, Estonia, Lithuania and Latvia (which had all gained their independence), renamed itself the Soviet Union. The deteriorated Ottoman Empire became Turkey and various other Middle Eastern countries.

The war in Europe quickly spread to non-European theaters, transforming the war into a global conflict.

In Asia and on the Pacific front, the conflict that arose in World War I was naval and/or consisted of Allied Powers conquering German colonies in the Pacific Ocean and China. Of these military actions, a particularly significant one was the deliberate and expertly maneuvered Siege of Tsingtao in what today is China. There were also lesser military engagements in German New Guinea at Bita Paka and Toma. The Allied Powers were able to topple other German or Austrian colonies in the Asian or Pacific region without death or wounding. The colonial powers all retained naval power in the Indian or the Pacific Ocean and therefore, naval warfare was commonplace in this region. The Allied Powers gave support to invasions of German-held territories and were charged with defeating the East Asia Squadron.

German Samoa, later called Western Samoa, was occupied by New Zealand on August 30, 1914. The Australian Naval and Military Expeditionary Force landed on the island of Neu Pommern (at that time part of German New Guinea, later to be called New Britain) on September 11, 1914. Following this, a German cruiser called *SMS Emden* defeated *Zhemchug*, a Russian cruiser, during the Battle of Penang on October 28. Japan took over German colonies in Micronesia, and following the Siege of Tsingtao, the coaling port called Qingdao, located on the Chinese Shandong peninsula.

In Tsingtao, Vienna refused to withdraw the *SMS Kaiserian Elisabeth*, an Austrian-Hungarian cruiser, causing Japan to declare war on Germany and Austria-Hungary. In defense of Tsingtao, in November 1914, the ship was sunk. Except for a few commerce raiders and holdouts in New Guinea, the Allied forces had seized every German territory in the Pacific region.

In response to rising Turkish and then Arab nationalism throughout the Ottoman territories in the Middle East, Arab leaders began advocating for the formation of a pan-Arab state. Initially, Arab nationalists had been content to demand greater autonomy within the existing political arrangements; in Paris in 1911, a group of Arab politicians and scholars met and formed the first nationalist movement called *Al Fatat*. Al Fatat held regular conferences in Paris to discuss how to identify and advance their goals. Towards the end of the First World War, however, with the Ottoman Empire losing ground, it cracked down on Al Fatat and other nationalist movements. In response, Arab nationalists decided to pursue full national autonomy.

Group photo of al-Fatat's members in 1919

In an attempt to gain independence, there was a widespread Arab Revolt in 1916 across Ottoman-controlled territories in the Middle East. The British fostered the Arab rebellion within the Ottoman Empire hoping that the large number of Arab soldiers serving in the Ottoman army would desert. The leader of it was Sharif Hussein, an ambitious governor of the Arab holy city Mecca, whom the British recruited to lead an uprising. He was promised that he would rule over an Arab nation, to be carved out of Ottoman territory, in return for his support, but this did not happen in the end. Tens of thousands of disenchanted Ottoman citizens joined the rebellion and claimed a large amount of Arab territory by 1917. The pivotal battle was the battle for the Ottoman port of Aqaba, which the Arabs claimed with assistance from the British and French. After the war, the British created new nations out of the territory which Hussein had expected to rule, thus severing their relationship with him.

The decision of the outside powers to partition the Arab World, and the wider Middle East, was largely taken without the consent of the powers that be in the region. Further, the Ottoman Empire was carved up in the wake of the First World War; even before its conclusion, the British and French had negotiated the *"Sykes-Picot Agreement,"* which delineated the two countries' respective spheres of influence in the former Ottoman lands when the war ended. This was further cemented by the League of Nations' "mandate system," whereby former Ottoman territories were *de jure* under the "guidance" of European powers, while *de facto* governed and divided by the European powers. The

United State Senate organized the "King-Crane Commission" to go to the non-Turkish former Ottoman lands and determine what the people of the region would like to see happen. They strongly advised against allowing the British and French to draw borders in the region, as it was inevitable that they would follow their "divide and conquer" colonial method of putting a majority group under the control of a minority group. Further, they strongly advised against the creation of a Jewish State in the Holy Land, owing to the resentment against the Jews on the part of the local populace.

During the First World War, over a million Armenian children, adults and elderly people lost their lives in an event called the Armenian Genocide. Armenia had been divided for centuries, with ethnic Armenian pockets in many neighboring nations. Armenia has been a sovereign nation since the collapse of the Soviet Union, but most ethnic Armenians live in Turkey, Iran, Lebanon, Egypt and other nations. In 1915, the Ottoman Empire expelled Christians living in their territory, including Armenians and other groups. They were forced on death marches into the Syrian Desert under armed guard and starved, raped and executed outright on the way. Estimates on the number of Armenians who perished in this event range from 800,000 to 1,500,000.

Though there was fear in Britain of revolt emerging in India, the opposite occurred. There was much loyalty and outpouring of support and goodwill from India to Britain because members of the India National Congress, among others, believed that this professing loyalty and support of the war effort would help push the cause of the *Indian Home Rule*. The British Army actually consisted of more Indians than British people at the beginning of the war; there were approximately 1.3 million Indian soldiers and laborers. They served throughout Europe, Africa and the Middle East and the central Indian government provided vast quantities of food, money and ammunition. On the Western Front, there were 140,000 Indian soldiers and in the Middle East there were close to 700,000. Indian casualties numbered 47,746 and the wounded numbered 65,126 by the end of the war. In spite of their loyal service, their death toll and suffering, Britain failed to grant independence or even any degree of self-government to the Indian people. This mistreatment fostered much disillusionment and hostility and would help fuel the movement for independence, primarily led by Mohandas K. Gandhi, which would eventually culminate in the *Indian Independence Act of 1947*.

The relationship of Europe to the world shifted significantly with the globalization of the conflict, the emergence of the United States as a world power, and the overthrow of European empires.

When World War I began, the United States initially maintained a policy of neutrality. President Woodrow Wilson was able to keep the United States neutral for two and a half years of the war; the United States did not enter the war until April of 1917. This was largely due to the fact that the United States, under Woodrow Wilson, sought to stay above the fray of European conflict and maintain their adherence to the "Monroe Doctrine" of non-intervention in extra-hemispheric wars. Also, there is much debate about the desire of the United States to sit the war out until such a time when American force would be decisive, and at such a time that the U.S. could shape the world order on what would later become known as "Wilsonian Liberalism."

American public opinion, including Irish Americans, German Americans, Swedish Americans and the majority of women and church leaders, was initially in favor of the neutral position. Except for a small population of Anglophiles who strongly supported the British, Americans generally were in favor of staying out of the conflict. Yet there were generally negative sentiments (specifically toward Germany) from Americans even before the start of the war. Wilson maintained a position of neutrality but offered Britain and France large-scale loans. As the war continued, and despite increasing calls for more national

President Woodrow Wilson of the United States

preparedness, Wilson made only minimal preparations to engage in war and the army remained in its peacetime condition, though there were enlargements of naval forces.

In early 1917, Germany again began waging unrestricted submarine warfare on commercial ships bound for Britain. This was understandable as by this point the United States was shipping vast quantities of arms to the Entente powers on ships that were flying under civilian flags. However, this unrestricted submarine warfare came to a head with the sinking of the ocean liner *Luisitania*, in which over one hundred American citizens perished (out of almost 1,200 passengers and crew). Further, the Germans angered the American public by sending the "Zimmerman Telegram" to the Mexican government, urging them to invade the United States, with Germany promising that if they won the war, they would return the territories of Arizona, New Mexico and Texas to Mexico. These events in tandem sparked public outrage and anger in the United States. President Wilson was spurred to ask Congress to go to war and Congress declared war on Germany in on April 6, 1917. Eight months later, the United States also declared war on the Austro-Hungarian Empire.

The United States emerged as a global power as a result of World War I. This was a result of America's new reputation as a powerful force which would intervene in global affairs, but it was also a result of a vacuum left by the removal of many of the original powers: Russia, Austria-Hungary and Germany. To a lesser extent, even the global hegemony of the victorious powers, France and England, also began to decline as major powers because the war strained their abilities to maintain their enormous overseas colonial empires. The Soviet Union was a byproduct of the war, but did not become a "superpower" until after (and as a result of) World War II.

It was not only military power arrangements which changed; the financial situation of the European powers, who had to import weapons and ammunition and fund huge militaries throughout all of the years of the war, contrasted starkly with that of the United States. While it did field a large military force, it was a net exporter of mass-produced war goods, from which it profited enormously. In addition, America was the primary lender of funds for the reconstruction of Europe as well as the debt imposed on Germany in the Treaty of Versailles. The balance of world trade was completely rebooted at the end of the war and America largely came out on top. America's war expenditure, relative to the size of its economy, was smaller than any of the European powers, which put it in a favorable position to be the creditor to European nations who would need to rebuild both their infrastructure and economies.

In diplomacy, America also became the unofficial world leader immediately after the war; the *Treaty of Versailles* was mainly President Wilson's initiative and his successor brokered the *Five Power Naval Limitation Treaty* in 1922. This has led some to argue that the United States, though they knew on which side they would fight, waited in joining the war effort so as to be in a favorable position to negotiate the peace.

Palace of Versailles upon signing of the Treaty of Versailles

By the end of the following decade, America—not European countries—had a market share on global trade. It had the largest navy and the largest military potential of any single nation. Beginning with the Woodrow Wilson presidency, America became the world's diplomatic leader. It was the world's main creditor. The European nations, in contrast, were not so much profiting from the tremendous income from their colonies, as much as they were trying to figure out a way to afford them and to maintain influence in the underdeveloped world.

In the aftermath of World War I, there were drastic social, cultural and political shifts throughout Europe, Asia, Africa and even in some places that were not a part of the three major continents who participated. As a result of the war, four empires collapsed, old countries were dismantled and new ones were created, boundaries were remapped, international organizations were formed and people began to subscribe to different ideologies. In Germany and the United Kingdom, World War I effected important political evolution by resulting in near-universal suffrage for the German and British populations. This primed these nations to become democracies which would hold mass elections.

Deterioration of four empires allowed for the establishment of several small countries in Eastern Europe. These nations were often populated by diverse ethnic minorities which were split by newly drawn borders from regions populated by their ethnic majority that they wished to be united with again. Czechoslovakia, for instance, was populated by Ruthenians, Poles, Germans and Ukrainians, Hungarians and Slovaks. There were many Minority Treaties which were sponsored in an effort to address this problem, but as the League of Nations declined throughout the 1930s, these treaties became decreasingly enforceable. The remapping of European borders and political modifications in the wake of World War I also resulted in numerous European refugees.

Populations of ethnic minorities located on the borders of these newly established states caused general instability. Though European borders were largely not altered between 1918 and 1935, many ethnic groups had been expelled from one country into another (for instance, the Sudeten Germans), and cooperation on a military or economic front between these countries was minimal. Based on this disquiet and lack of cooperation, defeated powers such as Germany and the Soviet Union remained capable of dominating the region once again. Though cooperating after World War I in the wake of their defeat, Germany and the Soviet Union ultimately were vying for the position of the dominant power in Eastern Europe.

The conflicting goals of the peace negotiators in Paris pitted diplomatic idealism against the desire to punish Germany, producing a settlement that satisfied few.

The Allied Powers began negotiations at the French Foreign Ministry on the Quai d'Orsay in Paris on 18 January, 1919. At first, there were 70 delegates from 27 nations who were participating. The defeated nations, including Germany, Austria and Hungary, were not included in the negotiations. Because it had already negotiated peace with Germany in the *Treaty of Brest-Litovsk* in 1918, Russia was excluded. The negotiators at Versailles later acknowledged that this treaty, in which Poland received large quantities of Germany's land and resources, was exceedingly harsh in regards to the economic toll it exacted on Germany.

First, two delegates each from the Unites States, Britain, France, Italy and Japan comprising the "Council of Ten" had a meeting in order to discuss the peace terms. The "Council of Ten" was reduced to the "Big Four" after Japan retreated from the negotiations and only one delegate from each remaining country participated in the talks. The "Big

Four" met in 145 closed sessions to determine major decisions the entire assembly would ratify. Besides issues dealing with Italy, conditions were negotiated in personal meetings between the leaders of the "Big Three" nations: British Prime Minister David Lloyd George, French Prime Minister Georges Clemenceau and U.S. President Woodrow Wilson.

"Big Four" at the Paris Peace Conference. Left to right: Lloyd George of Great Britain, Orlando of Italy, Clemenceau of France, and President Wilson

The "Plenary Conference" was a weekly meeting for minor nations to attend a general forum in which to discuss issues but not make decisions. The final treaty incorporated many recommendations from commissions formed by members of the Plenary Conference. The treaty contained many provisions; one of the most controversial was the requirement that Germany and her allies make reparation for damage caused during the war. This provision, Article 231, was later known as the War Guilt Clause and it forced Germany to surrender weaponry, concede significant portions of land and pay substantial amounts in reparations (in 1921 the total cost of these reparations would be estimated at 132 billion marks) to the countries who constituted the Entente powers.

With many negotiators advocating for competing and sometimes clashing goals, the resulting treaty was an unsatisfying compromise for all involved. The treaty neither conciliated nor pacified Germany, while at the same time Germany was not degraded to such a state that she would remain permanently weak. *The Locarno Treaties* would be signed on December 1, 1925 in an attempt to help solve problems that arose from the first treaty and improve the relationships of Germany with the other major European powers.

The reparation plan would be renegotiated leading to the formation of the Dawes Plan, the Young Plan and, finally, an indefinite postponement of payment at the 1932 Lausanne Conference.

Wilsonian idealism clashed with postwar realities in both the victorious and the defeated states. Democratic successor states emerged from former empires and eventually succumbed to significant political, economic and diplomatic crises.

Two events were pivotal to President Wilson's declaration of war against Germany: the sinking of the *Lusitania* and the Zimmerman telegram. Originally, America wanted no part of a European war. The American public saw no vested interest worth the death of their young men, and the American government, abiding by the Monroe doctrine, stated that America would not intervene in the territories of foreign powers. But when America was still neutral, Germany conducted a naval blockade of British waters which led to the torpedoing of the passenger vessel *Lusitania* in 1915, in which 114 Americans perished. This turned American public opinion against Germany, but did not immediately lead to a declaration of war.

Early in 1917, American intelligence intercepted a telegram from Germany's foreign minister to the government of Mexico, asking Mexico to enter the war on Germany's side and attack the United States. In return, should Germany be victorious, Mexico was to get back all of the lands acquired by the U.S. in the Mexican-American War: what was now Arizona, New Mexico, California and Texas. This and the continuation of the German submarine blockade outraged Americans further and triggered America's entry into the war on April 6th, 1917.

The Allies attempted to put forth the claim that Germany was the only major power involved in the war that harbored aggressive ambitions. However, the Bolsheviks disclosed details of a private treaty discussion that took place between the allies which showed the aggressive ambition of the Allies themselves. In response to this, the United States sought to remove the war from nationalistic arguments, conflicts and ambitions. President Wilson issued a statement, which later was referred to as the *Fourteen Points*, in January of 1918. In this speech, he set forth a plan of democracy, self-determination, free trade and open agreements and included a wish for a diplomatic end to the war, international disarmament, the formation of a League of Nations which could grant political independence and territorial integrity to states, the withdrawal of the Central Powers from occupied territories, the redrawing of Europe's borders along ethnic lines and the creation of a Polish state.

The numerous new (or restored) nations which were created out of the parts of the Austro-Hungarian Empire were nicknamed the "Shatter-belt" nations, named so because they were fragments of a larger whole. The naive assumption of the drafters of the Treaty of Versailles was that the presence of several smaller nations would form a buffer between the major powers, preventing them from being able to go to war with one another. The actual result was that the Shatter-belt nations were sitting ducks at the beginning of World War II and were rapidly gobbled up by Germany and the Soviet Union. The Shatter-belt included Poland, Austria, Hungary, Czechoslovakia, Yugoslavia, among other nations.

Edward M. House, U.S. political advisor

Wilson's Fourteen Points is also considered a response to the November 1917 Decree on Peace made by Vladimir Lenin. This decree outlined Russia's withdrawal from World War I and asked that territorial annexations not influence or prevent a fair and democratic peace. Wilson's speech was based upon the Inquiry, a team led by Edward M. House, the foreign policy advisor, and staffed by approximately 150 advisors. The Inquiry researched topics that were likely to come up in an anticipated conference dealing with the details of the peace. Though Europeans were generally in favor of Wilson's intervention, some Allied colleagues such as Georges Clemenceau from France, David Lloyd George of the United Kingdom and the Italian Vittorio Emanuele Orlando were less supportive and had little confidence in Wilson's idealistic pronouncements.

Late 1918 saw the formation of an independent Poland and a new Polish government. The Poles staged an uprising against Germany in December of 1918 and fighting stretched into February until an armistice was signed. This armistice gave the Poles control of the land but the area was still technically German property. Also in 1918, Mihály Károlyi became prime minister (and later president) of the first republic of Hungary, due to the success of the Aster Revolution in Budapest. Under Károlyi, disarmament of the Hungarian Army was carried out and Hungary was left devoid of a national defense, a new reality which the territory-hungry Yugoslavs, Poles and Czechoslovaks took advantage of.

Transylvania and other parts of Eastern Hungary were taken control of by Romania, whereas Czechoslovakia gained control of Upper Hungary; the northern regions and south Hungary fell under the control of a joint Serbian-French military. Each of these territories were home to majority populations from their respective occupying nations. However, each also had a significant Hungarian population because territories were occupied without consideration of ethnic boundaries. The subsequent annexations of these territories were backed by the post-War Entente.

The Communists in Hungary gained power in March of 1919. In April, Béla Kun briefly headed a government which he proclaimed the Hungarian Soviet Republic. Though Kun had an initial military victory in battle with the Czechoslovakian Army, his regime was ousted after a defeat at the hands of the Romanian Army in which Budapest was taken. When new Hungarian borders were established in the June 4, 1920 *Treaty of Trianon*, Hungary lost 71% of its territory and 66% of its population. Due to the border shifts, approximately one-third of the ethnic Hungarian population became part of minority enclaves in neighboring nations.

Hungary was now separated from its resources and raw materials, its entire industrial base and also its only seaport, the Adriatic-adjacent Fiume (known today as Rijeka). Therefore, the revision of the Treaty of Trianon was at the top of Hungary's political agenda. The exact process of revision was debated; some felt that Hungary's borders and the larger region should be restored to how it was before the Treaty of Trianon; others thought this restoration should only be applied to territories with a Hungarian ethnic majority. After the fall of Budapest to the Romanian Army, right-wing Hungarian military forces, led by Miklós Horthy, a former Austro-Hungarian admiral, took power. A monarchy was restored to Hungary after the 1920 elections for a unicameral assembly and Horthy was officially elected Regent.

Czechoslovakia and Yugoslavia were also created out of the ashes of the Austro-Hungarian Empire. While Poland and Hungary were failed attempts to unify single ethnic groups, Czechoslovakia and Yugoslavia were forced unions of several ethnic minorities with long histories of mutual hatred, in failed experiments at coexistence. Czechoslovakia was formed out of several ethnic territories, the main rivals being the Czech and the Slovak peoples. The presence of a German-speaking ethnic minority group that lived in a region known as the Sudetenland provided the pretext for the Nazi invasion of Czechoslovakia in 1938, and led to their espousing a policy of "lebensraum" (living space). Yugoslavia was initially called The Kingdom of Serbs, Croats and Slovenes and began its existence in 1922 with the Serbian monarchy becoming its rulers. In 1929, using the assassination of some deputies in the National Assembly as a pretext, King Alexander I abolished democracy and political parties. The dictatorship he created was invaded by the Germans in 1941 and then turned into communist Yugoslavia in 1945.

The League of Nations, created to prevent future wars, was weakened from the outset by the non-participation of major powers, including the United States, Germany, and the Soviet Union.

World War I was ended by the Paris Peace Conference and one of the results of this conference was the formation of the intergovernmental organization called the League of Nations on January 20, 1920. The international organization was the first of its kind to have the primary goal of peace promotion. In its Covenant, this goal was detailed as the intent to prevent conflict through collective safety and stability, disarmament and quelling of disputes using arbitration and negotiation. The goals of the League also incorporated the continued work on human rights issues such as labor conditions, just treatment of native inhabitants, human-trafficking, just treatment and return of prisoners of war, global health and protection of European minorities, as well as global issues such as drug-trafficking and the arms trade. The primary mission of the League of Nations was to prevent another world war. When World War II broke out, it was clear that the League had been unsuccessful.

Meeting of the League of Nations, 1921

The failure of the League of Nations can be attributed to a number of things, including general weakness within the organization. Though the League was supposed to represent and encompass all countries, many nations, including the United States, refused to join or joined and then withdrew after a short period of time (e.g., Italy and Japan). There is still much controversy over President Woodrow Wilson's refusal to join the League. Though President Wilson had been supportive of the League's formation and even helped to create it, the United States Senate voted not to join. Some believe that if the United States had been part of the League of Nations, it would have encouraged and stabilized France and Britain in cooperating with Germany, thereby ameliorating the conditions which led to the Nazi Party coming to power. On the other hand, it's possible that if the United States had been a member of the League it might have hampered the League's ability to deal with international crises because of an unwillingness to conflict with European states.

Germany was not allowed to join the League when it was formed in 1920 because Germany was considered the aggressor in World War I. Soviet Russia was similarly initially excluded because of its Communist government. During the 1930s, major powers withdrew, weakening the League more. Japan was originally a permanent Council member but withdrew in 1933 in response to the League voicing disagreement with the Japanese invasion of Manchuria. In 1937 Italy, who had also originally held a position as a permanent member of the Council, withdrew. Though Germany had been accepted into the League of Nations as a peaceful nation in 1926, when Hitler gained power in 1933, he withdrew Germany.

Like Germany and the United States, but for different reasons, the Soviet Union did not participate in the League of Nations. In 1922, at the outset of five years of communist revolutions and civil war, Russia and several of its neighbors became the Union of Soviet Socialist Republics, also known as the Soviet Union. The leaders of this new communist republic were not interested in joining a world organization like the League of Nations, in part because it was founded and led by free-market nations which communists saw as their natural adversaries, also because the communists were focused on spreading communism worldwide as their way of achieving what the League of Nations promised. The Soviet Union instead pursued individual secret negotiations with other governments and underground revolutionary groups, such as the German-Soviet non-aggression pact and the Soviet alliance with the anti-Franco republican forces in the Spanish Civil War.

The Versailles settlement, particularly its provisions on the assignment of guilt and reparations for the war, hindered the German Weimar Republic's ability to establish a stable and legitimate political and economic system.

A socialist revolution in Germany from 1918–1919 resulted in the abdication of Kaiser Wilhelm II, the installation of communist governments in several parts of the country, and the formation of the Weimar Republic. Under the threat of further Entente advance, the Weimar Republic was pressured into signing the Treaty of Versailles on June 28, 1919. This treaty mostly blamed Germany for the entirety of the war and Germany was required to pay 132 billion marks in reparations. As a result of this enormous debt, Germany was forced to print more money, causing the country's economy to spiral into hyperinflation between 1921 and 1923. In 1922, Germany was declared in default by the Reparations Commission, and January 11, 1923 saw the occupation of the Ruhr by French and Belgian troops until 1925.

Kaiser Wilhelm II of Germany

The Treaty of Versailles also stipulated that Germany would have to reduce the size of its military permanently. This reduction stipulated ranks of no more than 100,000 men and the destruction of all tanks, military aircraft and the U-boat fleet. Small segments of German territory were also portioned out to Denmark, Czechoslovakia and Belgium, while larger swathes of land were given to France and the reestablished Polish nation. German colonial possessions were parceled out among the Allied countries, with the United Kingdom gaining much of the German-colonized land in Africa. The aspect of the treaty that caused the most outrage was Germany being stripped of territory containing the German city of Danzig and the split between East Prussia and the rest of Germany–this was land that was given to the reestablished Poland. Adolf Hitler and the Nazi Party would gain political traction by speaking out and taking action against the treaty. Nazi propaganda catered to the sentiments of Germans, most of whom thought the treaty was unfair and refused to regard it as legitimate.

There are many factors which contributed to the failure of the Weimar Republic — economic problems, institutional problems and rise of specific individuals. The Weimar Republic contended with unprecedented levels of economic disarray; issues which had never been seen to such an extent in any Western democracy, including hyperinflation, hugely elevated unemployment rates and massive drops in living standards. Germany had a period of economic recovery from 1923 to 1929, until the 1929 stock market crash caused a worldwide depression. Germany, with its own economic turmoil and heavy reliance on the United States for loans, was especially affected by the depression. The number of unemployed Germans skyrocketed from 2 million in 1926 to 6 million in 1932. Citizens and political parties alike blamed the economic trouble on the Weimar Republic, with right-wing and left-wing politicians uniting in their wish to disband the Republic outright by means of continually deadlocking Parliament.

In the United States, economic stagnation prompted demands on Germany to start paying back American loans, but the Great Depression had further devastated the Weimar Republic. This severe economic depression made the Republic fragile and vulnerable to takeover by the Nazi Party. Germans were insulted by the Treaty of Versailles, they found it degrading that they were forced from land with resources and required to compensate billions of dollars to other countries. The treaty requirements bred resentment and the reparations were significant, though it is difficult to determine the exact amount of economic damage caused by the repayment, especially because Germany ultimately only paid a fraction of the costs.

The damage the reparations caused to Germany's economy was primarily due to decreased market loans, and the severe hyperinflation that resulted from the government having to print more money to finance the deficit. The German people were also nursing a collective psychological wound from an unexpected military defeat and the ensuing political chaos in 1919 which led to a rapid disintegration of their homeland. These events may have led to an extreme nationalistic fervor among the German people, which would then be exploited and manipulated by the Nazi regime.

In the interwar period. Fascism, extreme nationalism, racist ideologies and the failure of appeasement resulted in the catastrophe of World War II, presenting a grave challenge to European civilization.

World War I began in August of 1914, causing the political left in Italy to become harshly split. While the Italian Socialist Party (PSI) opposed the war outright, several

Italian revolutionary syndicalists gave their support on the grounds that the reactionary regimes of Germany and Austria-Hungary had to be defeated in order to ensure the spread and success of socialism. The pro-interventionist fascio named the *Fasci of Internation Action* was formed in October 1914, by Italian activist, lawyer and journalist Angelo Oliviero Olivetti. Benito Mussolini was the editor of the PSI's newspaper *Avanti!* but was fired for his anti-German rhetoric. Upon his removal from the editor position, he joined the interventionist cause in the Revolutionary Action, where the term "fascism" was first used. Fascism developed as a harsh authoritarian nationalism which emerged in opposition to liberalism, anarchism and Marxism.

From the fascist perspective, the First World War brought revolutionary change in warfare tactics and technology, shifted the meaning of society and the state, and in an atmosphere of total war and large-scale mobilization, had diminished the distinctions between combatant and civilian. As civilians had proven to be a vital economic necessity for a war effort, a sense of military citizenship developed in which every citizen had involvement with the military in some form during wartime. The First World War saw the emergence of powerful states that were able to mobilize millions of people to the front lines, provide supplies, resources and logistical support to those on the front lines and an

Benito Mussolini, Italian dictator

unprecedented level of government intervention in citizens' lives. Mass mobilization of a population during wartime and the technological advances in weaponry were viewed as the building blocks of a new era combining concentrated state power with mass control. This new era would triumph over the era of liberalism.

The emergence of fascism was greatly influenced by the October Revolution of 1917, in which Vladimir Lenin led the Bolshevik communists in a seizure of power in Russia. Mussolini, as the leader of the Fasci Revolutionary Party, praised the October Revolution in 1917, but changed his opinion of Lenin later on, viewing Lenin as a mere replication of Tsar Nicholas, the last emperor of Russia. Fascists began campaigning on anti-Marxist platforms after the end of the First World War. Fascism and Bolshevism shared certain elements, including advocacy for a revolutionary ideology, belief in the necessity of a vanguard elite, disdain for bourgeois values and totalitarian ambitions, while in practice both parties emphasized revolutionary action, proletarian nation theories, single-party states and party controlled armies. Animosity between anti-interventionist Marxists and pro-interventionist fascists had deepened to irreconcilable levels by the end of World War I.

One of the most negative ideologies shared by both communism (as put into practice by Stalin and Mao) and fascism was racism – a set of beliefs and practices that sought to implement unequal distribution of privileges, rights or goods among different racial groups. It was based on a desire to dominate and justified by a belief in the inherent inferiority of another race or ethnicity. Though these racist policies manifested themselves in different guises, the result of communist and fascist racist programs was often the same: the wholesale genocide of distinct groups of people

Communists sought to extinguish cultures and ethnicities in many regions that they came to control. In the Soviet Union, which consisted of many nationalities and ethnic minorities, suppression of local languages and cultural heritage was commonplace, leading in many examples to mass oppressions and even genocides (e.g., mass deportations of Tartars, Holodomor in Ukraine, extermination camps in Siberia). When Tibet was occupied by the Chinese communist regime, the indigenous culture of Tibetans was deliberately and ruthlessly crushed.

The Soviet regime, particularly under Stalin, took ruthless suppressive action when it thought it detected a counter-revolutionary threat. This often came in the guise of forced resettlement, an ancient Russian means of genocide by fiat. The most notable cases of resettlement were the dispersing of the Tatars, primarily located in Crimea, to Central Asia and the deportation of large Jewish communities in present-day Ukraine and the European portion of Russia to the Stalin-created Jewish Autonomous District in the Russian Far East. The latter deportation is one of the more heinous and underreported crimes of the Stalinist regime as the land in the aforementioned district was rocky with low nutrient content in the soil, which led to the malnourishment and starvation of generations of Jews sent to the region. This was all undertaken by the regime to root out potential sources of counter-revolutionary sentiments among the predominantly muslim Tatars or predominantly well-educated Jews.

Beginning in 1938 in Czechoslovakia, Hitler sent his military to occupy one "Shatter-belt" nation after another. The choice before the major democratic powers was to accept this or fight another global war only twenty years after the end of the first. The British Prime Minister of the time, Neville Chamberlain, chose to meet with Hitler to negotiate a solution. Germany was allowed to annex Czechoslovakia in exchange for a promise not to invade elsewhere. Hitler broke this promise, invading Austria and then Poland before Britain, France, Canada and Australia declared war on Germany.

Neville Chamberlain waves the Munich Agreement, signed by Hitler and himself

Historians have conventionally argued that Chamberlain's appeasement encouraged Hitler and a more bellicose approach would have discouraged him from invading Austria. But trying to evaluate "what if" scenarios in history is invalid. What is known is that Hitler was relying on secret alliances, which he had formed with four other leaders: Stalin, Mussolini, Franco and Hirohito. At the time of the Munich Conference (between Hitler and Chamberlain), Hitler was justified in believing that he could count on the United States remaining neutral, on Franco winning his civil war and Spain becoming a Nazi ally, and on the other three undemocratic powers being co-belligerents against only France and Britain. It is questionable whether under those circumstances, non-appeasement by only France and Britain would have worked any better than appeasement.

French and British fears of another war, American isolationism, and deep distrust between the Western democratic, capitalist nations and the communist Soviet Union allowed fascist states to rearm and expand their territory.

Though the sentiment was generally pacifist in the aftermath of the First World War, there were still nationalistic irredentist and revanchist feelings in certain European states. Due to the territorial and financial losses imposed on Germany by the Treaty of Versailles, these types of sentiments were especially strong. Due to the treaty, Germany lost approximately 13 percent of its territory, not including all of its colonial possessions. Limits were placed on Germany's military capabilities, German annexation of other territories or states was prohibited and harsh reparations were required.

With the dissolution of the German Empire during the German Revolution of 1918-1919, the Weimar Republic was created. During the time between the two World Wars, tension developed between the new republic and its neighbors on either side. As an Entente ally, Italy made decent post-war territorial gains, but many Italian nationalists were angry about the fact that Britain and France had made certain promises to Italy in order to persuade it to enter the war, and these were not fulfilled in the peace settlements. Over the three years between 1922 and 1925, Mussolini gained power in Italy, pushing an agenda of nationalism, totalitarianism, class collaboration and an aggressive expansionist foreign policy dedicated to propelling Italy into a role as a major power. Mussolini's agenda was targeted against socialist, left-wing and liberal forces and promised the creation of a "New Roman Empire." Part of the foreign policy Mussolini espoused included the conquest of Libya and Ethiopia.

Hitler's first attempt at overthrowing the German government was the Beer Hall Putsch in Munich in 1923 and was unsuccessful. Though ten years later his Nazi Party would win a democratic election and Hitler would be elevated to the position of Chancellor of Germany in 1933. Once acquiring office, he proceeded to abolish democracy, began an enormous rearmament of the military and continued to embrace extreme racist, radical revisionist rhetoric about the world order. This was the historical moment when political experts realized that another world war could be on the horizon. Meanwhile, France, in order to secure an alliance with Italy, allowed Italy to control Ethiopia. Tensions were again heightened in 1935 when, in response to Germany regaining legal control of the Territory of Saar Basin, Hitler repudiated the Treaty of Versailles outright and proceeded to introduce conscription and further accelerate his rearmament program.

In 1935 and in response to Germany's growing power, the UK, Italy and France formed the *Stresa Front*, an agreement against Germany. In June of the same year, the UK made an independent naval deal with Germany which went against prior restrictions. France and the Soviet Union, concerned about Germany's open intentions of taking over vast swathes of Eastern Europe, wrote a treaty of mutual assistance. It couldn't be signed and implemented, however, until it had passed through the bureaucracy at the League of Nations, which left it essentially toothless. The United States, becoming concerned with shifts taking place in both Europe and Asia, passed the *Neutrality Act* which made it illegal to trade weapons with any country involved in a war.

By establishing a military presence in the Rhineland in March 1936, Hitler again showed blatant disregard for the stipulations of the Versailles and Locarno treaties, though there was very little dissent against his actions from other European countries. In 1936, Germany and Italy formed the Rome-Berlin Axis in October, and Germany and Japan (and within the year, Italy as well) signed the Anti-Comintern Pact in November. A ceasefire between the Kuomintang and communist forces in China was decided in the wake of the Xi'an Incident in order to oppose Japan.

Joachim von Ribbentrop signs the Anti-Comintern Pact

Nazi Germany and the Soviet Union signed a non-aggression pact on August 23, 1939 in Moscow. It was named the *Molotov-Ribbentrop Pact* after the Soviet foreign minister Vyacheslav Molotov and the German foreign minister Joachim von Ribbentrop. For the Nazis, this pact was pragmatic. Many of those who held high rank in the German military had learned the lesson from the First World War that sustaining a two-front war, especially when that second front is located in Russia, is extremely difficult. The Nazis wished to appease the Soviet Union until such time that they could focus all their attention on defeating the Soviets with a military properly prepared to fight the unique threat posed by the Soviet military and the Russian climate. For the Soviets, this pact was necessary to buy time. The Soviets knew that they were not at a stage where they could successfully wage a war against the technologically far superior German war machine. Further, without a Polish buffer, which the pact allowed for, the land leading from the Soviet border to Moscow was, in the dry season, ideal for the Germans to carry out a land-based Blitzkrieg.

Germany broke this pact on September 1, 1939 due to the fact that they felt they could overrun Soviet defenses more quickly than their previous estimates had shown. This proved to be fatal for the Nazis as the Soviet willingness to sacrifice their own people in order to secure victory in the "Great Patriotic War" would ultimately prove too much for the German war machine to handle.

Germany's Blitzkrieg warfare in Europe, combined with Japan's attacks in Asia and the Pacific, brought the Axis powers early victories.

In 1937, the Japanese Empire was at war with the Republic of China and seeking to control the rest of Asia and the Pacific. This goal was sidetracked by the start of World War II when Germany invaded Poland on September 1, 1939, leading France and the United Kingdom to declare war on Germany. Japan entered into the Axis alliance with Italy and Germany, which had come to dominate a considerable amount of continental Europe via military campaigns between the latter part of 1939 and the beginning of 1941. Military technology, especially aircraft and tanks, had greatly improved since World War I. The Germans' primary military strategy was the Blitzkrieg (German for "lightning war"), whereby an offensive force led by a heavy concentration of armed foot soldiers supported by air strikes penetrates its enemy's line of defense in bursts, disorienting the enemy, who can then be taken off guard and encircled. The Germans also used a method known as Bewegungskrieg (maneuver warfare), another tactic which sought to surprise and disorient their opponents.

In June 1941, the Soviet Union was invaded by the European members of the Axis. The invasion required a significant portion of the Axis' military forces as it encompassed a massive area. In December 1941, Japan launched an offensive against the United States and European territories in the Pacific Ocean, and swiftly dominated a considerable amount of the Western Pacific region. In 1942, Japan suffered a key defeat at the Battle of Midway near Hawaii and Germany lost battles in North Africa and in the Soviet Union, which checked the Axis' previous advances. The Allies continued to experience success in 1943, defeating Germany in battles on the Eastern Front, securing the surrender of Italy and winning several battles in the Pacific; as a result, the Axis' strategy shifted to one of retreat. In 1944, the Western Allies regained France, which had been occupied by Germany, and the Soviet Union recovered all of its territorial losses and invaded Germany and its allies. During 1944 and 1945, the Japanese experienced setbacks in South Central China and Burma. The Japanese navy was losing to the Allies, who took critical islands in the Western Pacific arena.

Artistic representation of an attack on Japanese cruisers
during the Battle of Midway in World War II

American and British industrial, scientific and technological power and the all-out military commitment of the USSR contributed critically to the Allied victories.

In university history departments when the question of how the Allies won the Second World War is posed there is a common answer: the war was won with British brains, American money and Soviet blood. Without any one of these contributing factors, it is likely that an all-out defeat of the Nazis would have been impossible. German military technology was far superior to that of the Allies at the outset of the war; however, when the three aforementioned factors came together, the strength of the Nazi war machine could not only be defeated, but wholly eliminated. World War II military technology led to many of the technologies that we use in our everyday lives including plastics, computers, microwaves and jet engines, to name but a few.

During the war, aircraft were used for scouting, fighting, bombing and providing support to ground troops. Aircraft technology had improved significantly since the First World War. It was easier to move important supplies and equipment, and improved bombing accuracy meant that it was easier to hit specified targets. Anti-aircraft weaponry also improved, including defenses like radar and surface-to-air artillery. Jets were pioneered during World War II. While they did not have much impact on the outcome of the war because they were not introduced until near its conclusion, jets eventually became the standard craft of air forces around the world. Progress was also made in naval warfare, especially in terms of aircraft carriers and submarines. Although aeronautical warfare had scant success at the beginning of the war, the battles of Taranto (Southern Italy), Pearl Harbor (Hawaii) and the Coral Sea (the northeastern coast of Australia) established the aircraft carrier as more important than the battleship.

In the Atlantic, escort carriers were an integral piece of Allied convoys because they increased the effective protection radius and assisted in overcoming the Mid-Atlantic gap. In addition, carriers were more economical than battleships due to the lower cost of aircraft and the fact that they did not need to be as heavily armored. At the start of World War II, people expected submarines to play an important role in warfare because they had done so during the First World War. The British focused their efforts on developing anti-submarine weaponry and strategy, including sonars and convoys, while Germany concentrated on increasing its offensive use of submarines, with designs like the Type VII submarine and the use of "wolf pack" tactics. Allied innovations such as the Leigh light, hedgehog, squid and homing torpedoes eventually proved to be highly effective in countering Germany's submarine warfare improvements.

Land warfare, which had remained static during World War I, showed a rise in mobility and combined arms during World War II. The tank, which was mostly utilized for infantry support in World War I, improved in speed, armor and firepower and became one of the chief weapons of World War II. The Allied and Axis powers both devised ways of destroying each other's tanks, including indirect artillery, anti-tank guns, mines, short-range infantry anti-tank weapons and other tanks. Even with the large-scale mechanization that had occurred since World War I, ground troops remained the mainstay of all forces. Portable machineguns were widely used during the war, most notably the German MG34 and other sub-machineguns designed for combat in both urban and jungle settings. The assault rifle, which became the standard weapon for most armed forces after the war, was developed late in the war and incorporated many of the features of the rifle and sub-machinegun.

Also during the war, many countries sought to replace the big unwieldy codebooks used for cryptography with sophisticated rapid ciphering machines. The use of deception was another military intelligence tactic used by the Allies with great results, as in operations "Mincemeat" and "Bodyguard." Other technological and engineering achievements made during, or as a result of, World War II include the first programmable computers, guided missiles and modern rockets, the Manhattan Project's development of the atomic bomb, operations research and the development of artificial harbors and oil pipelines under the English Channel.

Emblem of the Manhattan Project

The Soviet Union began the war with a formidable military force, which was smashed by Hitler's surprise invasion on June 22, 1941. For the next two years, the Soviets were short on weapons and ammunition, while simultaneously working to rebuild their military and halt the Nazi advance. The nature of Soviet combat was that Soviet soldiers would use the only competitive edge they had, human bodies, against the most technologically advanced and well-trained military in the world. Soviet soldiers attacked German lines in droves, often with no artillery support from behind or hope of reinforcements when they became tired. It was not only those serving in the military or their families who suffered; a huge cost was exacted on the civilian populations of the Soviet Union.

In the Siege of Leningrad (now St. Petersburg) thousands of people were killed by the bombing campaign of the Luftwaffe and the starvation caused by the naval blockade of the former Imperial capital. Many citizens only survived by resorting to cannibalism, one of the most atrocious examples of attempting to force capitulation of an enemy through deliberate targeting of civilian populations. Residents of those regions which shared a border with Germany, particularly present-day Belarus, were gratuitously raped and murdered both in the Nazi invasion and during the Soviet advance on Germany. There is no doubt that though the Soviet Union was on the victorious side of the Second World War, the citizens of the Soviet Union paid a higher cost for this victory than the other allies.

Other factors that contributed to Allied success were American and British scientists and industrial capacity. Having been the two main nations to industrialize, comprehensively and early in history, paid dividends for these two nations in the Second World War. The size of America's resource base, industrial base, wealth and its population, made America able to produce a tremendous quantity of war material for its own formidable military while also being able to supply the allies with everything they needed.

Germany, Italy and Japan, on the other hand, were small nations, which were each resource-poor and had less industrial capacity than America and Britain. Britain, although small, had a strong manufacturing base and a tremendous wealth of scientific talent, in addition to being coal rich. Germany and Japan depended on the nations they occupied, such as Romania and Indonesia, respectively, for their fuel. When the allies bombed the oil production facilities and later liberated these nations, they lost much of their fuel supply. In contrast, the United States and the Soviet Union both have tremendously large oil reserves of their own that remained safely out of bombing range throughout the war due to their geographical positions. While Germany had a formidable scientific community which gave it some great military achievements, many of the best German scientists had been alienated by the Nazis before the war and ended up working on the side of the Allies instead. This ultimately contributed to America developing the atomic bomb before Germany could do so.

Fueled by racism and anti-Semitism, Nazi Germany—with the cooperation of some of the other Axis powers and collaborationist governments—sought to establish a "new racial order" in Europe, which culminated with the Holocaust.

During the Holocaust, Hitler's Nazi regime and its collaborators slaughtered about six million Jews in Germany and German-occupied areas. An additional five million non-Jewish people were murdered by Nazis during the war, making the total number of people killed by the regime and its supporters around eleven million. Nazism promoted several ideas about race, including that there was a racial hierarchy with the Aryan race (the "master race") at the top and the non-Aryan races, or "untermenschen" (German for sub-human), who were seen as a societal menace, at the bottom.

"Selection" of Hungarian Jews on the Ramp at the death camp Auschwitz-II (1944)

The systematic murder of Jews that took place from 1941 to 1945 was one of the largest genocides in history, and part of a wider Nazi program of oppression and killings of non-Aryan ethnic and political groups in Europe. Non-Jewish victims who were also targeted were Romanis (gypsies), ethnic Poles, communists, homosexuals, Soviet prisoners of war and people who were mentally or physically disabled. As stated above, about 11 million people were killed, a figure which includes around one million Jewish children. Nine million Jews lived in Europe prior to the Holocaust, and during the genocide about two-thirds of them were murdered. The Germans used about 42,500 facilities in Germany and German-occupied territories to concentrate, detain and murder Jews and other targeted victims. It is estimated that between 100,000 and 500,000 people directly participated in planning and carrying out the Holocaust.

The Holocaust occurred in stages. At first, the German government enacted laws, such as the Nuremberg Laws of 1935, to restrict Jews' participation in civil society. Concentration camps began to be erected in 1933 and ghettos were created at the onset of World War II in 1939. In 1941, as Germany invaded and acquired territory in Eastern Europe, specialized paramilitary units, known as *Einsatzgruppen*, were used to kill approximately two million Jews and partisans, often via mass shootings. By the end of 1942, targeted victims were regularly transported by train to extermination camps. Many did not survive the arduous and unsanitary conditions of the trip and if they did, they were killed in the gas chambers of the camp.

Jews forcibly opposed the Nazis throughout the Holocaust. For example, during the Warsaw Ghetto Uprising in 1943, thousands of scantily armed Jewish rebels held off the Waffen-SS for four weeks. In Eastern Europe, about 20,000 to 30,000 Jews actively fought the Nazis and their allies. Jews in France were also very active in the French Resistance, which carried out over a hundred guerilla actions against the Nazis and the Vichy French authorities. Despite the resistance, the Nazis' genocide continued until World War II ended in the spring of 1945.

As World War II ended, a Cold War between the liberal democratic West and the communist East began, lasting nearly half a century.

The Cold War, a non-violent period characterized by political and military tension between the Western Bloc (the United States, its NATO allies and others) and the Eastern Bloc (the Soviet Union and its allies in the Warsaw Pact), developed following World War II and lasted roughly from 1947 until 1991. It was called "cold" because there was no large-scale war between the Eastern and Western powers, though they each became involved with opposing sides in many regional wars, referred to as proxy wars, in Korea, Vietnam, Angola, and Afghanistan.

The Cold War ended the alliance the USSR and U.S. had formed against Nazi Germany during the Second World War. The two superpowers could not ignore their significant economic and political differences. The USSR was a single-party Marxist-Leninist state pursuing a planned economy and monitoring its media while professing state atheism and retaining the exclusive authority to establish and govern communities. The U.S., conversely, was a capitalist country that espoused the values of democratic elections (though African Americans were still discriminated against) and freedom of the press, alongside freedom of religion.

Many countries, including Egypt, India, Indonesia and Yugoslavia, sought to remain neutral during the Cold War in order to avoid provoking the disfavor of either superpower. The situation never devolved into war, but both the U.S. and USSR prepared their militaries for the possibility of an all-out nuclear world war. They each possessed nuclear arsenals that dissuaded an offensive because to do so would result in the annihilation of the attacker; this state of affairs was known as the "doctrine of mutually assured destruction." In addition to the cultivation of nuclear weapons and deployment of typical military forces, the Cold War was characterized by proxy wars, psychological warfare, the widespread use of propaganda and espionage, sports rivalries and technological competition like the Space Race.

The Second World War ended in 1945 and the Cold War began two years later. During this time, the USSR established its dominance over the states of the Eastern Bloc and the United States initiated the strategy of global containment in order to check Soviet power. To do this, the U.S. provided military and financial support to countries in Western Europe (for example, the U.S. supported the anti-Communist forces during the civil war in Greece) and established the NATO alliance.

Key events that exacerbated the Cold War were the victory of the communists in the Chinese Civil War, the outbreak of the Korean War (1950-1953) and the Soviet crackdown on the Hungarian Revolution in 1956. The USSR and the U.S. began to vie for influence in Latin America and the decolonizing states of Africa, the Middle East and Southeast Asia. The spread and acceleration of the conflict ignited further crises, including the Suez Crisis in 1956, the Berlin Crisis in 1961 and the Cuban Missile Crisis in 1962. A new phase of the Cold War, in which the Sino-Soviet split muddled relations among communist allies, while some U.S. allies (specifically France) displayed an increased independence of action, emerged following the Cuban Missile Crisis. During this time, the USSR also intervened in the 1968 Prague Spring liberalization campaign in Czechoslovakia, and the Vietnam War (1955–1975) concluded with the defeat of the United States-supported Republic of South Vietnam.

Berlin civilians watching an airlift plane during Berlin Blockade

By the 1970s, both the U.S. and the USSR wanted to find a way to foster a more stable international system, which led to a period of truce during which the Strategic Arms Limitation Talks (SALT) occurred and the U.S. opened relations with the People's Republic of China in a strategic attempt to balance with the Soviet Union. The period of détente came to an end in 1979, with the Soviet invasion of Afghanistan.

Tensions between the Cold War superpowers again became heightened during the early 1980s. In 1983, the Soviets downed Korean Air Lines Flight 007 and the "Able Archer" NATO military exercises took place. The United States increased diplomatic, military and economic pressures on the Soviet Union, which was already experiencing economic stagnation at the time.

In the mid-1980s, new Soviet leader Mikhail Gorbachev commended the liberal reforms of perestroika ("reorganization," 1987) and glasnost ("openness," c. 1985) and withdrew Soviet troops from Afghanistan. Simultaneously, national independence movements intensified in Eastern Europe, especially in Poland. Gorbachev would not employ Soviet troops to uphold the weakening Warsaw Pact governments, as the USSR had done in the past. This led to a series of revolutions in 1989 that peacefully (with the exception of the Romanian Revolution) deposed the communist governments in Central and Eastern Europe. In the Soviet Union, the Communist Party lost control and was outlawed after a failed coup attempt in August of 1991. This resulted in the USSR's formal dissolution in December of 1991 and the collapse of communist governments in other countries, including Mongolia, Cambodia and South Yemen. When the dust had settled, the United States was the world's sole superpower.

Despite efforts to maintain international cooperation through the newly created United Nations, deep-seated tensions between the USSR and the West led to the division of Europe, which was referred to in the West as the Iron Curtain.

The Iron Curtain was the term for the sociopolitical disagreement and physical border separating Europe into two regions between the end of World War II in 1945 and the conclusion of the Cold War in 1991. The expression stemmed from the Soviet Union's effort to keep its citizens and satellite states from engaging with Western and non-Soviet-controlled regions. Countries allied with or under control of the Soviet Union were located on the east side of the Iron Curtain.

Physical manifestations of the Iron Curtain emerged in certain countries in the middle of Europe; particularly, the Berlin Wall and its Checkpoint Charlie became an ultimate symbol for the Iron Curtain. Citizens of the Eastern Bloc were not allowed to travel freely to western countries because their governments forbade it. Non-physical manifestations of the Iron Curtain included: complete vacuum of objective information about the west (often filled by rampant propaganda about hardships of western people compared to abundance enjoyed by the Soviet peoples), absence of foreign goods in the market, as well as prohibition of western music and popular art.

The events leading to the destruction of the Iron Curtain began with Polish discontent, which spread to Hungary, the German Democratic Republic (East Germany), Bulgaria, Czechoslovakia and Romania—the sole European communist country to successfully topple its totalitarian government.

The Cold War played out on a global stage and involved propaganda campaigns; covert actions; limited "hot wars" in Asia, Africa, Latin America and the Caribbean; and an arms race, with the threat of a nuclear war.

The U.S. and its allies used the strategy of containment during the Cold War in an effort to check the spread of communism in response to the Soviets' attempt to increase their influence in Eastern Europe, China, Korea, Africa and Vietnam.

The Korean War was a result of containment policy. In June of 1950, Kim Il-sung's North Korean People's Army invaded South Korea, an attack that was conceived and coordinated by Stalin. At the time, the Soviets were refusing to attend UN meetings out of protest that Taiwan, but not China (a communist country) had been given a permanent seat on the UN Security Council. But even at that, Stalin was still surprised when the UN Security Council supported the defense of South Korea in response to the invasion. A UN alliance of troops from South Korea, the United States, the United Kingdom, Turkey, Canada, Colombia, Australia, France, South Africa, the Philippines, the Netherlands, Belgium, New Zealand and other countries was formed to halt the invasion.

North Korean People's Party soldiers with a wounded comrade during the Korean War

The Vietnam War, sometimes referred to as the Second Indochina War, was a proxy war that took place during the Cold War in Vietnam, Laos and Cambodia from November 1, 1955 until Saigon was taken on April 30, 1975. This conflict followed the First Indochina War (1946–54) and was waged between North Vietnam, who was supported by the Soviet Union, China and other communist allies, and South Vietnam, who was supported by the United States, the Philippines and other anti-communist allies. *The Viet Cong* (also known as the National Liberation Front) was a South Vietnamese communist common front, supported by the North, who engaged in a guerrilla war against the anti-communist forces in the area. The People's Army of Vietnam (the North Vietnamese Army) used more traditional tactics, committing larger units to battle.

As the war progressed, the Viet Cong's involvement decreased as the engagement of the NVA increased. During the conflict, the U.S. and South Vietnamese troops depended on air superiority and firepower to carry out search and destroy operations, which involved a combination of ground forces, artillery and airstrikes. Throughout the war, the U.S. carried out a large-scale strategic bombing initiative in North Vietnam. The U.S. government justified its participation in the war as a necessary effort to avoid a Communist takeover of South Vietnam. This was a component of the U.S.'s overarching "containment" policy, which sought to prevent the spread of communism outside of the USSR.

The Yom Kippur War was a short war for territory, fought in 1973 between Israel and its Arab neighbors – Egypt, Syria and Iraq. At the time, the Soviet Union actively supported the Arab nations mentioned, while the United States and Western Europe supported Israel. The three Arab nations were equipped with Soviet tanks and Mig fighters, though not the most up-to-date Soviet technology. These were no match for the French and American equipment used by Israel. Israel's air force had modern planes provided by the West, including the U.S. F-4 Phantom and the French Mirage fighters.

Afghanistan has seen many wars with modern Western powers and has a consistent history of not being conquered. The British attempted to conquer Afghanistan between 1839 and 1842 and were defeated by Afghan tribesmen. In 1981, the Soviet Union invaded Afghanistan in an attempt to prop up an allied communist dictator who was losing a civil war. They faced a relentless and resourceful insurgency from the Islamic Fundamentalist Mujahedeen, covertly supported by the United States and its allies. In 1989, the Soviets finally withdrew from Afghanistan. It was a period of Soviet reconciliation with the West and communism in Europe was on the verge of collapse. In 2001, Afghanistan was controlled by a rigid Islamic Fundamentalist regime who was the same group as the Mujahedeen, now calling themselves the Taliban, who protected themselves with the weapons the United States provided to combat the Soviets in the 1980s. Taliban-controlled Afghanistan would prove a stable base for Al Qaeda in their planning and implementing the 9/11 attacks on the United States.

The United States exerted a strong military, political and economic influence in Western Europe, leading to the creation of world monetary and trade systems and geopolitical alliances such as the North Atlantic Treaty Organization (NATO).

During the Cold War, the United States used its influence in Western Europe to develop an international system of geopolitical, financial and military alliances. For example, the North Atlantic Treaty Organization (NATO) was created by an intergovernmental military agreement based on the North Atlantic Treaty, signed on April 4, 1949. NATO is comprised of a system of collective defense whereby its members have pledged to defend each other if they are ever attacked by a non-NATO force. NATO was merely a political alliance until the Korean War inspired its members to add a military component, under the direction of two U.S. supreme commanders.

The events of the Cold War led to a competition with countries of the Warsaw Pact, which was formed in 1955. Questions about the strength of the alliances between European nations and the United States arose, as did concerns about the reliability of NATO in defending against a potential Soviet invasion. These doubts resulted in the French independently developing a nuclear deterrent and withdrawing from NATO's military structure in 1966 for the next thirty years. After the Berlin Wall fell in 1989, NATO became involved in the breakup of Yugoslavia and eventually carried out its first military interventions in Bosnia between 1992 and 1995, and later in Kosovo in 1999. NATO sought to improve its relations with the former Warsaw Pact nations and several of them became members of NATO between 1999 and 2004.

Crane removes Berlin Wall in 1989

The International Monetary Fund (IMF), located in Washington, D.C., is an organization of "188 countries working to foster global monetary cooperation, secure financial stability, facilitate international trade, promote high employment and sustainable economic growth, and reduce poverty around the world." It was created in 1944 at the Bretton Woods Conference and became operational in 1945, consisting of 29 member countries with a goal of reconstructing the international payment system. When it was created, the IMF's two main roles were to supervise the fixed exchange rate agreements between countries, which assisted national governments in managing their exchange rates and prioritizing economic growth, and to supply short-term capital to help with the balance of payments. This support was designed to check the increase of international economic emergencies. It was also envisioned that the IMF would assist in rebuilding the international economy, still fragile after the Great Depression and World War II. The IMF's role was fundamentally altered after the floating exchange rates.

After 1971, the IMF's role was profoundly amended due to floating exchange rates. It moved to examining the economic policies of states with IMF loan agreements to figure out if a shortage of capital was because of economic fluctuations or economic policy. In addition, the IMF studied what types of government policy would guarantee economic improvement. The IMF is currently tasked with promoting and implementing policies that decrease the incidence of emergencies among the emerging market countries, especially middle-income nations that are susceptible to major capital outflows. As opposed to only overseeing exchange rates, the IMF began to provide surveillance of overall macroeconomic performance in member states. Its responsibility increased because the IMF still currently manages overall economic policy, as opposed to just exchange rates.

The General Agreement on Tariffs and Trade (GATT) was an agreement among countries to regulate international trade. The GATT was designed to significantly lower tariffs and other barriers to trade, as well as to end preferential treatments. It was negotiated at the United Nations Conference on Trade and Employment, where an attempt was first made, but failed, to create the International Trade Organization (ITO). In 1995, the GATT was supplanted by the World Trade Organization.

Countries east of the Iron Curtain came under the military, political and economic domination of the Soviet Union within the Council for Mutual Economic Assistance (Comecon) and the Warsaw Pact.

The Cold War was initiated around 1947. Western nations had formalized an alliance through the creation of the North Atlantic Treaty Organization in 1949; the Soviet bloc responded by creating the Warsaw Pact. The Council for Mutual Economic Assistance (Comecon), an economic organization that existed from 1949 to 1991 and included the nations of the Eastern Bloc and numerous other socialist states, was initiated by the Soviet Union as a response to the Organization for European Economic Co-Operation that had been created in Western Europe. The Soviets used Comecon to check nations under their control from being swayed by the assistance the United States was offering under the Marshall Plan.

Comecon executive committee in 1964

The Warsaw Pact was a defense agreement between eight communist countries in Central and Eastern Europe. It was initiated by the USSR during the Cold War in conjunction with the Council for Mutual Economic Assistance (Comecon), which was the regional economic organization for the communist states of Central and Eastern Europe at the time. The Warsaw Pact was partly formed as a response to West Germany joining NATO in 1955 and the Paris Pacts of 1954, but its main motivation stemmed from the Soviets' hope to retain influence over the military forces in Central and Eastern Europe, which they believed essential to maintaining peace in Europe. Paradoxically, the Warsaw Pact's biggest military undertakings targeted its own members: Hungary in 1956 and Czechoslovakia in 1968. On 25 February 1991, Hungary withdrew from the Warsaw Pact; in July of that year, Czechoslovakia followed suit.

The collapse of the USSR in 1991 ended the Cold War and led to the establishment of capitalist economies throughout Eastern Europe. Germany was reunited, the Czechs and the Slovaks parted, Yugoslavia dissolved and the European Union was enlarged through admission of former Eastern bloc countries.

The world's political landscape, in addition to that of the Eastern Bloc, shifted in 1989 when the Iron Curtain fell. Germany was peacefully reunified in 1990 when the Federal Republic of Germany absorbed the German Democratic Republic. The following year, 1991, Comecon, the Warsaw Pact and the Soviet Union were all disbanded. Many European countries that had been under the control of the Soviet Union regained independence, including Belarus, Moldova, Ukraine, Latvia, Lithuania, Estonia, Georgia, Azerbaijan and Armenia. In 1993, Czechoslovakia uneventfully split into the Czech Republic and Slovakia. Many Eastern nations, including Bulgaria, the Czech Republic, Estonia, Hungary, Latvia, Lithuania, Poland, Romania and Slovakia eventually became members of the European Union.

The European Union was cautious about admitting the former communist countries as members following communism; each was experiencing different economic states and levels of political stability. East Germany, the post-communist country that was experiencing the most prosperity, became a member of the European Union by default when Germany reunified. Czechoslovakia was another post-communist country that was experiencing a certain amount of prosperity; however, other countries were not faring as well. Romania was enduring crushing poverty due to the policies pursued by its former dictator Nicolae Ceauşescu. As a result, Romania struggled to meet the EU admission condition that the country must create a free market economy.

Nicolae Ceauşescu, dictator of Romania

Western Europe feared that post-communist countries might become an economic liability because their diminished economic conditions made it difficult for them to pursue modernization policies and programs; however, On February 26, 2001 the Nice Treaty was signed, declaring that 10 new EU members would be admitted in 2004. On May 1, 2004, eight former members of the Warsaw Pact were admitted to the European Union: the Czech Republic, Slovakia, Latvia, Lithuania, Estonia, Hungary, Poland and Slovenia.

In the 1980s, there were strong-willed Western leaders in power who actively fought to end communism. In 1979, the staunch anti-communist Margaret Thatcher was elected in Britain and served as Prime Minister until the end of 1990. Ronald Reagan became the President of the United States in 1981 and also served for the entire rest of the decade. Along with other free-market conservatives in power in allied nations, Thatcher and Reagan formed an alliance that actively worked to undermine the Soviet Union from within, in contrast to the more benign approaches taken toward it by previous conservative leaders. By cutting off monetary aid and through other economic approaches, they brought about the financial collapse of the Soviet Union.

While Thatcher and Reagan played diplomatic hardball with the Soviets and greatly modernized their own nations' defenses, the Soviet Union had a change of leadership in 1984, to Mikhail Gorbachev. In 1984 Mikhail Gorbachev became the leader of the Soviet Union. He was a leader who was much more conciliatory towards the West and towards human rights and freedoms. Gorbachev stood in stark contrast to the anachronistic communist leaders who preceded him. The economic weakness of the Soviet Union and Gorbachev's change to a policy of non-intervention diminished the power of the Soviet communist party greatly and led to its collapse.

In 1989, as the Soviet Union was on the verge of dissolving, East Germans walked away from their own communist government en masse. In November, a border guard in Berlin opened a gate to the west and allowed thousands of East Germans to walk through. The East German security forces remained idle while people protested in the streets for freedom. East Germany collapsed, the Berlin wall was torn down by the hands of thousands of Germans from both sides, the government fell and East Germany was absorbed by West Germany, reunifying Germany rapidly.

However, integrating East Germany's economy and its other systems into those of West Germany was a puzzle. Since there had been no private property rights in East Germany under communism, there were no property values and no one had any capital with which to run a private business. The solution that was chosen was to put East German state property—its buildings, machinery, land and business apparatus—into a trust, and then sell it on the open market. The West German social assistance system was maintained temporarily and subsidized by the West German taxpayers. Although unemployment soared in the short run and at a time when the world was plummeting into a recession, in the long run the situation improved gradually and East Germans today have a much higher standard of living than they did under communism. The reunified Germany is now an economic leader in Europe and around the world.

Czechoslovakia had always been a forced union of different ethnic groups, the two largest ones being the Czech and the Slovakian groups. After World War II, it was liberated from the Nazis by the Soviet Union, which imposed its own dictatorship there. When the citizens protested for freedoms and democracy in 1968, Soviet military forces invaded and crushed the rebellion, resulting in a heavy loss of life. Late in 1989, citizens finally ended communism in a non-violent rebellion that became known as the *Velvet Revolution*. They swiftly chose its organizer, a playwright named Vaclav Havel as their first democratically elected president. One of Havel's first actions was to dissolve the nation into its ethnic constituencies: Czechoslovakia is split now into the Czech Republic with its capital in Prague and the Slovak Republic with its capital in Bratislava.

Throughout the 1990s, the conflicts in the Balkans served as motivation for the development of the EU's Common Foreign and Security Policy (CFSP). The EU failed to intervene at the outset of the conflict and UN peacekeepers from the Netherlands failed to avert the Srebrenica massacre that occurred in Bosnia and Herzegovina in July of 1995, which was the biggest mass murder in Europe since World War II. This meant that NATO eventually had to intervene and oversee a negotiation to end the war.

In response to the destructive impact of two world wars, European nations began to set aside nationalism in favor of economic and political integration, forming a series of transnational unions that grew in size and scope over the second half of the 20th century.

Following the Second World War, the integration of Europe was intended to counter the extreme nationalism that had previously had harmful consequences for the continent. The 1948 Hague Congress was significant in European federal history because it initiated the creation of the European Movement International and the College of Europe. In 1952, the European Coal and Steel Community, which was promoted as the initial step in the creation of a federation of Europe, was created. In 1957, the Treaty of Rome, which created the European Economic Community (EEC) and a customs union, was signed by Belgium, France, Italy, Luxembourg, the Netherlands and West Germany. Another pact, which created the European Atomic Energy Community (Euratom), a group designed to cooperate in developing nuclear energy, was enacted the following year in 1958. The new EEC was led by Walter Hallstein and Euratom was led by Louis Armand and later by Étienne Hirsch. Euratom was charged with integrating sectors in nuclear energy while the EEC was supposed to develop a customs union among its members.

Europe Congress in The Hague, 1948

Discord began to emerge in the 1960s, when France tried to check the supranational power; however, in 1965 an agreement was reached and the *Merger Treaty* of July 1, 1967 created a sole set of institutions for the three communities, which were known as the European Communities. The first merged Commission was led by Jean Rey. The union was able to increase its scope in 1989 when the Iron Curtain fell.

In 1973, the Communities were expanded to incorporate Denmark, Ireland and the United Kingdom. Norway could have joined, but Norwegian citizens voted not to. In 1979, the first direct, democratic elections to the European Parliament took place. Greece joined in 1981, Portugal and Spain joined in 1986. In the previous year, 1985, the *Schengen Agreement* paved the way for open borders without passport controls between most member states and even some non-member nations. In 1986, the European flag was adopted by the Community and the *Single European Act* was signed.

In 1995, Austria, Finland and Sweden were admitted to the EU. In 2002, euro banknotes and coins supplanted the national currency in twelve EU member nations. In 2004, Cyprus, the Czech Republic, Estonia, Hungary, Latvia, Lithuania, Malta, Poland, Slovakia and Slovenia were admitted to the EU, which at the time was the largest collection of countries to join at once. On January 1, 2007, Romania and Bulgaria joined the European Union. Also in 2007, Slovenia adopted the euro, as did Cyprus and Malta in 2008, Slovakia in 2009, Estonia in 2011, Latvia in 2014 and Lithuania in 2015. In June 2009, elections to the European Parliament took place, which resulted in the second Barroso Commission. In July 2009, Iceland sought membership in the EU, but it has since withdrawn its application. On December 1, 2009, the Lisbon Treaty, which included many EU reforms, was enacted.

François Mitterrand (left) and Helmut Kohl (right), architects of Maastricht Treaty

As the economic alliance known as the European Coal and Steel Community, envisioned as a means to spur postwar economic recovery, developed into the European Economic Community (EEC or Common Market) and the European Union (EU), Europe experienced increasing economic and political integration and efforts to establish a shared European identity.

The 1951 Treaty of Paris, ratified by Belgium, France, West Germany, Italy, the Netherlands and Luxembourg, created the European Coal and Steel Community (ECSC) in an attempt to bring peace and unity to Europe following the division and devastation experienced during World War II. The goal of the ECSC was to decrease European countries' rivalry over natural resources by establishing a common market for coal and steel. Four institutions were responsible for overseeing the ECSC: a High Authority (made up of independent appointees), a Common Assembly (made up of national parliamentarians), a Special Council (made up of national ministers) and a Court of Justice.

These four institutions eventually developed into the modern day European Commission, European Parliament, Council of the European Union and European Court of Justice. In 1957, the European Economic Community and the European Atomic Energy Community joined the ECSC and in 1967, all the institutions of the ECSC were incorporated into the European Economic Community, though the ECSC maintained an independent legal status. In 2002, when the Treaty of Paris expired, the ECSC was fully absorbed by the European Community.

The 1957 Treaty of Rome also established the European Economic Community (EEC), a regional organization with the goal of fostering economic integration among its member nations: Belgium, France, Italy, Luxembourg, the Netherlands and West Germany. In 1993, when the European Union (EU) was created by the *Maastricht Treaty*, it absorbed the EEC and changed its name to the European Community (EC), as the organization had expanded beyond its original six members and original economic goals. In 2009, when the *Treaty of Lisbon* was signed to amend the EU's constitution, the EC was fully incorporated into the EU and ceased to exist as its own entity.

There are various theories as to why the European Coal and Steel Community was created. The most common is that the United States and Britain believed that the best way to prevent all-out war on the continent was through the intermingling of economic dependence to such an extent that all-out war would result in total economic collapse. There has been significant evidence that this was the reason for the creation of the Community; however, recent scholarship has begun to show that there were more anti-communist undertones to the creation of the Community. These historians argue that the community was created largely as a means to support the creation of transnational industrial giants on the continent as a means to undermine the nascent and communist-leaning trade union movement on the European continent. There was a well-founded belief at the time that the Soviets wished to expand their sphere of influence into Western Europe and they believed that the trade union movements were the ideal means to do this. These scholars then argue that the Community was created as a way to prevent trade unions from becoming too strong in Germany, as these transnational industrial giants could source workers from France or vice versa. This point of view is gaining support in the European academic community and is championed by former Greek Finance Minister Yanis Varoufakis.

One of the major continuing challenges to countries in the EU is balancing national sovereignty with the responsibilities of membership in an economic and political union.

Members of the European Union share legislative power with that organization. The EU has the power to enact laws in certain policy areas, by which member states must abide while retaining the right to do their own legislation in other policy areas. The European Union is comprised of seven institutions: the European Parliament, the Council of the European Union, the European Commission, the European Council, the European Central Bank, the Court of Justice of the European Union and the European Court of Auditors. The European Parliament and the Council of the European Union share the power to inspect and amend laws, while the European Commission and the European Council share executive functions in a more limited capacity. The European Central Bank oversees the EU's monetary policy. The Court of Justice of the European Union is responsible for clarifying and enforcing EU legislation and contracts. The European Court of Auditors oversees the EU's budget. The European Parliament and the Council of the European Union each make up half of the EU's legislature.

Every five years, EU citizens elect the 751 Members of the European Parliament (MEPs) using a proportional representation electoral system. MEPs are elected on a national basis, but they sit by political affiliation as opposed to nationality. Every EU member nation has a set number of seats in the European Parliament and is divided into sub-national constituencies which do not influence the proportional nature of the electoral system.

The European Parliament and the Council of the European Union pass legislation together in nearly all areas using an ordinary legislative procedure. The European Commission is answerable to the European Parliament, and needs its authorization to take office. The president of the European Parliament serves as its speaker and external representative. The president and vice-presidents of the European Parliament are elected by the MEPs every two and a half years.

Two of the initial goals of the European Economic Community were to create a common European market and a customs union between its member nations. The EEC hoped a single market would promote the free circulation of goods, capital, people and services among EU countries, and that the customs union could apply a uniform external tax on the goods that entered the market so that once goods were admitted into the market, they would not be subject to customs duties, discriminatory taxes or import quotas as they circulated among member nations. The unhindered circulation of capital is meant to allow the transfer of investments, such as the purchase of property and shares among nations.

Prior to focused efforts to establish economic and monetary union in Europe, the emergence of the capital provisions had been slow. Since the 1993 Maastricht Treaty, the ECJ has made many judgments on this initially disregarded freedom. The unrestricted flow of capital is unique in that it is also extended to countries who are not members of the EU. EU citizens can also move freely between nations to live, work, study, etc. The unrestricted movement of people necessitated the loosening of administrative formalities and acknowledgement of professional qualifications granted by other countries.

Nationalist and separatist movements, along with ethnic conflict and ethnic cleansing, periodically disrupted the post-World War II peace.

Post–World War II Europe was generally peaceful, but there were nationalist and separatist movements and ethnic cleansings that took place.

Northern Ireland remains a constituent part of the United Kingdom, but has a significant nationalist minority who would prefer to be united with the Republic of Ireland. Catholics and supporters of the moderate Social Democratic and Labor parties in Northern Ireland are referred to as "nationalists" as they hope for unification with Ireland via non-violent means. The more aggressive strand of nationalism in Northern Ireland, which was originally advocated by Sinn Féin, is usually referred to as "republican"; however, modern-day Sinn Féin is a constitutional party dedicated to pursuing its goals in a peaceful and democratic manner.

On October 1 1999, Chechnya, which had effectively been independent in the wake of the First Chechen War (1994-96), was invaded by Russian troops in order to reestablish Russian control of the area. This war was largely undertaken as a response to a series of attacks within Russia, the most notable of which were a series of apartment bombings in Moscow, Buynansk and Volgodonsk, in which Russian civilians were targeted by Chechen terrorists. The Second Chechen War (1999-2009) was brutal and thousands of Chechen civilians were killed through the direct targeting of civilian populations by the Russian military. The war gained international attention due to its brutality; however, as all the battles occurred within the territory of the Russian Federation, there was little the outside powers could do to stop the bloodshed.

Russian offense ground battle in the Second Chechen War

ETA, the leading group of the Basque National Liberation Movement, is an armed Basque nationalist and separatist organization in northern Spain and southwestern France, which was founded in 1959. ETA was originally founded to safeguard traditional Basque culture, but has developed into a guerrilla group that wants the independence of the Greater Basque Country.

ETA has been designated as a terrorist group by Spain, the United Kingdom, France, the United States and the European Union as its actions have killed 829 people, injured thousands and kidnapped dozens since 1968. Over 400 ETA members are in prison in Spain, France and other countries. In 1989, 1996, 1998 and 2006, ETA declared ceasefires, which it later went back on; however, on September 5, 2010, ETA declared a ceasefire that has remained in force; on October 20, 2011, ETA announced it would fully cease further armed activity; and on November 24, 2012, it was reported that ETA wanted to negotiate a "definitive end" to its operations and dissolve the group.

The ethnic cleansing of Muslims that occurred during the Bosnian War led to the nearly total segregation of the country's religious communities into specific ethno-religious areas. This was done through establishing the state of Bosnia-Herzegovina as a Federative Republic, with the majority of those who are Orthodox Christians living in Bosnia's *Respublika Srpska* (Serbian Republic). The establishment of a Federal Republic in Bosnia was essential after the atrocities committed by Bosnian Serbs in the wars after the breakup of Yugoslavia. Bosnian Serbs, under the leadership of former Yugoslav military officers, waged wholesale genocide against the Muslim community of Bosnia. The most heinous of these atrocities was the shelling of the city of Srebrenica, where Dutch UN observers were used as human shields to prevent NATO bombing while the Bosnian Serbs devastated the civilian population of the city. With the 1995 Dayton Accords, it seemed as if the wars following the breakup of Yugoslavia were coming to an end. However, in 1999, a series of crises erupted in Kosovo, a Serbian controlled though predominantly Islamic, Albanian-populated city. Kosovo remains in a state of flux to this day and the NATO targeting of Serbia, including buildings in the capital of Belgrade, remain a strong point of contention in U.S.-Serbian and U.S.-Russian relations.

During the war in Kosovo in 1999, 218 out of 540 mosques (almost 40%) were demolished by state forces from the Federal Republic of Yugoslavia; a lot more were significantly damaged, as were many secular monuments of Ottoman culture. Though Yugoslavia signed the Kumanovo Agreement to end the conflict, it continued to conduct attacks, such as the burning of the Islamic Community of Kosovo, the official organization of Muslims in Kosovo, and its archives which inspired revenge attacks on dozens of churches. In August of 1999, the attacks finally stopped after pleas from Kosovo's political leaders and the Mufti (the leader of the Islamic Community of Kosovo).

The process of decolonization occurred over the course of the century with varying degrees of cooperation, interference or resistance from European imperialist states.

Decolonization refers to the withdrawal of a colonial power from territory it previously colonized and the procurement of political or economic independence by those colonies. It typically refers to the post-World War II decolonization of areas that had been occupied by European powers prior to the First World War. The United Nations Special Committee on Decolonization has said that during decolonization the colonizer must permit self-determination, but in reality decolonization can also come about from nonviolent revolutions or national liberation wars instigated by pro-independence groups. There have been several particularly active periods of decolonization in modern times: the breakup of the Spanish Empire in the 19th century; the breakup of the German, Austro-Hungarian, Ottoman and Russian Empires after World War I; the breakup of the British, French, Dutch, Japanese, Portuguese, Belgian and Italian colonial empires after World War II; and the breakup of the Soviet Union (which inherited the Russian Empire's holdings) after the Cold War.

At the end of World War I, President Woodrow Wilson's principle of national self-determination raised expectations in the non-European world for freedom from colonial domination – expectations that led to international instability.

The Treaty of Versailles is rife with references to self-determination. These were placed in it only for the benefit of the constituent parts of the defeated empires in Europe. European ethnic groups that had been vassals of extensive European Empires prior to World War I were granted their own nations: Hungary, Poland, Ukraine, etc. But colonial subjects outside of Europe would have been right to wonder why, if it was done for these people, it could not be done for them. National self-determination is explicitly mentioned in five of the points and is implied in almost all of them.

Much of the wording of the Treaty's fourteen points can easily be construed as giving a solid legal claim for the emancipation of all European colonies; Clause XIV, which established the League of Nations, says: "A general association of nations must be formed under specific covenants for the purpose of affording mutual guarantees of political independence and territorial integrity to great and small states alike." Although this is intended to create a forum for international diplomacy, consider the last half of it in the context of subjugated people: "guarantees of political independence and territorial integrity to great and small states alike." Clause V calls for a redistribution of colonies among the victorious nations, but its wording includes a pointed reference to the welfare of the people living in those colonies: "…the interests of the populations concerned must have equal weight with the equitable government whose title is to be determined." This is incompatible with the idea of colonized and subjugated people having fewer rights than the Europeans who form their governments.

The signing of the Treaty of Versailles

Most striking of all, the twelfth clause divests the former Ottoman Empire – the one power whose colonies were primarily outside of Europe – of its colonies with the following statement: *". . . the other nationalities, which are now under Turkish rule, should be assured ... an absolutely unmolested opportunity of autonomous development."* This certainly would have looked, to a colonial subject in Syria or Jordan, like a promise of national self-determination formalized in international law.

In the wake of World War I (in which colonial soldiers and laborers had participated and died in large numbers), independence movements entered a new phase, with increased activity and determination to achieve full national autonomy. The Pan-African movement, which had lost momentum in the beginning of the twentieth century, was reinvigorated. It held new congress meetings throughout the 1920s, but this progress stalled during the Great Depression and World War II. The Indian independence movement entered a new stage, motivated by two simultaneous events; the massacre at Amritsar, which occurred in the middle of the war, and the economic strain which the war caused the British. In addition, thousands of Indian colonial soldiers fought with the British – tens of thousands were killed – and over a million Indian laborers facilitated the British war effort. Indians felt that they should have earned the respect of the British. The Indian non-cooperation movement began in 1920 in the immediate aftermath of the Treaty of Versailles. Worldwide, non-violent non-cooperation movements, violent insurgencies and vigorous political campaigns began and did not stop until colonies began to be emancipated in the post-World War II period.

The League of Nations distributed former German and Ottoman possessions to France and Great Britain through the mandate system, thereby altering the imperial balance of power and creating a strategic interest in the Middle East and its oil.

At the Berlin Conference of 1884–1885, which took place during the Scramble for Africa (motivated by natural resources like rubber and gold) of the late nineteenth century, West European powers separated Africa and its resources into political partitions. By 1905, nearly all of Africa was under the control of West European countries, with the sole exceptions of Liberia, which was settled by African-American former slaves, and Ethiopia, which had successfully resisted the colonization attempts of Italy. Britain and France controlled the most areas in Africa, but Germany, Spain, Italy, Belgium and Portugal also operated colonies there. After World War I, international sentiment shifted away from supporting colonization and efforts were undertaken by the League of Nations to promote decolonization in Africa. Article 22 of the Covenant of the League of Nations established a number of mandates regarding decolonization. Decolonization continued to be promoted and supported by the United Nations.

Beginning in the early 16th century, vast areas of the Middle East were contested for by the Ottomans and Iranian Safavids who fought over them for centuries. By 1700, the Ottomans had been cast out of Hungary and power over the frontier had shifted decisively to the West. The British also established control of the Persian Gulf and the French expanded their influence into Lebanon and Syria (the Levant). In 1912, Italy annexed Libya and the Dodecanese islands, which were just off the coast of Anatolia, the center of the Ottoman Empire. In the late 19th and early 20th centuries, Middle Eastern rulers attempted to modernize their countries in an effort to compete more effectively with European countries. Oil was discovered in Persia in 1908, in Saudi Arabia in 1938, and in other areas of the Persian Gulf, such as Libya and Algeria. This led to increased American interest in the region due to the West's dependence on oil for fuel and the fact that Britain's influence in the region was decreasing.

First commercial oil well in Saudi Arabia, 1938

As a means to control the often restive populations of the region, the European powers, and later the United States, established and supported an imperial mode of "divide and rule" control of the region. This was done through the drawing of borders that did not correspond to any inherent ethnic or religious concentrations in the region. Examples of this include the creation of states such as Syria, Iraq and Saudi Arabia. Lebanon is an artificially created state in that it is multi-ethnic and multi-religion; however, this area has been historically diverse, which means that other than Shia Iranian intervention with the hopes of annexation, the state largely corresponds to realities that existed prior to the mandate system.

The most contentious state that began to form in the wake of the post-WWI mandates was the State of Israel. While the State of Israel was not explicitly created at this time, there was a call for the establishment of a Jewish State in the historical Holy Land on the West Bank of the Jordan River. This was an area that had been populated for hundreds of years by the Palestinians, who received their name from the Roman name for the region.

The policies that the Western powers began to support at this time eventually led to the creation of a Jewish State, but some historians hold an opinion that the way in which it was done provided the modus operandi for a large portion of the Islamic terrorism seen today.

The hangover from these post-WWI policies can be seen today in the majority of conflagrations in the region due to the policies which began in the wake of WWI. The artificial creation of states in which there is no distinct nationality, the outright support for the state of Israel and its displacement of the Palestinians, and the support of brutal dictators such as Muammar Gadhafi in Libya or Saddam Hussein in Iraq have led to disastrous results in the modern era.

Despite indigenous nationalist movements, independence for many African and Asian territories was delayed until the mid- and even late 20th century by the imperial powers' reluctance to relinquish control, threats of interference from other nations, unstable economic and political systems and Cold War strategic alignments.

Even though the decolonization process unfolded in the early 20th century, the imperial powers were reluctant to renounce their possessions and relinquish control of them. Many independence movements started within the African and Asian continents.

The Indian Independence Movement, which was made up of both peaceful and violent national and regional activities, sought to end first the rule of the East India Company (1757–1858) and later the rule of the British Raj (1858–1947). The first organized militant activities of the movement took place in Bengal. Later, the activities took on a political nature in the form of a mainstream attempt in the recently established Indian National Congress (INC), where prominent moderate leaders sought the basic right to sit for Indian Civil Service examinations, in addition to economic rights for the Indian people. From the 1920s onwards, the INC pursued the nonviolent policies promoted by Mohandas Karamchand Gandhi in hopes of gaining independence for India.

Independence campaigns by the Quit India movement (led by Gandhi) and the Indian National Army (INA) movement intensified during World War II and eventually led to the withdrawal of the British from India. The Indian Independence Act was established in 1947 and granted independence to India and Pakistan. India continued to be a dominion of the Crown until January 26, 1950, when its constitution was enacted and created the Republic of India while Pakistan was a dominion of the Crown until 1956 when its first republican constitution was adopted. In 1971, East Pakistan declared independence and became the People's Republic of Bangladesh.

The National Liberation Front was an Algerian socialist party established on November 1, 1954 in order to seek Algeria's independence from France. It was the leading nationalist movement throughout the Algerian War of Independence, which lasted from 1954 to 1962, and ruled Algeria as the sole legal political party until other parties were allowed to form in 1989. The Algerian War of Independence was an important and complex decolonization conflict, which involved the use of guerrilla warfare, maquis fighting, terrorism and torture by both sides. There was also a component of civil war between loyalist Algerians, who supported a French Algeria, and nationalist Algerians, who desired independence from France.

Leaders of the National Liberation Front

The Vietnamese communist revolutionary leader, Ho Chi Minh, was prime minister of the Democratic Republic of Vietnam (North Vietnam) from 1945–55 and president from 1945–69. He was instrumental in the creation of the Democratic Republic of Vietnam in 1945, the People's Army of Vietnam (PAVN) and the Viet Cong (NLF or VC) during the Vietnam War. He headed the Viet Minh independence movement from 1941 on, created the Communist-ruled Democratic Republic of Vietnam in 1945 and defeated the French Union's Far East Expeditionary Corps in 1954 at the Battle of Dien Bien Phu.

Period 4: 1914-Present

Key Concept 4.2: The stresses of the economic collapse and total war engendered internal conflicts within European states and created conflicting conceptions of the relationship between the individual and the state, as demonstrated in the ideological battles between liberal democracy, communism and fascism.

During World War I, states increased the degree and scope of their authority over their economies, societies and cultures. The demands of total war required the centralization of power and the regimentation of the lives of citizens. During the war, governments sought to control information and used propaganda to create stronger emotional ties to the nation and its war effort. Ironically, these measures also produced distrust of traditional authorities. At the end of the war, four empires dissolved–the German, the Austro-Hungarian, the Ottoman and the Russian Empires–but the democratic nations that arose in their place lacked a tradition of democratic politics and suffered from weak economies and ethnic tensions. Even before the end of the war, Russia experienced a revolution and civil war that created not only a new state, the Union of Soviet Socialist Republics (USSR, also known as the Soviet Union), but also a new conception of government and a socioeconomic order based on communist ideals.

In Italy and Germany, charismatic leaders led fascist movements to power, seizing control of post-World War I governments. Fascism promised to solve economic problems through state direction (although not ownership) of production. The movements also determined to defy the provisions of the Treaty of Versailles by rearming (a rapid military buildup) and by aggressive territorial expansion. The efforts of fascist governments to revise the Treaty of Versailles led to the most violent and destructive war in human history (World War II), a conflict between liberal democracies, those temporarily allied with communist Russia, and fascist states. When this conflict ended in the total defeat of fascism, Europe was devastated and the liberal, capitalist democracies competed with centrally directed communist states–the only viable alternatives left.

In the post-World War II period, despite the difference in ideologies, states in both the East and West increased their involvement in their citizens' lives through the establishment of welfare programs, the expansion of education, regulation and planning of the economy and the extension of cultural opportunities to all groups in society.

With the collapse of communism and the fall of the Soviet Union in the early 1990s, the liberal democracies of Western Europe celebrated the triumph of their political and economic systems, and many of the former communist states moved for admission into the European Union and NATO. By the late 1990s, it became evident that the transition from communism to capitalism and democracy was not as simple as it first appeared to be. The West also experienced difficulties because of economic recession and experimented with hybrid economies that emphasized the social responsibility of the state toward its citizens.

The Russian Revolution created a regime based on Marxist-Leninist theory.

Marxist-Leninist theory is Vladimir Lenin's adaptation of Marxism. Lenin's main disagreement with Marx was about how communism could be achieved in a capitalist nation. Marx wrote that capitalism would collapse under the weight of the conflicts it creates between workers and elites. He argued that there would be an incremental and natural transition from capitalism through different levels of socialism and, finally, to full communism. Lenin, while initially a strict adherent to this policy, eventually turned to a more revolutionary approach, arguing that the only way to replace capitalism with communism was through the use of force, which is what he accomplished in Russia.

Drawing of Vladimir Lenin, Russian politician and theorist

The Russian Revolution was actually two revolutions that took place in February-March and October of 1917, respectively. When they were over, the Tsarist autocracy had collapsed and the way had been paved for the Soviet Union to emerge. The February Revolution (which began in March according to the Russian calendar) took place in Petrograd (Soviet Leningrad and present-day St. Petersburg). The Russian military was weak and divided, decimated by World War I, and was unable to quell the revolution. The emperor, Nicholas II, abdicated and members of the Imperial Parliament, or Duma, took power and formed the Russian Provisional Government. The Provisional Government, which had state power, was tolerated by the Soviets (workers' councils), who were headed by radical socialist factions and supported by the lower classes and the liberals, but the Soviets demanded the right to have influence on the government and control certain militias.

The Provisional Government was headed by the pragmatic socialist Alexander Kerensky, whose father was a tutor to the young Vladimir Ulyanov (later to be known as Vladimir Lenin) in the provincial Siberian town of Simbirsk (now known as Ulyanovsk). Kerensky advocated socialist change; however, he was fully aware of the largely backward peasantry because of his own rural upbringing and participation in the "Narodnik" movement, which had advocated for the need to educate the peasants as a means to improve the conditions of the nation as a whole. Unfortunately for Kerensky, the pressures from France, Britain and the United States to remain involved in the First World War led to his abandonment of many of the principles he held in order to keep the outside powers content. This led to further disillusionment in the military ranks as they felt that once the Tsar was gone, they could return to Russia and cease fighting the Germans. Into this chaos of workers' strikes, disappointment in the army ranks, Western European demands and Germany's desire to topple the Provisional Government came the Bolsheviks and their leader – Vladimir Lenin.

It was not seen as a *fait accompli* that the Bolsheviks would take power over the Provisional Government, and there is still some debate as to how big of a role the Germans played in their success; however, what is clear is that amongst the ranks of the common soldier, there was widespread discontent with the Provisional Government. Due to this, Bolshevik agitators who had made their way into the ranks of the army from the outset of the war, began to stir up discontent among the rank-and-file Russian soldiers, eventually leading to widespread mutiny. At the same time, the leader of the Bolsheviks, Vladimir Lenin, found himself in neutral Switzerland, with the entire Eastern Front of WWI standing between him and the burgeoning revolution. The German military found a solution for this by means of armoring a single train car for Lenin and his group to make their way back to Russia as a means to spur on the revolution and demand an immediate end to the war, which in turn would drastically help Germany by focusing all their attention on the Western Front.

The October Revolution was led by the Bolshevik party and headed by Vladimir Lenin and the workers' Soviets. They overthrew the Provisional Government and established the Russian Soviet Federative Socialist Republic (SFSR). In 1918, the Bolsheviks moved the capital to Moscow, seized control of many government ministries and formed the Cheka to suppress any opposition that arose. In March of 1918, the Bolshevik leaders signed the Treaty of Brest-Litovsk with Germany in order to end the Russian involvement in World War I. Civil war successively broke out between the Bolsheviks (known as the "Reds"), anti-socialist groups (known as the "Whites") and the non-Bolshevik socialists. The Bolsheviks eventually defeated both the Whites and their socialist adversaries, paving the way for the Union of Soviet Socialist Republics (USSR) to be formed in 1922.

Emblem of the Russian Socialist Federative Soviet Republic

The victorious Entente powers were active in their attempts to overthrow the Bolsheviks, as was most clearly evidenced by their support for the Czechoslovak Legion that held the vital Trans-Siberian Railway for years and greatly prolonged the period of time it took the Bolsheviks to extend their rule throughout the vast Siberian and Far Eastern Regions. The then Secretary of the Navy and future Prime Minister of the United Kingdom, Winston Churchill, would go on to say later in life that one of his greatest regrets was not working hard enough to "smother the Bolshevik baby while it lay in its crib."

In Russia, World War I exacerbated long-term problems of political stagnation, social inequality, incomplete industrialization and food and land distribution, while creating support for revolutionary.

At the outset of Russia's involvement in World War I in August of 1914, the country's social and political unrest dissipated somewhat as people united against the threat of Germany; however, as the war continued and more Russian lives were lost in the conflict, people began to grow disillusioned with the Tsar and the government's ability to defend Russia's territory and people. Mutinies and rebellions broke out as soldiers rebelled against the poor conditions they faced in the army and the growing casualty rate.

Russian civilians were suffering as well. By the end of 1915, the Russian economy was greatly strained by the war, which was evidenced by food shortages, rampant price increases and diminishing incomes. These issues were especially problematic in the capital, St. Petersburg, due to distance from supplies and poor transportation networks. Bread, sugar, meat and other provisions were hard to come by and the people had to stand in very long lines in hope of getting them. It became increasingly difficult for Russian civilians to afford and procure food.

Unsurprisingly, from mid-1915, strikes and crime became more frequent, though people largely endured their suffering and combed the city for food. In St. Petersburg, working class women reportedly waited in food lines up to forty hours each week; they also resorted to begging, prostitution and crime in order to keep their families fed. The people began to blame Tsar Nicholas II for their dire circumstances, and what little support he had left eroded.

The Duma issued a warning to Tsar Nicholas in November of 1916, proclaiming that a constitutional form of government must be put in place in order to avoid further disaster in Russia. While the Tsar was open to this idea in principle, the general weakness of his character and the loss of his most trusted reformer, Peter Stolypin, to an assassin's bullet (in the presence of the Tsar) in 1911 strengthened his resolve to govern Russian in an autocratic manner. Towards the end of his reign, he began to increasingly rule the empire under the Russian tradition of *Pravoslaviye, Samoderzhavie, Narodnost'* (Orthodoxy, Autocracy, Nationality), which made him resistant to any of the changes needed to prevent the overthrow of the monarchy; Nicholas ignored the warning, which led to the collapse of his Tsarist regime during the February Revolution of 1917, and he and his family were executed the following year.

Military and workers' insurrections, aided by the revived Soviets, undermined the Provisional Government and set the stage for Lenin's long-planned Bolshevik Revolution and the establishment of a communist state.

The October Revolution, which was more organized than the February Revolution, marked the start of the spread of communism in the 20th century. Lenin's role in the onset of the revolution was at best marginal. He had contributed to the narrative of revolution and many agitated on his behalf; however, the massive discontent of the lower classes was largely spontaneous and the Bolsheviks could then present a ready-made narrative, which many of the already discontented would readily accept. Lenin was proclaimed a leader of the

Bolshevik Party, though he was not present for the takeover of the Winter Palace, which has led some to argue that it was really Trotsky who was at the helm of the revolution.

Order of the October Revolution

On November 7, 1917, Lenin, the Bolshevik leader, led leftist revolutionaries in an uprising against the Provisional Government, which they thought was ineffective. (The Julian calendar was still in use in Russia at the time, so references of the time give the date of the revolt as October 25.) The October Revolution built on the discontent of the initial February Revolution and ultimately replaced Russia's brief provisional parliamentary government with a government led by *soviets* (Russian word for "councils"), which consisted of local councils elected by workers and peasants. The Russian Civil War began straightaway when opponents of the Bolsheviks, liberal, moderate socialist and monarchist forces, who were known as the "White Army," waged war on the Bolshevik "Red Army."

Members of the soviets were freely elected at first, but the Socialist-Revolutionary Party, anarchists and other leftists stirred up opposition to the Bolsheviks among the soviets. The Bolsheviks eventually had little support beyond the industrialized cities of St. Petersburg and Moscow, so they banned non-Bolsheviks from becoming members of the soviets. This led to a lot of tension and civil unrest and many called for more political reform or "a third Russian revolution," for which there was significant support. The Tambov rebellion of 1919–1921 and the Kronstadt rebellion in March of 1921 were two significant anti-Bolshevik movements, but they were not coordinated effectively and were quelled by the White Army during the Russian Civil War.

The Bolshevik takeover prompted a protracted civil war between communist forces and their opponents, who were aided by foreign powers.

Following the Russian Revolution, the Russian Civil War began in 1918, which caused massive civilian suffering and death. The main players in the war were the Red Army ("Reds"), which was comprised of the uprising majority led by the minority Bolsheviks, and the "Whites," which were composed of army officers and Cossacks, the bourgeoisie and various anti-Bolshevik political groups. Great Britain, France, the U.S. and Japan supported the Whites with military aid, but the Reds had internal support and cohesion which was more integral; they were eventually able to defeat the anti-Bolshevik forces and retain control of Russia.

The Kronstadt Rebellion was a naval mutiny undertaken against the Bolsheviks by Soviet Baltic sailors, former Red Army soldiers and the people of Kronstadt near the end of the war. This was especially damaging to the Bolshevik cause, as the sailors of Kronstadt were seen as the vanguard of the revolution due to the part they played in the 1905 Revolution. The Tambov Uprising was seen as a further undermining of the Bolshevik cause as it was undertaken by former Bolsheviks. The uprising took place in the city of Tambov as a reaction to the Bolshevik government's attempts to seize all the grain supply in the territory under their control.

In order to improve economic performance, Lenin compromised with free-market principles under the New Economic Policy, but after his death, Stalin undertook a centralized program of rapid economic.

In response to the dramatic decrease of support for the Bolsheviks that was due to the extreme poverty experienced by many Russians as a result of the Russian Civil War, Lenin retracted the policy of War Communism and changed how he approached his New Economic Policy (NEP), which consisted of laws sanctioning the co-existence of the private and public sectors. The NEP sought to move away from full nationalization of particular components of some industries. It was chiefly a fresh take on agricultural policy. The Bolsheviks saw life in villages as conservative and a hindrance to the progress made during the October Revolution when they triumphed over the Tsar. Hence, the NEP only permitted private landholdings as opposed to collective farming.

Lenin increased free trade in markets in the hope of stimulating an increase in production in order to improve economic conditions. He ended grain requisitions and implemented a tax on peasants, which allowed them to retain and trade a portion of their crops. At first, this tax was paid in kind, but as the Russian currency stabilized in 1924, it became a cash payment. The peasants' incentive to produce a higher yield increased as a result of the tax, which led to a 40 percent increase in production following the drought and famine that occurred in 1921–1922. In addition to the NEP economic reforms, which sought more independent economy, NEP labor reforms married labor and productivity, which incentivized cost decreases and increased labor efforts. As a result, labor unions became independent civic organizations. Government positions were also opened up to the most qualified workers as a result of NEP reforms.

Lenin thought of the NEP as a strategic withdrawal from socialist policies, but maintained that it was entrenched in the stage of state capitalism, the last step before the evolution of socialism. He was aware that the implementation of full communism was impossible in the conditions Russia found herself in and to do so would be counter-productive. A fellow supporter of this notion was the leader of the Red Army, Leon Trotsky. He was a proponent of the idea that a relatively pragmatic program of socialism should be adopted until communism could spread to Britain and Germany, thereby beginning the takeover of communism on a global scale. This was opposed by the former seminarian and principal Bolshevik agitator in the Caucasus, Josef Dzhugashvili, by this time based in Moscow and known as Josef Stalin. He advocated for a stronger consolidation of power in the territories of the former Russian Empire, eventually to be expressed in his five-year plans and his promulgation of the notion of "communism in one country."

Stalin's economic modernization of the Soviet Union came at a high price, including the liquidation of the kulaks, famine in Ukraine, purges of political rivals, unequal burdens placed on women and the establishment of an oppressive political system.

Lenin had been of the opinion that the NEP should last for several decades or more, but in 1928, after just seven years of the NEP, his successor, Stalin, introduced full central planning, re-nationalized a lot of the economy and employed policies of industrialization. Stalin's collectivization of all agriculture was an especially notable deviation from the NEP methodology. The scale and influence of Russia's secret police and intelligence agencies grew under Stalin's leadership. Soviet intelligence forces established intelligence networks in many of the most powerful countries in the world, including Germany, Great Britain, France, Japan and the United States. Stalin used the Communist International movement to infiltrate agents and to bolster pro-Soviet and pro-Stalin sentiment within foreign Communist parties. In 1940, Stalin used a combination of secret police and foreign espionage tactics in order to have Leon Trotsky assassinated in Mexico.

Leon Trotsky, Bolshevik revolutionary

As head of the Politburo of the Central Committee of the Communist Party of the Soviet Union, Stalin maintained virtually absolute power during the 1930s, especially after he undertook the Great Purges of the party, which were justified as efforts to oust "opportunists" and "counter-revolutionary infiltrators." All who were viewed as a threat to the dictatorial rule of Stalin were eventually killed or exiled. His first victims were those of the "Right Opposition" and the "Left Opposition," both of which consisted of "Old Bolsheviks," who wished to move the country in either a slightly more right-wing direction or a slightly more left-wing direction. This resulted in arrests, false accusations of conspiracy, and the torture and summary execution of the majority of those who undertook the Bolshevik Revolution. The "Great Purge" eventually expanded even into Stalin's inner circle, leading to the arrest and execution of the NKVD Chief who began the purges, Genrik Yagoda, and his successor Nikolai Yezhov.

In the time period surrounding World War II, Stalin perpetrated a series of large-scale deportations that significantly influenced the ethnic makeup of the Soviet Union. Between 1941 and 1949, an estimated 3.3 million people were deported to Siberia and the Central Asian republics, where up to 43 percent may have perished due to disease and poor nutrition.

Stalin instituted the collectivization of agriculture in order to increase the output from large-scale mechanized farms, to have more political influence over the peasantry and to increase the efficiency of collecting taxes. Collectivization resulted in social changes on a magnitude that had not been seen since serfdom was abolished in 1861. It also resulted in worsening conditions for peasants, many of whom reacted to the changes with violence. The most notable instance of this was the "Holodomor" in Ukraine where collectivization, along with a desire on the part of the Politburo to quell Ukrainian nationalism, led to the death due to starvation of millions of people living in the Ukrainian SSR.

The ideology of fascism, with roots in the pre-World War I era, gained popularity in the environment of postwar bitterness, the rise of communism, uncertain transitions to democracy and economic instability.

Fascism's ideological beginnings have been traced to the 1880s, during which revolts against materialism, rationalism, positivism, bourgeois society and democracy were prevalent. The generation of intellectuals living at the end of the 19th century adhered to emotionalism, irrationalism, subjectivism and vitalism, and believed civilization was in crisis and needed a total overhaul. The fin-de-siècle intellectual school of the time thought individuals were only a piece of the greater collectivity, which should not be seen as an atomized numerical sum of individuals. They rejected the rationalistic individualism of liberal society and the dissolution of social links in bourgeois society.

Darwinian biology was one intellectual development that influenced the fin-de-siècle views. Others included: Wagnerian aesthetics, Arthur de Gobineau's racialism, Gustave Le Bon's psychology and the philosophies of Friedrich Nietzsche, Fyodor Dostoyevsky and Henri Bergson. Social Darwinism, which came to be widely accepted, did not make a distinction between the physical and social lives, and saw the human condition as a never-ending struggle to achieve the survival of the fittest. Social Darwinism's emphasis on biogroup identity challenged positivism's assertion that deliberate and rational choice determined human behavior. The idea that human behavior was governed by rational choice was rejected by new theories of social and political psychology, which said that emotion, as opposed to reason, was most influential in political issues. Nietzsche's assertion that "God is dead" overlapped with his attack on the "herd mentality" of Christianity, democracy and modern collectivism. Nietzsche's concepts of the *übermensch* and his promotion of power as a primordial instinct were very influential on many of the fin-de-siècle generation.

Friedrich Nietzsche

The notion of propaganda of the deed, which emphasized the importance of direct action as the key means of political action, was put forth by the anarchist Mikhail Bakunin. Because this idea sanctioned revolutionary violence, it was favored by the fascists. Fascism was influenced by Charles Maurras, a French nationalist and reactionary monarchist, who endorsed what he referred to as "integral nationalism," which called for the organic unity of a nation. Maurras maintained that a powerful monarch who had the ability to unite a nation's people was an ideal leader. He did not trust what he considered the democratic mystification of the popular will from which an impersonal collective subject was created. Maurras' nationalist ideas were idealized by fascists, but they were altered into a modernized revolutionary form that did not champion monarchism the way Maurras had.

The question of the legitimacy of political violence was discussed by the French revolutionary Georges Sorel, a syndicalist, in *Reflections on Violence* (1908). In this and other works, he promoted radical syndicalist action in order to stimulate a revolution to combat capitalism and the bourgeoisie. In *Reflections on Violence*, Sorel stressed the need for a revolutionary political religion. In *The Illusions of Progress*, Sorel criticized democracy as being reactionary, saying "nothing is more aristocratic than democracy." Fascism was influenced by the Italian Futurism Movement, which saw violence and war as natural consequences of modern civilization.

Fascist dictatorships used modern technology and propaganda that rejected democratic institutions, promoted charismatic leaders and glorified war and nationalism to lure the disillusioned.

Pageantry, rhetoric and other forms of propaganda were used by Italy's fascist regime in an attempt to unite and control the country. For example, it was promulgated that Mussolini, the head of the fascist party who became Prime Minister in 1922, was never wrong about anything. In 1935, a special propaganda ministry was created, and in 1937 the Ministry of Popular Culture was established. Mussolini's leadership and fascist propaganda served as unifying forces for Italy as a whole, despite the fact that citizens were often unhappy with their local officials. The Fascist movement was one of the most prominent to favor action and violence over negotiation.

Mussolini extended fascist propaganda to economic issues, referring to programs with such names as "the Battle of Wheat" and "the Battle of the Lira," as well as the military, through which he sought to become dominant on land, in the sea and in the air. War and killing were portrayed as the core of manhood and Mussolini proclaimed that individuals should be willing to kill or die for their fatherland, as the nation's well-being was more important than each individual's well-being.

Benito Mussolini, Italian dictator

Mussolini disdained liberal individualism and sought to make fascism an absolute totalitarian experience and not merely a political one. Fascism was portrayed as a way of life, not just a political party. Hence, liberalism's distinction between the private and public spheres was rejected and the corporatist state, as opposed to liberal democracy, was elevated to the role of unifying Italy.

Mussolini and Hitler rose to power by exploiting postwar bitterness and economic instability, using terror and manipulating the shaky and unpopular democracies in their countries.

Benito Amilcare Andrea Mussolini (1883–1945), known as *Il Duce* (Italian for "the Leader"), was an Italian politician, journalist and founder and leader of the National Fascist Party. Mussolini was Prime Minister of Italy from 1922 until ousted in 1943. He governed according to Italy's constitution until 1925, when he abandoned any democratic pretenses and instituted a legal dictatorship.

Mussolini was initially a prominent member of the National Directorate of the Italian Socialist Party (PSI), but was banished from the PSI in World War I because he disagreed with its stance on neutrality. Mussolini condemned the PSI and went on to found the Fascist movement. In October of 1922, Mussolini and his Fascist Party initiated the March on Rome in order to take control of Italy. He extinguished any opposition and consolidated his power in a one-party dictatorship by utilizing a secret police force and outlawing labor strikes. By 1927, Mussolini had taken legal and extraordinary measures to create a dictatorial authority with the hopes of eventually creating a totalitarian state. Mussolini ruled Italy until 1943, when he was overthrown by King Victor Emmanuel III. Subsequently, Mussolini led the Italian Social Republic, a German client regime in the northern part of Italy. He served in this capacity until his death in 1945.

Adolf Hitler (1889–1945) was an Austrian-born German politician. He led the Nazi Party (NSDAP), was Chancellor of Germany from 1933 to 1945 and had the title of *Führer* (German for "Leader") of Nazi Germany from 1934 to 1945. Hitler's policies and actions, including the Holocaust, in which millions of people were tortured and killed, led to the Second World War in Europe.

Prior to his rise to power in Germany, Hitler served as a soldier in the Austro-Hungarian Army in World War I. After the war he joined the German Workers' Party, which would later become the NSDAP, in 1919 and became leader of the NSDAP two years later in 1921. In 1923 Hitler tried to seize power of Germany by staging a coup in Munich, which became known as the "Beer Hall Putsch." He failed and was sent to prison as a result of the attempt. During his imprisonment, Hitler wrote an autobiography and political manifesto called *Mein Kampf* ("My Struggle"). He was released from prison in 1924 and began gaining popular support by using his compelling oratory skills and Nazi propaganda to criticize the Treaty of Versailles, which had been signed at the end of the First World War. The Nazi Party became the largest elected party in Germany, and in 1933 Hitler was made chancellor.

The Enabling Act was passed in order to transform the Weimar Republic into Nazi Germany, a single-party dictatorship based on the totalitarian and autocratic ideology of National Socialism. Hitler endorsed Pan-Germanism, anti-Semitism and anti-communism, and between 1933 and 1939, Hitler orchestrated rapid economic recovery from the Great Depression in Germany, the denunciation of the severe reparations imposed on Germany after World War I and the seizure of territories in which millions of ethnic Germans lived. All of these actions resulted in increasing popular support of Hitler.

Hitler wanted to oust Jews from Germany and create a New Order in opposition to what he considered the unfairness of Britain and France's dominant position in the post-World War I international sphere. In the background of apparent humane successes, the Nazis established a system of brutal forced labor camps to which they consigned all political opponents. They also gradually made Jews *personae non gratae* with the Nuremburg Laws, ending their rights to work and receive education.

Adolf Hitler, dictator of Nazi Germany

Franco's alliance with Italian and German fascists in the Spanish Civil War–in which the Western democracies did not intervene–represented a testing ground for World War II and resulted in authoritarian rule in Spain from 1936 to the mid-1970s.

Francisco Franco Bahamonde (1892–1975) was a Spanish general and served as dictator of Spain from 1939 until 1975 when he died. Franco was a staunch conservative, and was unhappy when the Spanish monarchy was replaced by a republic in 1931. The conservatives narrowly lost the 1936 elections in Spain, in which the leftist Popular Front came to power. That same year, Franco, along with other generals, staged a partially successful coup, which ignited the Spanish Civil War. The other generals died quickly and Franco was left as the head of his faction. The Spanish Civil War ended three years later, in April of 1939, with Franco emerging victorious. Half a million people had been killed in the war.

Both sides enjoyed foreign assistance during the war, despite a Non-Intervention Agreement that had been signed in August of 1936. Fascist Italy sent the *Corpo Truppe Volontarie* to support the nationalists, who were also later supported by Nazi Germany, who sent the Condor Legion to help. The nationalists were opposed by the Soviet Union and Spanish communists, socialists and anarchists. The United Kingdom and France both maintained strict adherence to the 1936 arms embargo, though volunteers from around the world joined the anti-Franco forces. The most notable of these was the young American author Ernest Hemingway, whose work as an ambulance driver for the Red Cross in Italy during the conflict led to his writing of the novel *For Whom the Bell Tolls*.

After the conclusion of the war, Franco set up an autocratic dictatorship, which defined Spain as a totalitarian state, and made himself Head of State and Government. He was known as *El Caudillo* (Spanish for "the Chief"). Only the *FET y de las JONS* political party, a combination of the Monarchist Party and Fascist Party that assisted Franco during the war, was legal during Franco's regime.

Franco sought to eliminate his political and ideological opposition by sending dissidents to concentration camps, forcing them to perform hard labor or killing them. These practices led to the deaths of between 200,000 and 400,000 people. During World War II, Franco maintained a policy of neutrality, with the exception of the Blue Division (when he allowed Spanish volunteer soldiers to fight USSR on in support of Germany). By the 1950s, the nature of Franco's regime had transitioned from a strict dictatorship to a semi-pluralist authoritarian system. Franco actively groomed the young King Juan Carlos I, who he thought could continue his dictatorial rule over the country.

Francisco Franco, Spanish dictator

After failures to establish functioning democracies, authoritarian dictatorships took power in Central and Eastern Europe during the interwar period.

Between the two world wars, many Central and East European countries were ruled by authoritarian dictatorships.

Marshal Jozef Pilsudski initiated the May Coup on May 12, 1926, in Poland, which overthrew the civilian government. His effort received support from leftist factions, who prevented the government forces from using railway transportation. Pilsudski was also supported by conservative landowners, which left the right-wing National Democrats as his only major opposition.

After the successful coup, Pilsudski instituted an authoritarian form of government known as the *Sanation* regime (because it was intended to be "healing"), which he led until he died in 1935. The *Sanation* regime was a reflection of Pilsudski's evolution from a center-leftist to a supporter of more conservative policies. Political institutions and parties existed, but the electoral process was rigged and any opposition was suppressed. Many leftists were imprisoned at the Bereza Kartuska Prison (about 3,000 people between 1934 and 1939) or other prison camps, and some were tried (e.g., the Brest trials) and received harsh sentences. Some sought to rebel against the authoritarian regime, such as in the 1937 peasant strike, but the military was employed to quickly quash any opposition.

Between the First and Second World Wars, Miklos Horthy de Nagybanya, an admiral and statesman, served as Regent of the Kingdom of Hungary. His government was conservative and irredentist and outlawed both the Communist Party and the Fascist Party in Hungary. Charles IV unsuccessfully sought to reclaim his throne from Horthy twice. In 1921, the parliament made the pragmatic sanction null, which effectively deposed the Hapsburgs. Horthy developed an alliance with Nazi Germany during the late 1930s. With Hitler's help, Horthy regained ethnically Hungarian lands that had been lost following World War I. Horthy sanctioned Hungary's participation in the German invasions of the Soviet Union and Yugoslavia. However, Horthy was hesitant to support Germany's military endeavors and the deportation of Hungarian Jews. He sought to make a covert deal with the Allies, which prompted a German invasion. In March 1944, Germany ultimately took control of Hungary.

From 1918 to 1938, Romania was a liberal constitutional monarchy, though it experienced the rise of nationalist, anti-Semitic parties, principally the Iron Guard, during that time. From 1938 to 1944, Romania was ruled by a dictator. King Carol II was the first dictator and he eliminated the parliamentary regime.

The Molotov-Ribbentrop Pact of 1939 between Germany and the Soviet Union specified the Soviet "interest" in Bessarabia. Carol II had lost a lot of territory due to his unsuccessful diplomacy, so the military supported General Ion Antonescu's effort to seize power. In June of 1941, under command of the German Wehrmacht, Romania entered World War II by declaring war on the Soviet Union in the hope of reclaiming Bessarabia and Northern Bukovina. Germany eventually gave Transnistria (the area between Dniester and the Southern Bug) to Romania. The authoritarian King Carol II abandoned his throne in 1940, and the monarchy was replaced by the National Legionary State, in which power was shared by Ion Antonescu and the Iron Guard.

Molotov and Ribbentrop, after signing the Molotov-Ribbentrop Pact

The Great Depression, caused by weaknesses in international trade and monetary theories and practices, undermined Western European democracies and fomented radical political responses throughout Europe.

During the 1930s, the world experienced the extensive economic depression known as the Great Depression. Its start varied from country to country, but in many it began in 1929, following the fall in stock prices in the United States that occurred in October of that year, and continued through the late 1930s. The Great Depression was devastating for both wealthy and struggling countries. The worldwide GDP decreased 15 percent between 1929 and 1932. Personal income, tax revenue, profits and prices all fell, and international trade decreased by more than 50 percent. The United States' unemployment rate rose to 25 percent and in some countries it reached as high as 33 percent.

Cities were hit hard, especially those dependent on heavy industry. New construction was also put on hold in a lot of countries. Rural areas and farmers also suffered; crop prices dropped about 60 percent. Those who worked in primary sector industries like mining and logging were hit hardest by the decreasing demand for their services and minimal existence of sources of alternative jobs. The negative impacts of the Great Depression continued in many countries until the onset of the Second World War, though some countries had started to improve a few years earlier, by the middle of the 1930s.

World War I debt, nationalistic tariff polices, overproduction, depreciated currencies, disrupted trade patterns and speculation created weaknesses in economies worldwide.

Economists have continued to debate the origins of the Great Depression, but most point to the 1929 stock market crash in the U.S. as the tipping point, which led to the deflation of assets and commodity prices, large decreases in demand and credit and decreased trade; rampant unemployment and poverty followed as a result. Demand-driven theories of the Great Depression are supported by Keynesian and Institutional economists, who maintain that the Depression was initiated by an extensive loss of confidence that led people to consume and invest less than they normally would following the 1929 stock market crash. Panic and deflation occurred and many people sought to protect against further loss by refraining from entering the markets. Deflation is when the price level of goods and services decreases and borrowers would have to pay back more valuable dollars than the ones they borrowed, as opposed to inflation, when value of the money diminishes into the future.

Monetarists argue that the Great Depression began as an ordinary downturn, but that monetary authorities made errors that led to a decrease in the money supply, which elevated the tenuous economic situation into a full-fledged recession. In agreement with monetarists are those pointing to debt deflation causing borrowers to owe an increasing amount in real terms. Many heterodox theories exist that deny the explanations of both the Keynesians and the monetarists. For example, some new classical macroeconomists say that certain labor market policies employed at the beginning of the Great Depression led to its continuation and severity.

Crowd gathers outside the Stock Exchange after the Crash of 1929

Dependence on post-World War I American investment capital led to financial collapse when, following the 1929 stock market crash, the United states cut off capital flows to Europe.

Economic historians note the impact of the large number of bank failures that occurred, mostly in rural areas of the U.S. The structural weaknesses of the rural economy meant that banks in rural areas were vulnerable to economic upheaval. In the late 1920s, farm prices decreased drastically and interest rates on loans increased dramatically, which made it difficult for farmers, many of whom were already in debt. Banks in urban areas also possessed structural weaknesses that made them susceptible to economic upheaval. Many urban banks did not maintain adequate reserves, invested heavily in the unpredictable stock market or made risky loans, especially to places like Germany and Latin America.

Together, the 1929 Stock Market Crash and the Great Depression created the biggest financial crisis that occurred during the 20th century. The Crash of October 1929 has become a symbol of the recession that crippled the world over the following decade.

Despite attempts to rethink economic theories and policies and forge political alliances, Western democracies failed to overcome the effects of the Great Depression and were weakened by extremist movements.

John Maynard Keynes was a British economist, who theorized in his book *The General Theory of Employment Interest and Money* that lower aggregate expenditures contributed to a big decrease in income and to the employment rate being well below average. In this way, the economy achieved "balance" through low levels of economic activity and high rates of unemployment. Keynes' theory was that to achieve full employment, governments should run deficits as their economy slows, because the private sector will not invest enough to maintain the normal levels of production necessary to help an economy recover from a recession. Keynesian economists say governments should increase government spending and/or cut taxes during times of economic crisis.

John Maynard Keynes, British economist

As the Depression continued, U.S. President Franklin D. Roosevelt attempted public works, farm subsidies and other programs and policies to stimulate the economy, though never fully abandoning an attempt to balance the budget. According to Keynesians, Roosevelt's actions improved the U.S. economy, but the government did not spend enough money to lift the economy out of recession until the outset of World War II.

The Great Depression began when Britain was still trying to recover from the staggering impact of the First World War, which had occurred more than a decade earlier.

The impact of the depression on the northern, more industrial areas of Britain was immediate and crippling because demand for industrial products drastically decreased. By the end of 1930, unemployment in Britain had more than doubled, from 1 million people to 2.5 million people, which was 20 percent of the insured workforce; exports had dropped in value by 50 percent. In some areas in northeast Britain, unemployment rose as high as 70 percent and the demand for shipbuilding fell 90 percent. Several hunger marches took place in Britain in the 1920s and 1930s, the largest of which was the National Hunger March in September/October of 1932.

It took a couple of years for the impact of the Great Depression to reach France, which it did in 1931. The depression in France was relatively mild compared to other countries: unemployment rates peaked at under 5 percent, production fell only about 20 percent below 1929 levels. France did not experience a banking crisis. However, the depression did have an extreme impact on the local economy. In response, riots occurred on February 6, 1934, and a new political party, the Popular Front, helmed by SFIO socialist leader Léon Blum, won the elections in 1936.

Postwar economic growth supported an increase in welfare benefits; however, subsequent economic stagnation led to criticism and limitation of the welfare state.

Between the end of the Second World War in 1945 and the early 1970s, many countries experienced a period of great economic expansion, also known as the postwar economic boom, the long boom and the Golden Age of Capitalism. West European and East Asian countries in particular enjoyed remarkable economic growth and employment levels. The Golden Age of Capitalism descended on many of the countries that had previously been ravaged by World War II, including Greece (the Greek economic miracle), West Germany (*Wirtschaftswunder*), France (*Trente Glorieuses*), Japan (the Japanese post-war economic miracle) and Italy (the Italian economic miracle). The development of these economies was largely due to the loans that the United States provided as a means to rebuild Europe after the war, from which the United States greatly benefited economically.

This expansion was checked in the early 1970s when the Bretton Woods system fell apart in 1971, an oil crisis occurred in 1973 and the stock market crashed again in 1973–1974, creating a recession.

Under the Marshall Plan the United States financed an extensive reconstruction of industry and infrastructure in western and central Europe and stimulated an extended period of growth, often referred to as the "economic miracle," which increased the economic and cultural importance of consumerism.

The Marshall Plan (officially known as the European Recovery Program, or ERP) was an American program, lasting from 1948 to 1952, by which the United States gave $13 billion (approximately $130 billion in current dollar value as of August 2015) in economic aid to Western European nations in order to help them rebuild their economies after the end of World War II. The U.S. embarked on the Marshall Plan, named for Secretary of State George Marshall, in order to help rebuild war-devastated areas, eliminate trade barriers, modernize European industries, increase Europe's prosperity and check the spread of communism. The Marshall Plan loosened interstate barriers, eliminated petty regulations that had formerly constrained business and promoted increased productivity, membership in labor unions and the implementation of modern business practices.

The Marshall Plan generally divided assistance between recipients on a per capita basis. More money was allocated to the major industrial powers, on the theory that their revival was a key predecessor of a wider recovery in Europe. Larger aid per capita was given to the Allied nations than was marked for countries that had been part of the Axis powers or had remained neutral during the war. The United Kingdom received the most money from the Marshall Plan (about 26 percent of the total amount allocated), followed by France (18 percent) and West Germany (11 percent). In total, about eighteen European countries received some sort of assistance from the Marshall Plan. The Soviet

*George Marshall
of the Marshall Plan*

Union refused the benefits it was offered and also prevented other Eastern Bloc countries, such as East Germany and Poland, from accepting assistance. The United States also provided comparable aid programs in Asia, but they were distinct from the Marshall Plan, which was directed at Europe.

The expansion of cradle-to-grave social welfare programs in the aftermath of World War II, accompanied by high taxes, became a contentious domestic political issue as the budgets of European nations came under pressure in the late 20th century.

The welfare programs of today are more widespread and inclusive than the poverty relief programs of the past were. The institution of social insurance, which emerged in Germany under Bismarck, was an important model for modern welfare programs. In his popular essay *Citizenship and Social Class* (1949), the British sociologist T.H. Marshall labeled modern welfare states as being characterized by a combination of democratic government, welfare programs and capitalist economies. He argued that citizens should have access to social rights, in addition to political and civil rights. Examples of states that put this into practice are Germany, the Nordic countries, the Netherlands, Uruguay, New Zealand and the United Kingdom during the 1930s.

The world-wide Great Depression, which condemned millions of people to unemployment and desolation, changed many people's attitudes about welfare programs. The welfare state was considered a "middle way" between communism and unregulated laissez-faire capitalism during the Great Depression. After World War II, many European countries expanded the social service offered to their citizens from partial or selective coverage to more complete "cradle-to-grave" coverage. Today, welfare states offer both cash benefits (pensions, unemployment benefits, housing benefits) and in-kind services (health care, childcare, post-secondary education). In the majority of Western and Northern Europe these programs are now seen as a vital component in the role of government.

Eastern European nations were defined by their relationship with the Soviet Union, which oscillated between repression and limited reform, until Mikhail Gorbachev's policies led to the collapse of communist governments in Eastern Europe and the dissolution of the Soviet Union.

Following World War II, Eastern European nations that had been overtaken by the Soviet Union were subject to the activities of the Soviet secret police, the NKVD (later renamed the KGB), which collaborated with local communists. Once the Red Army had cast out the Germans, the secret police began to arrest identified political enemies. The Communists, who were generally backed by the Soviets, came to power relatively gradually. They began by gaining control of the Interior Ministries, which controlled the local police forces, and seizing and reallocating farmland. Next, the Soviets and their agents took over the mass media, especially radio, as well as the education system.

The communists then took control of or supplanted the organizations of civil society, including church groups, sports teams, youth groups, trade unions, farmers' organizations and civic organizations. Finally, the communists undertook a large scale ethnic cleansing by resettling ethnic minorities far away, which often resulted in loss of life. For a while, cooperative non-Communist parties were allowed to exist. The communists remained highly popular because it was the Russians who had defeated Hitler and his Nazis. The stated goal of the communists was to assure long-term working-class harmony, but the Stalinist reality did not live up to these initial ideals.

All the countries in Eastern Europe, which generally meant the countries that had been freed and then occupied by the Soviet military, installed communist governments. These countries were theoretically independent from the Soviet Union, but in practice their independence was restricted – except in Yugoslavia, Albania and, to some extent, Romania. Stalin pressured these nations to refuse the assistance offered by the Marshall Plan and instead join the Molotov Plan, which grew into the Comecon (Council for Mutual Economic Assistance). Upon the creation of NATO in 1949, most Eastern European countries became members of the opposing Warsaw Pact.

Warsaw Pact Meeting, 1955

In 1989, after the collapse of the Iron Curtain, the political situation in Europe was altered and some of the previous members of the Warsaw Pact, including former Republics of the USSR, began joining NATO. The most notable of the former Warsaw Pact states to join NATO are Estonia, Latvia, Lithuania, the former Czechoslovak successor states of the Czech Republic and Slovakia, Bulgaria, Hungary and Poland. Further, with the fall of the Soviet Union, the former constituent republics gained independence. These former Socialist Republics within the Soviet Union are now Russia, Belarus, Ukraine, Latvia, Lithuania, Azerbaijan, Armenia, Georgia, Moldova, Kyrgyzstan, Tajikistan, Turkmenistan, Uzbekistan and Kazakhstan.

The Socialist Federal Republic of Yugoslavia was not a member of the Warsaw Pact. Instead, it was a founding member of the Non-Aligned Movement, which sought to avoid allegiance to either the NATO or Warsaw Pact blocs. The movement was successfully independent from both the Soviet Union and the Western bloc for most of the Cold War period, which allowed Yugoslavia and its other members to serve as business and political mediators between the blocs. In the early 1960s, the time of the Sino-Soviet split, the Socialist People's Republic of Albania severed its ties with the Soviet Union and chose to align itself with China. In September of 1968, Albania withdrew from the Warsaw pact due to the repression of the Prague Spring. In 1978, China and the Unites States established diplomatic relations and Albania severed its ties with China. Albania and especially Yugoslavia remained neutral for most of the Cold War, and thus were not joined with the Eastern Bloc.

Central and Eastern European nations within the Soviet Union bloc followed an economic model based on central planning, extensive social welfare and specialized production among bloc members.

The Soviet Union was the first country to implement a planned economy, in which the government had control over the production and distribution of goods. War Communism was the first instance of a planned economy in the Soviet Union; it included the nationalization of industry, centralized distribution of output, seizure of agricultural production and attempts to eradicate the circulation of money, private enterprises and free trade. In 1921, following the economic distress after World War I, Lenin supplanted War Communism with his New Economic Policy (NEP). The NEP made free trade and small business ownership legal; as a result, the Soviet economy improved rapidly.   Stalin abandoned the NEP when he took control of the country in 1928–1929 and imposed full adherence to central planning.

Joseph Stalin, Soviet dictator

To achieve that end, Stalin began to enforce the collectivization of agriculture and passed harsh labor laws. He mobilized resources in an effort to produce rapid industrialization in case of another war, which increased Soviet capacity in heavy industry and capital goods throughout the 1930s. Thus, the USSR was converted from a largely agrarian economy into an influential industrialized state, priming it to become a superpower after World War II. Between the 1930s and its collapse in the late 1980s, the operation of the Soviet economy stayed the same. The economy was centrally planned, implemented by Gosplan (the State Planning Committee of the Soviet Union) and organized into five-year plans. These plans were highly aggregated, provisional and open to impromptu intervention by superiors in the political leadership who controlled all important economic decisions.

Under these plans, resources and goals were generally denominated in rubles as opposed to physical goods. The use of credit was discouraged, but remained widely used. The distribution of output was made by fairly decentralized, unplanned contracting. In theory, prices were set by the government, but in practice prices were regularly negotiated, with unofficial horizontal alliances (between producers and factories, etc.) forming.

Education and health care, and numerous other basic services were funded by the state. Heavy industry and defense were designated as higher priorities than the production of consumer goods in the manufacturing sector. Consumer goods, especially in rural areas, were often hard to procure and not of high quality. Under the command economy, consumers had virtually no power over production, so their evolving demands (due to an increase in income) could not be satisfied by supplies at stringently fixed prices. In 1987, Mikhail Gorbachev tried to improve the economy by implementing perestroika. He loosened state control of enterprises, but did not yet permit it to be supplanted by market incentives, which led to a decrease in production output. The economy, which was already hurting due to a decrease in petroleum export revenues, started to fail. Prices remained fixed and property was mostly state-owned until after the dissolution of the Soviet Union.

After 1956, Soviet leader Nikita Khrushchev's de-Stalinization policies failed to meet their economic goals within the Soviet Union and prompted revolts in Eastern Europe.

When Stalin died on March 5, 1953, the Soviets could not agree upon a successor so the Communist Party officials elected to rule the Soviet Union jointly. Nikita Khrushchev eventually emerged as the Soviet leader in the mid-1950s. In 1956 Khrushchev gave what came to be known as the "Secret Speech," where he condemned the repression of Stalin's reign, ushering in an era of de-Stalinization. Many of the victims of the Purges of the late 1930s and early 1940s were "rehabilitated" during this period. Moscow saw Eastern Europe as a buffer zone for the defense of its western borders and guaranteed its control of the region by incorporating Eastern European countries into satellite states. The Sino-Soviet split occurred in the late 1950s due to the USSR under Khrushchev striving for reconciliation with Western powers, which Mao Zedong condemned. It resulted in division throughout the global Marxist-Leninist movement, with the governments of Albania, Cambodia and Somalia forming alliances with China rather than the USSR.

Khrushchev undertook "The Thaw," a complicated shift in political, cultural and economic policy in the Soviet Union. It included greater openness and contact with other countries and new social and economic policies with greater stress placed on commodity goods, which dramatically raised living standards while maintaining high levels of economic growth. In addition, censorship was relaxed.

Khrushchev's reforms in the agricultural and administrative sectors were largely unproductive. In 1962, a crisis arose between the United States and the Soviet Union over Soviet deployment of nuclear missiles in Cuba. The Cuban Missile Crisis was concluded with an agreement between the Soviet Union and the United States to remove their nuclear missiles from Cuba and Turkey, respectively. Khrushchev suffered much embarrassment and a decrease in prestige when it was eventually realized by the Soviets that the United States was already in the process of removing their missiles from Turkey because they were antiquated. He was eventually removed from power in 1964.

Following a long period of economic stagnation, Mikhail Gorbachev's internal reforms of perestroika and glasnost, designed to make the Soviet system more flexible, failed to stave off the collapse of the Soviet Union and the end of its hegemonic control over Eastern and Central European satellites.

Gorbachev made substantial alterations to the Soviet economy and party leadership, which are known as perestroika. For example, the glasnost policy permitted public access to information following a lengthy period of government censorship. Gorbachev also sought an end to the Cold War. The Soviet Union abandoned its nine-year war in Afghanistan in 1988 and started to remove its troops. The Iron Curtain fell with the fall of the Berlin Wall and the reunification of East and West Germany.

Mikhail Gorbachev, Soviet leader

In the late 1980s, the republics comprising the Soviet Union undertook legal proceedings to gain sovereignty over their territories. In order to do so, they cited Article 72 of the USSR constitution, which said that constituent republics were allowed to withdraw from the union. On April 7, 1990, a law was enacted which granted republics the right to legally secede from the Soviet Union if greater than two-thirds of the republic's residents voted to do so. In 1990, many republics undertook their first free elections in the Soviet era for their own national legislatures. Many of these legislatures then proceeded to enact legislation contradicting the Soviet Union's laws; this was referred to as the *"War of Laws."*

In 1989, the Russian SFSR, then the biggest republic in the Soviet Union, containing about half of its population, assembled a freshly elected Congress of People's Deputies with Boris Yeltsin as its chairman. On June 12, 1990, the Congress professed Russia's sovereignty over its territory and passed legislation that endeavored to supersede certain USSR's laws. After a landslide victory of Sąjudis (group that led the fight for independence) in Lithuania, the country announced its independence from the Soviet Union on March 11, 1990. A vote on whether or not to preserve the USSR was held on March 17, 1991 in nine republics (the rest boycotted the vote). A majority of people in those nine republics voted to preserve the Union, which provided Gorbachev with a small boost. In the summer of 1991, eight republics ratified the New Union Treaty, which would have loosened the Soviet Union.

Day of Lithuanian Independence in Šiauliai, 1990

The signing of the treaty was prevented by the August Coup—an attempted takeover by hardline members of the government and the KGB, who wanted to reverse Gorbachev's reforms and reaffirm the central government's control over the republics. After the coup failed, Yeltsin was lauded due to his decisive actions, which effectively ended Gorbachev's power and shifted the balance of power towards the republics. In August 1991, Latvia and Estonia declared their independence from the Soviet Union. Later that month, Gorbachev resigned as general secretary and soon afterward the Party's activities were indefinitely suspended—effectively ending its rule. By the fall, Gorbachev had lost all of his influence except in Moscow, where he still faced a challenge from Yeltsin, who had been elected President in June 1991.

The rise of new nationalisms in central and eastern Europe brought peaceful revolution in most countries but resulted in war and genocide in the Balkans and instability in some former Soviet republics.

Analysis of the secession of the 15 post-Soviet states is complicated. The Russian Federation is considered to be the principal successor to the Soviet Union as it maintained ownership of the former Soviet embassy properties, in addition to the old Soviet UN membership and permanent membership on the Security Council. The Baltic countries are considered to have *de jure* continuity with their pre-World War II governments through the non-recognition of Soviet incorporation that took place in 1940. The other 11 post-Soviet nations are thought of as newly-independent successors to the Soviet Union.

Four additional states claim independence from the other internationally acknowledged post-Soviet states, but their international recognition is limited: Abkhazia, Nagorno-Karabakh, South Ossetia and Transnistria. The most notable of these claims for statehood are in Nagorno-Karabakh and Transnistria. The issue of the status of Nagorno-Karabakh predates the Soviet Union; after World War I the territory was claimed by both ethnic Azeris and ethnic Armenians as part of their territory. After the fall of the USSR, it was officially under Azeri control, where it remains to this day. A war over the territory ended in 1994, with a tentative status quo still in place. The territory still belongs to Azerbaijan, although the population is almost 100% ethnic Armenian. There is a parallel government which calls itself the Republic of Nagorno-Karabakh; however, they receive only limited recognition as a legitimate state.

Transinitria is a breakaway republic in eastern Moldova. They seek to gain their independence from the predominantly Romanian-speaking Moldova, as Transnistria is one-third Russian and one-third Ukrainian; the majority of the population is Russian-speaking.

Another independence movement took root in the North Caucasus region of Chechnya. Their calls for independence have received little in the way of international recognition; however, post-Soviet Russia has waged two wars since independence to tame the restive republic. They have quieted down since the installation of the autocratic pro-Russian leader of the republic, Ramzan Kadyrov.

The fall of the Iron Curtain in 1989 altered the political landscape of the Eastern bloc and, in turn, the world. When Germany reunified in 1990, the Federal Republic of Germany took in the German Democratic Republic (East Germany). In 1991, Comecon, the Warsaw Pact and the Soviet Union were all disbanded. A lot of European countries that had been members of the Soviet Union regained their independence (Belarus, Moldova,

Ukraine, Latvia, Lithuania and Estonia). Czechoslovakia separated into the Czech Republic and Slovakia in 1993. Many of the new nations joined the European Union, including Bulgaria, the Czech Republic, Estonia, Hungary, Latvia, Lithuania, Poland, Romania and Slovakia.

Period 4: 1914-Present

> **Key Concept 4.3: During the 20th century, diverse intellectual and cultural movements questioned the existence of objective knowledge, the ability of reason to arrive at truth, and the role of religion in determining moral standards.**

The major trend of the 20th century European thought and culture moved from an optimistic view that modern science and technology could solve the problems of humankind to the formation of eclectic and sometimes skeptical movements that doubted the possibility of objective knowledge and of progress. Existentialism, post-modernism, and renewed religiosity challenged the perceived dogmatism of positivist science. While European society became increasingly secular, religion continued to play a role in the lives of many Europeans. Religious denominations addressed and in some cases incorporated modern ideas, such as tolerance toward other religions, as well as biblical and scientific scholarship that challenged the veracity of the Bible. The Christian churches made these accommodations as immigration, particularly from Muslim countries, altered the religious landscape, challenging Europe's traditional Judeo-Christian identity.

After World War I, prewar trends in physics, psychology and medical science accelerated. In physics, new discoveries and theories challenged the certainties of a Newtonian universe by introducing the ideas of relativity and uncertainty.

Psychology, which became an independent field of inquiry at the end of the 19th century, demonstrated that much human behavior stemmed from irrational sources. By the mid-20th century, dramatic new medical technologies prolonged life but created new social, moral and economic problems. During World War II, the potential dangers of scientific and technological achievements were demonstrated by the industrialization of death in the Holocaust and by the vast destruction wrought by the atomic bombs dropped on Japanese cities. It became clear that science could create weapons powerful enough to end civilization.

The art world in the 20th century was defined by experimentation and subjectivity, which asserted the independence of visual arts from realism. Futurism glorified the machine age; Dadaism satirized traditional aesthetics; and Expressionism and Surrealism explored the relationship between art and the emotions or the unconscious. In the interwar period, the slogan "form follows function" expressed a desire by architects to render the space in which we live and work more efficient. Throughout the century, American culture exerted an increasing pull on both elite and popular culture in Europe.

The widely held belief in progress, which had characterized much of 19th century thought, began to break down before World War I; the experience of the war intensified a sense of anxiety that permeated many facets of thought and culture, giving way by the century's end to the popularity of intellectual frameworks.

Major events and themes of the 20th century included World War I and World War II, decolonization, cultural homogenization through transportation and communications technology development, nationalism, world population growth, the Cold War and post-Cold War conflicts, awareness of climate change and environmental degradation and the emergence of the Digital Revolution. The century saw the first cross-continental and trans-oceanic global-scale total wars with World Wars I and II. International law recognized the right of nations to self-determine and nationalism proved to be a major geopolitical issue, with official decolonization and regional armed conflicts taking place, fueled by nationalistic fervor.

First transistorized computer in the U.S.A., completed in 1954

Huge shifts in culture, society, economics, ideology, politics, science, medicine and technology affected the way people were living in the 20th century. As technology advanced exponentially and in unprecedented ways, the common vocabulary began to

---

include terms like world war, ideology, nuclear war and genocide. The foundation of physical science was profoundly changed with discoveries and developments like the theory of relativity and quantum physics. Scientists accepted that the world and the universe were much more complex than they had previously known, and made it clear that contrary to what the science world may have believed at the end of the 19th century, scientific knowledge had a lot more than a few small blanks to fill.

The start of the 20th century saw transportation by horses, simple automobiles and freighters, but by its end humans were traveling by global commercial air travel, high-speed rail, cruise ships and even space shuttles. Automobiles and buses quickly became the standard and basic forms of personal transportation, replacing the horses that had done so for thousands of years. After the discovery of fossil fuel resources, this easily portable energy was exploited, allowing for the rapid advancement of technological developments, and also causing concerns about pollution and environmental detriment. In the 20th century, humans were able to land on and explore the moon for the first time.

World knowledge was more easily disseminated with the advancement of information technology (such as the Internet, computers, public education and paperback books), mass media and telecommunications. General welfare improved alongside advances in medical technology, and global life expectancy increased from 35 to 65 years during the course of the century. Conversely, warfare became more deadly and destructive than ever before due to technological advances. In World War II, 60 million were killed, and the creation of nuclear weapons gave humankind the means of quick annihilation.

The World Wars also ushered in a period where most of the world was not under imperial rule for the first time in human history. Expansion and colonization on the part of the traditional and historical imperial powers ended, and world affairs became more globalized and generally more cooperative. The last open declaration of war between major powers was in 1945. The world has become culturally homogenized to a certain extent since then due to communications technology, developments in worldwide transportation, international corporations, the dissemination and influence of Western culture and the end of the 20th century seeing, arguably, a true global economy.

When World War I began, Europeans were generally confident in the ability of science and technology to address human needs and problems despite the uncertainties created by new scientific theories and psychology.

Advances in technology and knowledge have always been present throughout the history of science. Scientific and technological innovations feed off one another and inspire fresh approaches to tough science problems. The scientific method having proven successful in the physical sciences, was then applied to other fields of study; these efforts resulted in the development of the social sciences.

Einstein published his general theory of relativity, represented by the famous equation $E = mc^2$ in 1905. It states that mass and energy are equivalent and means that when an object is at rest, it has a huge amount of potential energy. This seminal discovery was a paradigm shift in the field of physics and a major step towards general relativity and the theory of space-time in the next decade. In the same year, he published his *Theory of Special Relativity*, which has many fundamental implications; these are generally related to how our expectations of physical behavior of objects change the faster an object goes (the closer it comes to the speed of light) or the closer it comes to a massive gravitational

Albert Einstein, theoretical physicist

pull (especially in the case of a black hole, although these had not yet been discovered). In 1915, Einstein published his theory of general relativity, building on $E = mc^2$. This theory stated that space and time are unified (space-time) and that gravity bends space-time.

The interwar period was also a golden age of scientific discoveries. Ground was broken and new paradigms emerged in every major field, especially in cosmology and psychology. Rutherford's discovery of the neutron in 1920 was another pivotal moment in physics. Pluto was discovered by Clyde Tombaugh in 1930.

In cosmology, several of the most pivotal discoveries were made by the astronomer Edwin Hubble in the early 1920s. Hubble discovered that the universe was far vaster than just our galaxy and that the universe was expanding. A key component of these future discoveries was his pioneering work in finding a reliable way to measure the distances of stellar objects. Hubble decided to rely on a special type of star which is known to have a constant luminosity (the relationship of Cepheid variable stars, which had been discovered by Henrietta Swan Leavitt). This is called the "standard candle" measurement. Related to this, Hubble also discovered the red shift phenomenon in 1929, which enables us to measure the speed of objects relative to us by watching how light from them changes. The implications of Hubble's discoveries and theories were of course very important for cosmology. Without knowing the distances of objects and how fast they are moving, it is impossible to determine their mass, how much light they are radiating and everything else which can be derived from those two things. Without Hubble's standard candle measurement and red shift, cosmologists would not have been able to learn most of what they have learned since.

In 1900, Sigmund Freud published a pivotal work in psychology, *The Interpretation of Dreams*, which presented the theory that resolving internal conflicts is the primary focus and that dreaming has a central role in it. In psychology, Carl Jung published his theory of individuation in human development in *The Psychology of the Unconscious* in 1912. This was the first step in the creation of the field of analytical psychology by Jung. In the 1890s, Ivan Pavlov had performed his famous experiments with dogs, which led to the theory of classical conditioning.

Sigmund Freud, founder of psychoanalysis

Biologists also catapulted the field of psychology to new levels by discovering much about how the human brain works. In the early 20th century, neuroscience was recognized as a distinct field of study and ground-breaking discoveries were being made in that field. But not all of the discoveries were beneficial. The treatment of mental patients was in its infancy and many inhumane methods and inaccurate theories were employed for generations, causing damage to millions before research provided better answers.

Many people feared science because of the negative side effects of industrialization, early experimental failures and the unprecedented pace of change. In the early twentieth century, the industrial age was still new and while Europeans generally appreciated the good things which it brought, they also recognized its negative side effects painfully well – the unprecedented lethality of the negative side-effects of science, pollution, greed and overcrowding in the cities. The greatest contributor of all may have been World War I, so devastating largely due to new weapons developed by scientists. People broadly associated these negative side-effects with science, since it was the scientists who had enabled all the negative outcomes, as well as the positive ones.

Scientific experimentation was a new phenomenon; scientists were still working out many flaws. There were many early experimental failures which had devastating consequences and there were no established rules of experimental ethics, as there are today. The more drastic scientific failures, especially in the field of medicine, scared people: psychiatric treatment at that time often involved treatments which would be considered quackery today and damaged the patient instead of helping. Some of the most notorious examples are: electroshock therapy, lobotomy, incarceration of people with mental conditions in dungeon-like cells and physical abuse of in-patients.

The world also saw many lethal accidents occurring on a scale never experienced before, the result of unsafe machines such as steam engines exploding and trains colliding or derailing. During World War I, the Canadian city of Halifax was devastated when a French ship carrying tons of explosives and flammable acid collided with a Norwegian vessel. The resulting explosion was the World War I equivalent of an atomic bomb. It killed almost two thousand people instantly, destroyed a major part of the city and sent the anchor of one of the ships flying through the air to the opposite side of Halifax harbor, where it remains today as a memorial to the victims.

The growth in science in the years leading up to this point was the necessary condition for this tragedy to occur, and highlighted the need for creating safeguards in order to prevent unchecked scientific progress leading to unintended consequences.

Safeguards are developed by professionals who work in each free market industry, from experience and discussion, albeit with the aid of scientific knowledge. Their findings are reported to governments if and when politicians request them.

The fear of science was popularized in science fiction stories, which began in the industrial age and exploded in the World War I era. *The War of the Worlds*, written by H.G. Wells at the peak of the industrial age/early age of scientific experimentation, tapped into the pervasive fear that superior technology in the hands of an ill-intentioned enemy would be used to devastating effect. This fear would be somewhat realized in the real war of the worlds, World War I, which took place twenty years later. Radio (1938) and motion picture (1953) adaptations, using both actors and elaborate special effects, made the experience Wells wrote about much more "real" and frightening than reading words in a book.

Still from "The War of the Worlds" film (1953)

The pace of change which science brought to the world throughout the 20th century was far faster than anything Europeans had ever seen before. Human beings have an aversion to change, which has a natural psychological basis as well as a cultural one. Europeans feared – as many still do today – that the pace of intellectual change was getting out of control. This fear would peak with the development of the atomic bomb in the next period of history. The splitting of the atom could be used to modernize the entire world — or to annihilate it in a single day.

The effects of world war and economic depression undermined confidence in science and human reason, giving impetus to existentialism and producing post-modernism in the post-1945 period.

One of the key reactions to the two World Wars was the growing belief that the answers on how both individuals and society progress could not be found in science and strict rationalism alone. There was no means by which to express the horrors of the First World War in previously popular mediums, as the sheer tragedy of the events that occurred in that war were too great to comprehend.

This resulted in the rise of post-modernism. This was expressed in the arts, architecture and philosophy. The most poignant example of post-modern art was the Pablo Picasso painting *Guernica.* This piece was an imaginative representation of the Nazi Luftwaffe's bombing campaign on the civilians of Guernica, Spain in the Spanish Civil War. The civilian death toll and the sheer human cost of these events would have been impossible to express in the realistic styles of painting popular in earlier eras. As a result, Picasso painted a work that represented the horrors of the event in a manner that was only possible through the application of the post-modernist technique of disembodiment of the subject(s). There are many other examples of post-modernist art, but this is the most striking in showing the devastation visited upon humanity by scientific progress used for military purposes.

The most lasting tradition which the onset of post-modernity fostered was in the field of philosophy and the social sciences. Although the modern era predominantly focused on the scientific method and studies that relied upon empirical observation, the philosophers and social scientists of the post-modern period began to call these methods into question. The central focus of these authors tended to be the belief that there was no scientific means by which to approach society and/or culture. These things existed outside of the realm of empirical observation, as their meaning lay in power structures, narrative and historical traditions. There were many scholars of earlier eras upon whom the post-modernists would draw, including Karl Marx, Max Weber, Soren Kierkegaard, Freidrich Nietzsche and Ludwig Wittgenstein. Drawing on the philosophical lines of enquiry opened by these philosophers, Jacques Derrida was the first philosopher who can truly be called post-modern.

Derrida developed the notion of "deconstructionism," seeing a need to break down into its constituent parts an argument or idea as a means to understand the context in which it was formulated. The context in which the words written in a text have meaning are open to the interpretation of the individual reading it, which often leads to the (sometimes deliberate) misrepresentation of the point the writer is attempting to make. Derrida's work greatly influenced that of one of the preeminent philosophers of post-modernity, Michel Foucault.

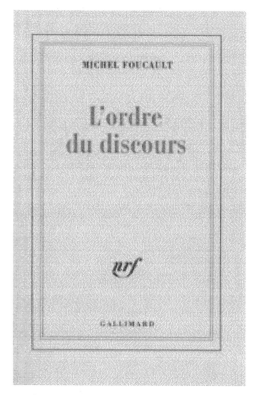

Foucault's "The Order of Things"

Foucault is considered to be one of the most impenetrable authors in western philosophy, due to the difficulty in understanding his writing and the many contradictions in the notions found therein. His critique of society is one that is still pertinent today, in that he saw that any given society tended to be a representation of the power structure of that society, which could only act at the behest of those who hold the power in the society in question. Flowing from this, he posited the notion that language, by its very nature, is a power structure that is used to keep people from expressing themselves in a manner that allows them to truly exercise their agency. His seminal works, *The History of Sexuality, Discipline and Punish, The Archaeology of Knowledge* and *The Order of Things,* along with his many lectures, has

created a body of work which is essential reading for those who are interested in understanding the world from a post-modern (though many of his earlier writings were distinctly modern) philosophical perspective.

The most influential movement in post-modern philosophy was that of the Frankfurt School, which was initially based at the Institute of Social Research at the Goethe Frankfurt University. The most influential of these authors were Theodor Adorno, Max Horkheimer, Herbert Marcuse and Walter Benjamin. They developed a larger field of enquiry which would eventually be called "critical theory." The name of the theory, to a large extent, sums up the goals of the Frankfurt School authors in that they were deeply critical of Western society. In essence, they felt that the strict rationality of Enlightenment society inevitably led to "the dictatorship of rationality" imposed through technological domination over both people and nature. They were crucial in formulating the opinion in the social sciences of the importance of narrative and the domination that an individual or group can have over society when they speak in the name of the whole.

The largest notion that began with the work of the philosophers above was the establishment of the idea that it is structures which govern society. The post-modernists, standing on the shoulders of the giants of previous eras such as Heidegger, Kierkegaard, Hegel, Kant and many others, began to challenge the notion that agency was the defining characteristic shaping society and the individual. They stressed the importance of understanding the narrative behind these structures as a means to liberate oneself from the domination of hegemonic societies. In the contemporary discourse, the narratives set up by the philosophers of post-modernity led to the creation of schools of thought such as post-Marxism, neo-Marxism, neo-Gramscianism and contemporary post-structuralism. That these schools of thought are now taken for granted in European universities has led to their being seen as the modern manifestation of "Continental Philosophy." It is important for the American student to note that the theories developed in and from post-modernism are still not widely accepted in American universities, where the tradition of analytic Anglo-American philosophy still prevails.

Science and technology yielded impressive material benefits, but also caused immense destruction and posed challenged to objective knowledge.

There were enormous advances in science throughout the century. Building off progress made in the 19th century, revolutionizing and radical developments were made in the life, human and physical sciences. Funding for science helped promote Big Science, especially after World War II. Mathematics branched out into more specialized and abstract studies. One of the defining aspects of the 1900s was the dramatic advancement of technology. In areas of communication, medicine, warfare and travel there were advances due to improved scientific practices and organized and concentrated research. Daily human life was greatly changed with advances in the medical field, communications and information technology, and transportation technology.

In the modern period of history, scientific discoveries reached a new point with unprecedented benefits made available, but the trade-off was an unprecedented risk. The splitting of the atom is key to both electricity generation (which can power a city) and to a bomb (which can instantly kill hundreds of thousands and level entire cities). Several European-born scientists worked on the creation of the atomic bomb which was used to level Hiroshima and Nagasaki. In the early 1980s, a nuclear reactor in Soviet Ukraine, built with inadequate safeguards, had a catastrophic meltdown which devastated the surrounding region. In 2011, a similar disaster at the Fukushima nuclear power plant in Japan poured huge amounts of radioactive material into the Pacific and, like Chernobyl, made a huge sector of the surrounding area uninhabitable.

Abandoned hotel in Chernobyl after the nuclear disaster

Oil has been a primary fuel source longer than nuclear power has. There have been many massive spills of oil, usually from ocean-going tankers but sometimes also at the sources where oil is mined. In the 1980s, the Exxon oil tanker *Valdez* collided with rocks in Alaska, creating a huge spill which devastated the environment. In 2010, a British Petroleum oil rig operating in the Gulf of Mexico had a catastrophic failure which cost the lives of eleven crew members and devastated the coastal environment of the entire Gulf region, especially in Louisiana.

The challenge to the certainties of the Newtonian universe in physics opened the door to uncertainty in other fields by undermining faith in objective knowledge, while also providing the knowledge necessary for the development of nuclear weapons and power.

The only time nuclear weapons have been used was by the United States against Japan at the end of World War II. A uranium fission bomb was detonated over Hiroshima, Japan by the U.S. Army Air Force on August 6, 1945. Three days later, a plutonium fission bomb was detonated over Nagasaki, Japan. About 200,000 civilians and military personal were killed in the attacks. Only a handful of countries possess nuclear weapons or seek them, and since the devastation of Hiroshima and Nagasaki, approximately two thousand nuclear weapons have been detonated for testing and demonstration.

The countries known to have carried out this type of detonation are the United States, the Soviet Union (and then Russia), the United Kingdom, France, the People's Republic of China, India, Pakistan and North Korea. Israel is believed to possess nuclear weapons but does not acknowledge it. South Africa, towards the end of its apartheid regime, lied about having nuclear weapons but its arsenals were disassembled. It did this to cooperate with the Nuclear Non-Proliferation Treaty and receive coverage by international safeguards. According to estimates of the Federation of American Scientists, based on data from 2012, there are over 17,000 nuclear warheads worldwide; 4,300 of these warheads are believed to be "operational."

Werner Heisenberg, Enrico Fermi, Niels Bohr and Robert Oppenheimer are representative examples of numerous scientists who played pivotal roles in the evolution and progress in nuclear power and technology. Werner Heisenberg was a prominent physicist who pioneered Quantum theory. Unlike many of his Jewish colleagues who had to flee Germany, he remained in Germany during World War II and led the German atomic energy project. In 1939, Niels Bohr brought news to Fermi that the Germans had achieved nuclear fission – a pivotal step in developing both nuclear power and an atomic bomb. He was subsequently employed in the Manhattan Project, where his major contribution was solving how to create modulated neuron initiators, a problem which had been vexing the scientists there.

Enrico Fermi was pivotal to the Manhattan Project. He was one of the first to alert western governments of the possibility of an atomic bomb and that the Germans had been making significant progress in that aim. The leader of the Manhattan Project scientific team was Robert Oppenheimer, who spent the rest of his life campaigning against the creation which he had made possible.

Medical theories and technologies extended life, but posed social and moral questions that eluded consensus and crossed religious, political and philosophical perspectives.

Medics and mobile hospital units trained for dealing with massive injuries and infection commonly seen in wartime conditions were first included in the military during the 20th century. The technology for prosthetic limbs and plastic surgery improved and was more readily available as thousands of injured and maimed troops returned from battle. New knowledge of plastic surgery was applied to cosmetic surgery and other elective surgery. New methods on preventing gangrene were invented by Alexis Carrel and Henry Dakin in World War I. They developed an irrigation method coupled with a germicide named Dakin's solution.

Roentgen's invention of the X-ray and the electrocardiograph were first used in World War I to monitor internal bodily functions. During the time between the two World Wars, the first anti-bacterial agents, such as sulfa antibiotics were discovered. During the Nazi regime, there was human experimentation: the Aktion T4 euthanasia program and the murder of patients (especially those with disabilities), among other atrocities. The Doctors' Trial was held to look at the inhumane acts of the Nazis as well as other cases and to develop a set of medical ethics and principles, such as the Nuremburg Code, to prevent a recurrence of such horrors. The Japanese created programs perpetrating biological warfare upon the Chinese, in China in 1937; Japanese doctors in Unit 731 performed vivisections on Chinese victims.

The difficulty of predicting characteristics of offspring on the basis of their heredity was more fully appreciated by the late 1920s. Eugenics was dismissed as unscientific based on its extremely simplistic theories. The Great Depression fostered discussion and criticism of the pervading idea that human worth was equal to economic value. Society rejected most ideas about "unfit" members of society and "racial hygiene" after becoming aware of the atrocities committed by Nazi Germany on those principles. Nazi leaders were tried at the Nuremburg Trials, which also resulted in formalized standards of medical ethics and policies and the 1950 UNESCO statement on race after the genocidal medical practices of the Nazis had been fully revealed.

The idea of eugenics reentered public discourse with advances in genetic engineering in the 1980s. These advances made it possible to produce genetically modified organisms, including food. The modification of the human genome was seemingly possible as endeavors like the Human Genome Project came into existence. In the modern research of the 21st century however, there was a more cautious attitude toward eugenics, which history had warned was something to fear, not to embrace. In Article 23 of the Convention on the Rights of Persons with Disabilities, disabled individuals are guaranteed protection from compulsory sterilization and of the right to adopt children.

Military technologies made possible industrialized warfare, genocide, nuclear proliferation and the risk of global nuclear war.

There was a shift during the history of warfare in the early 19th century and from the beginning of the Industrial Revolution to the Atomic Age. In this period, nation-states arose that created and equipped huge armies, navies and air forces using processes of industrialization. Armies were conscripted on mass levels, advances in rapid transportations (first on land, and then by sea and air) were created, telegraph and wireless communications were utilized and total war was first conceptualized and carried out in this era. Military technological advances took the form of chemical weapons, rifled breech-loaded infantry weapons capable of high rates of fire, high-velocity breech-loaded artillery, armored warfare, metal warships, submarines and aircraft.

After the first ever detonation of a nuclear or atomic bomb on July 16, 1945, the world entered the Atomic Age or the Atomic Era. In 1933, nuclear chain reactions were hypothesized and in December 1942, the first artificial self-sustaining chain reaction, called the Trinity test, occurred. The bombings of Hiroshima and Nagasaki ended World War II and were the first large-scale uses of nuclear technology. Previous to the end of the World War II, the coming of atomic power had been anticipated by scientists as a valuable tool of progress and modernity. After World War II, there were shifts in sociopolitical thinking which affected technology development. The promise of atomic power had soured for many due to social issues such as the massive death and destruction and lingering after-effects of radiation from the nuclear attacks on Japan, the dangerous U.S.-USSR nuclear arms race, the Chernobyl disaster, the Three Mile Island accident and the problems surrounding bomb plant cleanup and nuclear plant waste disposal and decommissioning.

Trinity atomic bomb, sixteen milliseconds after detonation

Organized religion continued to play an important role in European social and cultural life despite the challenges of military and ideological conflict, modern secularism, and rapid social changes.

In the 20th century, the secularization of Western society that started in the 19th century was challenging Christianity. However, Christianity was also being strengthened by its spread to other, non-Western regions of the world. After the Second Vatican Council of the Catholic Church, Christian ecumenism gained traction, beginning at the 1910 Edinburgh Missionary Conference. In both Protestant and Catholic Christianity, and especially in Anglicanism, the Liturgical Movement gained importance.

Meanwhile, Eastern Orthodox and other Christians were facing persecution in the communist countries of the Soviet Union and Eastern Europe, where atheism was state-promoted. Western and Eastern Christianity came to have much more contact as Russian Orthodox Christians migrated to Western Europe and the Americas to escape persecution. Even with this new influx of Eastern Christians to the West, church attendance in Western Europe declined more than in the East. In an attempt to modernize, the Roman Catholic Church adopted many reforms. Greater followings in mainland China, Taiwan and Japan were also acquired through Catholic and Protestant missions to the Far East.

Europe has experienced a general trend toward secularism and away from Christian teachings and general religious observance. The Enlightenment, which spurred a "secularization of society," is acknowledged as one of the factors responsible for the spread of secularism. According to the Gallup International Millennium Survey, less than half of the European population gave God "high importance," only about 40 percent said they believed in a "personal God" and only about one-sixth of Europeans regularly attend religious services.

The challenges of totalitarianism and communism in Central and Eastern Europe brought mixed responses from the Christian churches.

The relationship between totalitarian governments and the church was highly complex in the 20th century. Though there was a decline in the overall religiosity of the people of Europe throughout this period, the vast majority still held strict religious views. As a result, even under totalitarian and atheistic or quasi-atheistic governments, there was the need to maintain relations with the churches within their jurisdiction.

One of the most interesting relationships one could find in this era was that of the Catholic Church and the Nazi Government of Germany. After the war, the Catholic Church would be heavily criticized for its assistance in laundering wealth stolen from the Jews of Europe and factions that assisted in helping Nazi war criminals flee to South America. However, the Church suffered some persecution under the Nazi regime as well. Many Catholics found themselves alongside their Jewish compatriots in the concentration camps of Europe, and many influential Church officials did what they could to assist the Jews before they themselves were targeted. Despite the heroism on the part of the churchmen "on the ground" in areas under direct Nazi control, the hierarchy of the Church was culpable in some of the crimes the Nazis committed, and initially helped the Nazis in their rise to power by not speaking out against the early signals the Nazis gave as to their intent for the establishment of a worldwide Reich.

Another institution which was not vociferous in its criticism of Nazism was the German Lutheran Church. It is easy to criticize these institutions if one ignores the context of Weimar Germany; however, when one takes the conditions the Germans found themselves in, it is easy to understand how individuals could fall under the spell of a charismatic leader who promised he knew how to solve the problems of the day.

There is no religious figure who better embodies this reality than Martin Niemoller, Protestant pastor. When the Nazi Party first began he was openly supportive of the group, thinking that they could solve the problems of Weimar Germany. Niemoller was a leftist by nature and it is easy to forget that much of the early agenda and narrative of the Nazis was leftist in nature. It would turn out that this was merely a façade. However, it is only through historical analysis that we are able to make this judgment; history unfolds in a far different manner to those living through it than to those examining it in retrospect. Niemoller would eventually become vociferously anti-Nazi, and wrote a poem that came to symbolize the dangers of a tolerant attitude toward Nazism:

> *"First they came for the Socialists, and I did not speak out – Because I was not a socialist. Then they came for the Trade Unionists, and I did not speak out – Because I was not a Trade Unionist. Then they came for the Jews, and I did not speak out – Because I was not a Jew. Then they came for me – and there was no one left to speak."*

Niemoller spent much of the war in a concentration camp and only narrowly escaped the fate of the millions who perished under Nazi extermination. He spent the rest of his life campaigning for peace and against totalitarianism.

Arguably the most outspoken religious figure who criticized the Nazis was the Lutheran pastor Dietrich Bonhoeffer. From the moment Hitler came to power, he was deeply skeptical of the promises made by the Nazi Party, and gave a speech to this effect immediately after their rise to power. He eventually found safe passage to the United States, but his desire to assist the German people in defeating the Nazis led to his returning to the country on the last steamer to depart the United States for Germany until the end of the war. He worked with the resistance movement and continued to preach for a tolerant interfaith dialogue. He was eventually imprisoned by the Nazis in 1943. He was held near Berlin, then moved to a concentration camp where he was hanged as the Allies were advancing towards Germany.

Plaque commemorating Dietrich Bonhoeffer, Lutheran pastor and anti-Nazi dissident

Another influential figure in resisting totalitarianism was Pope John Paul II. Karol Jozef Wojytila, who would become Pope John Paul II, was born in Wadowice, Poland and would become a crucial figure in the dismantling of the "Iron Curtain." Polish by birth, he had a unique ability to reawaken a spirit of religiosity that had long been bubbling just below the surface in Poland. Many credit his historic visit to Poland in 1979 with awakening the Solidarnosch ("Solidarity") movement of Lech Walesa, which would eventually topple the Soviet-allied Polish government that had been in place since the end of World War II.

Reform in the Catholic Church found expression in the second Vatican Council, which redefined the Church's dogma and practices and began to redefine its relations with other religious communities.

Relations between the Roman Catholic Church and the modern world were uneasy, and were addressed by the Second Vatican Council. It was the second ecumenical council to take place in the Vatican at Saint Peter's Basilica, and was the 21st council overall. On October 11, 1962, through the Holy See, the council opened under the pontificate of Pope John XXIII and closed on the 1965 Feast of the Immaculate Conception under Pope Paul VI.

The council established several changes, including the call to holiness for everyone (even those who are not clergy), ecumenical efforts towards dialogue with other religions and the renewal of consecrated life by revising the charisma of the church. More specific changes included: vernacular languages being spoken in Mass instead of Latin, use of less ornate clerical regalia, Eucharistic prayers being revised, the liturgical calendar abbreviated and officiates began to face the congregation or the "East" and the Crucifix. Modern aesthetic changes were made to contemporary Catholic liturgical music and artwork, many of which are still a point of contention among devout Catholics.

Pope Paul VI delivers the ring to Cardinal Joseph Ratzinger

Of those who took part in the council's opening session, four have become pontiffs: Cardinal Giovanni Battista Montini, who on succeeding Pope John XXIII took the name of Paul VI; Bishop Albino Luciani, the future Pope John Paul I; Bishop Karol Wojtyła, who became Pope John Paul II; and Father Joseph Ratzinger, present as a theological consultant, who became Pope Benedict XVI.

Increased immigration into Europe altered Europe's religious makeup, causing debate and conflict over the role of religion in social and political life.

Immigration in the 20th century took on characteristics that had not been seen in the industrial era, notably the introduction of immigrants from completely different cultural contexts. As the 1960s ushered in a wave of decolonization, many of the citizens of the newly sovereign states sought to improve their living conditions by emigrating to their former metropoles. Thus, large numbers of people of Afro-Caribbean, Indian and Pakistani descent immigrated to the United Kingdom, while people from the Maghreb immigrated to France. This wave of emigration resulted in massive demographic shifts in the UK and France in particular, causing a backlash on the part of the traditional white population. Racist attacks were the norm in Britain in the 1970s and 1980s, eventually giving rise to the anti-immigrant "British National Party."

In France, the relationship between Frenchmen and their new immigrants was even more complex. The French colonization of North Africa, particularly Algeria, was seen as a unique "uplifting" component. The French believed that through exposing people to the ideas of French philosophy and the French revolutionary spirit, anyone could become a true Frenchman. This project was carried out to its fullest extent in Algeria, considered to be a sovereign territory of France as opposed to being a colony. While they were successful in establishing a lycees system of education and in promulgating the use of the French language, a large military presence was always necessary to prevent rebellion.

Ever since the French granted independence to their former territory after the end of the Franco-Algerian War, there has been a steady flow of migrants moving from Algeria to France. Many of these migrants held French passports, which gave them easy access. Once these migrants made their way to France, they found that even though they spoke French and had been educated in the French education system, the mainland population was not at all receptive to their presence.

The majority of these French Algerians, who were not of European ancestry, lived in *banlieues* (self-created ghettos) on the outskirts of major cities. In these highly concentrated immigrant areas, there has been an increase in religiosity due to the fact that they found themselves living in a society that was rejecting their very presence. This has meant that mosques and other religious organizations were often the only means for these individuals to feel a part of a group. At the same time, this increased religiosity of a select group of people has led to the rise of far-right anti-immigrant groups such as the Front Nationale, founded by Jean-Marie La Penne, and now run by his daughter Marine Le Pen.

In Britain, immigration from former colonies was also strong; however, those who lived in colonial possessions were not seen as British citizens and therefore their immigration was more difficult. There was a large immigration of individuals of Afro-Caribbean descent from the West Indies, along with Pakistanis and Indians from the Indian subcontinent. Immigrants from the West Indies have had their difficulties in adapting to life in Britain; however, as they share a Christian cultural context, they have largely thrived in the UK.

Those coming from India and Pakistan have had a more difficult time. This has proven especially true for those of an Islamic religion, particularly in those two to three generations removed from the actual migration. The first generation migrants worked diligently to establish themselves in the community and were largely successful in doing so, though they had to endure hostility on the part of the British; to many they were not welcome in the country. The first generations tolerated this as they figured that it was far easier than moving back to the economically impoverished land from which they came. However, the initial ostracizing of these migrant communities has largely continued, leading the succeeding generations, which had no experience with the difficulty of life on the Indian subcontinent, to turn to radicalization.

Many of these young people (mostly males) have turned to radicalization as a means to gain an identity. New immigrants from the Indian subcontinent do not accept them because they have never lived in the region, and the British do not accept them because they have a faith different from that of the majority of the population. This came to a head with the July 7, 2005 bombings of the London Underground and Bus Network, carried out by British-born Islamic Fundamentalists who had largely been radicalized on British shores.

During the 20th century, the arts were defined by experimentation, self-expression and subjectivity, with the increasing influence of the United States in both elite and popular culture.

The main events which led to the rejection of the physical and rational world depicted by the 18th century Enlightenment were new discoveries of relativity by Einstein, the psychological theories of Sigmund Freud and the unprecedented large-scale destruction of civilizations in the two World Wars that was made possible by rapid technological developments. 20th century art has followed a pattern of searching for new standards and endless possibilities, then repudiating that attempt and trying again. With this in mind, art movements such as Impressionism, Expressionism, Fauvism, Cubism, Dadaism, and Surrealism are not necessarily relevant outside of the time frame in which they existed. Other cultures' influence can be seen in Western art; for example, Picasso's work shows influences from Primitivism, Iberian sculpture and African sculpture.

Japonism and Japanese woodcuts (that were themselves influenced by Western Renaissance designs) influenced Impressionism and later artistic advances. Examples include Paul Gauguin's interests in Oceanic art, the popularity among the cognoscenti in early 20th century Paris of newly discovered African fetish sculptures, and other works from non-European cultures influencing the work of Picasso, Henri Matisse and many of their contemporaries.

The 19th century's search for truth gave us Modernism, but as the century progressed, it gave way to a realization that the ideal was unattainable. The unstoppable evolutions of science and technology were understood to be inevitable, leading to the late Modern and Post-modern periods. During these periods, cultures metamorphosed. Furthermore, the demarcation of one culture from another became more and more porous, leading it to be more readily understood in terms of a global, rather than regional culture.

New movements in the visual arts, architecture, and music demolished existing aesthetic standards, explored subconscious and subjective states, and satirized Western society and its values.

Fauvism, Cubism, Expressionism, and Futurism were all movements that blossomed in the early 20th century. Between 1910 and the end of the First World War, and after the peak of cubism, quite a few other movements came out of Paris. The Italian painter Giorgio de Chirico relocated there in July 1911; his brother Andrea already lived in Paris. Through Andrea, Chirico met Pierre Laprade, a member of the Salon d'Automne, where he showed three of his surreal works: *Enigma of the Oracle*, *Enigma of an Afternoon* and *Self-Portrait*. During 1913, he showed his art at the Salon des Indépendants and Salon d'Automne, where they were noticed by Pablo Picasso,

Portrait of Giorgio de Chirico, artist

Guillaume Apollinaire, and other artists. His gripping and mystifying paintings were inspirations to the burgeoning surrealist movement.

World War I ushered in an end to this period in art, but it also marked the beginning of some anti-art movements, such as Dada, which includes the art of Marcel Duchamp, and of Surrealism. Artist groups (like de Stijl and the Bauhaus) developed new concepts regarding the interrelation of the arts, architecture, design, and art education. Modern art was first introduced in the U.S. with the Armory Show of 1913 and through European artists who had relocated to the United States during the same period. However, it was only after World War II that the United Sates became a breeding ground for new artistic movements. During the 1950s and 1960s, Abstract Expressionism, Color field painting, Pop art, Op art, Hard-edge painting, Minimal art, Lyrical Abstraction, Fluxus, "Happenings," video art, Post-minimalism, Photorealism and various other movements all came about. Novel art forms claimed the attention of critics and curators in the later part of the 1960s and early 1970s, including land art, performance art and conceptual art.

In the latter part of the 1970s, cultural critics began talking about "the end of painting," with an increasing number of artists experimenting with new technologies like video. However, traditional painting regained its place in the art world during the 1980s and 1990s; this included neo-expressionism and the revival of symbolic painting. By the end of the 20th century, the concept of "the modern" was being questioned by many artists and architects who began to create typical "postmodern" works.

Throughout the century, a number of writers challenged traditional literary conventions, questioned Western values, and addressed controversial social and political issues.

The main periods for the Euro-American literary tradition — modernist literature and postmodern literature — are understood to be divided by World War II, and span roughly 1900-1940 and 1960-1990 respectively. What is called "contemporary literature" is typically thought of as post-1960.

Franz Kafka (1883 – 1924) was a German-language novelist and short story writer, often touted by critics as one of the most important authors of the 20th century. His literary works, such as *Die Verwandlung* (The Metamorphosis), *Der Process* (The Trial), and *Das Schloss* (The Castle), deal with topics like alienation, physical and psychological cruelty, parent–child issues, characters on frightening journeys, the complexities of government, and frightening magical transformations.

James Augustine Aloysius Joyce (1882 – 1941) was an Irish author and poet and is understood to be one of the most influential writers of the modernist avant-garde era in the early 20th century. Joyce is well known for his novel *Ulysses* (1922), in which the episodes of Homer's *The Odyssey* are given modern-day Dublin equivalents using different literary styles, perhaps the most famous being the stream of consciousness technique.

Erich Maria Remarque (1898 – 1970), was a German author who wrote many books about the horrors of war. The most well-known of these is the novel *All Quiet on the Western Front* (1928), about German soldiers in World War I. It was made into a movie that won the Academy Award for best picture of 1930. His depictions of the German military mentality and the rise of fascism were viewed negatively by the Nazis, who burned many of his books. Remarque later resided in the United States and Switzerland.

Jean-Paul Sartre, French philosopher and writer

Jean-Paul Charles Aymard Sartre (1905–1980) was a French philosopher, playwright, novelist, political activist, biographer, and literary critic. Sartre was one of the prominent figures of existentialism and phenomenology, and is considered one of the leaders in 20th century French philosophy and Marxism. His work continues to influence the disciplines of sociology, critical theory, post-colonial theory and literary studies. Another noted feature of Sartre was his open relationship with the key feminist theorist Simone de Beauvoir. He always chose to decline official honors, saying that "a writer should not allow himself to be turned into an institution," Sartre declined the Nobel Prize in Literature in 1964.

Period 4: 1914-Present

> **Key Concept 4.4: Demographic changes, economic growth, total war, disruptions of traditional social patterns and competing definitions of freedom and justice altered the experiences of everyday life.**

The disruption of two wars, the reduction of barriers to migration within Europe because of economic integration, globalization and the arrival of new permanent residents from outside Europe changed the everyday lives of Europeans in significant ways. For the first time, more people lived in cities than in rural communities. Economic growth—though interrupted by repeated wars and economic crises—generally increased standards of living, leisure time (despite the growing number of two-career families), educational attainment and participation in mass cultural entertainments. The falling of the birth rate to below replacement levels enhanced the financial well-being of individual families even as it reduced the labor force. To support labor-force participation and encourage families, governments instituted family leave policies that supported children and created large-scale guest-worker programs.

Europe's involvement in an increasingly global economy exposed its citizens to new goods, ideas and practices. Altogether, the disruptions of war and decolonization led to new demographic patterns – a population increase followed by falling birth rates and the immigration of non-Europeans – and to uncertainties about European's cultural identity. Even before the collapse of communism and continuing afterward, a variety of groups on both the left and right began campaigns of terror in the name of ethnic or national autonomy, or in radical opposition to free-market ideology. Other groups worked within the democratic system to achieve nationalist and xenophobic goals.

By the 1960's, the rapid industrialization of the previous century had created significant environmental problems. Environmentalists argued that the unfettered free-market economy could lead Europe to ecological disaster, and they challenged the traditional economic and political establishment with demands for sustainable development sensitive to environmental, aesthetic and moral constraints. At the same time, a generation that had never experienced either economic depression or a large-scale war came of age, critical of existing institutions and beliefs and calling for greater political and personal freedom. These demands culminated with the 1968 youth revolts in Europe's major cities and in challenges to institutional authority structures, especially those in universities.

Feminist movements accelerated the active participation for women in politics, and before the end of the century, several women had become heads of government or state. Yet traditional social patterns and institutions continued to hinder the achievement of gender equality. While these internal movements and struggles went on, immigrants from around the world poured into Europe, and by the end of the century, Europeans found themselves living in multi-ethnic and multi-religious communities. Immigrants defied traditional expectations of integration and assimilation and persisted in socio-cultural values different from those of 20th-century Europeans. Many Europeans refused to consider the newcomers as true members of their society. In the early 21st century, Europeans continue to wrestle with issues of social justice and how to define European identity.

The 20th century was characterized by large-scale suffering brought on by warfare and genocide as well as tremendous improvements in the standards of living.

World War II was the most lethal war in history in terms of the total number of people who died. Over 60 million people, about 3 percent of the world's population in 1940, perished as a result of the war. The statistics about the number of people killed by World War II are inconsistent, with estimates of the total number of deaths ranging from 50 million to over 80 million (these numbers include deaths that occurred due to war-related disease and famine) and the total number of military dead ranging from 21 to 25 million (these numbers include the deaths of about 5 million prisoners of war who perished in captivity).

American soldiers pay their respects at the World War II cemetery

The mid-20th century is historically unique in that its most important advances directly or indirectly resulted from economic and technological innovation. Economic development led to widespread changes in daily living, to a degree not seen before in the human history.

Throughout the 20th century, the world's gross domestic product (GDP) per capita increased by a factor of five, which was greater than in all earlier centuries combined (including the 19th century, when the Industrial Revolution took place). Many economists have argued that this assertion minimizes the magnitude of the economic growth that occurred during the 20th century, because numerous goods and services that were routinely consumed at the end of the century, such as improved medicine (which led international life expectancy to increase by over two decades) and innovations in communications technologies, had not been available for consumption at the beginning of the 20th century.

Despite economic growth, the gap between the world's affluent people and those who were poor (the vast majority) increased. Technological and medical advances had a big influence, even in the Southern Hemisphere. In the mid-20th century, large-scale industry and more centralized media made brutal dictatorships possible on a large scale but were less pervasive than the oppressive monarchies that had preceded industrialization and which led to unprecedented wars. However, the increased ability to communicate did contribute to democratization. Technological developments of the time included the development of airplanes, space exploration, nuclear technology, advances in genetics and the emergence of the Information Age.

World War I created a "lost generation," fostered disillusionment and cynicism, transformed the lives of women and democratized societies.

Earnest Hemingway, American writer

The generation that came of age during World War I is often referred to as the "Lost Generation," a term popularized by Ernest Hemingway, when he used it as one of two conflicting epigraphs for his first novel, *The Sun Also Rises* (1926). In the book, Hemingway attributed the phrase to Gertrude Stein, his mentor and patron at the time.

The "Lost Generation" could be said to broadly include creative figures like writers F. Scott Fitzgerald, T. S. Eliot, James Joyce, John Dos Passos, John Steinbeck, William Faulkner, Waldo Peirce, Franz Kafka, Henry Miller, Aldous Huxley, Louis-Ferdinand Céline, Erich Maria Remarque and the composers Sergei Prokofiev, Paul Hindemith, George Gershwin and Aaron Copland.

In Great Britain, the term has a slightly different meaning: it refers to those who perished in the First World War. Some historians also believe that it was used to refer particularly to the loss of upper-class young men, as the effects of this loss on the whole nation were particularly acute. The sons of the wealthy had high levels of education and a social background (families who were chiefs of industry, etc.) which meant that they had exceptional potential to lead and improve British society. The common sentiment that "the cream of our youth has been lost," reflected their bitterness at this irreplaceable loss.

A similar sentiment was held by all European nations. In most of them, particularly Russia, but also the other nations, the officers tended to come from educated and wealthy families – the nobility and the Kulaks, in the case of Russia – while the enlisted men were recruited from the peasantry, farmers and laborers. This very distinct social division was present in every European nation prior to World War I as a persistent remnant of medieval social hierarchies. In Russia, this tradition was ended by the Bolshevik revolution; in Britain, this cultural division continued alongside a flourishing democracy. All nations more strongly mourned the loss of thousands of promising future captains of industry, professors and politicians than the loss of a larger number of uneducated farm and factory laborers.

Communist and fascist movements throughout Europe fed on disenchantment with the existing governments in the wake of the slaughter of World War I. In two other powerful countries, Italy and Spain, fascist parties succeeded in seizing power. In contrast to this, democracy was modestly enhanced in the rest of Europe. Two distinct interpretations of democracy need to be considered separately here: democracy as a system of government and democratic rights for all, regardless of the political system. Politically, Britain and France had already become modern democracies before the war and continued to be so. The same can be said of some smaller nations which developed democracy early, such as the Netherlands and Switzerland. In Germany at the outset of the war, an attempt was made to create a democratic system, but it led to the election of fascists, eventually leading to the Nazis usurping power in 1933. Women were granted the right to vote with the founding of the Weimar Republic in 1918, but all citizens lost this right temporarily under the Nazis.

Cultural democratization – where it occurred – affected the lives of ethnic groups, laborers and women. New states were created (or recreated) in the wake of the war, some of which (e.g., Poland, Hungary, Ukraine) were an attempt to grant formerly subjugated ethnic groups their own sovereign nations. On the other hand, disparate ethnic groups were combined into hybrid nations like Yugoslavia and Czechoslovakia, though this had already been done in the case of the Austro-Hungarian Empire before the war. In the Soviet Union, workers were granted special privileges as the holdings of the wealthy were divided up and redistributed to the working class.

Ramsay MacDonald,
British Prime Minister

In Britain and other nations, there was a political backlash against conservative politicians and policies, driven by the Labour Party. The harsh reparations terms imposed by the Treaty of Versailles resulted in the loss of markets for British goods abroad, causing huge unemployment in the coal industry in particular. The result was the election of Britain's first Labour Party government in 1924 under Prime Minister Ramsay MacDonald and the replacement of the Liberal Party by the Labour Party as the alternative to the Conservatives.

The women's rights movements of Europe were fueled by disenchantment with the "old social order" and by the knowledge that the War could not have been won without the support of women in philanthropy and in predominately female work like nursing and textile mills.

The lives of European women were greatly transformed by the First World War, but differently in each nation. They obtained the right to vote in each nation eventually, but at very different times. In Britain, women obtained the right to vote incrementally, finally achieving parity with men in 1928. France and Italy, however, did not grant women this right until the end of the Second World War. Women began to enter the workforce in large numbers, as they were needed for the war effort, although afterwards they returned to non-working status in varying degrees. In Russia, for example, female participation in the labor force doubled, reaching almost half, during the war.

The main backlash women faced was from Europe's left-wing labor unions, which wanted to protect the jobs of their male members from women and were opposed to immigration for the same reason. This union reaction was most successful in Germany, where far fewer women had entered the labor force than had been the case in Britain and

Russia; Germany was on the losing side of the war, while the nations that had the highest degree of female participation in industry were on the winning side.

Attitudes towards women did not change dramatically anywhere in Europe, despite their pivotal contributions. Gender coding persisted as a norm into the 1970s; women were expected to be maternal and maintain the household, while men worked to earn the family's income.

World War II decimated a generation of Russian and German men; virtually destroyed European Jewry; resulted in the murder of millions in other groups targeted by the Nazis including Roma, homosexuals, people with disabilities and others; forced large-scale migrations; and undermined prewar class hierarchies.

About 27 million Soviets were killed during the war, a number that includes 8.7 million military casualties and 19 million civilian deaths. The largest number of military dead was 5.7 million ethnic Russians, followed by 1.3 million ethnic Ukrainians. A quarter of the population of the Soviet Union was wounded or killed during the war. Germany experienced 5.3 million military losses, mostly on the Eastern Front and during the final battles of the war in Germany.

Of the total number of deaths in World War II, about 85 percent occurred on the Allied side and 15 percent on the Axis side. Many of these deaths were the result of war crimes perpetrated by German and Japanese forces in the territories they seized. It is estimated that between 11 million and 17 million civilians perished as a direct or indirect consequence of the Nazi ideological policies, including the systematic genocide of around 6 million Jews (which came to be known as the Holocaust), along with a further 5 to 6 million ethnic Poles and other Slavs, homosexuals and other ethnic and minority groups. Hundreds of thousands of ethnic Serbs, along with gypsies and Jews, were murdered by the Croatian Ustaše in Yugoslavia, an ally of the Axis powers, in retribution-related killings just after the war's conclusion.

Axis forces used biological and chemical weapons during the war. The Germans tested such weapons on civilians and prisoners of war. The Soviet Union carried out the Katyn massacre of 22,000 Polish officers and the imprisonment or execution of thousands of political prisoners by the NKVD in the Baltic States and Eastern Poland, which was captured by the Red Army.

Pile of dead prisoners inside a Nazi concentration camp

Further war crimes committed by the Axis powers include the mass bombing of civilian targets, for example, the cities of Warsaw, Rotterdam and London – which included the targeting of hospitals and fleeing refugees by the German Luftwaffe. Tokyo and the German cities of Dresden, Hamburg and Cologne were bombed by the Western Allies, and may also be classified as crimes of war. The bombing of German cities by the Allies resulted in the destruction of over 160 cities and the deaths of more than 600,000 German civilians.

The German government, headed by Adolf Hitler and the Nazi Party, was responsible for the Holocaust, in which roughly 6 million Jews were killed, as were 2.7 million ethnic Poles and 4 million other people who were labeled "unworthy of life" (including the disabled and mentally ill, Soviet prisoners of war, homosexuals, Freemasons, Jehovah's Witnesses and Romany) as part of a program of deliberate extermination. About 12 million mostly Eastern European prisoners were used by the Germans as forced labor.

Along with the Nazi concentration camps, the Soviet gulags (labor camps) were the settings for the death of citizens of occupied countries like Poland, Lithuania, Latvia and Estonia, as well as German prisoners of war (POWs) and even Soviet citizens suspected of supporting the Nazis. Sixty percent of Soviet POWs, some 3.6 million people, held by the Germans died of starvation and disease or were murdered while in captivity during the war. Soviet ex-POWs and repatriated civilians were viewed suspiciously as potential Nazi collaborators, and some of them were sent to the Gulags after being investigated by the NKVD.

Mass production, new food technologies and industrial efficiency increased disposable income and created a consumer culture in which greater domestic comforts such as electricity, indoor plumbing, plastics and synthetic fibers became available.

20th century technology was characterized by its rapid development. Widespread acceptance and implementation of scientific methods and increased spending on research all contributed to the advancement of modern science and technology. New technology improved communication and transport, which in turn made it easier to spread technical understanding. Mass production brought automobiles and other high-tech goods to large numbers of consumers. Military research and development quickly led to innovations like computers and jet engines. Radio and telephones, already in use at the time, were greatly improved. Innovations in the fields of energy and engine technology included the peaceful use of nuclear power, which was developed after the Manhattan Project. The development of rockets during this time led to long range missiles and the space age.

Mass production refers to the production of massive quantities of standardized products, particularly through the use of assembly lines, one of the three main methods of production, along with job production and batch production. The ideas of mass production are applied to a variety of products, from fluids and particulates that are handled in bulk (food, fuel, chemicals and mined minerals) to discrete solid parts (fasteners) to the assembly of such parts (household appliances and automobiles). Mass production is a diverse field, but it can generally be differentiated from craft production and distributed manufacturing. It has been in use for centuries; there are examples of methods of production that can best be defined as mass production predating the Industrial Revolution. However, mass production techniques only became widely used and an important factor in the economy in the late 19th century.

Mass production became even more streamlined after the development of materials like inexpensive steel, high strength steel and plastics. Machining of metals was greatly improved by the use of high-speed steel and, later, very hard materials (e.g., tungsten carbide), which were used to cut edges. The use of steel components in fabrication was assisted by the invention of electric welding and stamped steel parts, both appearing on the industrial scene around 1890. Plastics such as polyethylene, polystyrene and polyvinyl chloride (PVC) can easily be formed into shapes by extrusion, blow molding or injection molding, resulting in extremely low manufacturing costs for consumer products, plastic piping, containers and parts. A very influential article that helped to define 20th century

America's perception of how mass production worked, based on correspondence with the Ford Motor Company, appeared in the 1926 *Encyclopedia Britannica Supplement*.

Mass production in a Ford factory

New communication and transportation techniques multiplied the connections across space and time, transforming daily life and contributing to the proliferation of ideas and to globalization.

One of the most obvious features of the 20th century was the dramatic technological innovation that occurred. Organized research and the practice of science led to improvements in the fields of communication, engineering, travel, medicine and warfare. The number and variety of household appliances increased dramatically due to technological improvements, the availability of electricity and increases in people's disposable income and leisure time. Appliances like washing machines, dryers, furnaces, exercise machines, refrigerators, freezers, electric stoves and vacuum cleaners became increasingly popular in the period from the 1920s to the 1950s. The microwave oven became commonplace about thirty years later during the 1980s.

During the 1920s, radio became popular as a form of entertainment. In the 1950s, television emerged as an innovation in the entertainment world. A further innovation, cable television, spread rapidly during the 1980s. Personal computers began to enter homes during the 1970s–1980s. During the 1960s, the age of portable music players emerged with the development of 8-tracks and cassette tapes, which slowly began to replace record players. During the late 1980s and the 1990s, CDs became the vehicle of choice for listening to music. Innovation in the distribution of music has continued to this day, with mp3s now being distributed digitally as a result of the proliferation of the Internet in the mid-to-late 1990s. In the 1970s, VCRs became popular, but were replaced by DVDs by the end of the 20th century.

In 1903, the first airplane was flown. Mass air travel became commercially viable within the next fifty years, accelerated by the innovation of the jet engine. Assembly lines, such as the one innovated by Henry Ford, allowed for the mass production of cars. By the close of the 20th century, billions of people had automobiles for their personal use. The existence of automobiles, motorboats and air travel facilitated an unprecedented degree of personal mobility. As a consequence of the increase in travel, motor vehicle accidents became the leading cause of death among young people in Western countries. The expansion of divided highways eventually reduced the rate of deaths due to motor vehicle collisions.

The triode tube, transistors and integrated circuits revolutionized computers, which led to a huge increase in the use of personal computers during the 1980s, and cell phones and the public-use Internet in the 1990s on. New materials, notably stainless steel, plastics, polyethylene, Velcro and Teflon, came into widespread use. Aluminum became an inexpensive metal and eventually was the second most used metal behind iron. Semiconductors were used in electronic objects. Thousands of new chemicals were developed for use in industrial processes and for consumer use at home.

Lives were defined by family and work responsibilities, economic changes and families.

The two world wars completely transformed the common conception of everyday life and familial roles. Employment stabilized and could be counted on as a steady source of income during periods of economic growth. Women were granted many of the rights they had sought for so long and their roles in families and in society were enriched and transformed. Along with their roles as wives and mothers, women became increasingly active in both public and political life. Society in the post-war period came to be defined by work responsibilities, family involvement and often an active presence in public life.

During the world wars, women became increasingly involved in military and political mobilization, as well as in economic production.

Women have had diverse military experiences. Historically, they have played a major role domestically during times of war; however, by the 18th century, some women were accompanying armies in combat missions, though usually to do the cooking and laundry on these expeditions. Nursing became a major wartime role for women starting in the mid-19th century, when Florence Nightingale established a nursing corps in the Crimean War. Women's chief role in World War I (1914-1918) was to work in munitions factories, on farms and to perform other jobs that became vacant due to men leaving to serve in the military. Women played a vital part in food rationing during wars. World War II (1939-1945) marked a decisive

Florence Nightingale, founder of modern nursing

turning point of women's involvement during military conflicts, with millions of women handling important roles on the home front, such as working in munitions factories and otherwise taking the place of men who were on active duty. Volunteer roles for women also expanded.

The biggest change was that millions of women began to serve in regular military units, most often in clerical roles, so that men could be relieved of them and become combatants. Some women (particularly in the Soviet Union, Germany and Britain) were assigned limited combat roles, often in anti-aircraft units, where they shot down enemy bombers while at the same time remaining safe from capture. Women of the Soviet Union played a significant role in front-line combat, in comparison to other nations. The Soviets had an all-female paratrooper unit which ran over 1,100 missions against the Germans, and several of the Soviet Union's most effective snipers and fighter pilots were women. Underground and resistance movements made extensive use of women in support roles.

After 1945 the role of women was sharply reduced in all major armies; however, in the 1970s, women again played an increasing role in the militaries of major nations, including roles as combat pilots; the first female American combat pilots were trained in 1974. These new combat roles were highly controversial, raising issues of gender identity (perhaps not so much for the women as for those male soldiers who felt their masculinity threatened if women could perform the same tasks just as well).

In Western Europe through the efforts of feminists, and in Eastern Europe and the Soviet Union through government policy, women finally gained the vote, greater educational opportunities and access to professional careers, even while continuing to face social inequalities.

During the First World War, women entered the labor market in unprecedented numbers, many times in new sectors, and for the first time demonstrated the value of their contributions to the world of work. The war also widowed large numbers of women, who were bereaved and short on household income. The number of men who were killed and wounded shifted demographic compositions. War also divided feminists, with many women being opposed to the war, while others were actively involved in the "white feather" campaign. Feminist theorists such as Francoise Thebaud and Nancy F. Cott have cited traditional imagery and literature promoting motherhood as a conservative reaction to World War I in some countries. The emergence of these attitudes during wartime has been termed the "nationalization of women." In the years between the World War I and World War II, feminists struggled to overcome male bias in the business world.

In the early 1960s, second-wave feminism began in the United States. While first-wave feminism was largely centered on suffrage and the legal obstacles to gender equality (i.e., voting rights, property rights), second-wave feminism expanded the debate to include sexuality, family, the workplace, reproductive rights, and legal and de facto inequalities. Second-wave feminism allowed women to make workplace, military, media and sports gains, brought attention to marital rape and other domestic violence issues. It led to the establishment of rape crisis centers and battered women's shelters, as well as changes in the divorce and child custody laws.

The major feminist political effort in the United States was the attempt to pass the Equal Rights Amendment (ERA) to the Constitution; however, it was shot down by anti-feminists (led by Phyllis Schlafly) who made the argument that the ERA would mean that women could then be drafted into the military. This wave of feminism eventually spread throughout the western world and beyond. In America, the movement persisted through the early 1980s; however, it subsequently grew into a strong worldwide movement in Europe and parts of Asia, such as Turkey and Israel.

With economic recovery after World War II, the birth rate increased dramatically (the Baby Boom), often promoted by government policies.

After the Second World War in 1945, there was a period of fiscal prosperity known as the postwar economic expansion (also called the postwar economic boom, the long boom, and the Golden Age of Capitalism). The expansion is typically defined as spanning from 1945-1952, with overall growth continuing until 1971. (There is some debate on how to date the period, with booms occurring at different times in different countries, some starting as early as 1945 and overlapping with the rise of the East Asian economies into the 1980s or 1990s.) The boom could be said to have lasted until the early 1970s, marked by the end of the Bretton Woods system in 1971, the 1973 oil crisis, and the 1973-1974 stock market crash, which all contributed to a recession.

One critical component to the economic boom in Europe was the Marshall Plan, an aid initiative implemented by the United States in April 1948 that distributed $13 billion dollars (modern day equivalent of about $128 billion U.S. dollars) to war-ravaged nations that joined the Organization for European Economic Co-operation to aid in their recovery. This aid money helped to rebuild war-ruined infrastructure, modernize outdated industrial and business practices by using more efficient models, reduced trade barriers and established institutions that coordinated the European economy as a whole.

Individually, key European nations implemented their own recovery initiatives in addition to the Marshall Plan's financial support from the U.S. West Germany reformed their currency in 1948 and, beginning in the 1950s (with the support of labor unions), took on technological modernization, postponed wage increases, minimized strikes, devised an employee-employer grievance resolution system and put worker representation in the boardrooms of large corporations.

France's economic growth was encouraged by productivity gains, an increase in the number of average working hours, an increase in both manufactured goods and agricultural exports. In Italy, an increased demand for iron and steel worldwide spurred their metal industry, and investments flowed into the country via the European Common Market.

In western countries, the end of the Second World War brought about a baby boom, as well as an economic one. While there is a degree of vagueness about the exact dates of the postwar baby boom, the most cited dates are from the years immediately after the war and ending over a decade later, when birth rates began to decrease in 1957. In countries with extensive damage from the war, post-war economic hardships and displaced populations (such as Germany and Poland), the baby boom did not begin until years later.

Sweden modernizes the Stockholm metro, 1957

Following World War II, the majority of European nations increasingly adopted policies that bolstered the social services offered to the public. These policies included the offering of cash benefits (pensions, unemployment benefits, housing benefits) and in-kind services (health care, childcare, post-secondary education). For most participating nations, these programs are now seen as a vital component in the role of government.

New modes of marriage partnership, motherhood, divorce and reproductive technology gave women more options in their personal lives.

The feminist movement has effected change in Western society, including women's suffrage, greater access to education, more equitable pay with men, the right to initiate divorce proceedings, the right of women to make individual decisions regarding pregnancy (including access to contraceptives and abortion) and the right to own property. From the 1960s on, the campaign for women's rights was met with mixed results in the U.S. and the U.K. Other countries of the EEC agreed to ensure that discriminatory laws would be phased out across the European Community. Some feminist campaigning also helped reform attitudes to child sexual abuse. The view that young girls' flirtatiousness was responsible for men having sex with them came to be replaced by an attitude that men were responsible for their own conduct. The Convention on the Elimination of All Forms of Discrimination Against Women (CEDAW) was an international convention adopted by the United Nations General Assembly and described as an international bill of rights for women. It came into force in 1979 in those nations ratifying it.

Many things changed the nature of marriage partnerships after the war, some immediately and some in the long term since the war. The old assumption that men worked while women stayed at home to parent and maintain the house became obsolete over the long period since the war. This was largely because of economic realities that required women to work, but also because of female political activism. Increased tax burdens over the long term forced most families to choose between having fewer children and having both parents work to maintain the standard of living they were accustomed to. The rights and equality of gay people emerged as a political issue in Western Europe in the 1960s.

Economic realities since the end of the war, particularly a dramatic rise in taxation in developed nations, has meant that in many low-income and even middle-income families, one wage earner is no longer able to sustain the family. The general reactions to this have been either to accept a lower standard of living in order to facilitate large families where one parent can stay at home and parent several children, to choose not to have children or limit the number of children they have, or for both parents to work (which usually means forfeiting "quality time" with their children in order to maintain the standard of living and have several children).

In the immediate postwar years, citizens of western democracies expected life to continue as it had before the war; they desperately wanted to return to "normalcy." Taxation was not yet dramatically higher, and in fact the size of government even temporarily receded as defense needs lessened. As a result of this sudden influx of millions of young men returning home from the front and wanting to resume normal lives, there was a postwar baby boom. The traditional gender-coded family was the understood norm, but only for a short period after the war. In the long term, since the end of World War II, there has been a diminishing marriage rate, an increase in the divorce rates, a drop in western birth rates and changes in the amount of time householders spend working.

Divorce carried social stigma in the early 20th century in Europe, and continues to do so among a minority of Europeans. When a woman initiated a divorce suit, she was thought of more negatively than a man who initiated one. Activists have worked hard to change European attitudes towards female divorcees. Today, women in Europe who initiate a divorce have much greater social acceptance and active sympathy from people around them than their women in the 1940s, 1950s and 1960s.

One underreported cause of the high postwar divorce rate is Post-Traumatic Stress Disorder (PTSD). Tens of millions of men returned from the battlefields of World War II having had emotionally shattering experiences; many more Europeans had survived the horrors of Nazi and Communist concentration camps. These people returned to normal life with severe emotional trauma, which in many cases would today be diagnosed as PTSD and treated as such. However, in the 1940s and 1950s, there was no such designation as "Post-Traumatic Stress Disorder." Even to the extent that postwar

Assistance dog aids a veteran with post-traumatic stress disorder

psychologists could recognize serious symptoms of trauma, treatment was not widely available and the inhibiting cultural expectations of the time were such that people did not discuss their problems openly and were expected to cope with them by themselves. But a fact unspoken even to this day is that in postwar homes, alcoholism, spousal abuse, child abuse and dysfunctionality were a common consequence of PTSD, which explains the high rate of family break-ups after the war.

Inter-ethnic marriages increased greatly after the war. Displaced persons settled in new countries after the Second World War and married. Soldiers abroad met women in the countries they were serving in and this produced thousands of marriages. Although this is a progressive development, it often triggered racial tension within communities and families. Despite the revelation of Nazi atrocities and contact between millions of soldiers and the foreigners whom they liberated, Europe's ancient racist traditions endured. Racism was fueled by the war precisely because members of different cultures had been fighting apocalyptic wars with each other for years. This often resulted in unfriendliness toward or outright rejection of spouses with different ethnicities and religions by the relatives of their partners.

With the increasing divorce rates, the legal freedom and the need of single women to work to support themselves, and the decision to have a two-income family, millions of European women entered the workforce. This change happened particularly over the course of the 1960s, 1970s and 1980s. The division of labor within households was accentuated by the increased entry of women into the workplace in the 20th century. In two-career couples, both spouses spend on average about equal amounts of time working, but women still spend more time on housework than men.

Motherhood has changed as women have entered the workforce while continuing to have children. Issues which have arisen from this include day care, maternity leave and the difficulty of rising to the top executive levels of a large organization while needing to divert time to maternity leave and parenting. Politicians have attempted solutions in the form of maternity leave laws and subsidized child care programs. Children of two-income households suffer from having less contact with their parents; this cannot be blamed on women entering the workforce, since it is just as conceivable that a one-income household could include a stay-at-home father instead of the traditional stay-at-home mother. Lack of contact with their parents frequently manifests itself in antisocial behavior and disengagement from school; however, there are many two-income households that raise children successfully.

Factors which seem to make a difference are the presence of large extended families with many supportive relatives, adequate income levels and various forms of stability, such as established family routines and parents not changing jobs or having frequent work-related travel absences. Single motherhood became much more common due to the increasing rates of family dysfunction, divorce and greater sexual freedom, which came with the long-term cultural changes. This, of course, was one compelling reason for more women to enter the workforce, particularly since child support laws lagged in implementation and enforcement, far behind the increasing number of abandoning fathers. In Europe today, both governmental and private support systems are in place for single parents to a far greater extent than they were in the 1940s.

As western women acquired access to more dependable birth control, both family planning and their career potential increased. In the last three decades of the 20th century, this movement (which actually started in the 1900s in the United States under Margaret Sanger and elsewhere under Marie Stopes) gave women an entirely new freedom though the ability to control when and under what financial circumstances they would start their families. This gave them the power to plan their lives much more intentionally, making it possible to have both a career and a family.

Abortion is a controversial aspect of reproductive rights because many people, due to religious or other moral values, see it as a killing. Both sides of that debate have produced compelling arguments. In the Soviet Union, abortion law took a roller coaster ride; it was legalized unconditionally by Lenin, then made illegal again by Stalin in order to promote population growth, then made legal once and for all in 1955. In Western Europe, it was legalized at different times in different nations. For example, Sweden was the first to make it legal in 1938. Britain legalized it in 1968.

In vitro fertilization was another technology given to women by medical research. This technology gave childbearing ability to many women who otherwise would not be able to become mothers due to health conditions, advancing age or other reasons.

Women attained high political office and increased their representation in legislative bodies in many nations.

The increased participation of women in the European work force led to the entry of women into politics as well. The right to participate had been legalized in most of Europe in the early twentieth century, thanks to the hard work and personal sacrifice of women's rights activists. But participation lagged because cultural pressures and traditional assumptions persisted. Another generation of female ground-breakers of a different kind dealt a fatal blow to this cultural barrier. Not all were left-wing; many of the most dynamic and effective leaders were leaders of European conservative parties.

Margaret Thatcher,
Prime Minister of Great Britain

Margaret Hilda Thatcher (1925–2013) was the Prime Minister of the United Kingdom from 1979-1990 and the Leader of the Conservative Party from 1975-1990. She both held the position of Prime Minister the longest of any 20th century prime minister and was the only woman to do so in history. Nicknamed the "Iron Lady" by a Soviet journalist for her uncompromising political strategy, she put into practice policies that came to be termed *Thatcherism.*

Her most popular achievements include the restoration of the British economy and competitiveness, dramatically increasing funding for health care and education while at the same time cutting taxation rates, and liberating the Falkland Islands after they were invaded by Argentinian dictator Leopoldo Galtieri.

Mary Therese Winifred Robinson was the seventh President of Ireland (from 1990-1997) and the first female to hold the office. She was also the United Nations High Commissioner for Human Rights from 1997-2002. She distinguished herself as an academic, barrister, campaigner and member of the Irish Senate from 1969–1989. As an independent candidate (nominated by the Labor Party, the Worker's Party, and independent senators), she beat Fianna Fáil's Brian Lenihan and Fine Gael's Austin Currie in the 1990 presidential election, becoming the first elected president in the office's history that did not have the support of Fianna Fáil. She is most well-known for her Irish presidency, her transformation of Ireland, and liberalizing a previously conservative, low-profile political office.

Édith Cresson was the first (and only woman to date) to have been the Prime Minister of France (from 1991-1992). In her biography, *Edith Cresson: la femme piégée* (1993) by Élisabeth Schemla, it is argued that Cresson's failure and low approval ratings were due to the misogyny of the French political class, the Socialist elites, and even the French media. Cresson's political career ended later in a scandal during her tenure as the European Commissioner for Research, Science and Technology.

Mary Robinson (left) receiving the Presidential Medal of Freedom in August 2009 from U.S. President Barack Obama (right)

New voices gained prominence in political, intellectual, and social discourse.

The lives of Europeans would forever be changed by the tragedies of two world wars, the economically-driven disintegration of migration barriers, globalization, and the permanent residencies taken up by non-Europeans. More people were living in cities than in rural areas for the first time in its history. The economic growth led to more participation in mass cultural entertainment, greater education opportunities and increased standards of living and leisure time. While it reduced the labor force, the lowering of birth rates had the side effect of increasing the disposable income of individual families. Governments implemented policies that supported child-bearing and child-rearing to encourage families that would one day add to the workforce.

The increasing globalization of the economy exposed Europe's citizens to new products, ideologies and customs. However, decolonization, the disruptions of war and lowered birth rates with population growth largely due to immigration, led to uncertainties about Europe's cultural identity. There were many campaigns of terror stemming from the struggle for ethnic or national independence, or in radical opposition to free-market ideology – both before the collapse of Communism and after. Still others chose to work within the democratic system to advance their nationalist agendas.

By the 1960s, significant environmental issues were being given recognition as a byproduct of the swift industrialization of the last century. Environmentalists challenged the status quo economic and political structures by demanding sustainable development, arguing that an untrammeled free-market economy could lead Europe into an ecological disaster. During this time, a generation that had never experienced either a war or an economic depression came of age; they criticized the established institutions' beliefs while at the same time protesting for greater political and personal freedom, culminating in the 1968 youth revolts in Europe's major cities.

More participation in politics was fostered by the feminist movement. Before the end of the century, several governments had women as heads of state. However, customary social patterns and traditional institutions still hindered gender equality. As Europe's internal struggles and movements continued, immigrants from around the world were entering its borders; by the end of the century, Europeans were residing in multiethnic and religiously tolerant communities. However, these immigrants did not assimilate or follow the usual expectations of integration and possessed different values than those of 20th century Europeans, and many nationalists were unwilling to consider the newcomers part of their society. This struggle of to maintain a traditional "European" identity continued into the early 21st century.

Green parties in Western and Central Europe challenged consumerism, urged sustainable development, and, by the late 20th century, were cautioning against globalization.

Green politics is associated with issues surrounding the environment and (in modern times) also social justice and nonviolence. Thus, a Green Party is a political party formed along these principles. It is the Greens' belief that such issues are the foundation of world peace because they are inherently related to one another. Typically, Green parties are inclusive of social-democratic policies and form coalitions with leftist parties. Almost ninety countries around the globe now have Green parties, many of them members of Global Greens.

*Logo of Green Italia,
European green political alliance*

After the many new social movement and the rise of environmental awareness, Green parties of Europe began to be formed in the late 1970s, with Belgium having the first one. Belgium elected Green members to its parliament. Due to having many Green seats in its local council, the party had the balance of power in the city of Liege. In 1979, groups in West Germany that felt underrepresented politically formed a coalition to contest the European Parliament elections of the same year. They did not win any seats that year, but this association morphed into a formal party that later won a breakthrough in the German national elections of 1983. Even thought they were not the first Green party in Europe to have members elected, they attracted a lot of media attention and were perceived to have been. That was largely due to their charismatic leader Petra Kelly, who may have been interesting to the media because she had an American stepfather, although she was German. Kelly's Green party, founded in 1980 (later called the Alliance '90/The Greens after its merger with the Alliance 90), has become one of Europe's most important Green parties due to its recruitment ability and its role in establishing Green parties in other countries such as Spain.

The "PEOPLE" Party that was formed in Coventry in 1972 was the predecessor of the Green party in the UK. It changed its name twice, first to the Ecology Party in 1973, and then to the Green Party in 1985.

In 1984, there was an agreed-upon platform on which Greens would run its members as candidates for the new European Parliament; this led to the first Green members being elected to it (two members from Belgium, two from the Netherlands, and an impressive seven members from Germany). However, even having eleven elected members of the European Parliament was not enough for the Green party to form a parliamentary group of their own; they instead formed alliances with members of the European Parliament (MEPs) from Italy and Denmark, as well as regionalists from Flanders and Ireland to create the Green Alternative European Link group (GRAEL, also known as the Rainbow Group). These groups were responsible for responding politically to the fight against nuclear energy (1986 was the year of the Chernobyl disaster), pollution, cruelty to animals and the demolition of Brussels. A pan-European alliance that unites most European Green parties was formed after the many years of cooperation.

In the contemporary context, most Western European nations currently have an active Green Party movement, which usually receives enough votes to meet the bar for inclusion in the Parliament in question. Contemporary Green parties are often seen as the furthest "left" option that a voter has, most notably with the "Greens" in the United Kingdom.

The modern Green movement in Europe tends to be ideologically neo-Marxist with the issue of environmentalism as the "bait" to garner a larger portion of the vote than they would have running on a strictly neo-Marxist platform. Though these parties have never won a significant majority to be able to form a government of their own, they have begun to be able to change the narrative of politics. These pushes have not only been visible in the environmental sphere, as their desire to challenge consumerism, urge for sustainable development and warn the public of the exploitation inherent in globalism have all shaped the political discourse in European capitals.

Gay and lesbian movements worked for expanded civil rights, obtaining in some nations the right to form civil partnerships with full legal benefits or to marry.

The lesbian, gay, bisexual, and transgender (LGBT) social movements advocate for the equality and acceptance of the LGBT population. There is a long history of such campaigns for what is sometimes called gay rights, gay and lesbian rights, or just LGBT rights. There are many LGBT groups that are active worldwide but there is no central organization that unities all LGBT people or their interests.

LGBT equality march in Moscow, 2012

Social equality is commonly touted as the goal of most LGBT movements in history. Many advocate for society at large to rid itself of homophobia and bigotry, though some have been focused on building LGBT communities for internal support. These movements can be comprised of political activism (lobbying, street marches) or cultural activities (social groups, media, art, research). There are debates within the LGBT community about how to best reach their overall goals of political and social equality, as well as strategy, and even who comprises the members of the movement that they represent.

Debates occur about what lesbians, gays, bisexuals, transgender people, intersex individuals have in common in terms of political goals. Within the LGBT communities, there were controversies when leaders of the gay and lesbian movements in the 1970s, 1980s, and 1990s made an effort to shield the public from masculine lesbians, feminine gay men, transgender people, and bisexuals.

There was a kind of identity politics assumed by these LBGT movements of the past that views gay, bisexual and/or transgender individuals as a set class of people, a clearly defined minority group or groups. However, those employing this tact seek liberal political goals of equality and freedom of choice, and desire to merge with the political mainstream.

So called "conversion therapies," which attempt to change gay, lesbian and bisexual people into heterosexuals, are generally opposed by the LGBT community; they argue that sexual orientation and gender identity are innate and are unable to be consciously altered. The advocates of such techniques are often religiously motivated, viewing anything other than heterosexuality as immoral.

The movement has had success in Europe; while not all European governments yet recognize same-sex marriage, thirteen do. These thirteen European governments constitute the majority of governments which have granted formal legal recognition of gay marriages. Many other European governments have recognized LGBT marriage as a separate category called "civil unions."

Intellectuals and youth reacted against perceived bourgeois materialism and decadence, most significantly with the revolts of 1968.

In 1968, the protests that were part of a worldwide upsurge in social concerns, often marked by active resistance against military pursuits and the bureaucratic elites, were generally responded to with increased political oppression. In the United States, such protests were the turning point for the civil rights movement and created new movements like the Black Panther Party. The protests against the Vietnam War that began around this time escalated into a broad movement in reaction to the Tet Offensive. These occurred all over the United States and even in London, Paris, Berlin and Rome.

A widespread socialist movement rose in the U.S. as well as in most European nations. For example, in May 1968 in France, students found common cause with the wildcat strikes (the strikers numbered around ten million French workers), and for a few days the movement seemed like it might have the power to depose the government.

Other notable protests occurring in capitalist nations in 1968 were over foreign dictatorships, state oppression and colonization. Examples include the start of "the Troubles" in Northern Ireland, the Tlatelolco massacre of hundreds of protesters in Mexico City and the rise of guerrilla warfare in opposition to the military dictatorship of Brazil.

Protests also occurred in socialist nations over restrictions on freedom of speech and other civil rights abuses by the communist bureaucratic and military elites. Protests occurred in central and eastern Europe, especially in the Prague Spring in Czechoslovakia and in Warsaw, Poland, and in Yugoslavia.

Student demonstration in Oaxaca City commemoration of the Tlatelolco massacre of 1968

The environmental movement can trace its early stages to these protests of 1968; it grew out of the anti-nuclear movement. In 1968, France became especially concerned with the environmental concerns of the time, and the French Federation of Nature Protection Societies and the French branch of Friends of the Earth were created, and the French scientific community organized Survivre et Vivre, or "Survive and Thrive." This same year, the Club of Rome was established. Students protested against hydroelectric plants in Sweden. Environmental activists in Denmark and the Netherlands protested against pollution.

In 1986, the Civil Rights Movement of Northern Ireland began. However, it resulted in the violence now called "The Troubles."

Because of the economic growth of the 1950s and 1960s, numerous "guest workers" from southern Europe, Asia, and Africa immigrated to Western and Central Europe; after the economic downturn of the 1970s, these workers and their families often became targets of anti-immigrant agitation and extreme nationalist political parties.

Greece, Ireland, Italy, Norway, Portugal, Spain and the United Kingdom had been the traditional source of emigrants to the Americas and Australia until the late 1960s and 1970s. Some went to other European nations such as France, Switzerland, Germany and Belgium. However, once living standards in these nations rose, they themselves became a destination for emigrants, especially coming from Morocco, Somalia and Egypt to Italy and Greece; from Morocco, Algeria and Latin America to Spain and Portugal; and from Ireland, India, Pakistan, Germany, the United States, Bangladesh and Jamaica to the United Kingdom.

In France, the National Front is a socially conservative, nationalist political party that practices "dirigisme" (where the state has jurisdiction over investment). It was founded in 1972 in order to unite a number of French nationalist movements of the time. Initially, the National Front only called for immigration to be lessened, viewing immigration as a minor issue. However, in 1978, with the entrance of Jean-Pierre Stirbois and his "solidarist" group, excluding non-European immigrants increasingly became a major issue in the early 1980s.

More recently, the National Front's issues with immigration have narrowed to a single one–Muslim immigration into France from North Africa, West Africa and the Middle East. However, since the 1999 split (when opponents of Jean-Marie Le Pen's National Front voted Bruno Mégret to lead a splinter group within the party) and in comparison to proposals of Mégret's MNR or Philippe de Villiers's Movement for France, the National Front has made an effort to appear more moderate on issues of immigration and Islam. The National Front does not advocate the repatriation of legal immigrants any longer but it does support the deportation of criminal, illegal or unemployed immigrants.

Marine Le Pen, after becoming the leader of the National Front in 2011, refocused the party's efforts on the apparent threat to the French Republic's secular values. Le Pen has criticized the Muslim community for what she views as their intention to eventually impose their values on France. She advocates a pro-active stance against immigration to Europe by Tunisian and Libyan immigrants following the Arab Spring rebellions.

The Freedom Party of Austria (FPO) is an Austrian right-wing, populist political party, founded in 1956 as the successor to the Federation of Independents or VdU. They are the ideological descendants of the pan-German and national-liberal movement that dates back to the 1848 revolutions. It wasn't until the 1980s that immigration became a real political issue in Austria. Under Haider's leadership, immigration went from being politically unimportant to the FBO before 1989, to being their tenth most important issue in 1990, and their second most important issue in 1992.

Logo for the Freedom Party of Austria

The "Austria First!" initiative of 1993 tried to collect signatures for an immigration reform, saying "Austria is not a country of immigration" and "the protection of cultural identity and social peace in Austria requires a stop to immigration." They claimed that the initiative was not explicitly against foreigners, but intended to maintain the cultural identity of native Austrians. However, during the late 1990s, the FPO heavily criticized the radicalization of Islam, and subsequently inveighed against "Islamization" and the Muslim community in general.

We want to hear from you

Your feedback is important to us because we strive to provide the highest quality prep materials. If you have any questions, comments or suggestions, email us, so we can incorporate your feedback into future editions.

Customer Satisfaction Guarantee

If you have any concerns about this book, including printing issues, contact us and we will resolve any issues to your satisfaction.

info@sterling-prep.com

Image Credits

Period 1

Marcus Tullius Cicero. Capitoline Museum, Rome. *Library of General and Practical Knowledge: Demolition of World Literature*. Vol. 5. 1905. Wikimedia Commons

Dante Alighieri. Doré, Gustave, 1800s. *The Comedy of Dante Alighieri*. Viajando Nas Palavras. Wikimedia Commons

Marsilio Ficino. Imagines Philogorum, by Alfred Gudeman, Berlin/Leipzig: 1911. Bolognese. Print. Ser. 3. Wikimedia Commons

Portrait of Lorenzo the Magnificent. Agnolo Di Cosimo, 1400s. Uffizi Gallery, Florence. *Lorenzo the Magnificent*. By Hugh Ross Williams. Wikimedia Commons

Library of General and Practical Knowledge: Demolition of World Literature. Vol. 5. 1905. Wikimedia Commons

The Great German in the Picture. Schönitzer, Michael, 1936. Wikimedia Commons

Portrait of Erasmus of Rotterdam Writing. Hans Holbein the Younger, 1523. Color on paper mounted on pine wood. Kunstmuseum Basel, Basel, Switzerland. Wikimedia Commons

Small Prison Scene. Joseph Wright of Derby, c. 1789. Oil on canvas. Yale Center for British Art, New Haven, Connecticut. Wikimedia Commons

Michelangelo Buonarroti. Jacopino Del Conte, c.1535. Oil on canvas. Wikimedia Commons

Sistene Chapel Ceiling. Michelangelo Di Lodovico Buonarroti Simoni, c. 1508–1512. Gold and plaster. Sistene Chapel, Rome. Wikimedia Commons

The Trevi Fountain in Rome. Piranesi, Giovanni Battista, 1773. Copper engraving. Private Collection. Wikimedia Commons

Nicolaus Copernicus. Flack, J. C., 1600s. Reproduction of line engraving after J. Flack. Wellcome Library, London. Wikimedia Commons

Page xii of *De humani corporis fabrica*. Andreas Vesalius, portrait. By Andreas Vesalius (1534 edition). Public domain

Portrait of René Descartes (1596–1650). Hals, Frans, c. 1649. Oil on panel. Statens Museum for Kunst, Copenhagen. Wikimedia Commons

Portrait of Isaac Newton. Sir Godfrey Kneller, 1689. Oil. Wikimedia Commons

Christopher Columbus at the Court of the Catholic Monarchs. Cordero, Juan, 1850. Oil on canvas. Museo Nacional De Arte, Mexico City. Wikimedia Commons

Portrait of Maximilian I (1459–1519). Joos Van Cleve, 1530. Oil on panel. Rijksmuseum, Amsterdam. Wikimedia Commons

Wallenstein: A Scene of the Thirty Years War. Crofts, Ernest, 1884. Oil on canvas. Leeds Art Gallery: The Bridgeman Art Library, Leeds. Wikimedia Commons

Negotiating the Religious Peace of Augsburg. c. 1500s. *Descriptive Democracy and Revisionary Democracy*. Word Press. Wikimedia Commons

Allegory of Good and Bad Government in Siena (Detail). Lorenzetti, Ambrogio, c. 1338–1340. Fresco. Public Palace, Sienna. Wikimedia Commons

Cover page of 1550 edition of Machiavelli's *Il Principe and La Vita di Castruccio Castracani da Lucca*. Public domain.

The Swearing in of the Peace Treaty between Spain and the United Provinces in the Town Hall of Munster, May 15, 1648. c. 1648–1670. Oil on copper. Rijksmuseum, Amsterdam. Wikimedia Commons

Illustration of a 17th-century pikeman. Hewitt, John. *Ancient Armour and Weapons in Europe: From the Iron Period of the Northern Nations to the End of the 17th Century*. Oxford and London: J. Henry and J. Parker, 1860. Print.

Polish Husaria. Husarz-Stefano Della Bella. Polish Life in the Past Centuries. By Wladyslaw Lozinski. 5th ed. Warsaw: 1907. Bella, Stefano Della. Wikimedia Commons

Portrait of King Charles I in His Robes of State. Van Dyck, Anthony, 1636. Oil. Royal Collection of the United Kingdom, London. Wikimedia Commons

Sir Thomas Fairfax. Hollar, Wenceslaus, c. 1607–1677. University of Toronto Thomas Fisher Rare Book Library: Wenceslas Hollar Digital Collection, Toronto. Wikimedia Commons

Prince of Orange Landing at Torbay. Miller, William, 1852. *The Art Journal*. Vol. IV. London: George Virtue, 1852. Wikimedia Commons

Treaty of the Pyrenees. Jacques Laumosnier, 17th Century. Tessé Museum, Le Mans. French Ministry of Culture, *Jaconde*. Wikimedia Commons

Luther Posting His 95 Theses in 1517. Pauwels, Ferdinand, 1872. Wikimedia Commons

Sir Thomas More. Hans Holbein the Younger, 1527. Oil on oak panel. Frick Collection: Living Hall, New York City. Wikimedia Commons

Presbyterians, a Popular Narrative of Their Origin, Progress, Doctrines, and Achievements. Hays, George Pierce, 1892. New York: J.A. Hill. Wikimedia Commons

Teresa of Ávila. Rubens, Peter Paul, c. 1615. Oil on panel. Kunsthistorisches Museum, Vienna. Wikimedia Commons

The Peace Portrait of Elizabeth I. Marcus Gheeraerts the Elder, c. 1580–1585. Oil on panel. Private Collection, United Kingdom. Wikimedia Commons

Ville Assiégée Pendant La Guerre Des Paysans 1525. Grien, Hans Baldung, 1535. *National Library of Strasbourg University*. Strasbourg University. Wikimedia Commons

King Louis XIV of France. Griesinger, Theodor, 1874. British Library, London. *The Maitressenwirthschaft in France under Louis XIV. & XV.* Superb ed. Vol. 2. Wikimedia Commons

The Peace of Westphalia. Anselm Van Hulle, 1717. Peace Palace Library, The Hauge. Wikimedia Commons

Paris through the Centuries : National History in Paris and the Parisians, since the Founding of Lutèce until Today. Genouillac, H. Gourdon De. Paris: F. Roy, 1879. Wikimedia Commons

Philip II of Spain. Van Baerland, Adriaan, and Jan Moretus. N.d. Serbian Printing. 1600. *Dukes of Brabant Chronicle*. Wikimedia Commons

Admiral Gaspard II De Coligny. Clouet, François, c. 1565–1570. Oil on panel. Saint Louis Art Museum, St. Louis, Missouri, United States. Wikimedia Commons

Portrait of Willem I of Nassau, Prince of Orange and Stadhouder (1533–1584). Mor, Antonis, 1555. Oil on panel. Gemaldegalerie Alte Meister, Kassel, Kassel, Germany. Wikimedia Commons

Hungarian Medieval Ducat. Bartolomeu Drágfi De Beltiug, 1491. Gold. Wikimedia Commons

Portrait Drawing of the Head of Spanish Conquistador Hernán Cortés. Reich, Jacques. *Appletons' Cyclopædia of American Biography*. Vol. 1. 1900. Wikimedia Commons

An 1887 Illustration of En:Bartolomeu Dias' Two Caravels, the São Cristóvão and the São Pantaleão. Whymper, Frederick, 1887. British Library, London. *The Sea: Its Stirring Story of Adventure, Peril & Heroism*. Vol. 2. 1887 Wikimedia Commons

Ellis's History of the United States. Edward S. Ellis, Minneapolis: Wester Book Syndicate, 1899. Wikimedia Commons

The Conquest of Tenochtitlá. C. Late 17th Century. Library of Congress: Jay I. Kislak Collection: Rare Book and Special Collections Division, Washington, D.C.

Destruction of the Spanish Armada. Gartner José De La Peña, 1892. Oil on canvas. Museo De Málaga. Wikimedia Commons

Our Country. Lossing, Benson J., New York: Johnson and Bailey, 1895.

The Gazebo, 1857 (The Garden Arbor). 1857. *The Gazebo*. 1857. Wikimedia Commons

Engraving of the East India House (17th Century). Mid-17th century. Amsterdam. *East India House (1606)*. Amsterdam Monuments. Wikimedia Commons

Portrait of Miguel De Cervantes Y Saavedra (1547–1615). Juan De Jauregui Y Aguilar, 1600. Oil on panel. Real Academia De La Historia, Madrid. Wikimedia Commons

American's Story for America's Children: The Early Colonies. Pratt, Mara L. Boston: D.C. Heath & Company, 1901.

Farmers in the Delivery of Their Taxes to the Landlords. Woodcut. Niederstätter, Alois. 15th Century. Picture Archive of the Austrian National Library, Vienna. *A Century of Austrian History 1400–1522.* Vienna: 1996. Wikimedia Commons

The Jaquerie Revolt. 14th century. *Grandes Chroniques De France.* Gallica. Wikimedia Commons

St. Macarius of Ghent Giving Aid to the Plague Victims. Jacob van Oost II, 1673. Oil on canvas. Louvre Museum, Paris. Wikimedia Commons

Guillaume Farel. Bachelin, Auguste, 19th century. Neuchâtel. *Public University at the University of Neuchâtel.* The University of Neuchâtel. Wikimedia Commons

Portrait of André Tiraqueau. Amman, Jost, 1574. Engraving. German Research Foundation Virtual Archive. Wikimedia Commons

A Scene on the Ice. Avercamp, Hendrick, c. 17th century. Watercolor. Teylers Museum, Haarlem, the Netherlands. Wikimedia Commons

Preparation for witch burning in 1544. Impression by Jan Luiken, 17th century. Public domain, via Wikimedia Commons

Period 2

Queen Elizabeth I. C. 1575. Oil on panel. National Portrait Gallery, London. Wikimedia Commons

Ivan the Terrible Shows His Treasures to the English Ambassador Horsey. Litovchenko, Alexander, 1875. Oil on canvas. State Russian Museum, St. Petersburg, Russia. Wikimedia Commons

Portrait of Louis XIV. Lefébvre, Claud, c. 1670. Oil on canvas. Palace of Versailles, Versailles. Wikimedia Commons

Wilhelm Roscher, Woodcut. Dreihundert Berühmte Deutsche. Klinkicht, Moritz. By Karl Siebert. Stuttgart: Greiner & Pfeiffer, 1912. Wikimedia Commons

Prince Henry of Prussia (1726–1802). Johann Heinrich Tischbein the Elder, 1769. Oil. National Museum in Berlin: Picture Gallery, Berlin. Wikimedia Commons

Stanislaus August Poniatowski King of Poland. Pichler, Johann Peter, c. 1791–1793. Auction House: Con Morenberg. *Arcadja.* Wikimedia Commons

Peter the Great. Sir Godfrey Kneller, 1698. Oil on canvas. Royal Collection, United Kingdom. Wikimedia Commons

Portrait of Catherine II of Russia. Levitzky, Dmitry Grigorievich, 1794. Oil on canvas. Novgorod Art and History Museum, Oblast, Russia. Wikimedia Commons

King Charles I of England, Elbow. Anthony Van Dyck, c. 1632. Color on canvas. Kunsthistorisches Museum, Vienna. Wikimedia Commons

East Front of the Bank of England. Shepherd, Thomas H., 1828. British Library: Mechanical Curator Collection, London. *Metropolitan Improvements; or London in the 19th Century*. By James Elmes. Wikimedia Commons

Jean-Baptiste Colbert. Helmolt, H.F., ed. History of the World. New York: Dodd, Mead and Company, 1902. Wikimedia Commons

Description of a Slave Ship. 1789. Wood engraving. British Museum, London. Wikimedia Commons

A Popular History of the United States. Bryant, William Cullen and Sydney Howard Gay. New York: Charles Scribners' Sons, 1881.

Allegorical Representation of the Dutch Republic as a Ship. Schillemans, Frans, and Jacobus Oorloge, 1620. Engraving. Rijksmuseum, Amsterdam. Wikimedia Commons

English Ships and the Spanish Armada, August 1588. English School, 1588. Royal Museums Greenwich, London. Wikimedia Commons

East India House. Thomas Malton the Younger, c.1748–1804. Yale University: Yale Center for British Art: Paul Mellon Collection, New Haven, Connecticut. Wikimedia Commons

Portrait of René Descartes. Jan-Baptist Weenix, c. 1647-1649. Centraal Museum in Utrecht, Netherlands. Wikimedia Commons

Voltair at the Age of Twenty-four, Detail. Workshop of Nicolas De Largillière, 18th century. Oil on canvas. Carnavalet Museum: Salon Voltaire, Paris. Wikimedia Commons

Portrait of Montesquieu. French School, 1728. Palace of Versailles, Versailles. Wikimedia Commons

Quentin De La Tour, Maurice. *Portrait of Jean-Jacques Rousseau*. Late 18th Century. Musée Antoine-Lécuyer, Saint-Quentin. Wikimedia Commons

Mary Wollstonecraft. Opie, John, c. 1797. National Portrait Gallery, London.

Madame Roland. Album of the Centenary: Great Men and Great Events of the French Revolution (1789–1804). Rousseau, H., and E. Thomas. By Augustin Challamel and Desire Lacroix. Paris: Jouvet & Cie, 1889. Wikimedia Commons

The Tatler. Steele, Richard. Ed. Joseph Addison, 1709–1711. *University of Otago: Library: Special Collections*. Wikimedia Commons

The Supper Philosophers. Huber, Jean, 18th Century. Etching. *France Belgium Luxembourg Switzerland*. Frederic Fabre. Wikimedia Commons

Encyclopaedia or a Systematic Dictionary of the Sciences, Arts and Crafts. Diderot, Denis, and Jean Le Rond D'Alembert, eds., 1751. Wikimedia Commons

Portrait De Pierre Bayle. Savart, Pierre, 1774. Engraving. National Library of Paris, Paris. Wikimedia Commons

Portrait of John Locke. Sir Godfrey Kneller, 1697. Hermitage Museum: Collection of Sir Robert Walpole, Houghton Hall, St. Petersburg, Russia. Wikimedia Commons

Profile of Adam Smith. Caldwell and Davies, John Horsburgh, R.C. Bell, and James Tassie, 1787. Harvard Business School: Vanderblue Collection, Cambridge, Mass. Wikimedia Commons

Portrait of David Hume. Ramsay, Allan, 1766. Oil on canvas. Scottish National Gallery, Edinburgh. Wikimedia Commons

Return of Roger Williams from England with the First Charter, 1644. Grant, C.R., 1886. *The Providence Plantations for 250 Years, Welcome Arnold Greene.* Wikimedia Commons

Las Meninas. Diego Rodríguez de Silva y Velázquez, c. 1656–1657. Prado Museum, Madrid. Wikimedia Commons

Portrait of Daniel Defoe. c. 17-18th centuries. National Maritime Museum, London. Wikimedia Commons

Portrait of John Dryden. Sir Godrey Kneller, and Gérard Edelinck, c. 1700. Justin F. Skrebowski Prints and Pictures, Oxford and London. Wikimedia Commons

The Early Poems of Alfred, Lord Tennyson. Tennyson, Alfred Tennyson, and W.E.F. Britten. London: Methuen, 1900. Restored by Adam Cuerden. Wikimedia Commons

View of the Royal Baths Palace in Summer. Zaleski, Marcin, c. 1836–1838. National Museum in Warsaw, Warsaw. Wikimedia Commons

The Popular Science Monthly. Thomas Robert Malthus, 1909. Ed. J. McKeen Cattell. Vol. 74. New York: Science, 1909. *Internet Archive.* Wikimedia Commons

John Loudon McAdam. Turner, Charles. British Museum, London. Wikimedia Commons

Nicholas Barbon, English Economist, Physician and Financial Speculator. 18th Century. United Kingdom. *Insurance Hall of Fame.* Claire and Joseph Smetana, Griffith Foundation for Insurance Education, St. Johns University School of Risk Management, and the University of Alabama. Wikimedia Commons

Portrait of Josiah Wedgwood. Reynolds, Joshua, 18th century. Oil on canvas. Wikimedia Commons

The History of the Fabian Society. Pease, Edward R. New York: E.P. Dutton, 1916.Wikimedia Commons

History of the World. Helmolt, H.F., ed. New York: 1901. *University of Texas Portrait Gallery.* Wikimedia Commons

Pen drawing. *Journal of the History of Medicine and Allied Sciences.* Sir George Chalmers. *James Lind.* By A.E.A. Hudson. Ed. A. Herbert. 1956. Wikimedia Commons

Great Britain and Her Queen. Keeling, Annie E. London: Kelly, 1897. *Project Gutenberg.* Wikimedia Commons

Period 3

Industrial scene from the United Kingdom showing ironworks. Nant Y Glo, Monmouthshire. Gastineau, Henry G., and Samuel Lacey, 1830. Black and white print on engraving. National Library of Wales, Aberystwyth. Wikimedia Commons

Cupola Furnace. MacFarlane, Walter, 1917. California Digital Library. *The Principles and Practice of Iron and Steel Manufacture.* 5th ed. New York, Bombay, and Calcutta: Longmans, Green, 1917. Wikimedia Commons

"The Panic – Run on the Fourth National Bank, No. 20 Nassau Street." Frank Leslie's Illustrated Newspaper 4 Oct. 1873. *Library of Congress: Prints and Photographs Division.* Wikimedia Commons

Alphonse de Lamartine. Faces of the Politicians of the Day. By Hocquart. Paris. 1843. Lacoste. Wikimedia Commons

Portrait of Prince Klemens Wenzel Von Metternich, German-Austrian Diplomat, Politician and Statesman. Lawrence, Thomas, 1815. Oil. Kunsthistorisches Museum, Vienna. Wikimedia Commons

Indian cotton excise duty cartoon. By Swain (Punch, January 19 1895) [Public domain], via Wikimedia Commons

John Wilkinson (1728–1808), The Ironmaster. Abbott, Lemuel Francis, 18th century. Oil on canvas. Wrexham County Borough Museum, Wrexham. British Broadcasting Company. Wikimedia Commons

Joseph Wilson Swan. c. 19th century or early 20th century. Wikimedia Commons

Engraving of Charles Goodyear. Jackman, William G. Library of Congress: Prints and Photographs Division, Washington, D.C. New York: D. Appleton. Wikimedia Commons

Guglielmo Marconi, Portrait, Head and Shoulders, Facing Left. Pach Brothers, 1908. Library of Congress: Prints and Photographs Division, Washington, D.C. Wikimedia Commons

The Principles of Scientific Management. Taylor, Frederick Winslow. Düsseldorf: Verlag Wirtschaft Und Finanzen, 1996. Wikimedia Commons

Enterprise Cotton Mill, Kings Mountain, N.C. 1897. Government and Heritage Library, State Library of North Carolina, Raleigh, N.C. *Annual Report of the Bureau of Labor Statistics of the State of North Carolina.* North Carolina, Department of Labor, 1897. Wikimedia Commons

Portrait of Karl Marx. Mayall, John Jabex Edwin, 1875. International Institute of Social History, Amsterdam, the Netherlands. Wikimedia Commons

Caricature of John Bennet Lawes (1814–1900), English Entrepreneur and Agricultural Scientist. Chartran, Théobald, 1882. *Vanity Fair.* July 8, 1882. *Smithsonian Institution Libraries: Galaxy of Images.*

Members of the Irish Women Workers' Union on the Steps of Liberty Hall. c. 1914. National Library of Ireland on the Commons, Dublin. Wikimedia Commons

Knoxville Whig Steam Printing Ad. Brunlow & Haws, 1866. Library of Congress: Chronicling America Directory, Washington, D.C. *Knoxville Whig.* Brunlow & Haws, 1866. Wikimedia Commons

Family Group at a Harpischord. Troost, Corenlius, 1739. Oil on canvas. Rijksmuseum Twente, Enschede. Wikimedia Commons

Kitchen Still Life with Female Figure and Parrot. Horemans, Peter Jakob, 1760. Oil on canvas. Staatsgalerie: Bavarian State Painting Collections, New Castle Bayreuth. Wikimedia Commons

British Museum, London, England. C. 1890–1900. Photomechanical Print: photochrom, color. Library of Congress: Prints and Photographs Division: Photochrom Print Collection, Washington, D.C. Wikimedia Commons

Photograph of Thomas J. Barratt. W. & D. Downey, 1914. The Illustrated London News Archives. *The Illustrated First World War.* ILN Limited. Wikimedia Commons

A View in Whitechapel Road. Caricature by H. T. Alken, 1831 [Public domain], via Wikimedia Commons

Depiction of the Irish Potato Famine. 1849. *Illustrated London News. Internet Archive.* Wikimedia Commons

Grand Duchess Helena Pavlovna of Russia. Ritt, Augustin Christian, 18th century. *Invaluable Auction.* Invaluable, LLC. Wikimedia Commons

French Philosopher Antoine-Louis-Claude Destutt De Tracy. 19th Century. Engraving. National Library of France, Paris. Wikimedia Commons

Emile Durkheim. Early 20th century. *Marxists Internet Archive.* Wikimedia Commons

Les Belles Femmes De Paris. Messieurs De Balzac, Roger De Beauvoi, and Raymond Brucker. Paris: Au Bureau, 1839. Wikimedia Commons

French Philosopher and Sociologist Georges Sorel. Early 20th Century. *Flag Blackened.* Pierre J. Proudhon. Wikimedia Commons

Double Portrait of Jacob and Wilhelm Grimm. Grimm, Ludwig Emil, 1843. *Expedition Grimm.* Project 2058 GmbH, Bonn. Wikimedia Commons

Italian Statesman Giuseppe Mazzini. Time, Inc. 1860. *Life Magazine.* Wikimedia Commons

Struck, Hermann. *Portrait of Theodor Herzl.* c. 1920–1930. Jewish Museum, Berlin. Wikimedia Commons

Portrait of Auguste Comte. Etex, Louis Jules, 19th century. Oil on canvas. Temple of the Religion of Humanity, Paris. Wikimedia Commons

Thomas Robert Malthus. Popular Science Monthly, 1909. Ed. J. McKeen Cattell. Vol. 74. New York: Science, 1909. *Internet Archive*. Wikimedia Commons -- (Author was in italics)

Congress of Vienna (1815). Hoechle, Johann Nepomuk, c. 1820. Wikimedia Commons

Meyers Konversations-Lexikon. Ferdinand Lassalle, 1906.4th ed. c. 1885–1890. Wikimedia Commons

Emmeline Pankhurst. Matzine, Chicago, 1913. Library of Congress, Washington, D.C. Wikimedia Commons

Lord Castlereagh. Historic Memoirs of Ireland. Barrington, Jonah. London: R. Bentley, for H. Colburn, 1833. British Library. Wikimedia Commons

Marie Louise Says Farewell to Her Family. Pauline, Auzou, 1812. Castles of Versailles and Trianon, Versailles, France. Wikimedia Commons

The Oath. Tsokos, Dionysios, 1849. National Historical Museum, Athens. Wikimedia Commons

Louis Philipee D'Orléans, Duc De Chartres in 1792. Cogniet, Léon, 1834. Oil on canvas. *Palace of Versailles*, Versailles, France. *Joconde Database*. Wikimedia Commons

Charge of the Light Cavalry Brigade, 25th Oct. 1854, under Major General the Earl of Cardigan. Simpson, William, 1855. *Library of Congress*, Washington, D.C. Wikimedia Commons

Treaty of Paris, 1856. The History of the World; A Survey of a Man's Record. Helmolt, Hans F., ed. New York: Dodd, Mead, 1907. *Internet Archive*. Wikimedia Commons

Portrait of Count Camillo Benso Di Cavour. Gordigiani, Michele, c. 1850-1860. Oil. National Museum of the Risorgimento, Turin. Regione Piemonte.

First Russian Revolution. Gospolitizdat, M., 1905. Wikimedia Commons

The World's Work: A History of Our Time. Julcy, P. A. Portrait of Count Sergei Yulyevich Witte, c. 1905. Doubleday, Page, 1905. Wikimedia Commons

Illustrated World History. 6th ed. Stockholm. 1879. Wikimedia Commons

Emperor Franz Joseph of Austria, in Uniform. C. 1905. *Library of Congress*, Washington, D.C. *The Globe and Mail*. The Globe and Mail, Inc. Wikimedia Commons

Congress of Berlin, 13 July 1878. Von Werner, Anton, 1881. Oil on canvas. *Berliner Rathaus*, Berlin. Wikimedia Commons

Portrait of the Future King Leopold II, King of the Belgians. De Keyser, Nicaise, 1853. *Belgian Royal Collection: Palace of Brussels*, Brussels. Wikimedia Commons

John Bull Is Unfazed by Reports That France is to Make a Power Moved in Sudan. Commentary on the Fashoda Incident. Welsh Newspapers Online. Staniforth, Joseph Morewood. Wales: *National Library of Wales*, 1989. Wikimedia Commons

Portrait of Joseph Chamberlain. The World's Work: A History of Our Time, c. 1903. Vol. 7. New York: *Doubleday, Page & Company*. 1903. Wikimedia Commons

Minie Balls. The Wonders of Science 1867–1891. Figuier, Louis. Vol. 3. Fig Tree, 1891.

Studio Portrait of Louis Pasteur, Restored. Nedar, 1895. Wikimedia Commons

Robert Koch. Images from the History of Medicine, c. 1900. U.S. National Library of Medicine. Active Media Group. Wikimedia Commons

Berlin Conference, 1884. History of the World (textbook), 1897. Wikimedia Commons

Vladimir Ilyich Lenin. Soyuzfoto, c. 1920. Library of Congress, Washington, D.C. Wikimedia Commons

Photograph of Jules Verne. Nadar, c. 1878. *Jules Verne: A Biography.* London: Macdonald and Jane's, 1976. Wikimedia Commons

"Femmes de Tahiti ou Sur la plage" by Paul Gauguin (1891). Public domain via Wikimedia Commons

A Natal Zulu Chief. The Story of an African City (On the rise and progress of Maritzburg), by INGRAM, Joseph Forsyth (pg. 42). Original held and digitized by the British Library. Wikimedia Commons

Sepoy Mutiny, 1857. By Granger [Public domain], via Wikimedia Commons

The New fighting the Old in early Meiji Japan circa 1870. By unknown Japanese artist (Printing Museum News N36). Public domain.

An attack on Beijing Castle during the Boxer Rebellion. By Torajirō Kasai [Public domain], via Wikimedia Commons

Erlkönig. Von Schwind, Moritz, 19th century. Austrian Gallery, Vienna. Wikimedia Commons

An Officer of the Imperial Horse Guards Charging. Géricault, Théodore, 1812. Oil on canvas. Louvre Museum, Paris. Wikimedia Commons

American Bookmen: Sketches, Chiefly Biographical, of Certain Writers of the 19th Century. DeWolfe Howe, M. A. New York: Dodd, Mead, 1898. *Internet Archive.* Wikimedia

Portrait of Auguste Comte. Etex, Louis Jules, 19th century. Oil on canvas. The Bridgeman Art Library: Temple De La Religion De L'Humanite, Paris.Wikimedia Commons

Charles Darwin. The Descent of Man and Sexual Selection. Paris: C. Reinwald, 1881. *University of Illinois Urbana-Champaign.* Wikimedia Commons

A Portrait of Karl Marx. Mayall, John Jabez Edwin, 1875. International Institute of Social History, Amsterdam, Netherlands. Wikimedia Commons

Portrait of Honoré De Balzac. St. John, J. Allen, and Louis Boulanger. Musee De Tours. *The Works of Honore De Balzac.* Vol. 1. Philadelphia: Avil, 1901. Wikimedia Commons

Charles Dickens. Watkins, George Herbert, 1858. National Portrait Gallery, London. Wikimedia Commons

Portrait of the Philosopher Georg Wilhelm Friedrich Hegel, Berlin 1831. Schlesinger, Jakob, 1831. Oil. Alte Nationalgalerie, Berlin. Wikimedia Commons

Henri-Louis Bergson. "*Henri Bergson – Facts.*" Nobelprize.org. Nobel Media AB 2014. Wikimedia Commons

French Philosopher and Sociologist Georges Sorel (1847–1922). Early 20th century. *Flag Blackened.* Pierre J. Proudhon Memorial. Wikimedia Commons

Albert Einstein. Turner, Oren Jack, 1947. Library of Congress, Washington, D.C. Wikimedia Commons

Impression Sunrise. Monet, Claude, 1872. Oil on canvas. Musée Marmottan Monet, Paris. Wikimedia Commons

Period 4

American soldiers wounded in France during World War II. By Sgt. J.A. Marshall [Public domain], via Wikimedia Commons

Archduke Franz Ferdinand of Austria. Pietzner, Carl, 1919. Library of Congress: Prints and Photographs Division, Washington, D.C. *The War of the Nations.* New York: New York Times, 1919. Wikimedia Commons

Otto Von Bismarck as Member of the Regional Parliament of Prussia 1847. 1915. *Bismarck. The Iron Chancellor Life in Nearly 200 Rare Images along with an Introduction.* By Hermann Montanus, Verlagsbuchhandlung Siegen and Leipzig. Ed. Walter Stein. 1915. Wikimedia Commons

Serbian Volunteers at the Border with Bulgaria. 1913. *Serbo-Bulgarian War in 1913: Najnovi Songs, the Level Descriptions of Battles and Various War Notes.* Ed. M. Milanovic. 1913. Wikimedia Commons

A Brigadier of the 1st Regiment of French Chasseurs D'Afrique with His Horse. Battle of the Marne. Gervais-Courtellemont, Jules, 1916. Bibliotèque nationale De France, Paris. Wikimedia Commons

The Four Military Representatives of the Supreme War Council, Versailles, Their Co's, Secretaries, and Interpreters in Session. Olivier, Herbert A., 1919. Imperial War Museum, London. Wikimedia Commons

The Ottoman Representative Signs the Sèvres Treaty. Asbarez Armenian News, 1920. *Asbarez.* Wikimedia Commons

Group Photo of Al-Fatat's Members at a Resort outside of Damascus. 1919. Online Museum of Syrian History. *Syrian History.* Comp. Haykal Media. Wikimedia Commons

Congress of Europe in The Hague. Snikkers and Anefo. 1948. The Hague. National Archive.

American Forces Radio and Television Service. Mitterrand: United States. Department of Defense. U.S. Military. By James Cavalier. American Forces Network Online. Wikimedia Commons

Former German Chancellor Helmut Kohl. Kohl: White House Photograph Office. 1984. Ronald Reagan Library: University of Texas. Wikimedia Commons

Russian offense ground battle in the Second Chechen War. Source: photographer.ru via Wikimedia Commons

The Signing of Peace in the Hall of Mirrors, Versailles, 28th June 1919. Orpen, William, 1919. Oil on canvas. Imperial War Museum, London. Wikimedia Commons

The First Commercial Oil Well in Saudi Arabia, Which Stuck Oil on March 4, 1938. 1938. *World Oil.* Comp. Gulf Publishing Company. Wikimedia Commons

Six Leaders of the FLN before the Outbreak of the "Revolution of November 1, 1954." 1954. *Algerian Ministry of Mojahedin.* Wikimedia Commons

Vladimir Lenin. Ten Days That Shook the World. Reed, John, and Clive Weed. New York: Boni and Liveright, 1919. Wikimedia Commons

State Emblem of the Russian Socialist Federative Soviet Republic. Lobachyov, Vladimir. Digital image. 1918–1920.

Order of the October Revolution. Tupolev, Public Joint Stock Company. United Aircraft Company. Wikimedia Commons

Photo of Leon Trotsky. McBride, Isaac, 1920. Barbarous Soviet Russia. Wikimedia Commons

Friedrich Nietzsche. Hartmann, F., c. 1875. Basel. Wikimedia Commons

Benito Mussolini. Mussolini Reviews 5th Alpine Mobile Black Brigade. 1945. Brescia. Wikimedia Commons

Adolf Hitler, Head-and-shoulders Portrait, Facing Slightly Left. Bain News Service, 1923. Library of Congress: George Grantham Bain Collection, Washington, D.C. Wikimedia Commons

Francisco Franco in 1923. Government of Spain, 1923. Wikimedia Commons

Molotov and Ribbentrop, after the Signing of the Soviet-German Treaty of Friendship and the Border between the USSR and Germany. Fund TSHAKFD, 1939. Moscow. Wikimedia Commons

A Solemn Crowd Gathers outside the Stock Exchange after the Crash. 1929. *Official Social Security Website of the United States.* Wikimedia Commons

John Maynard Keynes: Detail of a Photograph with Jane Christian Smuts. 1933. National Portrait Gallery, London. Wikimedia Commons

George Marshall. U.S. Army Center of Military History. United States. U.S. Army. U.S. Army Center of Military History. Federal Government. Wikimedia Commons

Warsaw Pact Meeting, 1955. Central Intelligence Agency. United States. Central Intelligence Agency. Executive Office of the President of the United States. Flickr. Wikimedia Commons

Joseph Stalin. The History of the Civil War in the U.S.S.R. Gorky, Maksim. Moscow: Co-operative Pub. Society of Foreign Workers in the U.S.S.R., 1937 Wikimedia Commons

Michail Gorbachev. White House Photograph Office. Executive Office of the President of the United States. *Reagan Library University of Texas Archives.* 1985. Wikimedia Commons

Day of Lithuanian Independence in Šiauliai, Lithuania. Lazdynas, Rimantas, 1990

TRADIC (for TRAnsistor DIgital Computer or TRansistorized Airborne DIgital Computer). 1955. *Radio-Electronic Engineering Magazine.* 5th ed. Vol. 24. New York: Ziff-Davis, 1955. Wikimedia Commons

Albert Einstein during a Lecture in Vienna. Schmutzer, Ferdinand, 1921. National Library of Austria, Vienna. *Internet Archive.* Wikimedia Commons

Sigmund Freud, Founder of Psychoanalysis, Smoking Cigar. Halberstadt, Max, 1922. *Politiken.* Wikimedia Commons

The War of the Worlds. Paramount Pictures, 1953. Wikimedia Commons

Foucault's "The Order of Things." L'ordre Du Discours: Leçon Inaugurale Au Collège De France Prononcée Le 2 Décembre 1970. Paris: Gallimard, 2009. Wikimedia Commons

A Room inside an Abandoned Hotel Room in Pripyat. 2011. Markosian, D. One Day in the Life of Chernobyl. *Voice of America News.* Wikimedia Commons

Trinity Site Explosion, 0.016 Second after Explosion, July 16, 1945. Brixner, Berilyn, 1945. *Los Alamos National Laboratory.* Wikimedia Commons

Dietrich Bonhoeffer Plaque. Koreng, Ansgar, 1945. Zion Church, Berlin. Wikimedia Commons

Pope Paul VI Delivers the Ring to Cardinal Joseph Ratzinger. N.d. *Newsletter.* Vol. 49. Paul VI Institute of Brescia, 1977. Wikimedia Commons

Portrait of Giorgio De Chirico. Van Vechten, Carl, 1936. Library of Congress, Washington, D.C. Wikimedia Commons

Jean-Paul Sartre. N.d. *Archive Daily Clarin.* Buenos Aires, Argentina. 1983. Wikimedia Commons

American soldiers pay their respects at the World War II cemetary. U.S. Army. National Archives and Records Administration. 1945. Wikimedia Commons

Ernest Hemingway Portrait 1918. 1918. National Archives and Records Administration: JFK Library, Boston. Wikimedia Commons

James Ramsay MacDonald in 1916. Bain, 1916. Library of Congress, Washington, D.C. Wikimedia Commons

WWII Europe: Germany: Concentration Camps: "Piles of Dead Prisoners" 1945. National Archives and Records Administration: Franklin D. Roosevelt Library, Hyde Park. Wikimedia Commons

Workers on the First Moving Assembly Line Put Together Magnetos and Flywheels for 1913 Ford Autos. 1913. National Archives and Records Administration. Wikimedia Commons

Florence Nightingale. Great Britain and Her Queen. Keeling, Annie E. London: Kelly, 1897. Wikimedia Commons

Constructing the Stockholm Metro in 1957, Svenska Dagbladet, Herman Ronninger. 1957. Wikimedia Commons

Project Rover Assistance Dog. United States. National Institute for Occupational Safety and Health. By Project Rover. Wikimedia Commons

Margaret Thatcher, Former UK PM. Trikosko, Marion S., 1975. Library of Congress: Prints and Photographs Division, Washington, D.C. Wikimedia Commons

Mary Robinson receiving the Presidential Medal of Freedom in August 2009. By U.S. federal government (2009 Presidential Medal of Freedom Ceremony). Public domain.

Logo of Green Italia. European Greens. Digital image. *Green Italian European Greens.* Wikimedia Commons

Column Equality March on General Democratic March in Moscow on 6 May 2012. 2012. Wikimedia Commons

Central Kiosk Socket Oaxaca City during the Student Demonstration in Commemoration of the Slaughter of Students in Tlatelolco Mexico in 1968. Chapulinera, 2004. Wikimedia Commons

Logo FPO Carinthia. Freedom Party. Digital image. *FPO Carinthia.* Freedom Party in Carinthia. Wikimedia Commons

Made in the USA
San Bernardino, CA
02 May 2018